THE BRITISH CABINET
SYSTEM

THE BRITISH CABINET SYSTEM

Martin Burch
and
Ian Holliday

Department of Government   University of Manchester

PRENTICE HALL
HARVESTER WHEATSHEAF

LONDON   NEW YORK   TORONTO   SYDNEY   TOKYO   SINGAPORE
MADRID   MEXICO CITY   MUNICH

First published 1996 by
Prentice Hall/Harvester Wheatsheaf
Campus 400, Maylands Avenue
Hemel Hempstead
Hertfordshire, HP2 7EZ
A division of
Simon & Schuster International Group

Typeset in 10/12pt Times
by Dorwyn Ltd, Hants

Printed and bound in Great Britain by
T.J. International Ltd, Padstow, Cornwall

Library of Congress Cataloguing-in-Publication Data

Burch, Martin.
The British cabinet system/Martin Burch, Ian Holliday.
p.cm.
Includes bibliographical references and index.
ISBN 0-13-206194-5 (alk.paper)
1. Cabinet system–Great Britain.   I. Title.
JN405.B873   1995   95-4954
320.441–dc20   CIP

British Library Cataloguing in Publication Data

A catalogue record for this book is available
from the British Library.

ISBN 0-13-206194-5

2 3 4 5   00 99 98 97

Contents

□

Figures and tables

Figures

Tables

□

Acknowledgements

Some of the material in this book was presented in lectures and seminars at the Department of Government, University of Manchester. We are grateful to the many students who witnessed and aided our attempts to impose some order on it. We are particularly grateful to those students who presented case studies of the cabinet system at work to seminars, and thereby helped us to refine what has since become Chapter 8 of the book. In 1993–4, they were Matthew Bulmer, Piers Burgess, Jon Greenwood, Robert Hamilton, Matthew Hardy, James Howlett, George Hutchinson, Kerrie Jopling, Tom Kujawa, Francis Land, Neil Lea, Camilla Marsh, Thomas O'Brien, James Perry, Matthew Seager and Jonny Whitehead. In 1994–95, they were James Anderson, Paul Attwood, Gareth Barnes, Mary Barnes, Martin Blanche, Norbert Böhnke, Sophie Caston, Suzanne Gilhooly, Allison Graham, Joost Misell, Linda Olanipekun, Rupal Patel, Alice Rigby, Daniel Roseman, Julian Sinclair, Leahn Stanhope, Daniel Stiassny, Lucy Stokoe, Jonathan Sumberg, Abha Thakor, Paul Wolstenholme and Richard Wynn-Davies. At a very late stage, we received highly efficient research assistance with our case studies from Garrath Williams.

In the course of our research, we conducted interviews with former or serving cabinet ministers, cabinet system officials, whips and back-bench MPs. We are grateful to them all for invaluable information and insights into the cabinet system. We would also like to thank officials in the Cabinet Office and Treasury for providing us with statistical information and other material on the cabinet system. Assistance with some interview expenses was provided by ESRC (R000231012) and Nuffield Foundation grants to Martin Burch.

We thank Simon Bulmer and Andrew Gray for commenting on parts of the manuscript, Brian Hogwood for providing data for Table 1.2, John Griffith, Michael Ryle and Sweet and Maxwell for permission to reproduce Table 1.1, the Treasury for providing the data for Table 2.1, and our publisher's anonymous reviewers for their helpful comments on the final draft of the book. We owe a very great debt of gratitude to Michael Lee, Michael Moran and Maurice Wright, all of whom read and made detailed comments on a draft of Part 1 of the book.

We remain responsible for everything that follows.

□

Abbreviations

ASI	Adam Smith Institute
BC	British Coal
BL	British Leyland
BMA	British Medical Association
BP	British Petroleum
C&E	Customs and Excise
C&L	Coopers and Lybrand
CAP	common agricultural policy
CBI	Confederation of British Industry
CC	Chrysler Corporation
CID	committee of imperial defence
CIG	current intelligence group
CMO	concerned ministers only
COI	Central Office of Information
COREPER	committee of permanent representatives
CPRS	central policy review staff
CPS	Centre for Policy Studies
CRD	Conservative research department
CSD	Civil Service Department
CUK	Chrysler UK
DEmp	Department of Employment
DEn	Department of Energy
DES	Department of Education and Science
DfEE	Department for Education and Employment
DHSS	Department of Health and Social Security
DoE	Department of the Environment
DoH	Department of Health
DoI	Department of Industry
DTI	Department of Trade and Industry
DTp	Department of Transport
EC	European Community
ECJ	European Court of Justice
EEC	European Economic Community
EMS	European monetary system
EMU	economic and monetary union
ERM	exchange rate mechanism

EU	European Union
FBI	Federal Bureau of Investigation
FCO	Foreign and Commonwealth Office
FMI	financial management initiative
FPP	first past the post
G5	Group of Five
G7	Group of Seven
GCHQ	Government Communications Headquarters
GDP	gross domestic product
HMO	health management organisation
IEA	Institute of Economic Affairs
IMF	International Monetary Fund
IR	Inland Revenue
JIC	joint intelligence committee
MAFF	Ministry of Agriculture, Fisheries and Foods
MI5	security service
MI6	secret intelligence service
MoD	Ministry of Defence
MP	Member of Parliament
MPO	management and personnel office
MTA	medium term assessment
MTFS	medium term financial strategy
NCT	new control total
NEB	National Enterprise Board
NEC	national executive committee
NIO	Northern Ireland Office
NHS	National Health Service
OPSS	Office of Public Service and Science
OPS	Office of Public Service
OSA	Official Secrets Act 1911
PES	public expenditure survey
PLP	Parliamentary Labour Party
PMEU	prime minister's efficiency unit
PMPU	prime minister's policy unit
PPS	parliamentary private secretary
PR	proportional representation
PSBR	public sector borrowing requirement
PSIS	permanent secretaries' committee on the intelligence services
SNP	Scottish National Party
STV	single transferable vote
TGWU	Transport and General Workers' Union
TUC	Trades Union Congress
UK	United Kingdom
UKRep	UK permanent representative, Brussels
US	United States
UUP	Ulster Unionist Party
VAT	value added tax

□

A note on cabinet committees

Where possible in the text, we identify cabinet committees from our period 1974–95. *Ad hoc* committees take the designation GEN or MISC followed by a number. Standing committees are identified purely by letters. Only one official standing committee is identified in the text. It is EQ(S), which shadows OPD(E). The many ministerial standing committees featured in the text are listed below. Bracketed dates indicate the relevant year or years of the committee's existence. Committees to which no date is attached were in existence in July 1995, and are listed in Cabinet Office (1995c).

E   economic policy (1979–80)
E(LF)   local government finance (1984–6)
EDC   competitiveness
EDCP   coordination and presentation of government policy
EDE   environment
EDH   home and social affairs
EDH(D)   drug misuse
EDI   industrial, commercial and consumer affairs (abolished 1995)
EDI(P)   public sector pay (abolished 1995)
EDP   economic and domestic policy
EDR   regeneration (abolished 1995)
EDS   science and technology (abolished 1995)
EDX   public expenditure
EY   economic policy (1976)
FLG   queen's speeches and future legislation
FLQ   queen's speeches and future legislation (1978–89)
ID   industrial development (1974)
IS   intelligence services
LG   legislation
NI   Northern Ireland
OD   defence and overseas policy (1982)
OPD   defence and overseas policy
OPD(E)   European questions
OPD(T)   terrorism
OPDSE   European security (abolished 1995)

Introduction

In formal terms, Britain is one of the most centralised states in the modern democratic world. Constitutionally, governing power and authority have for more than three centuries been concentrated in a Parliament possessing unlimited sovereignty. Since the eighteenth century, when the doctrine of parliamentary sovereignty was first put fully into effect, formal centralisation of power in Parliament has often been reinforced in practice by subordination of the legislature to the executive. In the eighteenth century, the chief threat to effective parliamentary sovereignty was posed by the monarch. As this threat was slowly reduced by the assertion of parliamentary rights, so a new mechanism by which the exercise of power might be transferred from legislature to executive developed. This was the emergence of a strong and disciplined party system in the middle decades of the nineteenth century, which checked formal parliamentary sovereignty and effectively delivered power once more into the hands of the executive. This informal change has meant that for more than a century the British executive has usually dominated Parliament, and has therefore been able to pass most of its desired legislative programme through it.

At the centre of the British executive throughout the period marked by the existence of a disciplined party system has stood cabinet. In the high Victorian era, this committee of leading government ministers had minimal institutional support. In subsequent years, the apex of the British executive has been institutionally transformed. It now comprises cabinet, cabinet committees, Cabinet Office, Prime Minister's Office, parts of the Treasury, the major government law offices, and parts of the machinery which manages the executive's immediate support base, the governing party in Parliament (Figure 0.1).

It is this core or central executive, the cabinet system, which is analysed in this book. It is the very heart of the centralised British state, and is therefore of major concern to any student of British politics. The cabinet system, increasingly known to insiders as 'the centre' (Wakeham, 1994: 476), is far more substantial and complex than is generally recognised. To understand its nature, it must be analysed as a complete system. Only if this is done can the

1

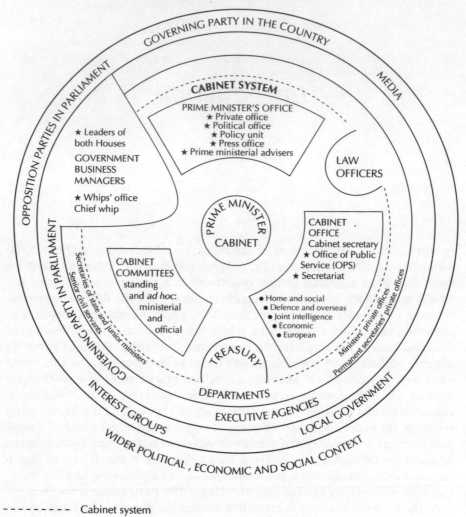

GOVERNING PARTY IN THE COUNTRY

MEDIA

OPPOSITION PARTIES IN PARLIAMENT

CABINET SYSTEM

PRIME MINISTER'S OFFICE
★ Private office
★ Political office
★ Policy unit
★ Press office
★ Prime ministerial advisers

★ Leaders of
both Houses

GOVERNMENT
BUSINESS
MANAGERS

★ Whips' office
Chief whip

LAW
OFFICERS

PRIME MINISTER
CABINET

CABINET
OFFICE
Cabinet secretary
★ Office of Public
Service (OPS)
★ Secretariat

CABINET
COMMITTEES
standing
and *ad hoc*:
ministerial
and
official

● Home and social
● Defence and overseas
● Joint intelligence
● Economic
● European

Secretaries of state and junior ministers
Senior civil servants

GOVERNING PARTY IN PARLIAMENT

Ministers' private offices
Permanent secretaries' private offices

TREASURY

DEPARTMENTS

EXECUTIVE AGENCIES

LOCAL GOVERNMENT

INTEREST GROUPS

WIDER POLITICAL, ECONOMIC AND SOCIAL CONTEXT

- - - - - - - - - Cabinet system

Figure 0.1   The cabinet system

significance of particular aspects, such as prime minister and cabinet, be fully grasped. In this book, we seek to present a comprehensive analysis of the cabinet system by investigating all the parts that constitute it.

Analysis of the cabinet system

The cabinet system has only recently begun to be subjected to the degree of analysis that its importance in the British political system warrants. Bagehot, whose classic 1867 study *The English Constitution* rated that importance higher than any other, himself remarked on this relative neglect: 'The most curious point about the Cabinet is that so very little is known about it' (Bagehot, 1963: 68). His own attempt to fill the gap in public knowledge comprised a eulogy which has continuing fame to this day. Cabinet, Bagehot wrote (1963: 68), is 'a *hyphen* which joins, a *buckle* which fastens, the legislative part of the State to the executive part of the State'. Writing at a time when cabinet government was experiencing its most gilded age, Bagehot described a cabinet of great power and also substantial informality (see Chapter 1). As it happens, he actually said very little about its real operating conventions.

In subsequent years cabinet slowly changed, but on the whole analysis of it did not. Two major studies were Sir Ivor Jennings' *Cabinet Government*, published in 1936, and A. B. Keith's *The British Cabinet System*, which appeared in 1938. Each was largely formal in approach, and failed to examine the reality of cabinet system operations. Not until 1962, when J. P. Mackintosh published *The British Cabinet*, did a credible analysis appear. With its broad historical sweep and detailed investigation of cabinet through the ages, Mackintosh's book was soon recognised to be a classic. An informed but neglected account, Hans Daalder's *Cabinet Reform in Britain 1914–1963*, was published soon after, in 1964.

Since the early 1960s numerous studies have appeared. Some explore the full cabinet system, others focus on aspects of it. Mosley (1969), Rush (1984), Madgwick (1991) and James (1992) provide detailed descriptions of those parts of the central executive which are well documented from secondary sources. Gordon Walker (1972) provides an informed insider's account. Naylor (1984) offers an indispensable history. Hennessy (1986) presents a wide range of interview material in his analysis of cabinet. A collection edited by Rhodes and Dunleavy (1995) provides a more analytical but fragmentary survey of core executive operations. Together, these accounts have substantially extended our understanding of cabinet.

However, possibly the most significant development in the past 20 years of cabinet studies has been publication of a series of ministerial memoirs, following the path-breaking posthumous publication of *The Diaries of a Cabinet Minister* by Richard Crossman (1975, 1976, 1977). This had a major constitutional impact, paving the way for other insiders to reveal more about the workings of the cabinet system. Among Labour ministers, Barbara Castle (1980, 1984) and Tony Benn (1989, 1990) have both published detailed ministerial diaries. Joel Barnett (1982) and Edmund Dell (1991) have published revealing ministerial memoirs. The accounts of the last two Labour prime ministers, Harold Wilson (1974, 1979) and James Callaghan (1987), are more traditional in approach, though an analysis of British governance by Wilson (1976) is highly perceptive. Among Conservative cabinet ministers no contemporary diarist has gone into print, but detailed memoirs have been published by James Prior (1986), Nigel Lawson (1993), Kenneth Baker (1993),

Margaret Thatcher (1993) and Geoffrey Howe (1994). Although few of these accounts indulge in systematic reflection on the nature of the British cabinet system, they are genuinely indispensable to contemporary analysis of it.

In this context, our aim in this book is to provide an analytical account both of the range of cabinet system operations and of specific instances which reveal notable features of the functioning of that system. Our survey of the range of cabinet system operations comprises Part 1. A series of 14 case studies comprises Part 2. In both Parts 1 and 2, the accession to office of Harold Wilson's minority Labour government in March 1974 serves as a starting point.

This date is in some senses arbitrary, but is in no sense entirely so. Cabinet system institutions have evolved slowly during the period since a recognisably modern cabinet system was created in 1916. In many ways this has been a continuing process which has placed an accumulation of functions and oversight responsibility in cabinet system organisations. Yet within this cumulative process there have been critical moments when a significant change in the character of the system has taken place. The second world war, and the subsequent Attlee administration, were the occasion for introduction of the extensive modern system of cabinet committees which has had enormous consequences for the distribution of power within the cabinet system. Similarly, in and immediately prior to 1974, an increase in external pressure on the cabinet system caused a number of organisational changes to be brought to fruition, thereby generating an important alteration in its character. Harold Wilson testifies to the important growth in pressures experienced by cabinet system institutions in or around 1974: 'The enormous increase in the work load on ministers, senior officials and the machine itself following the oil crisis . . . if it could be statistically measured, must be, I would estimate, between thirty and fifty per cent' (Wilson, 1976: 67). This step change in pressures on the cabinet system, and resultant alterations made to the system itself, is our first reason for taking 1974 as a starting point.

The second reason is that the period from 1974 to 1995 provides us with a long perspective on the contemporary cabinet system. The third is that this period of more than 20 years provides extensive evidence of cabinet system operations during two Labour (Wilson, Callaghan) and two Conservative (Thatcher, Major) administrations. The fourth is that the many ministerial memoirs listed above constitute a superb resource and make possible a form of contemporary analysis which has previously not been feasible. To fill gaps in accounts given in published sources, we have interviewed key individuals. The book draws, but is not based, on a series of interviews with practitioners carried out over the period 1988 to 1994. In total, 43 former cabinet ministers (19 Conservative and 24 Labour) were interviewed, plus 16 serving or retired senior officials experienced in cabinet system operations. Interviews were also carried out with party officials, former government whips and back-benchers in the House of Commons.

4

Methodology

Analysis of a limited set of organisations such as those which constitute the cabinet system raises two universal problems concerning methods and emphases in research. A concentration on internal dynamics means both that the importance of external factors tends to be downgraded, and that the significance of internal factors tends to be exaggerated. A particular problem in analysing the kind of small group, face-to-face politics which characterise the cabinet system is that the importance of individuals tends to be highlighted. This frequently results in accounts which place a predominant emphasis on the role of 'great' men and women in shaping and determining events. As Dunleavy and Rhodes (1990) argue, cabinet studies have a marked tendency to pay excessive attention to the position of prime minister and to undervalue broader influences. Our intention is to strike a more plausible balance between individual and contextual factors.

This is not to deny that the role of individuals within the cabinet system is important. It is rather to make the point that the exact way in which the cabinet system works varies in relation not only to the particular individuals involved, but also to the precise circumstances in which they are working, and the specific matters or issues with which they are dealing (Hill, 1991: 244–5). Crucially, variation takes place within, and is shaped by, established institutional parameters. The key task is therefore to develop a satisfactory analytical means of taking account of the inevitable fluidity which this broad array of factors generates. We do this by examining the established framework within which these highly variable factors operate.

Our approach is to recognise that cabinet system actors operate within a series of limits which are both internal and external to that system. Internal limits comprise abiding organisational patterns and established ways of working. They shape behaviour, and provide the immediate context within which opportunities to exercise individual initiative arise. Opportunities may be exploited by individuals if they are well placed, able and minded to act. External limits comprise the economic, social and political context within which all cabinet system actors operate, and of which they are often forced to be deeply conscious. In our way of looking at things, the role of the individual is conditioned by and secondary to these limits and constraints. In formal terms, the approach we adopt marries institutional analysis with a policy process perspective.

Institutional factors provide an established and stable part of the context within which actors are obliged to operate. They do not constitute the whole of that context, but they are crucial because they mediate other pressures generated by wider economic, social and political forces. The institutional context which we seek can be derived from analysis of the development of the institution in question, of organisations and positions which constitute it, of values and practices which apply within it, of links and processes centred on it, and of tasks and networks which are employed in the handling of its business.

It is a central proposition of institutional analysis that institutions help to shape not simply actors' behaviour, but also the strategies and goals they pursue (Thelen and Steinmo, 1992; March and Olsen, 1989; Vickers, 1967; Simon, 1947). Institutions also provide actors with many of the resources necessary to exercise individual initiative, and they condition opportunities to do so. In summary, it can be said that institutional factors help to condition, guide, channel and facilitate actors' behaviour.

A policy process approach enables us to add to this picture an analysis of ways in which the various institutional elements which constitute the cabinet system operate when it comes to handling business and carrying out regularised tasks such as the legislative programme for a parliamentary session and the annual spending round. Case studies centred on particular policy issues allow more variable factors such as issue, circumstance and the role of the individual to be addressed.

Analytical focus

Our institutional approach to analysis of the cabinet system is applied at several levels.

First, we describe and examine the structure of the cabinet system. Many organisations are highlighted, notably the Prime Minister's and Cabinet Offices, as are arenas in which issues are considered, such as cabinet and its committees. We also examine the leading established positions within the cabinet system, and the formal powers and staff resources attached to them. In addition, we investigate the ethos, conventions and codes which prescribe how individuals holding cabinet system positions should act. In developing our analysis, we make a distinction between formal, semi-formal and informal aspects of the cabinet system. Whereas formal aspects of the system are established organisations and arenas, such as the system of standing and *ad hoc* committees, semi-formal aspects are more transient groups, such as working parties, which may be set up from time to time. Informal aspects comprise personal contacts developed by individuals engaged in or connected with activities which take place in formal and semi-formal structures.

Second, we examine how this structure creates opportunities for individuals to take initiatives. By analysing the incidence of these opportunities, important aspects of the pattern of cabinet system relations are revealed. We refer to this aspect of the cabinet system as its disposition. Our focus on disposition is a natural corollary of the argument that institutions shape and constrain behaviour. Once it is accepted that institutions are not neutral in either their composition or their consequent effect on actual behaviour, notions of partiality and disposition arise (Hammond and Thomas, 1989: 156–7). Institutions are bound to operate in a selective and partial way, and to advantage some office holders. Effective exploitation of that advantage will allow certain interests and policy initiatives to prevail over, and sometimes at the cost of, others (Seidman, 1970: 14). The spirit of this line of analysis is captured in Schattschneider's (1960: 71) famous observation that *'organization is the mobilization of bias*. Some issues are organized into politics while others are organized out' (his italics; see also Crenson, 1971).

Third, we investigate further elements which affect the disposition of the cabinet system. Our contention is that the disposition of an institution is not to be found solely in its structure. Processes are also relevant. To the extent that they follow regular patterns, processes advantage some positions over others. In particular, processes of business management are not purely mechanistic, and are therefore not neutral in their consequences. Instead, they can greatly influence outcomes (Plott and Levine, 1978: 146). Processes can be operated to assist, retard or suppress a proposal. In this way, a task as apparently innocuous as handling the flow of material through the cabinet system can have an important effect on whether, how, when and by whom decisions are reached. It can also affect the number and type of actors drawn into policy making and able to make a contribution to it. Some are fully drawn in, some are merely consulted, others are excluded altogether. Similarly, some are better positioned to manage cabinet system processes than are others.

Fourth, we examine wider factors. Some actors are in better positions than are others to alter cabinet institutions themselves, and the procedures and processes whereby they operate. While some are merely advantaged by institutional structure and established processes, some others are advantaged by their ability to shape this structure and its processes. Some potentially significant actors enjoy an advantage in both spheres.

Finally, we put our many elements of structure and disposition together to analyse the pattern or distribution of power potential in the cabinet system. The concept of power potential is central to this book. It refers not to actual exercises of power, but to the potential to exercise power which is invested in a position. The difference between power and power potential is that power potential is not always realised. An individual's impact on policy outcomes depends in part on circumstance, which is conditioned by a range of external factors. When circumstances are right, opportunities to act expand. They may or may not be taken up. If they are taken up, the action undertaken may or may not be effective. Within the framework of an institution, it is the coming together of position and resources on the one hand, and propitious circumstances on the other, which creates opportunities for individual action. This is, however, only one stage in a much longer sequence, which thereafter centres on characteristics of the individual occupying an advantaged position, such as his or her willingness and ability to act (see Chapter 7). In focusing on power potential, we seek merely to identify positions which have enhanced opportunities to exercise power.

We use the concept of power potential in conducting the general institutional analysis undertaken in Part 1 because we believe that this kind of

7

analysis cannot provide a picture of actual exercises of power. It can, however, identify those actors within the cabinet system who are well placed to take initiatives, and who thus have power potential. It can also indicate alterations in power potential over time. In Part 2 we are able to isolate, by means of institutional criteria, significant exercises of power in concrete cases. These are judged in terms of an individual's impact on policy outcomes. Yet what this analysis reveals is the variability of individual impact in distinct circumstances. While it is thus possible to map power potential in the cabinet system, it is not possible to construct a simple power model.

Organisation of the book

The two parts of the book have distinct tasks. In Part 1, the conditioning framework of established institutions, values, practices, processes and networks is set out. In this part of the book we move progressively from tangible aspects of the cabinet system to more variable features. Chapter 1 is preparatory. It examines development of the modern cabinet system from the nineteenth century to 1974. Subsequent chapters examine key features of the post-1974 cabinet system. Chapter 2 investigates the formal organisational structure of the contemporary cabinet system. Chapter 3 analyses the values and practices which pervade it. Chapter 4 examines communication links and processes for handling business in the system. Chapter 5 looks at a series of networks and tasks which are centred on the cabinet system. Chapter 6 assesses the mechanisms which have been developed to manage the two major constraints which the cabinet system faces, time and money. Chapter 7 considers the impact of more variable factors, parties and individuals, on the operation of the cabinet system. Part 2 concentrates on case-study analysis of the cabinet system at work, and enables us to consider in detail the role of variable factors in cabinet system operations. We focus in particular on the role of the individual. Chapter 8 presents 14 case studies of cabinet system activity during the period 1974–95. Chapter 9 draws lessons from those cases, using an institutional approach applied throughout the book.

Part One

1

□

Origins and development

The contemporary British cabinet system is the central part of a set of governing institutions which has developed over several centuries. At no point has the British political system experienced revolution in the modern sense of the term. At no time, in consequence, have the basic principles on which the system operates been subjected to fundamental review and alteration. To some extent, evolutionary change of course characterises all political systems. None is ever completely refashioned. Yet in very few comparable systems have so few systematic attempts been made to reshape the polity. British institutions, unlike those in many other countries, have developed in strictly evolutionary ways, and still bear clear marks of previous centuries.

The evolutionary nature of British institutions is a key point of orientation for analysis of the cabinet system, for that nature characterises cabinet just as much as all other branches of the polity. This set of institutions can trace its origins to the governing practices of the late seventeenth century, when the restoration monarch Charles II created a stable group of ministerial advisers from parliamentary forces and trusted courtiers (Mackintosh, 1977: 35–8). More fancifully, antecedents can be found in the medieval King's Council of baronial support (Rush, 1984: 8; Punnett, 1976: 165–6). However, the precise extent to which precedents can be identified in earlier centuries is not relevant to this analysis. What is important is that the core notion of evolutionary development be established at the outset.

Within a generally evolutionary history there have, however, been step changes in development of the cabinet system when decisive attempts to formalise emergent practices have been made. Yet important as some alterations to cabinet institutions and practices undoubtedly have been, they cannot be said to have effected a full-scale revolution at the heart of British government. Rather, they represent successive systematisation at the centre of a state which throughout has remained imbued with earlier traditions. Crucially, while there have been important changes in staffing, organisation, process and procedure, the underlying principles of British government have survived substantially intact throughout its modern history. Those principles are multiple, and often overlap in part with operating principles found in other state systems. The ethos of the British system – infused as it is with important residues from earlier, pre-democratic times – is, however, unique.

In this chapter, we examine the origins and development of the cabinet system in the period up to 1974. We begin by analysing the underlying principles of the British central executive.

Underlying principles of the British central executive

Seven main principles underlie operation of the British political system. Each has deep historical antecedents.

Fundamental to the system is the concept of a unitary state, in which formal authority is concentrated at the centre and a single source of executive power is identified. This concept derives from the constitutional convention of the sovereignty of Parliament which, among other things, holds that Parliament is the primary source of legal authority (Street and Brazier, 1985: 28–9). Parliamentary omnicompetence raises a key question: who or what controls Parliament? At least since mid-Victorian times, when a disciplined parliamentary party system emerged, it has been the governing party in Parliament and, through party management, the executive which have been largely predominant (Cox, 1987: 5). The character of its relationship with Parliament is the key to executive dominance.

A second core principle is that within the central state decision making is, and for many years has been, concentrated on a relatively small group usually comprising the prime minister, senior ministers and senior aides and officials. The size of this group has grown over the years, and its exact boundaries have fluctuated according to the issue being handled. Nevertheless, key personnel at the very centre remain remarkably small in number. Moreover, this small group has always operated on a close interpersonal basis, and has tended to be somewhat isolated and self-contained, operating discreetly outside the gaze of public and media.

Reinforcing this insularity is a third principle, exclusiveness. This principle derives from a central characteristic of English elite relations, and has become embedded in the British way of governing. A clear distinction is drawn between insiders and outsiders, and trust is readily accorded only to the former (Heclo and Wildavsky, 1981: 2–14). British secrecy laws are merely an overt expression of this distinction. The 1920 revision of the Official Secrets Act, for example, was promoted by the desire to maintain the exclusive nature of cabinet and committee business (Roskill, 1972: 131).

A fourth principle is that, within the small group, executive power has always been focused on a predominant individual, initially the monarch,

10

subsequently the prime minister. This concentration of authority in a single person, however, has never been absolute. Indeed, Britain has no significant tradition of absolutism. Instead, the authority of the singular executive has always been diluted by the need to share power with a wider governing group and to maintain elite support and consent.

This is closely related to the fifth principle of the British system, the compromised nature of the executive. Although the executive has traditionally been top–down in its mode of operation, it has also had to remain responsive to the power base which sustains it. This should not however disguise the fact that the central executive has usually been as much concerned to manage its power base as to react to it. Although the power base has shifted over time, from court to parliamentary faction to party (with the electorate operating intermittently as a wider shaping factor), the attempt to manipulate that power base has been persistent, and remains one of the key tasks facing the modern central executive.

A sixth principle underlying the British executive system is a highly compartmentalised government structure, which creates separate power centres and sources of information, advice and policy initiative. The division of British government into distinct departments and agencies is long standing, and was certainly fully established by the first half of the nineteenth century (Parris, 1969: 82). By this time the British tradition of departmental autonomy and respect for ministerial lead in areas of departmental responsibility was also fully established. This is enshrined in the convention that ministers are individually responsible to Parliament for the work of their departments (Marshall, 1989: 17). This departmentalism has resulted in an executive which is composite in nature, and has a strong impulsion to satisfy the interests of parts at the cost of the whole.

This tendency towards disaggregation is partly counteracted by the final principle upon which the British system is based, a strong emphasis on the unity of the group. This is expressed in the central convention of collective responsibility, whereby once a decision has been reached the executive attempts to speak with one voice and dissenting ministers are expected either to accept the decision or resign (Brazier, 1988: 129–30).

There is clear conflict between some of these principles. In particular, the emphasis on singular leadership, the collective aspiration towards cabinet government, and the individual reality of ministerial representation of departmental interests are in evident tension. Many debates about cabinet government focus on precisely this tension.

The important point is that most of these operating principles were set in a pre-modern age. On the one hand, they were established prior to the institution of liberal democracy, and thus predate the mass franchise, mass parties and mature interest groups. On the other, they were in place before emergence of the large-scale modern state, which characteristically generates a vast amount of business, as well as complex and specialised policy

11

making spanning departmental boundaries. Evolutionary development carried pre-modern principles into the modern age. Reform of the cabinet system in the period up to 1974 did little to alter these underlying principles. In substance, they remained substantially intact. A transformed and more extensive central executive was simply grafted on to them.

The most significant step change in development of the modern British cabinet system was made in 1916, when Lloyd George acceded to the premiership. However, before investigating the post-1916 cabinet system it is important to analyse its previous shape and nature.

The central executive prior to 1916

The Victorian and Edwardian periods witnessed what we now consider to have been the classic period of cabinet government (Mackintosh, 1977). In earlier times, the most important locus of power had been the crown, and such cabinets as gradually began to emerge in the seventeenth century were clearly circumscribed by the authority of the monarch. In later times, cabinet government was again to be circumscribed by fragmentation, specialisation and sheer weight of business. In the period roughly from 1832 to 1916 – that is, from the first Reform Act to Lloyd George's assumption of the premiership – cabinet was the central locus of power in the British state. In the first half of this period it held the initiative in producing legislative proposals, but did not exercise full control of Parliament. In the second half, it established clear dominance over the legislature. Throughout, it tended to operate as a genuinely collective body. It is in this sense that the period is thought to have been one of real cabinet government.

Even within these years, cabinet faced challenges to its authority. Piecemeal development of a mass franchise after 1832 gradually helped to release the House of Commons from influence by both the monarch and the House of Lords. Increased party discipline and cohesion in the late nineteenth century helped to secure cabinet control of the Commons (Hanham, 1966). Yet gradual widening of the franchise weakened cabinet in relation to the prime minister, whose position was enhanced as incumbents exploited their status as national party leaders (Mackintosh, 1977: 308–21). Simultaneously, the increase in government responsibilities prompted in part by extension of the franchise vastly expanded the amount of business flowing through the cabinet system, and resulted in decisions being either taken or significantly shaped outside cabinet itself. In no sense, then, was this a period of complete cabinet dominance. Instead it was a period in which cabinet found itself on a slippery slope, its central position being undermined from both above and below.

Cabinet procedures were nevertheless substantially unaffected by the gradual slide from (brief) political pre-eminence. Throughout this period, cabinet tended to operate as a genuinely collegial forum in which privileged gentlemen debated the major political questions on fairly equal terms, and reached properly collective decisions (Daalder, 1964: 10). There were, of course, failures to attain this ideal. On the one hand, suspicions were sometimes aired that ministers had either deliberately failed to bring important questions to cabinet, or that factions within cabinet had sought to lead debate in a certain direction and thereby determine cabinet decisions. On the other, cabinet almost always functioned sub-optimally, notably towards the end of the period. Its members were often briefed poorly or not at all, and frequently gave cabinet discussion less than their undivided attention. During Lord Rosebery's premiership of 1894–5 one cabinet meeting was devoted chiefly to discussion of a Juvenal satire (Daalder, 1964: 27). Henry Campbell-Bannerman, Liberal prime minister from 1905 to 1908, found cabinet 'tedious and discursive' (Naylor, 1984: 19).

Indeed, prior to the 1916 reforms, cabinet was almost comically inefficient in its conduct of business. It often operated without an agenda and hardly ever kept minutes, the only regular record of debate – instituted by Lord Melbourne in 1837 – being a letter sent by the prime minister to the monarch at the end of each cabinet (Wilson, 1975: paras 303–5). Sometimes ministers distributed memoranda for discussion, but this was not a regular practice and no central means existed for recording decisions and circulating papers (Wilson, 1975: paras 306–11, 331). Often, as is only to be expected in a system run on such lines, it was unclear even to participants what conclusions had been reached. When John Bright resigned his cabinet post in 1882, the secretary of another cabinet member, Lord Hartington, wrote to prime minister Gladstone's private secretary to ask 'what the devil was decided, for he be damned if he knows' (Naylor, 1984: 19). A cabinet system run on the informal and trusting principles of a gentleman's club was certain to descend into this type of confusion from time to time.

While, therefore, cabinet modes of operation may have been congenial to many ministers, they were placed under mounting strain as the pressure of business coming to cabinet increased. This increase is extremely difficult to quantify, but is clearly indicated by the growth in parliamentary business and public spending which have taken place during the twentieth century (Tables 1.1 and 1.2). To some extent, cabinet adapted to this situation by taking more time for preparation, increasing the use of memoranda and making more frequent use of committees (Mackintosh, 1977: 290). The extent to which business was coordinated at all relied very much on the activities of private secretaries attached to the prime minister (Jones, 1987: 39). However, the approach was piecemeal and erratic.

By the start of the twentieth century (if not earlier), cabinet had four major weaknesses. It was deficient in competence, for it did not have sufficient information and advice to reach decisions on complex and technical matters. It was deficient in capacity to handle the quantity of business which was beginning to pass through the system and require attention. It was deficient

Table 1.1 Volume of public legislation passed by Parliament (including delegated legislation), 1900–87.

Year	Public General Acts and Measures		Statutory Instruments	
	Number	Pages (a)	Number	Pages
1900	63	198	N/A	N/A
1910	38	214	303	922
1920	82	560	2472	1753
1930	42	805	1166	1966
1940	61	506	2223	1685
1950	51	1001	2144	4067
1960	67	1176	2496	2820
1970	61	1516	2044	6835
1980	70	2876	2051	7424
1981	72	2276	1892	6558
1982	59	2130	1900	5572
1983	62	1541	1966	6439
1984	62	2876	2065	6099
1985	76	3233	2082	6518
1986	72	2847	2356	N/A
1987	57	1538 (b)	2279	N/A

Source: Griffith and Ryle (1989: 288).

(a) The growth of the statute book in recent years is partly accounted for by exceptionally large consolidation Acts; for example, the Income and Corporation Taxes Act 1988 had 1041 pages.
(b) Published in A4, and therefore with fewer pages.
N/A: not available.

in coordinating capability, and in ever more apparent ways failed effectively to oversee government business. It was deficient in directional ability, being unable to give a clear lead to the overall system of government.

The 1916 reforms of the central executive

In modern times, the key step change in development of the central executive was made in December 1916, when the demands of total war triggered fundamental reorganisation of a central executive already showing signs of an inability to cope with pressures generated by an expanding state machine. Only from this date was a recognisably modern cabinet system established at the heart of British government. However, although it took the stimulus of total war to trigger significant reform of the British cabinet system, it is clear that the changes made in December 1916 – or something very similar to them – would have had to come sooner or later. As it was, the brutal reality of the first world war, and the extent of the mobilisation which it required, proved too much for the Edwardian cabinet system to cope with. As Lord Curzon, a member of the war cabinet, remarked in the House of Lords in June 1918, 'the

Table 1.2 Public expenditure in real terms and as a percentage of GDP, 1890–1992.

Year	Public expenditure £m (1992 prices)	As % of GDP
1890	7731	9.7
1895	9658	11.2
1900	15727	15.9
1905	13859	13.4
1910	15219	13.8
1915	45584	35.2
1920	31217	28.2
1925	30765	26.1
1930	34774	27.4
1935	36511	26.6
1940	104931	62.4
1945	116407	66.2
1950	74254	39.6
1955	83099	38.7
1960	94961	39.3
1965	121766	41.6
1970	153840	46.7
1974	189167	51.9
1975	195013	53.9
1976	193200	51.9
1977	182503	47.9
1978	189530	48.4
1979	199081	49.5
1980	204569	51.9
1981	208678	53.5
1982	214458	54.0
1983	218171	53.0
1984	220210	52.5
1985	223795	51.2
1986	224621	49.5
1987	222923	46.9
1988	221422	44.4
1989	227387	44.6
1990	230860	45.0
1991	238823	46.1
1992	254126	49.4

Source: Brian Hogwood.

old Cabinet system had broken down, both as a war machine and as a peace machine' (Naylor, 1984: 15). Reform simply had to happen.

It was triggered by Asquith's resignation in December 1916, when reform of the machinery of cabinet was a central issue (Daalder, 1964: 39). A systematic rethink was quickly managed almost in its entirety by two men. One was David Lloyd George, who replaced Asquith as prime minister. The other was Maurice Hankey, from 1908 to 1912 assistant secretary, and from 1912 secretary, of one of the few parts of the cabinet machine to operate according to modern bureaucratic principles, the committee of imperial defence (CID). Within days of Lloyd George's assumption of the premiership Hankey had been appointed secretary to the cabinet (or cabinet secretary) with a remit to establish an efficient set of operations at the core of British government.

Lieutenant Colonel Hankey, not a civil servant but a member of the armed forces, set about creating a new cabinet system based on the staff and methods developed by the CID (Roskill, 1970: 338). These methods reflected a military concern for confidentiality, organisation and clear lines of communication and direction. At the heart of the new system was a five-man war cabinet with executive authority, a cabinet secretariat located close to Downing Street in Whitehall Gardens, and a network of cabinet committees. Lloyd George also instituted a prime minister's secretariat – or 'Garden Suburb' – in the grounds of 10 Downing Street (Turner, 1982).

Equally important as these reforms in organisation were changes in the way in which the cabinet system operated. Breaking with precedent, Hankey instituted the keeping of systematic records of cabinet proceedings in the form of minutes and conclusions expressing a clear decision (Daalder, 1965: 49). In addition, he regularised distribution of memoranda and created central records and indexes to assist continuity of administration (Wilson, 1975: para. 325). What has been described as 'the ending of Cabinet informality' was thereby brought to pass (Naylor, 1984: 16). Genuinely bureaucratic principles were embedded at the core of British government for the very first time.

The cabinet system in the inter-war period

The 1916 reforms succeeded both in creating a measure of order and in substantially increasing institutional capacity at the centre of British government. Lloyd George believed them to have established 'virtually a new system of Government in this Country' (Naylor, 1984: 26). The Haldane report on the machinery of government agreed: 'during the war an entirely new type of Cabinet has been evolved, with new methods of procedure' (Ministry of Reconstruction, 1918: para. 8). In essence, the reforms effected systematisation of the core executive, and a greater centralisation of power within it.

Not surprisingly, the 1916 reforms provoked resistance from departments dispossessed to a greater or lesser degree by the new centralisation. Most concern was expressed by the Treasury, historically the nodal point of all domestic administration, and therefore the department with most to lose from new coordinating (potentially also controlling) mechanisms (Roskill, 1972: 125–6). Indeed, after war was over the Treasury moved in September 1919 to have its permanent secretary named official head of the civil service in order to secure formal recognition of its pre-eminent place in the administrative hierarchy (Naylor, 1984: 70–1). With the fall of Lloyd George in October 1922, the fate of his reforms became even more uncertain as elite opinion turned against not only the man, but also many of his works (Roskill, 1972: 304–21). Already, in June 1922, Parliament had launched a major debate on the cabinet secretariat, and many MPs had taken the opportunity to denounce the centralisation of power which it was widely held to have effected (Roskill, 1972: 280–2).

With Lloyd George's replacement as prime minister by Andrew Bonar Law, the 1916 reforms came under further pressure as the Treasury saw its chance to take control of the competitor body. It seems that what Sir Warren Fisher, permanent secretary to the Treasury, had in mind was a takeover bid whereby the cabinet secretariat would be incorporated into his central department of state (Naylor, 1984: 101–7). However, Hankey was able, first, to secure Bonar Law's support for the secretariat and, secondly, to conclude an agreement with Fisher whereby the Cabinet Office reverted to being a subordinate department of the Treasury, but in practical terms retained its independence (Roskill, 1972: 315–19). Even though the secretariat suffered a staff cut from 123 in 1922 to 39 in 1923 (Wilson, 1975: annex 7(a)), it had survived its greatest threat. Only on the occasion of Hankey's own resignation in 1938 was a further, largely token, attempt made to bring it under Treasury control. In effect, the key battle to secure the future of the secretariat had been fought – and won – in 1922. The implicit deal which had been struck confirmed the Treasury as primary department of state and the cabinet secretariat as the key agent of central coordination within the cabinet system.

Not all aspects of the 1916 reforms survived Lloyd George. He sought initially to extend the practice of a small executive cabinet – which is what the war cabinet was – into peacetime. This idea was quickly undermined and the coalition cabinet reverted to type in November 1919 with a membership of 19. Similarly, although Lloyd George maintained his prime ministerial secretariat in post-war years, it was formally abolished when he fell in 1922. The only two features of his system which did survive were therefore the cabinet secretariat and procedures associated with it, and the greater and more systematic use of cabinet committees. Even the latter practice diminished as wartime experience receded in the 1920s. The two enduring features owed their continued existence in the post-war world chiefly to eminent utility or, as Hankey put it, 'force of circumstances' (Roskill, 1972: 325). In the long term, it was these two innovations which were key.

They were added to in the years following Lloyd George's departure from government. In the 1920s it became standard practice for private secretaries to the prime minister to be civil servants, rather than personal aides, on secondment from their departments for two to four years (Jones, 1987: 43). Of particular significance in its impact on the cabinet system was the election in 1923 of the first (albeit minority) Labour government under Ramsay MacDonald. Again, the change was both beneficial and lasting. Labour ministers brought to the practice of government a very different experience from that of almost all their predecessors. In particular, their working knowledge of party and trade union committees enabled them to make an original contribution to the functioning of the cabinet system. Hankey believed their 'team work' to be 'excellent', and considered theirs to be 'a very business-like government' (Roskill, 1972: 366–7). Usually on the advice of Hankey or other secretariat members, specific procedural innovations were made by the first MacDonald cabinet to ensure timely notification and circulation of cabinet papers (Daalder, 1964: 65). Fuller interdepartmental consultation, notably with the Treasury and the law officers, was also established before issues came forward for decision (Roskill, 1972: 366). In addition, the MacDonald government innovated in the sphere of press relations by issuing a communiqué after each cabinet meeting. This practice was written out of the rules by Hankey once the Labour government had left office (Wilson, 1975: para. 513), but it did not prevent MacDonald from making the further innovation, in 1929, of appointing George Steward press relations officer. Steward was maintained in office by Baldwin in 1935 and created chief press liaison officer by Chamberlain in 1937. Perhaps the most important impact of the MacDonald cabinet was practical. In demonstrating that a bureaucratic machine might function smoothly, the first Labour government set standards for subsequent governments to meet. The cabinet secretariat, operating as guardian of the institutional memory, ensured that those standards deemed workable were communicated to successor cabinets.

By the end of the inter-war period, then, the twin innovations of a cabinet secretariat and systematic use of cabinet committees were embedded in the governmental practice of the British central executive. The secretariat had established itself as the key coordinating agent in the cabinet system. By 1938 its staff level had grown to 126, close to that achieved in the first world war (Wilson, 1975: annex 7(a)). Hankey, in more than 20 years' service as cabinet secretary, had become the embodiment of permanent government in Britain. Other members of the secretariat were also highly influential. Notable among them was Hankey's deputy, Tom Jones, a key figure in the domestic arena, and close confidant of prime minister Stanley Baldwin (Ellis, 1992). Cabinet procedures were also substantially under the control of the cabinet secretariat, which had secured their progressive documentation from January 1917 onwards. Such documents were usually submitted to (and occasionally amended by) each cabinet in the form of 'Instructions to the Secretary' (Wilson, 1975: para. 201). However, over time alteration of the rules became increasingly the province of prime minister and cabinet secretary. By the close of the inter-war years the secretariat was a fully established part of the cabinet system.

Similarly, cabinet committees, having fallen into partial disuse in the 1920s, had become by the late 1930s an established feature of the institutional landscape. By the time Britain again went to war, five cabinet committees had developed standing status, remaining in place even with a change of government. From 1935, a king's speech committee, charged with drafting the proposed legislative programme for each parliamentary session, was also fully instituted (Wilson, 1975: para. 207). Generally chaired by the prime minister, the five cabinet committees operated in the spheres of foreign policy, defence plans, defence policy and requirements, national expenditures and general purposes. It seems likely that the continuity provided by the long period of national government in the 1930s was the decisive condition for their emergence (Naylor, 1984: 256).

The cabinet system during the second world war

Little more than 20 years after the demands of the first total war in British history had prompted creation of the modern cabinet system, mobilisation of the nation in a second war effort was required of the central executive. Again, pressure of war quickened development of the cabinet system, and changes made in the space of a few war years proved to be decisive steps in its evolution.

The impact of war on the cabinet system in the 1940s was, however, different from that experienced a quarter of a century earlier. Under Lloyd George, the primary aim had been to introduce central coordinating and controlling capability across the whole range of government business. Under Churchill, reform centred on developing mechanisms which were already established, and on separating domestic from foreign and military policy. Again, a war cabinet – this time of between eight and 11 members – was instituted to set war aims and direct war policy. In the domestic sphere, policy debate and decision were devolved to a series of cabinet committees centred on the small and overarching lord president's committee. Created in late 1940, this was chaired initially by Sir John Anderson and, from 1943, by the deputy prime minister and Labour Party leader, Clement Attlee (Wilson, 1975: para. 950). Under its auspices, in 1941, statistical and economic sections were established to advise on the main lines of home policy. The effect was to create a dual structure for separate management of domestic and overseas concerns (Daalder, 1964: 211–12, 257). This distinction has remained, in one form or another, ever since.

Four other lasting innovations in the structure and procedure of the cabinet system were also developed during the second world war. The first and most important was increased official involvement in committee business. Until the 1940s, all committees other than those under the ambit of the CID were strictly ministerial in membership, though on occasion officials did attend. With the onset of war, a series of double-decker committees was created as official committees started to mirror ministerial ones. Subsequently free-standing official committees were created (Wilson, 1975: para. 933). The second innovation was introduction of the MISC and GEN series of *ad hoc* committees (Wilson, 1975: para. 934). Although this series was not used extensively, a precedent had been set which was to be substantially extended in the post-war period. The third innovation was institution of a separate legislation committee, charged with detailed legislative scrutiny before submission of bills to Parliament (Wilson, 1975: para. 946). The fourth was permission for committees to decide policy on behalf of cabinet (Gordon Walker, 1972: 41). Each of these innovations was developed by subsequent administrations. Each clearly transferred some power from full cabinet to its committees.

The cabinet system from 1945 to 1974

The story of cabinet system development in the post-war period is one of expansion and consolidation. The trend is persistent in broad outline over the long term. As before, the driving force was as much administrative necessity as political programme. A key problem which faced the central executive in the early post-war years was further expansion of business, much of it generated by enlargement of the welfare state. A great deal of this business was handled in committee. In Attlee's six-and-a-half years as prime minister 466 cabinet committees of all types (ministerial and official, standing and *ad hoc*) were established (Hennessy and Arends, 1983: 9). In the quest for enhanced central control of an increasingly unwieldy government machine, Attlee, assisted by cabinet secretaries Edward Bridges until 1947 and Norman Brook thereafter, created the first full-scale version of a recognisably modern cabinet system. Their approach centred on systematic organisation of the committee system.

Two key committees were the lord president's committee, which presided over domestic policy (as in the war), and a new economic policy committee, established in 1947. Attlee also appointed a number of ministerial coordinators to chair committees and oversee business in particular fields, and he made a deliberate attempt to draw junior ministers into the work of cabinet committees (Daalder, 1964: 103–7). On appointment as cabinet secretary, Brook regularised the practice of providing steering briefs for the prime minister and other committee chairmen to assist them in the handling of business. The outcome of these reforms was that many decisions were either predetermined or, indeed, taken outside cabinet (Butler, 1975). In addition, the flow of business through committees was facilitated, and the position of committee chairs enhanced.

One further important innovation made in 1945 was full establishment of the office of Downing Street press secretary. During the second world war, Churchill had dispensed with the press relations function undertaken by Steward in the 1930s. Attlee reintroduced it, and expanded the office. When Francis Williams was appointed adviser on public relations to the prime minister in

1945, he took charge not simply of lobby briefings, but also of broader aspects of the presentation of government policy. Although Churchill, on returning to office in 1951, again dispensed with the post, he was obliged in May 1952 to appoint Thomas Fife Clarke to a similar position, though it was located outside Number 10 and in the service of the government as a whole. No subsequent prime minister has dispensed with the office of Downing Street press secretary, and under the likes of Harold Evans (1957–64), Joe Haines (1969–70, 1974–6) and especially Donald Maitland (1970–4) the office was both systematised and expanded (Harris, 1990: 74–9; Seymour-Ure, 1989: 34). Ever since Attlee's time, with the sole exception of Churchill's premiership, the task of presenting the government's public position has been increasingly drawn into the cabinet system, and centred on the Prime Minister's Office.

Churchill also sought to reverse the trend of cabinet system development in other spheres. On entering office, he attempted to restore the position of cabinet as the major forum for policy discussion and coordination. In contrast to Attlee, he sought not to use a large cabinet and extensive committee system. Drawing on first-hand experience of the war years, he instituted a system of ministerial overlords who were to operate in peacetime much as members of his war cabinet had operated in wartime. The experiment was a failure, and soon disintegrated when departmental ministers refused to toe lines set by their ministerial overlords. Moreover, Churchill's lack of interest in domestic policy meant that in this sphere, at least, policy remained largely the province of responsible ministers. Churchill also tried to cut the number of cabinet committees, especially official ones, but an extensive system was soon revived simply to deal with the volume of business (Daalder, 1964: 120). The effect of Churchill's tenure was initially to restore some control to cabinet and to slow the trend of cabinet system evolution, but only on an intermittent and temporary basis.

Thereafter extension and consolidation of the cabinet system continued in a piecemeal fashion. The Eden (1955–7), Macmillan (1957–63) and Douglas-Home (1963–4) premierships saw progressive and largely hidden enlargement of cabinet system operations. An important series of innovations took place which helped to systematise procedures within the cabinet system. Throughout the 1950s, cabinet secretary Brook and his aides quietly developed codes and instructions governing officials' work in the Cabinet Office. This work continued into the 1960s. The result was further to institutionalise procedures and practices which had become accepted in the period after 1916. For the cabinet secretariat, the period was one of struggle to stem the proliferation of cabinet committees, which under pressure of business were constantly in danger of expanding well beyond their initial boundaries. The Macmillan period also saw the beginnings of what was later to become the political section of the Prime Minister's Office with the appointment of an outsider, John Wyndham, to Number 10, and the use of aides from Conservative Central Office to help with speech writing (Jones, 1987: 45).

The position of prime minister in relation to departments was also inadvertently enhanced, following changes in procedures governing prime minister's questions in the House of Commons. In July 1961, a twice-weekly parliamentary slot devoted solely to questions to the prime minister was created (Dunleavy, Jones and O'Leary, 1990: 128). This ensured that prime minister's questions on the order paper were actually put and answered, contrary to the previous situation when such questions were rarely reached (Wilson, 1976: 132). Subsequently, all prime ministers, in preparing for these engagements, required to be thoroughly briefed on a range of previously notified questions. By the early 1970s at the latest, it had become common practice for questions to the prime minister to take a stylised form, allowing an open-ended supplementary to be put (Griffith and Ryle, 1989: 259). Taken together, these developments meant that the prime minister had to answer questions on a wide range of potential topics. The consequence was that the legitimate right of the Prime Minister's Office to require information on a regular basis from departments was substantially enhanced.

Further expansion and consolidation took place in Cabinet Office functions, notably in the fields of foreign and defence policy. These date from 1957 when, in the wake of the Suez crisis, the joint intelligence committee (JIC) was taken out of military control, placed in the Cabinet Office, and reconstituted as a cabinet committee (Cabinet Office, 1993: 11). Further reform along these lines took place in April 1964, following the 1963 review of defence administration (Ministry of Defence, 1963). A standing cabinet committee on defence and overseas policy, and a separate secretariat were both created (Lee, 1990: 236). Then, between 1961 and 1963, the Plowden reforms of the public expenditure process were introduced (Treasury, 1961), creating the potential for a more systematic and central role for cabinet, and from time to time its committees, in the planning and control of public spending (Thain and Wright, 1995: ch.3). This potential was not, however, significantly realised until 1992 (see Chapter 6).

These tentative attempts to enhance central capacity were extended further under the first Wilson administration (1964–70). During these years there was a doubling in the number of senior staff employed by the Cabinet Office, and an expansion of its functions. The work of its secretariats became more specialised as organisation by policy sector was developed. In general, more power was devolved to deputy secretary level and some of its secretariats assumed a limited, but more substantial, policy role. In 1964 the post of chief scientific adviser to the cabinet was created (Healey, 1990: 251). An economic secretariat was instituted following creation of the Department of Economic Affairs in the same year (Lee, 1990: 236). In 1968 intelligence assessment staff were brought into the office under the auspices of the JIC and an expanded and reorganised intelligence and security secretariat. Also in 1968, the Cabinet Office was given its own vote in the supply estimates for the first time, and as a consequence emerged as an entirely free-standing institution (Lee, 1974:

165). Increasingly, Cabinet Office officials began to take from the Treasury responsibility for chairing interdepartmental committees. These changes amounted to a considerable enhancement of the position and status of the Cabinet Office. A trend was beginning to emerge whereby those functions which persistently crossed many departments were gradually drawn within the ambit of cabinet system agencies. The position of the Treasury was also bolstered when Wilson (1974: 722) promoted chief secretary John Diamond to cabinet in 1968. This experiment was discontinued in 1970, but became established practice after 1977 (see Chapter 2).

Under Wilson, the formal position and resources available to the prime minister were also augmented. The Ministers of the Crown Act 1964 increased the maximum number of permitted ministerial appointments from 70 to 91, thereby expanding the patronage available to the prime minister (Pollitt, 1984: 185). The Downing Street press and political offices were substantially reorganised, giving the presentation of government policy, if not its generation, more central direction (Jones, 1987: 46). Wilson also moved to strengthen the position of arenas outside the cabinet. In 1967, he placed clear new limits on the right of a minister to appeal from cabinet committee to full cabinet by ruling that a matter could only be taken to cabinet with the agreement of the committee chair (Gordon Walker, 1972: 44). This cut the amount of business going to cabinet, and made it more difficult for issues to be reopened at that level. It also served to strengthen the position of the prime minister, and those key ministers who held committee chairs. His ruling was not followed slavishly by the 1970 Heath government, but effectively it encapsulated practice thereafter (Hogwood and Mackie, 1985: 51; Cabinet Office, 1992a: para. 4). Other innovations of the Wilson years drew more functions and directive capacity into offices and positions within the cabinet system. In line with the recommendations of the Fulton committee, a Civil Service Department (CSD) was created in 1968 to manage the civil service under a minister for the civil service directly attached to Number 10. This enhanced the potential of the prime minister to intervene in civil service matters, and brought this area of activity more ostensibly into the prime ministerial domain. The recruitment of outside advisers, or 'irregulars', to assist the work of some ministers was for the first time allowed on a significant scale, but importantly all were subject to the agreement and approval of Number 10 and the Cabinet Office (Klein and Lewis, 1977).

This process of growth, consolidation and extension of cabinet system institutions continued during the Heath premiership (1970–4). A further doubling of senior Cabinet Office staff took place, as did further refinement and development of the secretariats. A science and technology group was established in the Cabinet Office to provide and coordinate advice to ministers (Gummett, 1991: 23). In 1972, a civil contingencies unit was set up in the office to deal with strikes and national emergencies (Hennessy, 1986: 21). It drew together functions previously held by a number of departments. In 1973, a fully-fledged European secretariat was created under a deputy secretary to handle relations with the EEC, and to coordinate departmental responses consequent on Britain's membership of the Community.

Heath also moved to augment the position of cabinet. He extended the advisory facilities available to it by creating, in 1971, the central policy review staff (CPRS). The think tank (as it was widely known) comprised some 24 individuals located in the Cabinet Office. They were given the task of providing cabinet with advice on a range of matters, notably strategic and policy issues (Blackstone and Plowden, 1988). Jones (1987: 40), however, claims that the CPRS worked chiefly for the prime minister. Under Heath an attempt was also made to report most committee decisions to cabinet. This practice tended to decline during his period in office, and was not maintained by his successors (Hogwood and Mackie, 1985: 51–2). In fact, the Heath government made extensive use of cabinet committees, and greatly extended the number and deployment of both official and mixed committees. Heath's period in office also witnessed an acceleration in the trend whereby junior ministers were given, in agreement with the prime minister, specific portfolios within a department. One consequence of this was that junior ministers were more extensively drawn into the work of cabinet committees (Theakston, 1987).

Extension of the range of activities located in cabinet system institutions, and gradual reordering of processes and procedures from the late 1950s onwards, took place largely under the cabinet secretaryship of Sir Burke Trend. He was assisted from 1972 by his deputy Sir John Hunt, who in 1973 took over as cabinet secretary. Their work, plus that of successive prime ministers, their advisers and other cabinet system officials, meant that the central executive which faced the oil shock and economic downturn of 1973–4 was substantially different from that which had emerged from the second world war. A systematic cabinet committee system was fully established, and the size and specialised nature of the cabinet secretariats had been expanded. Procedures had been documented and more firmly established. Staffing levels in cabinet system institutions had increased, and the facility to gather information from departments had been augmented. The Cabinet Office had emerged as an autonomous entity, and a small but increasing number of functions had been placed in it. The Prime Minister's Office remained somewhat underdeveloped, but there were also increasing signs of change here. This enhancement of central capability had been gradual and intermittent, but the overall trend had been one of expansion and consolidation.

Continuity and change in the cabinet system

Analysis of the period from 1916 to 1974 reveals a slow accretion in the size, complexity and status of the cabinet system. These changes did not, however, lead to a significant alteration in the principles underlying the central executive.

The predominance of executive authority remained. The tendency towards small-group and exclusive politics still applied. The emphasis on a singular, though highly compromised and constrained, executive endured. The practice of operating from the top down, while taking account of the party support base, persisted. The departmentalism inherent in the system continued to militate against a more corporate, unified and collective approach. Thus, the picture is one of both continuity and change. While institutions, processes and procedures changed dramatically over the period underlying principles remained largely intact, if a little threadbare. Yet the elements of the system which did change generated a clear alteration in the disposition of central government, biasing the system more overtly in favour of cabinet system institutions. Several aspects are of note.

One is that by 1974 the capacity of central cabinet system agencies – Cabinet Office and Prime Minister's Office – had been increased. The 60-year period after 1916 witnessed both stagnation and even cuts in central capacity, but the long-term trend was clearly in the direction of enlargement. It was visible in increased staffing levels, expanded functions, greater policy specialism, and an increasing central requirement to vet, approve or be informed about certain types of departmental actions. Moreover, the development of documentation and its management by the secretariats placed control and supervision of the flow of business more firmly at the centre. In sum, the position of central personnel was enhanced over the period, as was the power potential vested in these central offices.

A second clear change significantly affected the internal distribution of power potential within the system. This was decline in the position of cabinet as the central controlling element at the apex of British government. Part of its power had moved upwards to the central offices just described. Part of it had moved downwards to committees and, even, to individual departments. Given the increased pressure of business during the course of the twentieth century, this shift in emphasis was perhaps inevitable. The failure of attempts made by Churchill and Heath to return to more cabinet-based government indicates this.

A third change, hinted at already, affected departmental autonomy. However, this was by no means change in a single direction. On the one hand, departmental autonomy was reduced by the increased capacity of the cabinet system. Even the Treasury lost some activities to the centre. On the other, departmental autonomy expanded with the increase in government business and consequent overload at the centre. The net effect of these opposed changes was that departments were increasingly drawn within the ambit of the cabinet system on a series of strategic matters, but saw their power increased in areas of specific and subsidiary importance. The historic tension between collective and departmental government persisted.

These many and often contradictory changes were prompted by a multitude of factors. Among them were administrative necessity, pressure of events, party political ideas and pet individual projects. The important point is that reasons for change were as much administrative as either party political or individual. Many reforms were generated by the underlying administrative dilemmas inherent in big government. Much of the impulsion behind the changes reflected various and cumulative attempts to solve the problems of capacity, competence, coordination and direction which had been so manifest in 1916.

2

□

Organisations and positions

Expansion of the cabinet system, under pressure of expansion of the state itself, has inevitably increased the number and complexity of its constituent parts. In this chapter we analyse the formal organisational structure of the contemporary cabinet system, focusing on agencies and arenas within which issues are considered and key established positions contained within them. Positions are examined in terms of formal powers and number and nature of support staff. The chapter does not consider semi-formal and informal aspects of the system, which are addressed in Chapters 4 and 5. Our examination allows us to draw rudimentary conclusions about the opportunities that the cabinet system's formal structure offers for the exercise of individual initiative. It also permits us to identify changes in the formal structure in the period since 1974, and positions which have become more advantaged as a result.

The main agencies which we subject to detailed analysis are the Prime Minister's Office, Cabinet Office, Treasury, elements of the central executive concerned with government business management, and cabinet system law offices. Within each of these agencies we identify leading positions. We do not, therefore, analyse in this chapter the individual functions of all cabinet ministers, for we do not consider all of them on the basis of their formal positions to be consistently central actors in the cabinet system. Instead, we focus on those whose formal position places them in a strategic position within that system. The arenas we investigate are cabinet and its committees, both ministerial and official. Here we do give some attention to ministers, individually as committee chairs and collectively as members of cabinet and cabinet committees.

Prime Minister's Office

The Prime Minister's Office at 10 Downing Street divides into five parts: private office, political office, press office, prime minister's policy unit

27

(PMPU), and a number of free-standing advisers. The prime minister's room at the House of Commons is fully integrated with it for communications and office facilities (Wilson, 1976: 60). The Prime Minister's Office is smaller than the offices of many other heads of government (Jones, 1985a: 73). The German chancellor has a staff of 450 and the American president a staff of 400 (Müller-Rommel, 1993: 134–5). The 107 Downing Street staff registered under Major in 1993 was thus small in international terms, despite being a record for the contemporary period. Key staff (excluding typists, messengers and so on) numbered approximately 34 out of Major's total of 107.

The prime minister's private office serves as the main access point to the prime minister, and as the transmission point from the prime minister to other parts of the cabinet system and government departments. It is staffed by career civil servants, who usually serve for between two and three years on secondment from other departments, before returning to senior posts (Jones, 1985a: 77). The number of senior private secretaries in the office has not changed a great deal in the post-war period. In 1945 there were four. In 1995 there are six. However, since 1945 organisation of the office has become more structured and the number of support staff has increased. In 1995, with the exception of the principal private secretary, each main secretary covers a particular area of prime ministerial business. Two private secretaries are responsible for overseas affairs. The other three private secretaries cover economic affairs, parliamentary affairs and home affairs and diary. A further secretary assists the diary secretary and another, not located in the private office, deals with appointments. Two further assistant secretaries make up the complement of key positions (Cabinet Office, 1995a: col. 517). In addition to organising the flow of business to and from the prime minister and keeping the diary, private secretaries brief the prime minister and keep notes on his or her meetings and conversations (Jones, 1987: 51). The private office also plays a key role in briefing the prime minister for prime minister's questions in the House of Commons, and is an important liaison with Buckingham Palace.

The political office was first fully established by Wilson in 1964, although its origins may be traced somewhat further back (see Chapter 1). This is a small unit usually consisting of a political secretary and the prime minister's parliamentary private secretary (PPS) whose job, like that of other ministers' PPSs, is to liaise with back-benchers on an informal basis. The political office also handles the prime minister's relations with party headquarters and the mass party in the country, and deals with all correspondence of a party political nature. The prime minister's constituency secretary is sometimes located in the political office. This office has always been funded in part from party or other external sources.

The press office, or section, deals with media relations and is headed by the prime minister's press secretary, his deputy and eight other press secretaries. The essence of the press secretary's role is fourfold (Seymour-Ure, 1991: 6).

He acts as spokesman for the government, as adviser on media relations, as intermediary (or agent) with the news media, and as coordinator of the government's information services. There is an implicit tension in each of these roles between prime ministerial and cabinet functions. Over time, the press secretary has become increasingly identified with the prime minister (Seymour-Ure, 1991: 14–16).

The PMPU was first established by Harold Wilson in 1974 in line with the Fulton committee's recommendation that policy advisers be appointed to the Prime Minister's and Cabinet Offices (Wilson, 1976: 98). It is staffed either by outsiders or by civil servants on secondment, though all are employed as civil servants for the duration of their PMPU work. The unit has always been small. Under Wilson and Callaghan, it had eight or nine full- and part-time members. Under Thatcher, it was initially reduced to about four people, including one or two civil servants (Jones, 1985a: 91–2). Following abolition of the CPRS in 1983 (Blackstone and Plowden, 1988: ch.9), it was returned to its 1970s dimensions. Under Major, these dimensions have been increased. In 1995, the PMPU has retained a complement of eight desk officers, but has bolstered its support staff to five. In its early years under Labour, the unit concentrated on forward policy analysis over the medium to long term (Donoughue, 1987: 20ff.). Its main focus was economic policy (Willetts, 1987: 44). Under Thatcher, it developed a more departmental role, attempting not only to monitor government economic strategy, but also to develop new policy ideas in the fields of economic and domestic policy. If these were approved by the prime minister, the PMPU would then liaise with departments to determine whether they could be developed further. Under Major, the PMPU is less an initiator and more an evaluator of policy developed by departments. It has nevertheless played an important role in initiating some key policies in the Major era, notable examples being council tax, the Citizen's Charter and the government's approach to the Maastricht treaty negotiations in 1991 (Seldon, 1994: 158). Subsequently the PMPU has continued to take a significant interest in the European dimension to British politics and policy, a central concern of the Major government.

In addition to each of these formal organisations within the Prime Minister's Office some prime ministers, in both recent and earlier times, have had a series of largely free-standing advisers. Nowadays such individuals might be drawn into the work of the PMPU, or report directly to the prime minister. Use of prime ministerial advisers was developed particularly under Thatcher, who appointed special advisers in the fields of government efficiency, overseas, defence and economic policy. The most notorious of these was Sir Alan Walters, who on a periodic basis until 1989 served as special economic adviser. Major has continued this practice by employing advisers on foreign affairs, efficiency and competition policy.

The key position in the office is, of course, that of prime minister. The main powers vested in the prime minister are:

(i)   appointment of cabinet ministers, other ministers and top civil servants;
(ii) management of cabinet, its committees and the business that flows through them;
(iii) supervision of the civil service;
(iv) management of the machinery and structure of government;
(v)   oversight of security service operations;
(vi) appointment to public bodies;
(vii) distribution of honours; and
(viii)dissolution of Parliament (Brazier, 1988: 66–91; King, 1991).

In piecemeal fashion, each of these powers has been attached to the premiership, or significantly expanded, in the period since 1916.

Many commentators argue that in practice these prime ministerial powers are heavily constrained (Brown, 1968a, 1968b; Jones, 1985b; Wilson, 1976). This is an obvious but cardinal point. On the one hand, it is very clear that the prime minister has the right to intervene extensively in the work of the cabinet system. On the other, even the most active prime minister will face real-world constraints that simply cannot be overcome by a single individual. These are of two main kinds. Political constraints require the prime minister both to balance his or her ministerial team, and to ensure that government policy initiatives are broadly in tune with the mood of ministerial colleagues, party and public. Resource constraints are possibly more pressing, and are generated in particular by the prime minister's shortage of time, energy and information. The capacity and competence of immediate aides working for him or her also limit prime ministerial activism.

The position of principal private secretary is also important. This civil servant oversees the Prime Minister's Office, and controls papers which go to the prime minister. Depending on the extent of personal rapport between them, the principal private secretary can also become a key adviser on policy matters. Individual private secretaries are certainly important within their own field of responsibility, and in the small-group politics of the Prime Minister's Office may develop a wider importance. Under Thatcher, for example, the private secretary responsible for overseas matters, Charles Powell, was an especially close confidant and adviser (Ranelagh, 1992: 11, 254–7).

Other members of the Prime Minister's Office may become important from time to time, but the precise degree of influence often depends on individual chemistry. Most likely to become key prime ministerial advisers, even cronies, are the PPS, head of the PMPU, chief press secretary and free-standing advisers. Under Thatcher, Ian Gow (PPS) at the start of her premiership, Bernard Ingham (chief press secretary) virtually throughout it, and Sir Alan Walters (prime ministerial adviser) at intervals during it were certainly key figures (Ranelagh, 1992). Under Major between 1990 and 1994, Sarah Hogg (head of the PMPU) and Gus O'Donnell (chief press secretary) were judged to be amongst the most influential figures in Number 10 (Seldon, 1994: 158–9).

More generally, many of the individuals who serve in the Prime Minister's Office may develop initiatives in their own right, in conformity with what they understand to be the prime minister's wishes.

Change since 1974

In the period since 1974, the Prime Minister's Office has clearly expanded. The most important change has been creation of the PMPU. Thatcher's appointment of an efficiency adviser who reported directly to her (and headed an efficiency unit based in the Cabinet Office) was also an important innovation which has been retained. However, real significance attaches not so much to change in the size of the Prime Minister's Office, but to alteration of its operations and functions. To begin with, the status of the entire office as an established part of British central government has been enhanced. In 1977, for the first time, it was given a designation separate from the Cabinet Office in the *Civil Service Year Book*. More importantly, the relationship between the Prime Minister's Office and other parts of the British state has changed in recent years. In particular, the increase in advisory staff which has taken place has enhanced the prime minister's ability to know what is happening in other parts of the government machine. Interviews and published sources (Fowler, 1991; Lawson, 1993; Prior, 1986; Wass, 1984: 33; Young, 1991) reveal that there has been an increasing tendency for business to flow to the Prime Minister's Office, and for ministers to feel the need to consult Number 10 before launching significant departmental initiatives. These developments have enhanced the position of the Prime Minister's Office at the hub of the system, and expanded the potential of the prime minister and his or her staff to oversee government strategy, to monitor departmental work and to initiate policy from the centre. Each of these potentials remains limited, but each has certainly expanded in the last 20 years.

External changes, by combining to bolster his or her political standing, have also served to alter the power potential of the prime minister. The entire contemporary period has seen a major development of international summitry, both within the European Union (EU) and outside it in fora such as Group of Seven (G7) meetings (King, 1991; James, 1992; Lee, 1995). Such summitry often involves negotiation and agreement at prime ministerial (or equivalent) level, and has necessarily extended prime ministerial involvement and initiative in the foreign and international economic policy domains (Wass, 1984: 33). In addition the contemporary mass media, especially television, have tended to focus attention on the prime minister as representative of the government as a whole (Cockerell, 1988). Both developments have resulted in a significant enhancement of the singular position of the prime minister (Foley, 1993). Their net effect on the prime minister's power potential is, however, difficult to estimate. The requirements of international summitry

31

have increased demands on the prime minister's time and energy, while increased media attention has both enhanced the prime minister's position in a period of government success and weakened it in a period of government failure. Prime ministers may now take more of the credit, but they must also shoulder more of the blame.

Change since 1974 has consolidated and extended initiatives taken in earlier years. The cumulative result has been an enhancement of the power potential located in the positions of prime minister and the top members of his or her staff. The effect of change has been marginally to reduce the administrative deficit of offices directly supportive of the prime minister, although in comparative terms the position still appears to be under-resourced. The validity of this judgement depends very much on the extent to which other agencies in the cabinet system can be considered to work primarily for the prime minister. Most relevant in this regard is the Cabinet Office.

Cabinet Office

The Cabinet Office is located at 70 Whitehall. A single corridor provides direct access from it to 10 Downing Street. It comprises the cabinet secretariat and the Office of Public Service (OPS (until July 1995 the Office of Public Service and Science (OPSS)). The secretariat is responsible for organising the flow of business through cabinet and its committees. It is divided into five main subsidiary secretariats, each of which has a particular area of responsibility. In 1995, four of these cover economic policy, home and social affairs (including legislation), defence and overseas affairs and European affairs. A further, joint intelligence, secretariat plus an assessments staff deal with national security and intelligence information (Cabinet Office, 1993: 12). A telecoms secretariat also exists, but is not a policy division (Cabinet Office, 1995a: cols 67–8). OPS is charged with most of the functions relating to operation and management of the civil service (including the Next Steps programme), with raising the standard of public services (which is still held to include services provided by privatised utilities), and with responsibility for senior public appointments and promotion of greater openness in government. OPS is headed by a cabinet minister who answers to the deputy prime minister and prime minister.

In 1994 the Cabinet Office had a staff of more than 2200, the vast majority of whom worked in OPSS (see Table 2.1). Many were support staff engaged in typing, general clerical duties and messenger services. Senior administrative staff (from principal to permanent secretary, grades 7 to 1) numbered 134. Of these, about 28 were employed in the secretariats (PMS, 1995: 34–7). However, in the secretariats there was a far higher proportion of the top two grades of civil servant (deputy and under secretary) than in the rest of the Cabinet Office. The respective ratios were 1:3 and 1:7. It is important to note

Table 2.1 Staff employed in the Cabinet Office and Treasury, 1974–94.

	Cabinet Office	Treasury
1974	600	1000
1975	629	1065
1976	685	1144
1977	660	1143
1978	622	1063
1979	630	1052
1980	586	1026
1981	591	1006
1982	554	4177
1983	547	3992
1984	1669	3671
1985	1648	3385
1986	1680	3363
1987	1709	3359
1988	1574	3132
1989	1619	3181
1990	1484	3135
1991	1513	3008
1992	1476	2846
1993	2324	1946
1994	2204	1385

Figures indicate staff in post at 1 January 1974–83 and at 1 April 1984–94. Cabinet Office includes MPO from 1984, Central Statistical Office until 1990 and OPSS from 1992. Treasury includes ex-CSD staff from 1982.

Source: Treasury.

that most important secretariat staff are not permanent employees of the Cabinet Office, but are instead on secondment from departments of state, usually for between two and three years at a time. Only the cabinet secretary at the peak of the office, and support staff at the bottom, are in place for longer periods (Burnham and Jones, 1993: 307).

The key formal positions in the Cabinet Office are cabinet secretary, deputy and under secretaries who head each of the secretariats, ministerial and official heads of OPS and the deputy prime minister. The cabinet secretary is formally responsible for coordinating the handling of government business at the supradepartmental level, for revising and monitoring cabinet system rules, for investigating alleged breaches of them, for coordinating the oversight of expenditure on, and management of, government security and intelligence operations (Cabinet Office, 1993: 17), for overseeing the honours system, and for general organisation of government. The cabinet secretary is also consulted on a wide range of public appointments and is involved in selection of top civil servants. As head of the home civil service, he is responsible on the official side for its overall management. Formally, these powers are carried out in support of, and in consultation with, the prime minister.

In coordinating the flow of business through the cabinet system the cabinet secretary is assisted by senior officials in the secretariats. The heads of the economic and defence and overseas secretariats tend to provide broad assistance in managing this task, thereby generating oversight capacity in the domestic and foreign spheres of cabinet system business. In effect the head of the home and social affairs secretariat comes under the responsibility of the deputy secretary in charge of the economic secretariat. By contrast, the heads of the European and joint intelligence secretariats tend largely to operate within their own spheres of responsibility.

The ministerial head of OPS currently has the title chancellor of the Duchy of Lancaster and minister of public service and has a seat in cabinet. He is assisted by a junior minister. The ministerial head of OPS is formally responsible to cabinet, the deputy prime minister and the prime minister, who is lead minister in charge of the civil service. The permanent secretary to the OPS is heavily involved in management of the civil service, and in efficiency of government questions.

Assessment of the importance of key Cabinet Office positions is difficult. On the official side, the cabinet secretary is potentially enormously influential. The orthodox view is that the responsibilities vested in his position, and in all other civil service posts, are exercised on the initiative of ministers (and notably in this area the prime minister). However, for a number of reasons the cabinet secretary and his top colleagues are likely to become influential in their own right. This is partly because some of the tasks with which they are charged, such as management of the flow of business through the cabinet system, are very specialised, and are thus likely to be resistant to full political control. It is also because, in an informal sense, the cabinet secretary in particular is highly likely to develop a close personal relationship with the prime minister of the day. Deputy secretaries in the secretariats are also likely to be influential.

On the ministerial side, the deputy prime minister and the head of OPS are in key positions within the central executive, but the extent to which they are able to exploit their positions depends on the relationships they develop with the prime minister of the day and, to a lesser extent, with the cabinet secretary. The appointment of Michael Heseltine as deputy prime minister in July 1995 indicates the increasing importance of these key cabinet system positions in overseeing the government's central, cross-departmental programmes, and in coordinating government business in general. Although Heseltine's appointment was in some ways a political act, it did build on an established trend. David Hunt, who was chancellor of the Duchy of Lancaster from 1994 to 1995, already undertook some of the functions now fulfilled by Heseltine.

In assessing the importance of key Cabinet Office positions, a central question has to be addressed: in whose interests are Cabinet Office powers being wielded? Crudely, does the Cabinet Office primarily serve the cabinet or the prime minister? No clear, dichotomous answer to this question is possible. However, what can be said is that the chief focus of attention of key Cabinet

Office actors tends to be the prime minister. In an informal sense, the cabinet secretary is seen increasingly as the prime minister's permanent secretary. Certainly at interview ministers confirmed the growing impression that the prime minister has first call on the time of Cabinet Office officials.

Change since 1974

These arguments are reinforced by analysis of change in the Cabinet Office since 1974. The period has witnessed important alterations in the structure and operation of the Cabinet Office, and in key positions within it. The most visible trend in the years since 1974 is growth in the sheer size of the office, mainly through creation of new functions or transfer of existing ones from elsewhere. As shown in Table 2.1, in the space of 20 years the number of staff employed in the Cabinet Office has nearly quadrupled. At the same time, the range of functions placed within it has been greatly expanded. Many new functions bring important responsibilities for oversight of the entire government machine into the office. One set of examples is the government's internal efficiency programme created in 1979, the financial management initiative (FMI) launched as an expansion of it in 1982, and the Next Steps programme of executive agencies launched in 1988. Further examples are transfer of civil service management and training responsibilities to the management and personnel office (MPO) of the Cabinet Office following abolition of the CSD in 1981, the increase in its responsibility for coordination of security and intelligence information which took place in 1983, and its responsibility for oversight of the Citizen's Charter initiative, launched in 1991. The creation of OPSS in 1992 involved a further accretion of functions, drawing in some activities from outside the Cabinet Office. OPSS assumed responsibility not only for civil service administration, but also for science functions which previously were located in the Department of Education and Science (DES). Responsibility for science and technology policy, which was overseen previously by a Cabinet Office secretariat, was also transferred to OPSS. In addition, the OPSS's civil service administration functions were consolidated to include not only efficiency drives, staff recruitment and training and development but also oversight of the central government's market-testing programme. Other such functions were either developed or created when OPSS was established. A clear example was the 'open government' programme, launched in 1992. The creation of OPSS could thus be seen in part as an attempt to regularise earlier changes, and in part as an extension of Cabinet Office capability. The changes made in July 1995, when OPSS became OPS, comprised a transfer of science functions to the Department of Trade and Industry (DTI), a shift of the competitiveness and deregulation division from the DTI to OPS and an enhancement of central coordinating capacity under the general oversight of the deputy prime minister.

Further changes since 1974 have taken place within Cabinet Office secretariats. Here policy responsibilities have been extended to encompass development of cross-departmental policy issues. On occasion, changes of this kind have been temporary. The devolution unit of the late 1970s and special inner-city and urban-policy units in the 1980s are examples. Other changes have been more permanent. Since 1973, British membership of the EU has allowed the European secretariat to assume a key coordinating and briefing function. Important changes have also taken place in secretariat planning and management of the flow of business through the cabinet system (see Chapter 4). However, it has not all been a story of expansion. One element of the pre-1974 Cabinet Office was lost in 1983 when Thatcher abolished the CPRS. This weakened the collective resource base of ministers and, by removing an alternative support staff, strengthened the disposition of the Cabinet Office machinery to operate more clearly on behalf of the prime minister.

In the course of these changes the formal position of the cabinet secretary has been greatly enhanced. When the CSD was abolished in 1981 he was made joint head (with the first permanent secretary to the Treasury) of the home civil service. In 1983, he assumed the position of sole head of the home civil service, a position which has been retained ever since. This increase in formal responsibilities has meant that the cabinet secretary is now able to spend only half his time on cabinet system business (BBC, 1988), thereby reducing his capacity for involvement in this sphere. One consequence of these linked changes has been a reorganisation of secretariat workloads, and an increase in the autonomy of deputy secretaries (Seldon, 1990: 105), who now tend to liaise directly with the prime minister rather than via the cabinet secretary. Other official changes resulted from the creation of OPSS and subsequently OPS, and of new positions within them.

Judged purely in organisational terms, the period since 1974 has thus witnessed significant development of the Cabinet Office. In some respects, this development can be captured in increased staffing levels. However, more important is the accumulation of functions and powers of general oversight of government business which lies behind much of that increase. During the period, links between the Cabinet and Prime Minister's Offices have also been refined and developed, with the result that the two offices today form a significant core at the heart of government.

Treasury

This accretion of functions in the Cabinet Office has been partly at the cost of other government departments. It has always been the case that some departments which are formally outside the cabinet system have played a leading role within it. Among those most frequently mentioned are the Treasury and the Foreign and Commonwealth Office (FCO) (Dunleavy and Rhodes, 1990:

3). In fact, of these two, only the Treasury is drawn on a consistent basis into the whole range of government activity. In comparative terms, it is unusually powerful. The functions which it discharges cover all of government economic policy. These functions are split between the Ministry of Economics and the Ministry of Finance in Germany, the Department of Finance and the Treasury Board in Canada, and the Department of Finance and the Treasury in Australia. Only France among G7 nations has a Ministry of Finance which equals the British Treasury in taking sole responsibility for macro-economic policy (Lawson, 1993: 272; Pliatzky, 1989: 4–6). In practice, however, the Japanese Ministry of Finance fulfils a similar function.

The Treasury's crucial location within the cabinet system derives both from its responsibility for economic policy and from its control of the government's purse strings. Consequently, it is a vital player in almost all policy discussed within the cabinet system. Staffed by about 1400 officials and support staff (see Table 2.1), it is divided into four main divisions. These are finance, public expenditure, government economic service and civil service management and pay. Of particular importance within the cabinet system is the Treasury's public expenditure division.

The structural underpinnings of the Treasury's central role in the cabinet system are substantial. Not only does Treasury approval need to be acquired before any new spending proposal can be passed by cabinet committee (or, indeed, cabinet itself), it also has the formal ability to vet any new proposal before it is put into the cabinet system (Lawson, 1993: 273). The Treasury has also acquired the unique right to appeal from cabinet committee to full cabinet on expenditure grounds. In addition to each of these powers, one of the Treasury's main policy contributions, the annual revenue budget, is unique among major government initiatives in not being developed formally in the cabinet system at all (see Chapter 6). Instead, the budget is strictly a Treasury matter and only involves other government departments, and even the prime minister, on Treasury terms. Only at the budget cabinet, now held on the morning of the day on which the chancellor reads his budget statement to the House of Commons, are other government ministers informed of the full contents of the revenue budget (Brazier, 1988: 99).

The key Treasury ministers who are extensively drawn into the cabinet system are chancellor and chief secretary, both of whom are members of cabinet. The chief secretary in particular is responsible for public expenditure. Between them, these two ministers hold membership of most cabinet committees, and all with important spending implications (see Chapters 5 and 6). Theirs are weighty voices in each and every case. Treasury personnel are also a major presence on official cabinet committees, and play leading roles in the central executive network. Among top civil servants, the first permanent secretary to the Treasury can be considered second in rank only to the cabinet secretary. The Treasury also has two other permanent secretaries, one of whom is responsible for public expenditure.

Change since 1974

The Treasury has always been a powerful department, but its central position was greatly extended after 1945 mainly as the result of two developments. On the one hand the Keynesian revolution, reinforced by developing concern from the late 1950s with Britain's relative economic decline, inevitably enhanced the role of the leading economic department of government. On the other, the drive to institute effective public expenditure controls from 1976 further increased Treasury status.

In the period between 1974 and 1995, the Treasury's power potential initially increased but then suffered a measure of decline. The late 1970s saw an increase in Treasury influence, as public spending was placed under ever tighter control. The chief secretary was brought into cabinet in 1977, making the Treasury the only department which, since that date, has continuously had two ministers in cabinet. The Treasury's sole right of appeal from committee to full cabinet was established by the early 1980s. In 1981, following abolition of the CSD, civil service pay and some management functions were shifted into the Treasury, thereby further enhancing its status.

However, the late 1980s and early 1990s then witnessed a decline in some aspects of the Treasury's power potential. One minor, but telling, shift took place in the sphere of macro-economic policy, as the PMPU gradually became a source of alternative economic advice, especially under Thatcher. In 1993, nearly 900 staff engaged in developing government information and computer systems were transferred to the OPSS in the Cabinet Office (see Table 2.1). In October 1994, the Treasury announced plans to slim its senior staffing level by about a third, and to transfer management of civil service pay to the Cabinet Office. In July 1995 a powerful standing ministerial committee on competitiveness, chaired by the deputy prime minister and covering broad areas of industrial policy, was created. This could present a threat to the Treasury's traditional hold on economic policy. Finally, gradual creation of executive agencies under the Next Steps initiative has led to a reassessment of the Treasury's role in controlling the details of public spending, and to a commitment by it to allow departments greater autonomy in determining how they spend money allocated to them. Whether this and the transfer of staff imply that the Treasury will become less of a central player in the cabinet system is hard to judge. Its role in day-to-day expenditure control may be reduced, but its control over general economic and expenditure strategies may be enhanced.

Government business managers

A crucial element of the cabinet system is those offices and individuals which manage links with Parliament, and in particular with the governing party in

Parliament. Here organisational involvement is focused on the whips' offices in the Commons and Lords, and such bodies as the Privy Council Office and the Lord Privy Seal's Office in Whitehall. The individuals linked to these offices are known collectively as the government's business managers. Most important within this group are the leaders of the Commons and Lords, usually given ministerial titles such as lord president of the council and lord privy seal, and members of the whips' office, notably the chief whip, his deputy (there is yet to be a female chief whip), and the chief whip's private secretary.

When also lord president of the council, the leader of the Commons is responsible for the work of the Privy Council Office, located at 68 Whitehall. The precise duties of this office are not relevant to this analysis. What is significant is the institutional support it provides for one of the leading government business managers. Similarly, when the leader of the Lords is also lord privy seal, as he often is, his small private office within the Privy Council Office is devoted to business management functions. Total staff numbers in the Privy Council Office at the end of 1994 were 33. Of these, some seven or eight individuals in the lord president's private office, and five individuals in the lord privy seal's private office, were engaged in parliamentary business. Formally, these offices, in tandem with the home and social affairs secretariat in the Cabinet Office, are responsible for planning and managing passage of the government's legislative programme, and for dealing with general parliamentary matters (see Chapter 6). In discharging their functions, the leaders of the Commons and Lords liaise closely with the chief whip's office in each House. When Parliament is in session, staff from their private offices frequently work afternoons in the Palace of Westminster to assist in coordinating government business.

Government whips are often formally members of the Treasury Board, though they are not part of the Treasury in a departmental sense. The chief whip has an office in 12 Downing Street. Other whips' offices are in the Houses of Parliament. Under the deputy chief whip in the Commons there are a further 12 whips. Under the chief whip in the Lords there are a further five whips. The government chief whip relates formally to the cabinet system. His deputy acts as the coordinating agent between the chief whip in Downing Street and the whips' office in the House of Commons. On a daily basis it is the deputy chief whip who is in charge of this office. The chief whip is not usually a formal member of cabinet, but he attends on a regular basis because the first item on the agenda is always parliamentary business. Although this item is introduced by the leader of the Commons, the chief whip has to be available to comment on his report. He then habitually stays for the rest of the meeting, and can be called upon to express views on matters which arise. He has no right to intervene in cabinet discussion. The chief whip can attend most cabinet committee meetings, and is formally a member of both legislation committees and of EDCP committee, which deals with the coordination and presentation of government policy, EDH, which deals with home and social affairs, and OPD(E), which deals with European questions. He receives papers from many cabinet committees.

Change since 1974

In the period since 1974 the work of government business managers has changed only gradually. Between 1974 and 1976, Bob Mellish became the first chief whip ever to have a formal seat in cabinet. This experiment has not been repeated in subsequent years. The main characteristic of the period is a sustained attempt to regularise business management processes, and to coordinate them more effectively around the prime minister as party leader. Under both Thatcher and Major, for example, processes of consultation with backbench Conservative MPs, often through the 1922 Committee, have become more regularised (see Chapters 5 and 7). Heseltine's role as deputy prime minister and chair of EDCP is the latest attempt to coordinate this government business management function.

Law officers

Within the cabinet system, law officers and their departments play an important role in advising ministers on the legal dimensions of proposed legislation and other matters. The attorney general is the government's principal legal adviser. He has formal responsibility for provision of legal opinions to the government and, with his fellow law officers, is responsible for instituting legal proceedings on behalf of the government. In fulfilling his functions the attorney general is assisted by the solicitor general, to whom he is able to delegate business. Although both law officers are members of the government, they are not members of the cabinet (Street and Brazier, 1985: 392). However, one or other of these two law officers attends full cabinet when necessary to give advice on law (Rawlinson, 1989: 97). Each is only called to speak on specific items.

The attorney general plays a key role in drafting bills, and is a member of six important cabinet committees dealing with legislation and leading overseas and domestic issues. He also attends as appropriate the ministerial committee on the intelligence services (IS). The solicitor general is a member of the cabinet committee on drug abuse (EDH(D)). The attorney general is unusual in being one of the few government ministers who can be drawn into the work of any committee, and will be called routinely to give an opinion if significant legal questions arise in the course of a committee's deliberations. To this end, he and his staff maintain close contacts with members of the cabinet secretariats (Edwards, 1984: 187).

The law officers are part of a network of approximately 1000 lawyers in government departments. Only very rarely will many of these lawyers be involved in cabinet system activity. The law officers themselves are usually drawn into the work of the cabinet system on cross-departmental legal matters, and are also the final court of appeal within Whitehall on strict points of law (Edwards, 1984: 185). Former solicitor general Lord Howe (1994: 55) writes that 'The two Law Officers are *the* source of considered legal opinions for the Cabinet'. A small legal secretariat to the law officers (until the early 1990s the Law Officers' Department) provides institutional support to both the attorney general and the solicitor general. At the start of 1995 it had a staff of about 30, of whom 12 were lawyers on secondment from departments.

Separate law officers, the lord advocate and the solicitor general for Scotland, perform parallel functions with regard to questions of Scottish law and legislation. The lord advocate is involved in the cabinet's legislation committee network (see Chapters 5 and 7). The Lord Advocate's Department in London, the smallest government department, is the principal institutional support for the Scottish law officers (Brazier, 1988: 121). In June 1995 its total staff numbered 20, of whom nine were legally qualified (in Scottish law). In contrast to practice in the legal secretariat to the law officers, lawyers in the Lord Advocate's Department are not on secondment from other government departments but are instead permanent employees. Like their counterparts in England and Wales, the lord advocate and solicitor general for Scotland are members of the government, but not of the cabinet.

Change since 1974

Since 1974 the involvement of law officers in cabinet system decision taking has been enhanced. This is partly because British membership of the EU since 1973 has meant that the jurisdictions of the European Court of Justice (ECJ) have become pertinent to British law making. It is also a product of the trend towards increased questioning of the legality of government actions in the courts (Wade and Forsyth, 1994: 1012–14). In the mid-1980s, it thus became accepted procedure for papers entering the cabinet system to show that any possible threat of litigation had been considered before the matter in question was determined in cabinet or cabinet committee. A consequence of the growth in workload is that staffing levels have increased from three professional legal staff in 1967 to seven in 1984 (Edwards, 1984: 186) and to the present complement of 12. The role of the law officers has also been subtly changed since 1974 as their ministerial duties have increasingly taken priority over their crown functions (Rawlinson, 1989: 241).

Cabinet and cabinet committees

To this point, the focus of this chapter has been agencies that constitute the cabinet system, and key positions within them. The final element of our analysis is formal arenas within which individuals from those organisations, and others, interact. At the formal level two types of cabinet system arena exist: cabinet and cabinet committees. Other formal arenas can be found outside the cabinet system, notably interdepartmental committees, of which there are a vast number dealing with matters of interest to two or more departments. The distinguishing feature of cabinet as opposed to inter-departmental committees is that the former are recorded in the cabinet secretary's committee book, and serviced by Cabinet Office secretariats. These committees are therefore managed and organised from within the cabinet system.

Cabinet is conventionally seen as the formal locus of power in the British political system, executive authority being placed by an assortment of Acts of Parliament in its 20 or so members. They are chosen by the prime minister, and hold the senior ministerial posts in government. Some are heads of major departments. Others are non-departmental ministers. All traditional author-ities set cabinet at the heart of their accounts of the British polity. However, as was noted in Chapter 1, decision-taking responsibility has gradually shifted during the course of the twentieth century. What was once in formal terms a system firmly centred on cabinet has now become a much more fragmented one focused on a range of committees (Biffen, 1992: 52). This shift in the balance of the system has for some time been recognised in rules governing the conduct of ministers, which state that committees have full authority to take decisions without reference to cabinet (Cabinet Office, 1992a: para. 4). It is for this reason that it is now essential when discussing cabinet to speak of cabinet *and* its committees. Cabinet itself has been reduced to four major functions. It provides ministers with information. It decides issues which have proved impossible to settle at a lower level in the government system. It takes final (and often no more than ratifying) decisions on some major policy issues, such as public expenditure proposals and white papers outlining significant proposals for policy change. It is a forum for discussion of difficult political matters, and a sounding board for the leadership group. Only very occasion-ally does cabinet review overall strategy.

Cabinet committees divide into types according to two main distinctions. One relates to membership, and divides committees by their ministerial or official composition. The other relates to status and divides committees into standing and *ad hoc*. Standing committees tend to be more permanent, and deal with a range of business arising within the remit of the committee. Some standing committees have sub-committees which report as necessary to them, but which often decide matters in their own right. *Ad hoc* committees tend to be more temporary, and are usually set up to deal with a single issue. These two different dimensions generate four main types of committee – standing ministerial and official, and *ad hoc* ministerial and official – though on occa-sion a fifth type, attended by both ministers and officials, is set up (Hennessy, 1986; Benn, 1992). Mixed committees of this kind deal mainly with technical

Table 2.2 Ministerial standing committees of cabinet, July 1995.

Chair	Designation and policy areas				
Prime minister *John Major*	EDP: Economic & domestic (13)	OPD: Defence & overseas (8)	OPDN: Nuclear defence (5)	NI: Northern Ireland (9)	IS: Intelligence services (6)
Deputy prime minister *Michael Heseltine*	EDE: Environment (15)	EDL: Local government (18)	EDCP: Co-ordination and presentation of government policy (6)	EDC: Competi-tiveness (19)	
Lord president *Tony Newton*	EDH: Home & social affairs (21)	FLG: Future legislation (10)	LG: Legislation (13)	EDH(H): Health strategy (15)	EDH(D): Drug misuse (10)
	EDH (W): Women's issues (15)				
Other ministers (as indicated)	EDX: Public expenditure (7) *Chancellor of the exchequer*	OPD(E): European questions (20) *Foreign secretary*	OPD(T): Terrorism (9) *Home secretary*	EDL(L): London (12) *Environment secretary*	

Source: Cabinet Office (1995c).

The numbers in brackets refer to the designated membership of the committee (including the chair), though other ministers can be invited to attend if matters come up which are relevant to their areas of responsibility. Sub-committees are distinguished by a bracketed initial after the main initials, e.g. EDH(H), but they do not necessarily report to their 'main' committee. Sub-committees often have one or two junior ministers on them, as do EDL, FLG and LG.

issues. An example is the committee created by the Callaghan government in 1977 to consider the international implications of nuclear policy (Benn, 1990: 100). Standing committees are designated by a series of initials: EDP (economic and domestic policy) is one example (see Table 2.2). *Ad hoc* committees are designated by the prefix MISC or GEN, followed by a number. The prefix changes with each change of prime minister (not general election). The number counts from zero each time. Thatcher's first *ad hoc* committee took the designation MISC 1. By the end of her second term in June 1987, she had reached a total of about 200 (Seldon, 1990: 114). Major's first *ad hoc* committee was identified as GEN 1. By July 1995, after more than four years in office, his total had reached 34. About one-third of these were ministerial. In April 1995, the only three extant ministerial *ad hoc* committees were GEN 27 (sanctions against Yugoslavia with a membership of 6), GEN 29 (competitiveness with a membership of 6) and GEN

34 (card technology with a membership of 14) (Cabinet Office, 1995b). These were no longer extant in July 1995 (Cabinet Office, 1995c).

Ministerial committees either take decisions or prepare business for decision at a higher level (possibly cabinet). Official committees mirror ministerial committees, and prepare papers and clarify options for their consideration. On occasion official committees may take decisions in their own right. Official committees are usually mirrored by more *ad hoc* working parties of officials (Benn, 1992: 55). These working parties are commonly chaired by an under or assistant secretary. Usually only one or two members of the official committee which they serve are members of such working parties (Heclo and Wildavsky, 1981: 86).

Key positions in the cabinet system's formal arenas are occupied by those individuals who chair leading committees, and those officials who oversee the flow of business through committees (see Chapter 4). On the ministerial side, this means that the prime minister and other senior ministers are in a particularly strong position. In addition to the prime minister, the group of senior non-departmental ministers who chair a range of cabinet committees is small. Since July 1995 it has consisted of the deputy prime minister and the lord president of the council. Senior departmental ministers, such as the chancellor of the exchequer and the foreign secretary, may also chair committees, and are likely to be important figures. On the official side, the chairs of official committees which shadow the main ministerial committees, plus their own sub-committees, are key. In this respect the lead individuals are cabinet secretary, senior members of the cabinet secretariats and sometimes senior officials from the lead department and especially the Treasury. In addition, officials in strategic organisational positions are important, as they brief committee chairs about the handling of business and assist them in determining the exact flow of business through the committee. In this regard, key positions are held by the cabinet secretary (again), top secretariat officials and even on occasion experienced committee clerks. The formal powers vested in committee chairs and those advising them include some say in the nature and timing of matters to be brought to the committee, the way in which business is conducted and the manner in which it is determined and recorded. As was noted in Chapter 1, since at least the late 1960s (Gordon Walker, 1972: 44; Hogwood and Mackie, 1985: 51), chairs of ministerial committees have been allowed considerable discretion to determine whether a matter can be taken on appeal to cabinet (Cabinet Office, 1992a: para. 5).

Change since 1974

Over time cabinet itself has become marginalised, though it can – and does – still take major decisions. Soon after the start of our period, its regular meetings were cut from more than 60 a year to around 45. In the 1980s, the annual average was cut further to about 40: one Thursday morning cabinet per week during the parliamentary session. This level has been maintained in the 1990s. The post-war record of 108 cabinet meetings set in 1952 (Hennessy, 1986: 100) is therefore unlikely to be superseded now. Each cabinet begins by considering a range of set items: parliamentary business, foreign affairs and on occasion European affairs and home affairs. These are sufficiently broad to enable members to raise matters of concern, but they often take up the majority or all of what is usually a one-and-a-half to two-hour meeting. The lower frequency of meetings, combined with the limited amount of time available in cabinet for new agenda items, have contributed to a situation in which cabinet, as the formal focus of political power in the British system, is much diminished (Wakeham, 1994: 479).

Recent years have also witnessed some decline in the frequency of cabinet committee meetings. The reduction began at the start of the Thatcher premiership. By the end of Thatcher's first term, the total annual number of cabinet committee meetings (both ministerial and official) had been cut by one-third from its late 1970s levels. The frequency of cabinet committee meeting was reduced further during the rest of the 1980s, with the result that by the end of the decade the average annual frequency of meetings was little more than half that registered in the late 1970s. The most precipitate fall was in numbers of ministerial committee meetings. Under Major there has been no reversal of the trend decline in overall frequency of cabinet and cabinet committee meetings, though some of the trends witnessed in the Thatcher decade have been altered. Whereas ministerial standing committees have been used more extensively in the early 1990s than was the case in the late 1980s, a striking fall of some 50 per cent in the number of meetings of official standing committees has taken place. Indeed, under Major the annual number of cabinet committee meetings, taking ministerial and official together, has continued to fall. In addition, very few *ad hoc* committees have been created under Major and his period in office has seen a progressive reduction in the number of standing ministerial committees, from 26 in 1992 to 19 after July 1995. The result has been a more streamlined and regularised cabinet committee system.

It is still valid to argue that business is handled less in cabinet and less in cabinet committee than was once the case. In the period since 1974, formal cabinet has been progressively used less and less. Since 1979, the use of formal cabinet committees (both ministerial and official) has been substantially reduced. Business has either reverted to departments, or been handled informally within the cabinet system. Much informal contact at ministerial level, whether it be by correspondence, telephone, or face to face, of course takes place within the context of the cabinet committee structure. This, however, does not alter the fact that it happens outside formal cabinet system arenas. Changes in the way in which business is processed are analysed in Chapter 4, but it is worth noting here that they reflect deeper and more lasting factors than the style of any given prime minister. The speed and efficiency of decision taking are enhanced if issues are explored and developed before they are taken into formal arenas. It may also be politically useful to the leadership group to bypass formal arenas and established positions before taking business into the cabinet system. In consequence, to the extent that business is handled outside the formal arenas of the cabinet system – in, for example, bilateral and trilateral meetings and ministerial correspondence – there are less opportunities for fully collective discussion within the system. We explore semi-formal and informal aspects of the cabinet system in Chapters 4 and 5.

The formal cabinet system and power potential

Conventional accounts of the formal structure of the cabinet system tend to highlight the positions of prime minister, a small number of key ministers, cabinet acting collectively, and some key officials. This chapter demonstrates that the formal structure of the cabinet system is far more complex and comprehensive than is suggested by such accounts. The number of functions that are located in the cabinet system, and the multiplicity of formal cabinet system arenas within which key personnel interact, mean that a large range of formal organisations and key positions have to be brought within analysis. While the positions identified in conventional accounts are obviously important, they therefore need to be both added to and in some cases subjected to important qualification.

We have sought to do this in this chapter. Our analysis shows that in formal terms lead positions within the cabinet system comprise prime minister and key staff, chairs of ministerial committees, cabinet secretary, chairs of official committees, top personnel in cabinet secretariats, top Treasury ministers and officials, government business managers and government law officers. The precise distribution of power potential between these positions depends to a large extent on the nature of the issue at hand. However, in formal terms this list of key positions is comprehensive. Notwithstanding the formal location of decision-taking authority in cabinet, it is also only within this group that those who have a significant opportunity to restructure the distribution of power potential within the formal cabinet system are to be found. Not all of the key actors identified in this chapter have this opportunity, and even those that do are not able to exercise it at will.

Change in the distribution of power potential within the formal cabinet system in the years since 1974 has to be understood in the context of two broader developments. One is continuation of the trend, noted in Chapter 1, towards settling business in departments, or ensuring that it is substantially refined before entering the formal cabinet system. Change of this kind has been assisted by increased use of semi-formal and informal aspects of the cabinet system (see Chapters 4 and 5). The other is an increasing concern with government efficiency, which has brought new managerial functions into the central executive. This development is not unique to Britain. In many states 'new public management' has resulted in an enhancement of central capability (Greer, 1994: 8).

In this context, the distribution of power potential within the formal cabinet system has changed in two main ways. First, the period has been marked by growth in the number of formal powers, functions and staff located within it. One feature of this growth has been a clear extension of the specialist and oversight functions placed within the cabinet system. Secondly, the operations of the cabinet system have been systematised and increasingly coordinated. In general, change has advantaged central coordinating elements within the cabinet system. As a result, the positions of a small core group of individuals – notably the prime minister, certain key ministers in charge of cabinet committees and party management, the cabinet secretary, and a small group of civil servants in the Prime Minister's and Cabinet Offices – have been enhanced.

Investigation of the formal structure of cabinet system organisations and positions thus reveals that something resembling a central executive department is gradually emerging at the heart of the British state. It comprises the Prime Minister's and Cabinet Offices. Our period has been marked by an increase in the functions of these twin executive offices, and by an extension of the power potential of leading actors within them. The establishment of OPSS in 1992 and the appointment of a cabinet minister within the Cabinet Office might be seen both as a recognition of this change, and as an attempt to institutionalise it within the established conventions of British government. The changes made in July 1995, when Michael Heseltine was appointed deputy prime minister and OPSS was restructured as OPS, are a further development of this kind. Future governments may dispense with the position of deputy prime minister and even with the organisation OPS, but the functions which they fulfil have been progressively consolidated with the cabinet system during our period and, in one form or another, seem likely to remain there.

3

□

Values and practices

Underlying the formal structure of organisations and positions in the British cabinet system is a set of values and practices which conditions the behaviour of participants. It is a central assumption of institutional analysis that, over time, institutions develop operating values and practices which are inculcated into members through acculturation, education or experience, and thereby shape and steer their work (March and Olsen, 1989: 22; Peters, 1994: 10). Like other established institutions, the British central executive has developed accepted modes of behaviour, which limit options available to individuals. In examining the distribution of power potential within the cabinet system, our next task is to investigate the values and practices that pervade it.

Values and practices come in a variety of forms. Some are no more than generally accepted ways of acting. Others are precise documented rules which set out expected modes of conduct. The spectrum of positions which lies between these two extremes is difficult to divide into neat categories. However, it is possible to isolate three main ways in which behaviour within any mature institution is structured. At the least precise end of the spectrum is ethos: this constitutes the guiding philosophy of an institution. It pervades its workings, and is inculcated into personnel in the form of broad understandings about proper ways of doing things. Conventions have greater precision. They are clearly articulated general precepts 'regarded as obligatory' which may nevertheless be ambiguous and uncertain in exact meaning and applicability (Street and Brazier, 1985: 52). Operating codes are more precise still, taking the form of precise rules and regulations. Ethos, convention and code are the three key analytical terms employed in this chapter; in reality, the three overlap and interact. There is substantial interplay between them. Change can occur on any dimension, and is unlikely to be confined to that on which it originates.

The restrictions imposed by ethos, convention and code help to shape behaviour, but they do not determine it. Even the most precise rule is not fully comprehensive in coverage, for none can anticipate the full range of situations in which it might be applied. Furthermore, hardly any rule is enforced on a consistent basis. There will always be areas of ambiguity and neglect, so that even the most routine and rule-governed task provides some room for individual discretion (Hill, 1972). In consequence, rules are always partial, and the process of applying them is always compromised. Scope for individual initiative always exists.

Implicitly at least, this point is frequently made about the world of high politics represented by the British cabinet system, within which individual discretion is often said to be marked. The prime minister is usually the chief focus of such interpretations (Crossman, 1963; Mackintosh, 1977). In arguing that no rule is ever rigid, and that each is in fact malleable to a greater or lesser extent, we do not seek to align ourselves with this school of thought. Our main concern is to qualify it, first by acknowledging that rules are indeed always open to negotiation and alteration, and second by maintaining that the many values and practices which pervade the British cabinet system are, nevertheless, an important constraint upon all individual initiative (including that of the prime minister).

No body of institutional values and practices is set in stone. Codes, conventions and even ethos can be altered both over time, and even at a set point in time, by individual action. Alongside our recognition of the constraint imposed by institutional values and practices on individual autonomy we seek, therefore, to investigate opportunities for alteration of them, whatever precise form they may take. This we believe to provide an important opportunity for individual initiative for, if values and practices shape behaviour, the ability to alter them is significant.

Our aim in this chapter is thus to analyse both the underlying ethos of the contemporary cabinet system and the conventions and codes which also structure activity within it. This task almost inevitably has a historical dimension. It is not possible to investigate current values and practices without considering ways in which they have evolved. Furthermore, it requires us to investigate means by which the values and practices of cabinet government are passed from one generation to the next. Entrants to the cabinet system do not write on a clean sheet. They take their places in a set of institutions which has developed ways of doing things. We therefore look towards the end of the chapter at this important transmission process by analysing ways in which newcomers are made aware of the dominant values and practices of the set of institutions which they are joining. Finally, we consider opportunities open to individuals to alter the values and practices of the cabinet system.

General institutional values and practices

The values and practices which pervade the British central executive are variants of the values and practices which pervade the state apparatus as a whole. It is essential to give some consideration to this wider background before examining the ethos, conventions and codes of the cabinet system itself. We therefore begin by reviewing briefly those values and practices of the British state which especially affect the operation of the cabinet system. Two stand out: secrecy and civil service neutrality.

Secrecy is fundamental to the ethos of British central government (McEldowney, 1994: 275). Ponting (1986a: 133) states that 'Secrecy is at the heart of the way in which Whitehall works'. Hennessy (1990: 346) argues that it is the primary civil service value, 'the bonding material which holds the rambling structure of central government together'. Secrecy has consequences both for the exclusiveness of the system and for the manner in which business is conducted within it. It allows a clear distinction to be drawn between insiders and outsiders, and places strong restrictions on access to material.

This element of the ethos of central government has gained expression in a series of conventions. Central to them is the convention of confidentiality, which holds that all relations within central government are confidential and should not be revealed except in particular circumstances (Marshall, 1989: 3–4). Both Labour and Conservative governments have resorted to litigation in attempts to protect this principle. On the part of ministers, it is secured by means of the Privy Council oath which all are obliged to take, and by which all remain bound even after they have left office. It requires ministers to 'keep secret all Matters committed and revealed' to them (Hennessy, 1990: 349). Confidentiality also stretches across administrations. By convention, ministers may not see cabinet and other papers of former administrations, nor advice submitted directly to them (Hunt, 1989: 75–6). This convention is only overruled when a change of administration, but not governing party, takes place between general elections, and thereby generates continuity on the part of ministerial personnel. Further manifestations of secrecy and exclusion reside in the 'need to know' principle, whereby certain types of information are distributed on a selective basis only to those deemed to need to see them.

Rules about secrecy are communicated to ministers and civil servants in a series of specific (and almost draconian) codes. Most notorious in this regard are Britain's five Official Secrets Acts, passed in 1889, 1911, 1920, 1939 and 1989. All civil servants must sign a declaration under the Official Secrets Act. Ministers are invited to sign a declaration that they have read the relevant provisions of it (Ponting, 1986b). Within departments, internal rule books, which enshrine their own versions of the British commitment to secrecy, are always in existence. Since 1990 the Major government has diluted the application of secrecy rules. This has not involved any change in statutes but rather an informal commitment to more open government, and release of more background information. One consequence has been that for the first time the full list of existing ministerial committees of cabinet has been published, as has been the ministerial guide book, *Questions of Procedure for Ministers*.

Political neutrality evidently applies solely to civil servants. It holds that senior civil servants (principal – or grade 7 – and above) should have no party political affiliation, and are expected to serve any political master (Drewry and Butcher, 1991: 129). It is a feature which helps to distinguish the British system from many others. Elsewhere, it is often common practice to staff the top ranks of the state bureaucracy with political appointees. In Britain, incoming governments are expected to work with and through career civil servants bequeathed to them by their predecessors. Only in one or two instances has the principle been breached explicitly. Chief press secretary is one office which has changed with each change of prime minister (not simply government) throughout the post-war period. The recruitment of policy advisers on a regular basis from 1974 onwards has also breached the precept. In the main, however, the principle of neutrality continues to be strictly applied. This convention dates from creation of the modern civil service, and with it the Civil Service Commission in 1855 (Hennessy, 1990: 368). It is now a central aspect of the ethos of British central government. It has generated a panoply of rules proscribing party political activity of almost any kind on the part of senior civil servants.

The principle of civil service neutrality has clear consequences for cabinet system operations. A number of party political tasks relating to the management of the governing party in Parliament are coordinated within the system, but cannot involve civil servants. In consequence, it has become established practice that in these areas ministers are assisted by special or party-appointed personnel. Civil servants absent themselves from any such discussions. The principle of civil service neutrality is one of the justifications for preventing civil servants from taking an active part in cabinet and ministerial committee discussions.

In addition to the general civil service values and practices of secrecy and neutrality, two further conventions underpin the workings of central government and especially concern cabinet system operations: collective and individual ministerial responsibility (see Chapter 1).

The convention of collective responsibility emphasises that power is exercised by ministers collectively. It embodies many sets of practices, including the expectation that a government will resign if it loses a vote of confidence in the House of Commons (Marshall, 1989: 3–4). From the point of view of cabinet system operations, the key principle contained in the convention of collective responsibility is unanimity. This holds that ministers may disagree until a decision is reached in cabinet or ministerial committee, but must then support the decision before both Parliament and the general public, or resign (Cabinet Office, 1992a: paras 17, 18). Although this aspect of the convention has been breached informally by almost all modern governments, it has only formally been suspended on three occasions this century (Street and Brazier, 1985: 193–4). These were in 1932, when MacDonald's national government agreed to differ in public over the issue of protectionism; in 1975, when

Wilson's Labour government was allowed to split over the EEC referendum; and in 1978, when Callaghan's Labour government was publicly divided over direct elections to the European Assembly.

Individual responsibility is the convention that ministers are responsible to Parliament for the work of their departments and any other duties placed upon them (Cabinet Office, 1992a: para. 27). It is intended to ensure account-ability, but also helps to sustain departmental autonomy. Although the convention was once based on an expectation of resignation, it now secures little more than answerability to Parliament (Wright, 1977).

As noted in Chapter 1, there is a clear tension between the conventions of collective and individual responsibility. One emphasises the group, the other the individual. It is a major task of cabinet system officials, particularly in the secretariats, to try to balance the contradictory requirements of these two conventions. The accepted practice is that one minister and department will take the lead on an issue. Moreover, it is a rule that, while decisions may be reached collectively, they are normally announced and explained as the decision of the minister concerned (Cabinet Office, 1992a: para. 18). This is further reflected in the organisation of business by cabinet system officials, who are expected to ensure that relevant and interested ministers and departments are fully consulted and involved when matters are discussed (see Chapter 4).

These, then, are the general institutional values and practices which, while relating to the whole of central government, particularly affect operation of the cabinet system. Often they have found expression in clear conventions or even precise codes. Nevertheless, at the centre of British government a unique set of values and practices is grafted on to these more general ones. We now turn to investigate them in more detail, breaking them into ethos, conventions and codes.

Ethos in the British cabinet system

The ethos of the British central executive is most clearly revealed in the work of officials employed in its oldest sections: the Cabinet Office and the prime minister's private office. Ministerial as well as other, non-civil service, advisory personnel who have a more temporary standing have to come to terms with this ethos, though from time to time they may attempt to shape or alter it.

An essential feature of Cabinet Office ethos is the priority given to efficient handling of business. 'All senior officials,' writes Lee (1990: 235), 'wish to be remembered for their procedural efficiency.' The secretariats place primary emphasis on ensuring that business passes through cabinet and its committees in an organised and effective manner. Memoranda must always be available, decisions must be taken and recorded, minutes must be distributed on time and to all the right people. Officials emphasise the importance of a 'quick turnaround' of material flowing into and out of the Office. Particular pride is taken in drafting accurate minutes and conclusions, in circulating them within 24 hours of meetings, and in briefing committee chairs effectively. Officials are also concerned to see that proper procedures have been followed, and especially that consultation requirements have been fulfilled before a memorandum is submitted to cabinet or its committees.

In relation to this task of ensuring the smooth flow of business, four further characteristic points are emphasised by secretariat officials. One is a stress on the reactive nature of work undertaken. This is peculiar to the central executive. In departments, civil servants are held to be neutral in a political sense. However, in a policy-making sense it is recognised that they can seek to advance a particular line without compromising the convention of civil service neutrality. Indeed, officials are widely expected to 'fight the departmental corner'. In the central executive this is not the case: officials consider themselves to have only a limited policy role. 'We are,' they say characteristically, 'very much concerned with process rather than substance. We may shape policy, but we do not initiate it.' This is further reflected in the second characteristic, even-handed treatment of departments. Secretariat officials are, they claim, merely 'holding the ring' and 'ensuring that everyone is heard' at the centre of British government. This impartiality is in no sense seen to be compromised by the practice of seconding officials from departments to the Cabinet Office. The implication of both these claims is that secretariat officials carry out what are fundamentally coordinating and machine management roles.

The third and fourth characteristics of secretariat officials are their contentions that legal questions tend to dominate the work they do, and that the agenda to which they work largely sets itself (Lee, 1990: 236). The core claim is that cabinet system business tends to be routine, and reactive to policy matters flowing up from departments. The emphasis is on impartial coordination with little opportunity to influence policy content.

In the prime minister's private office civil servants' self-understandings are slightly different, for here the chief purpose is to serve the prime minister and to protect the limited resources which reside in his or her person. Probably most important among these is time. Officials therefore feel fully justified in organising the prime minister's timetable, in controlling access to him or her, and in filtering the information and advice which reach him or her. The objective is to ensure that the prime minister is sufficiently informed, without being over-burdened with material. Selection thus becomes a key task. In undertaking it, members of the private office distinguish between papers and persons that the prime minister must see, and those that he or she is likely to want to see. This latter activity requires some assessment of the 'prime minister's mind', the range of issues about which the prime minister is likely to be particularly concerned. In fulfilling these tasks private office personnel, though civil servants, are claimed to require a degree of political sensitivity, a detailed knowledge of and good connections into departments, and an ability to spot and alert the prime minister to any 'danger signals' which seem to be emerging (Rose, 1980: 27).

As public explanations of the work which central officials undertake, these contentions are probably to be expected. To get a full picture of their self-understandings it is, however, necessary to dig deeper. Over the years secretariat officials and indeed some members of the Prime Minister's Office, notably in the PMPU, have slowly developed policy competence which points to a different picture. In fact, it is now acknowledged even by secretariat officials that some parts of the Cabinet Office operate not reactively but 'proactively' (Seldon, 1990). In particular, the European secretariat is said by the nature of the policy areas in which it is involved to fulfil functions which require its officials to take a stance, and to assist actively in policy formulation as well as coordination (see Chapter 5). The point has more general, though less substantial, application across the office. Indeed, the development of separate secretariats has promoted a degree of specialisation which allows officials at the centre to become members of relatively stable policy networks. No longer are they mere generalists surveying the entire range of government policy and seeking to ensure that all parts of it cohere. Lee (1990) is right to caution that it is still too early to be entirely confident about this, but it does seem that part of the ethos of the central executive is now changing, as officials at the centre become specialists in distinct areas of policy. This trend implies a different kind of central executive from one which genuinely does no more than 'hold the ring'.

The contention that the agenda sets itself is also disputable. The gradual development of planning procedures within the Cabinet Office has provided secretariat officials with the opportunity to play a more directive role in managing government business. Most important in this regard is increased planning and monitoring of business flows over the short and long terms by secretariat officials. The former are managed by means of a weekly business meeting, the latter by means of a 'forward look' three- to six-month rolling programme of future business (see Chapter 4).

The ministerial element in the central executive, and the non-civil service advisers who enter it through the PMPU, are a much more temporary feature. Consequently, they have made little evident contribution to the ethos of the cabinet system. At the centre of British government there has never been a distinct ministerial ethos, with the exception that the prime minister can be expected to seek to balance conflicting departmental interests in order to ensure the coherence and unity of the government. Generally, ethos tends to be built within departments. There is no question that the PMPU exists purely to serve the prime minister of the day, though exactly how this is done can vary.

Ethos at the centre in the cabinet secretariats and the Prime Minister's Office is, then, slowly changing. As the potential for intervention in departmental spheres increases, so the ethos of the central executive is gradually becoming more 'proactive'. This applies particularly to those spheres, such as European affairs, in which cabinet system actors have taken more responsibility for policy coordination and development.

Conventions in the British cabinet system

Along with this gradual shift in ethos, conventions in the British central executive have also been slowly changing. For many years cabinet system conventions have related to two main issues: powers vested in the prime minister, and the flow and handling of business.

Many conventions relating to the prime minister derive from the royal prerogative. Exercised uniquely by the monarch in earlier times, the royal prerogative has gradually been divided between monarch and premier in more recent times. Evolutionary processes of democratisation have not deprived the monarch of a series of privileges, immunities and duties. They have, however, ensured that many powers have passed to the functioning executive where they are now exercised, by convention, by the prime minister. In the domestic sphere, powers to appoint and dismiss ministers and to dissolve and prorogue Parliament are derived from the prerogative. Other domestic powers, such as restructuring of departments, diffusion of government information and regulation of the civil service, also fall partly or wholly within its scope. In the sphere of external relations prerogative powers are preeminent, and cover matters such as declaration of war, conclusion of treaties and recognition of new states (Street and Brazier, 1985: ch.6).

The prime minister's exercise of these prerogative powers – and of some others, such as having final say on the cabinet's agenda – predates creation of the modern cabinet system in 1916. Of subsequent origin are a series of powers that by convention are exercised by the prime minister. In addition to those prime ministerial powers listed in Chapter 2, these hold that the prime minister has effective control over the Cabinet Office, and that he or she oversees government information services (Street and Brazier, 1985: 173–9). Since 1916 there has, in fact, been an increase in prime ministerial powers.

Three major precepts concerning the flow and handling of business are so well established as to deserve the label of convention. First, for many decades it has been accepted that business should be settled at the lowest possible level. In ascending scale, this means in department, in interdepartmental committee, in cabinet committee and, as a last resort, in cabinet itself. The clear expectation is that only significant items of collective concern and issues that cannot be resolved elsewhere will be brought into the system. Secondly, and consequentially, it is established practice that cabinet committees are authorised to take decisions in their own right (see Chapter 2). Thirdly, it is now expected that business coming into the system will be as refined as possible before it reaches a formal point of decision in cabinet or its committees. This refinement now covers requirements for prior consultation between departments and agencies, detailed specification of options, and even indication of the kind or nature of decisions that need to be taken.

This set of conventions clearly creates opportunities for selective central executive intervention in the policy process. As the set has expanded during the course of the twentieth century, so possibilities for intervention have increased. This is not to argue that cabinet system personnel operate as controllers of the entire business of British government. With staffing levels as they currently are, they never could. Yet the potential for selective intervention in the format and flow of business has undoubtedly increased in recent decades.

Codes in the British cabinet system

Some central executive systems, like the governing institutions of which they are the core part, are codified extensively. In Austria, Finland and Germany, for example, detailed rules of procedure are laid down in statutes and even, to some degree, in the constitution (Burch, 1993: 101–5). In Britain, few statutes apply. Cabinet is only mentioned in passing in three Acts of Parliament, and did not feature at all in the laws of the land until 1937 (Street and Brazier, 1985: 172). However, the absence of a legal framework does not mean that the British system operates without rules. Indeed, there are a great many formal codes. As most are confidential their content cannot be known in detail, and the extent to which they are actually applied can usually only be estimated. Yet taken together these codes constitute a considerable set. Almost all tasks undertaken in central government are governed by rules.

In addition to the rule books used in the rest of the civil service (Hennessy, 1990: 357) the cabinet system has its own particular versions. Handbooks exist for the guidance of staff in both the Cabinet and the Prime Minister's Offices. To cite just a few examples, the cabinet secretary's private office keeps a substantial *Precedent Book*, which is a collection of documents and precedents gathered together over the years; there is a 32-page handbook for the guidance of committee clerks which outlines established procedures; there are memoranda on reproduction, circulation and disposal of cabinet documents and on use of official cars and travel by rail and air; and there is a guide to minute taking which describes the accepted format of cabinet conclusions and committee minutes. These, like other guidelines, have been expanded and refined over the years. The committee clerks' guide was first collected as a single printed document in 1954 and has since been amended, in line with changing practice, by heads of the committee clerks' office. The most recent version of the guide to minute taking was drafted by cabinet secretary Sir Robert Armstrong in the 1980s.

The only central executive rule book to have been published – for the first time in 1992 – is *Questions of Procedure for Ministers* (Cabinet Office, 1992a). This is usually one of the first cabinet papers to be distributed after a change of prime minister. It is sent on behalf of the prime minister to all ministers (including whips) and permanent secretaries. *Questions* is perhaps the closest document to a cabinet system handbook which exists.

Questions can trace its origins to Hankey's 1917 document, 'Instructions to the Secretary' (see Chapter 1). This and other guidelines were, however, greatly expanded during Churchill's wartime administration. Then, Cabinet Office officials amassed a set of directives agreed by Churchill and Attlee as part of a general drive to create a central record of good governing practice. When Attlee himself became prime minister in 1945, guidance for ministers was distributed in two documents which together consisted of 37 paragraphs covering eight pages. In 1946 the two documents were consolidated into a single document of 46 paragraphs and 10 pages. By 1949, *Questions* had expanded to 65 paragraphs. In 1952 it was reduced to 46 paragraphs. By 1966 the document had grown to 85 paragraphs covering 16 pages. In 1976 it had expanded to 132 paragraphs and 27 pages (Lee, 1986; Hennessy, 1986: 8; Ponting, 1986b). The 1992 version covers 38 closely-typed pages and contains 134 paragraphs.

Though similar in terms of number of paragraphs to the 1976 document, the 1992 version differs from it in important respects. Most of the differences seem to derive from the public nature of the 1992 document. In comparison with what is known of the 1976 version (Ponting, 1986a), that of 1992 is rewritten for public presentation and contains a more extensive self-justification at the start (para. 1). Its most notable omission is material dealing with security in the conduct of government business. By contrast, seven paragraphs of the 1976 document are devoted to this issue. Additions in 1992 are rules governing the presentation and timing of government announcements (para. 29) and a substantial section outlining the prime minister's responsibility for the overall organisation of government (paras 32–8).

Only some of the range of issues addressed by *Questions* are relevant to the cabinet system and the disposition of power potential within it. What is nevertheless clear from this document is that the principle of settling business at the lowest possible level in the system is fully enshrined in its detailed prescriptions. The document confirms the committee-based nature of the cabinet system. Paragraph 4 empowers committees to take decisions without reference to cabinet. Appeals from committee to cabinet, it further states, 'must clearly be infrequent' (para. 5). Advice on whether to allow them will be given to the prime minister by the committee chairman. In fact, as paragraph 5 indicates, only Treasury ministers have an automatic right of appeal to cabinet (on expenditure grounds).

Questions thus reaffirms strongly the principle of settling business at the lowest possible level, and provides a set of injunctions to ensure that the central executive is not overloaded. These include the requirements that any paper submitted to cabinet or cabinet committee should contain:

(i)   Treasury approval (if necessary);
(ii) approval of the government's law officers (again if necessary);
(iii) an indication of likely impact on UK obligations as a member of the EU; and
(iv) a summary of any accommodation problems which might arise.

Major additions in this regard in the 1980s and 1990s have concerned the expectation that consideration will be given to:

(i)   the possibility of judicial review (which first emerged in the mid-1960s, but only really developed in the mid-1980s);
(ii) consistency with the European Convention on Human Rights;
(iii) value-for-money implications (including an evaluation of how the proposal is to be implemented, when, and at what cost);
(iv) business impact; and
(v)   environmental impact.

Papers are now also required to address presentational questions, and to contain a draft announcement where appropriate (paras 8 and 22).

Questions also addresses a number of issues relating to the smooth flow and timing of business through the cabinet system. Business for cabinet and cabinet committee should be notified at least seven days in advance. Memoranda should be circulated at least two working days (and preferably also a weekend) in advance of meetings (para. 6). Guidance is also given on the form that memoranda and minutes should take. A 24-hour period must be allowed for amendments to minutes (paras 11–12). Guidance is also given on the principle of confidentiality, and on the need for ministers to ensure that the internal process through which a decision has been made is not disclosed (para. 17). Proper precautions should also be taken to ensure that cabinet and cabinet committee documents are secure (para. 19).

In addition to providing evidence about the administrative characteristics of the cabinet system, *Questions* throws light on the position of actors at the centre of the executive. It states clearly that the prime minister is 'responsible for the overall organisation of the Executive', and for the allocation of functions between ministers and departments (para. 32). A small number of ministerial tasks *must* be undertaken in consultation with central actors. Due warning of, and discussion with, the law officers (para. 22) is unusual in being couched in such language. (It did not carry this emphasis in 1976.) However, the use of 'should' in almost every other part of the document does little to obscure the potential for intervention which exists. The range of matters on which consultation with central actors is expected is detailed in Table 3.1.

The operations of the British central executive are, then, substantially codified. Nevertheless, it must be recognised that part of the importance of *Questions*

Table 3.1 Matters requiring consultation with central actors.

Activity	Cabinet system action required
Ministers on appointment retaining connections with Lloyds	PM's permission required
Any changes that affect the allocation of functions between ministers	PM's approval
• transfer of functions to a non-departmental public body	PM's approval
• transfer of functions between junior ministers in a department involving a change in ministerial titles	PM's approval
• creation of new functions within a department	PM's approval Also permanent secretary must *consult* head of civil service. Cabinet secretary should be notified as should officials in machinery of government division of Cabinet Office
Arrangements for supervising the work of a department when the minister is absent	PM's approval
PPS's access to information graded secret	PM's approval
Appointment of PPSs by ministers	PM's approval (and also consult chief whip)
PPS accompanying minister on visit abroad	PM's approval
Ministers' appointment of special advisers	PM's approval
Cabinet members wishing to be absent from UK (except for ministers on official business to EC countries, NATO and WEU)	PM's approval. Also inform chief whip and cabinet secretary
• Payment of expenses for minister's spouse on official visits abroad	PM's approval
• Payment of expenses for minister's special adviser abroad	PM's approval
• Ministers' out of London engagements, weekend and holiday arrangements	Inform cabinet secretary
Appointment of chair, deputy and other members of royal commission	Consult PM
Appointment of nationalised industry boards	Consult PM
Appointment of public bodies, chairs and deputy chairs of regional health authorities	Consult PM (inform chief whip of all of these). Also inform public appointment unit, OPS and head of home civil service
• Ministers proposing to set up a royal commission	Consult PM
• Ministers proposing to set up an independent council of inquiry	Consult PM
Ministerial announcements which either affect the conduct of government as a whole or have a constitutional character	Consult PM
• Ministers publishing articles or books outside the strict confines of their departments	Consult PM
• Ministers wishing to make a complaint about the media to the media complaints authority	Requires authority of PM. Also need to consult: • Number 10 press secretary • cabinet secretary

Table 3.1   (cont.)

• Minister wishing to address press lobby	Consult Number 10 press office
• Minister intending to broadcast on TV or radio in ministerial capacity	Inform Number 10 press office
• Former minister writing ministerial memoirs	Submit manuscript to cabinet secretary (if in doubt consult PM)
Doubts about relinquishing directorships, investments, etc.	Consult PM
On all critical issues involving legal considerations	Law officers must be consulted
All important government announcements, including oral statements, written answers, white papers or press conferences	Leader of House, chief whip, Number 10 press office should be given at least 2 working days' notice
• Timing should be approved by	Private secretaries to PM, leader of House and chief whip

Source: Cabinet Office (1992a).

PM = prime minister; PPS = parliamentary private secretary.

lies not in what it does cover, but in what it does not. It has, for instance, nothing to say about the appointment, terms of reference and membership of cabinet committees. It also makes no mention of official committees: who establishes them, and what they should do. These matters are left to be determined at prime ministerial and cabinet secretariat level. Much of this type of activity is governed by established practices and may be inherently difficult, or even impossible, to codify. The point remains that in such circumstances opportunities for the exercise of individual discretion are enhanced.

We must emphasise here a point made earlier: no rule is ever followed to the letter at all times. *Questions* itself makes a rather modest statement of intent: the purpose of the document is said to be to 'give guidance by listing the rules and precedents which may apply' (para. 1). Lee (1986: 347) argues that *Questions* is not in daily use as a repository of rules, but should rather be seen as a 'document which is consulted . . . after any event which raises questions of ministerial propriety'. However, the document covers a great deal more than matters relating to ministerial propriety, and is of particular importance in regard to the preparation and flow of business. Secretariat officials state that rules of this kind are not rigidly applied, but are generally followed by departments when they compile and draft memoranda. They are sometimes stretched at the margin by time pressures. Requirements of consultation and evaluation which must precede submission of a cabinet paper are not always met, though necessary consultation with Treasury officials must be undertaken. The rules contained in *Questions* represent an outline of established practice which should be followed in normal circumstances.

Transmission processes within the British cabinet system

Any analysis of values and practices must consider means by which they are transmitted from one generation to the next. In the case of the central executive this is again a dual operation, for actors who become members of that executive have often already served a long apprenticeship in other parts of the British government machine. This is usually as true of ministers as it is of officials. Much acculturation therefore takes place outside the central executive, and needs no more than slight refinement in that executive itself.

Within British government as a whole, the most important transmission procedure would seem to be learning from experience and from those in more senior positions. Despite the growth of in-service training, these remain standard practices within the British civil service, and it is by these means that new entrants and juniors absorb the values and practices which are established within the service (Drewry and Butcher, 1991: 110; Sisson, 1959). The point also applies, though to a lesser extent, to ministers who on entering office for the first time need to learn how the system works (Heseltine, 1987: 10–12). Nevertheless, some individuals occupy key positions within any such learning process, and are recognised as those who transmit the guiding philosophy of an organisation.

In the British central executive, the individuals who occupy these sorts of positions tend to be senior civil servants either in departments (notably principal private secretaries and permanent secretaries), or within the cabinet system (notably the cabinet secretary, other secretariat officials and the prime minister's principal private secretaries). Their likely impact is determined in large part by the material with which they have to work. A very fresh government, like Wilson's in 1964, is likely to require more guidance than a more seasoned one (Crossman, 1975: 21 30). Indeed, on both sides – ministerial and official – entrants to the commanding heights of the central executive often have prior experience of that executive at a lower level. Of the three most recent cabinet secretaries, Hunt and Butler had previously served in the Cabinet Office, and Armstrong and Butler had experience as principal private secretary to the prime minister. Indeed, the major acculturation point for most members of the secretariat tends to be a ministerial private office. Such offices are essential parts of the network which connects into the cabinet system (see Chapter 4). Consequently, when a senior official joins one of the secretariats, the general rule is that there is only a couple of days' hand-over. Thereafter, assistance and advice are given by more established members of the office, sometimes at a fairly junior level, such as committee clerk. Similarly, most cabinet ministers have served as junior ministers earlier in their careers and it is at this level that they learn about the procedures of the cabinet system by being drawn into cabinet committees and other aspects of interdepartmental business (Clark, 1993: 87; Kaufman, 1980: 69–76). On entering office such junior ministers may be briefed by the cabinet secretary.

Transmission procedures mainly, therefore, involve a long process of learning by experience. By these means, participants are schooled in the accepted ways of working within the institution. Formal codes certainly operate as reference points for the inexperienced, but they are unlikely to be the main source of induction into the system for either ministers or officials. They are, however, important in that they embody expectations about how things should be done.

The capacity to alter values and practices

As values and practices shape behaviour, those able to alter them hold, at least in theory, key positions. Yet the ability of any one individual to alter significantly the values and practices of a set of institutions as established as the British cabinet system is likely to be limited. Clearly, codes are easier to change than is ethos, and the impact of any formal change in codification is likely to be felt fully only when it has percolated through the entire system to affect both conventions and ethos. That said, opportunities for individual impact do exist in this sphere, for the lesson of history is that key individuals have, on occasion, made a difference. The most celebrated example of an individual's impact on ethos is Hankey. Hankey did not in any sense 'create' the ethos of the modern cabinet system. On the one hand, he worked with the grain of cabinet ethos as it was in 1916 and refashioned it. On the other, a number of other individuals helped him to fashion the particular ethos of the modern Cabinet Office. Yet his was undoubtedly a significant influence.

At the level of codes, opportunities open to officials to 'change the system' would seem to exist. In the early years of the modern cabinet system, procedural changes were debated by each incoming cabinet. From at the latest Attlee's time, compilation of *Questions* and other formal codes has been a task undertaken chiefly by the cabinet secretary and his officials, in consultation with the prime minister. However, the procedure is generally one whereby changes are made at the margin as new requirements arise. Possibly the greatest opportunities to alter these documents arise when there is a change of government. Any new prime minister is unlikely to have either the time or the inclination to give such detailed procedural matters much thought. He or she is also likely to feel constrained in this sphere, for few new prime ministers feel able to make fundamental changes to procedures which have developed over decades.

Some change in cabinet system values and practices is driven by circumstance. Lee (1986: 348) makes the fair point that 'behind each rule there nearly always stands a case'. The rules of any system are of course updated from time to time in order to close any perceived loopholes. The sections of *Questions* dealing with ministerial memoirs (paras 19 and 98) were altered following publication of the Crossman diaries and the Radcliffe committee's report on the subject in 1976 (Radcliffe, 1976: appendix 2). The sections dealing with the confidentiality of law officers' advice (paras 23 and 24) may have been tightened following the Westland affair in 1986. Yet it seems likely that on occasion Cabinet Office staff do have the opportunity to change the rules which structure activity in the central executive, and historical precedent shows that that opportunity has indeed been utilised (Ellis, 1992; Naylor, 1984; Roskill, 1972).

Change since 1974

Change in cabinet system values and practices in the period since 1974 is extremely hard to identify. This is because by their very nature values and practices alter only slowly over time, and rarely experience step change. Nevertheless, within a graduated and largely continuous process it is possible to identify some changes that fall very clearly within our period.

One is a general, and in some ways limited, relaxation of secrecy rules. In part this change has resulted from the judicial decision relating to publication of Crossman's diaries. In part, it has flowed from the moves towards 'open' government taken by the Major government after 1992, which since April 1994 have been enshrined in a code of practice on open access covering all departments. A second change is increased questioning of the convention of individual ministerial responsibility. This has most recently been accentuated by the transfer of departmental service delivery activities to separate executive agencies undertaken under the Next Steps programme. However, such questioning has not yet prompted a significant reinterpretation of the convention. A third change affects rules governing business entering the cabinet system, which is now subject to greater consultation with cabinet system officials. The main impact of this change has been to increase cabinet system awareness of activities undertaken on its margins. The most notable feature of cabinet system values and practices is nevertheless their continuity over time and during our period.

Conclusion

Examination of values and practices reveals to a greater extent than perhaps anything else the extent to which the cabinet system is highly institutionalised. A wide range of activities is covered by accepted procedures, many of which are written down and codified. The values and practices which have been analysed in this chapter are thus deeply embedded features of Britain's executive institutions. They have developed cumulatively, and are therefore characterised by substantial inertia. They express in a very strong sense established ways of doing things, and reflect in some detail the historical traditions of the

British state. They also reflect, at least in part, the requirements imposed on British government by administrative necessity.

The continuity which the values and practices of the cabinet system represent generates a clear bias in favour of existing procedures. It is within this context that the pattern of advantage created by cabinet system values and practices is best analysed. Three main points about institutional bias may be made. The first is that individuals who are steeped in the values and practices of the British state possess an advantage over those who are not. In general terms, this means that officials usually (but not always) have some initial advantage over ministers, because they tend to be the more permanent participants. The second is that individuals who are predisposed to work with the grain of cabinet system institutions possess an advantage over those who are not. If they succeed at all, individuals such as Benn or Thatcher tend to attain their goals despite cabinet system values and practices, rather than because of them. The third is that those who have the ability to transmit or, better still, alter aspects of cabinet system values and practices possess an advantage over those who do not. Much transmission of cabinet system values and practices is undertaken by experienced and established personnel, and often happens unconsciously.

Change in cabinet system values and practices is often incremental. Nevertheless, over time small and accretive alterations can constitute a significant shift in the disposition of the system. Deliberate alteration to those values and practices really only takes place at the level of codes. Here, the cabinet secretary and prime minister, plus lead officials in the cabinet secretariats and Prime Minister's Office, are in key positions. One important repository of cabinet system codes, *Questions of Procedure for Ministers*, is generally held to be in the preserve of the prime minister and cabinet secretary. The generation and development of such codes is not subject to collective ministerial oversight.

4

☐

Links and processes

The British cabinet system is not only structured by formal organisations and positions (Chapter 2) and infused by a distinct set of values and practices (Chapter 3). It also operates at semi-formal and informal levels. We investigate these levels in this chapter, focusing on links which stretch from the cabinet system to many parts of central government, and on the way in which business is managed in the cabinet system. In investigating links we look in particular at the lines of communication which reach from the cabinet system across much of Whitehall. We use a simple policy process model to look at organisation and management of the flow of business through cabinet and its committees.

The importance of adding semi-formal and informal aspects of the cabinet system to its formal dimension was noted in our Introduction. By semi-formal aspects we mean transient groups which are set up from time to time. Such groups range from large to small. To qualify as semi-formal aspects of the cabinet system, they must hold prearranged meetings on notified topics, and a note taker must be present. Although such groups are established within the general framework of cabinet system activity they are not entered in the cabinet secretary's committee book, and are not necessarily serviced by the cabinet secretariat. They tend to centre on a key cabinet system actor, in most cases a leading official or senior minister. They are frequently established to discuss a matter at a preliminary stage, possibly before it is developed further in a department or sent for consideration to a formal cabinet committee. When semi-formal groups centre on the prime minister they are often serviced by one of his or her private secretaries. Informal aspects of the cabinet system comprise personal contacts that develop between individuals engaged in or connected with activities taking place in formal and semi-formal structures. The 'Whitehall village' interpretation of central executive operations is now well established (Heclo and Wildavsky, 1981: 2; Bruce-Gardyne, 1986: 2–3; Ponting, 1986a: 90). It holds that the more formal relations within government are underpinned by close informal contacts, friendships and acquaintances. In all organisations, a substantial amount of business is

65

is conducted through such channels. Often, a decision can be shaped or even determined in moments before or after formal meetings, during a chat in the corridor, by telephone, or over lunch.

Different personnel are often drawn in at different levels of cabinet system activity. It is not always the case that membership of a formal structure also constitutes membership of semi-formal ones. Similarly, some influential personnel (such as unofficial ministerial and prime ministerial advisers) only have access to the informal structure. Moreover, the development of policy content and handling may move from one structure to another. In the 1980s it was often the case that an issue would move from informal to semi-formal structures before being formally determined or ratified in the formal structure of cabinet and its committees (Prior, 1986: 135–6; Burch, 1990). Although this mode of operation was particularly developed during Thatcher's premiership, it was by no means unique to her. In 1977, for example, Callaghan established an economic 'seminar' to oversee sensitive aspects of exchange-rate policy (Callaghan, 1987: 476–7; Donoughue, 1987: 101–2). Under the chairmanship of the prime minister, this usually brought together the chancellor of the exchequer, cabinet secretary, officials from the Treasury and Bank of England and prime ministerial advisers. Thatcher chaired a group with a similar membership in the 1980s. Under Major, the tendency to determine matters informally has continued, though the approach is quite different.

Facilitative links centred on the cabinet system

While an awareness of the informal dimension is essential to understanding any organisation it is difficult to analyse in general terms, as much depends on circumstances and individuals. There are, however, four relatively established sets of links which facilitate information flows into and out of the cabinet system. Each is focused directly on the cabinet system and underpins its operations. These links are the private office grapevine, links between permanent secretaries, links centred on the Cabinet Office secretariats, and links between ministerial advisers. There are, of course, many other sets of links in Whitehall, but these four are the key ones focused on the cabinet system.

The private office grapevine – according to Kaufman (1980: 48) one of the most powerful in Whitehall – links officials in all government departments. Its members are lead officials in ministerial private offices, who have a dual loyalty on the one hand to their department and on the other to their minister (Henderson, 1987: 1). The power of this grouping derives from the fact that private offices are the chief point of contact between ministers and the rest of the government machine. Bruce Gardyne's (1986: 33) sardonic judgment is that 'The Private Office is the sole channel of communication permitted with the outside world'. The focus of this 'bush telegraph' is the prime minister's private office (Jones, 1985a: 79). Cabinet Office secretariats that are mainly engaged in handling business, and the cabinet secretary's private office, are also central to it. Contacts generated by this grapevine enable cabinet system officials to gather information and to monitor activities informally across the rest of Whitehall. They also provide cabinet system staff with opportunities to influence the flow of information around Whitehall. Finally, they help to generate a cabinet system conditioning of departmental perceptions of the political world. Nearly all prime ministerial messages are sent around Whitehall in the form of memoranda and telephone calls by means of this grapevine.

The second set of links engages the 38 permanent secretaries of government departments. At its core are the 18 most senior permanent secretaries, most of whom head a major government department. Based on informal contacts which often run through permanent secretaries' private offices, this set of links finds formal expression in a regular Wednesday morning permanent secretaries' meeting, chaired by the cabinet secretary. This meeting features in some accounts as a key policy forum within British central government. Haines' (1977: 16) contention is an extreme example: 'If the Whitehall machine has a collective "line" on policy, and it often does, it is at these meetings that it will emerge.' The reality is rather different. According to the present cabinet secretary, Sir Robin Butler, it is in fact very rare for serious policy questions to be discussed at the permanent secretaries' meeting (BBC, 1988). Instead, the meeting provides an opportunity to keep in touch and tends to focus on managerial matters, such as relationships with the parliamentary ombudsman or House of Commons public accounts committee, some civil service matters or the division of functions between departments. On occasion, issues thought to be of general interest are reported. On the whole, however, permanent secretaries are not keen to divulge the departmental line (unless they consider it likely to reflect well on both themselves and their department). This is, then, essentially a managerial board, which meets on a weekly basis. Two-thirds attendance is the norm. Although the Wednesday morning meeting is a focal point, the main contacts in this grapevine take place by means of a vast array of *ad hoc* links, often undertaken by telephone, which permanent secretaries maintain with their colleagues. This set of links tends to centre on the office of the cabinet secretary.

The third set of links centres on secretariat officials, notably the deputy and under secretaries who head those secretariats which are primarily concerned with handling business: defence and overseas affairs, economic, and home and social affairs. If business requires it, the cabinet secretary, his private office and heads of other secretariats, notably European, may also be drawn to the centre of this grapevine. Its key task is to gather intelligence about material entering the cabinet system. It seeks both to gain advance warning of business which might need to enter the cabinet system at some future point in time, and to check that business which is about to come into the system is indeed in a fit state to do so. To accomplish these tasks, core personnel maintain links with ministers' private offices, permanent secretaries' offices and relevant policy divisions within departments. Chairs of official committees, and working parties of officials which often feed into them, are involved in this grapevine. On the ministerial side only chairs of cabinet committees (including the prime minister) are drawn into it. Usually the point of contact is their private offices.

The fourth set of links involves ministerial or special advisers, of whom there are currently some 30 spread across government departments, plus about eight members of the PMPU. As ministerial advisers are a comparatively recent innovation (see Chapter 1), this grapevine has only developed in recent years. Furthermore, although the increase in numbers of advisers at the start of our period has seen this grapevine grow in importance subsequently, it remains a great deal less significant than the other sets of links already described in this chapter. Indeed, despite sporadic attempts to coordinate ministerial advisers, little success has been achieved. When Donoughue was in charge of the PMPU in the 1970s, efforts were made to secure coordination through that unit. Similar attempts were made when Redwood was head of the PMPU in the 1980s. Since 1979 more consistent attempts have been made to coordinate contacts through Conservative Central Office and in particular the Conservative research department (CRD), which supplies many advisers to Conservative ministers. However, a weekly Thursday meeting at the CRD, chaired by its director, is usually very poorly attended and is unlikely to undermine the firm ministerial loyalty felt by advisers.

Together, these sets of facilitative links constitute key intelligence channels into and out of the cabinet system. Although they are of differential importance, they are central elements in the informal context within which the handling of business discussed below takes place. Since 1974, the main change in these facilitative links has seen them become more focused on cabinet system institutions.

Processing policy material in the cabinet system

The picture presented thus far is rather static. In this second part of the chapter, we therefore move to consider cabinet system operations in a more dynamic way, by analysing the flow of policy material through the system. Our interest lies not in the content of policy, but in processes developed to handle its passage through the cabinet system.

We begin by presenting a model of the orthodox pathway taken by business passing through the cabinet system (Figure 4.1). It highlights the extent to which policy making is expected to be led by departments. This route is one which may or may not comprise initial cabinet system involvement in approving a broad proposal. The issue next enters a lead department or, if it has not yet been considered by the cabinet system, originates in a lead department. It

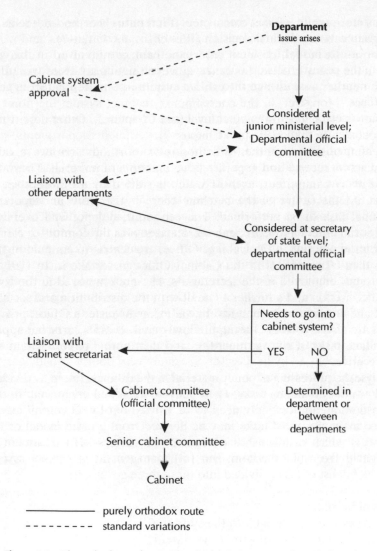

Department
issue arises

Cabinet system
approval

Considered at
junior ministerial level;
Departmental official
committee

Liaison with
other departments

Considered at secretary
of state level;
departmental official
committee

Needs to go into
cabinet system?

Liaison with
cabinet secretariat   YES   NO

Cabinet committee   Determined in
(official committee)   department or
                                 between
                                 departments
Senior cabinet committee

Cabinet

——————— purely orthodox route
- - - - - - - - standard variations

Figure 4.1 The orthodox pathway taken by business passing through the cabinet system.

is normally handled at junior ministerial level, usually through a departmental committee of civil servants. Here options are worked out, possibly in liaison with other departments (though this may happen later). The issue is then taken to secretary of state level for further refinement and liaison with other departments. At this point at the very latest, usually earlier, a decision is taken whether or not to engage the cabinet system. If the issue does enter the cabinet system it normally goes to a cabinet committee mirrored by an official committee. The cabinet committee can be *ad hoc* or standing. The issue may then go to a more senior cabinet committee. If it is entirely orthodox, the issue will then go to cabinet for final decision (Wakeham, 1994: 476–7).

In the orthodox model, business enters the cabinet system at a relatively late stage in the policy process. In reality, however, significant issues are often drawn in far earlier, and engage the cabinet system intermittently throughout their existence. Moreover, in the contemporary cabinet system the point of final decision is usually below cabinet level (see Chapter 2). Other departures from orthodoxy also take place (see Chapter 9).

In processing business, whether by orthodox or unorthodox pathways, cabinet system actors receive and generate large amounts of material. They also coordinate many committees, each of which is staffed by a different set of individuals. At the centre of the machine there is therefore an important organisational task to be performed. The economic, defence and overseas, home and social affairs and European secretariats, plus the committee clerks' and distribution sections in the Cabinet Office, are central to conduct of this task. Less than 60 personnel in the Cabinet Office undertake it. In 1991, in addition to staff employed in the secretariats, 11 were employed in the committee clerks' section and a further 17 dealt with the distribution and security of cabinet and committee documents. In the Prime Minister's Office, private office staff are also involved. Often quite lowly civil servants carry out apparently mundane tasks of sifting, recording and distributing papers within the central executive.

We analyse the processing of policy material in the cabinet system by dividing it into 11 key policy handling tasks. These may be identified in any mature and sizeable institution, and certainly need to be carried out by all central executives. Three main groups of tasks may be derived from a basic model of the policy process which distinguishes (i) sources of business, (ii) treatment of business within the cabinet system, and (iii) management of cabinet system outputs. The full list of tasks, divided into these three groups, is:

- Sources of business
  - Entering external material into the system
  - Originating material from within the system
- Treatment of business within the cabinet system
  - Collecting material
  - Interpreting material
  - Distributing material
  - Prioritising material
  - Reaching decisions
- Management of cabinet system outputs
  - Recording decisions
  - Distributing decisions
  - Formulating consequences of decisions
  - Monitoring implementation of decisions

The revealing point is that apparently simple administrative tasks can have policy consequences. Such tasks are not always neutral in their impact on policy. The process by which policy is made creates opportunities for intervention, and its consequent impact on policy can be significant. Some effects may be unintended, resulting from the established way in which business is handled. Others may be more intentional, as individuals choose to exploit opportunities placed before them.

Controlling sources of business in the cabinet system

A vast amount of material flows through the cabinet system. 'Cabinet papers' – those which are recorded by the secretariats – include agenda for cabinet and its committees, memoranda relating to agenda items, papers circulated by ministers in response to memoranda, minutes of cabinet committees and conclusions of cabinet. The secretariat itself produces handling briefs, which are given only to committee chairs. Annual flows of these papers are substantial. Brazier (1988: 116) cites Tony Benn's calculation that, in 1977, 1800 such papers were circulated to all cabinet ministers. It is certain that this figure does not include minutes of all ministerial and official committees or secretariat briefings to committee chairs. The grand total is thus likely to be higher than Benn's 1800, though it is also said to be falling in the contemporary period, as less formal business is transacted by the cabinet system. In principle, there are two main sources of this material: external and internal. External material usually comes from government departments. Internal material is generated by a wide range of bodies within the cabinet system.

Government departments are the most important agents in generating policy material for consideration by the cabinet system. Very few non-governmental agencies – such as pressure groups – are able to deal directly with the cabinet system. Instead, most must work through departments. Government departments therefore act as important gatekeepers into the system. They are usually major sources of information and advice, and also develop policy initiatives of their own accord (Smith, Marsh and Richards, 1993). Moreover, as the orthodox model shows, the standard practice is for departments to take the lead in generating proposals and providing advice. Departments also normally draft the main memoranda discussed in cabinet and cabinet committees.

Not all departmental initiatives feed into the cabinet system. Indeed, most policy issues that fall within the responsibility of a single department need not engage the system at all, but can be handled in-house. The clearest exceptions to this rule are items involving important new policy, spending commitments or legislation, all of which are likely to trigger movement into the central executive. Policy initiatives which might escape the cabinet system are those which

71

have implications for more than one department, but which can be handled either at official level, through interdepartmental committees, or through inter-ministerial contacts. Some departmental 'initiatives' which do feed into the cabinet system may have been originated by cabinet system actors in the form of manifesto commitments, or ideas generated at the centre which are subsequently devolved to departments for detailed development.

The bulk of the material entering the cabinet system has, then, departmental 'origins' (though it may in fact have been prompted by central executive initiative). However, some important business originates fully within the cabinet system. One potentially important source is the prime minister and his or her office. Indeed, there has been a trend in recent years for individuals grouped around the prime minister to become increasingly important policy initiators. Under both Wilson and Callaghan between 1974 and 1979, Harold Lever held a roving brief in the economic sphere, and was a source of creative policy proposals. In the 1980s, Thatcher was very keen to encourage similar *ad hoc* interventions, and often did so by setting up semi-formal committees chaired by herself. The increase in Downing Street resources, notably development of the PMPU since 1974, has made this sort of central initiative easier. Thatcher in particular exploited it to set policy going from Number 10, and on occasion required departments to do little more than work out the details of a fixed policy line. However, even under a strong-willed and interventionist prime minister, this remained a marginal development.

Certain departments are more likely than others to deliver issues into the cabinet system, because of the nature of the business they handle. Some departments have a focus of interest which is inherently more interdepartmental than that of others. The DTI is, for example, much less self-contained than is the Ministry of Defence (MoD). Some departments have an unusually large legislative output: the Home Office produces far more legislation than does a department such as Transport (Van Mechelen and Rose, 1986: 53). Some departments produce more business with significant new spending implications than do others. The major welfare departments are, for example, more likely to be drawn into the cabinet system on these grounds than is the FCO.

The precise rate at which business flows into the cabinet system from government departments is policed chiefly by the cabinet secretariats. Officials are acutely aware of timetabling possibilities. A series of preconditions must be met by any business coming into the system (see Chapter 3). In particular, liaison with other departments which might be affected, and with the Treasury if there are expenditure implications, must be undertaken prior to entry.

Other sources of initiative are cabinet committees, whether ministerial or official. However, it is less usual for policy proposals to be initiated by such committees, which deal most frequently with business already in hand. On occasion, an initiative may nevertheless emerge as a consequence of consideration of another policy matter. In the Cabinet Office, the main committee-based secretariats dealing with overseas, economic and domestic affairs do not initiate policy in any substantial sense (see Chapter 3). In spheres such as EU affairs and civil service management there has, however, recently been a considerable and sustained extension in the cabinet system's ability to initiate policy (see Chapter 5).

Policy initiation in the British system remains a predominantly departmental matter. Nevertheless, change is discernible, and has tended to operate in recent years to strengthen the resources and opportunities available to individuals at the very heart of the cabinet system. In particular, individuals grouped around the prime minister and, in selected fields of policy, within the Cabinet Office have extended their potential to become policy initiators.

Treatment of business within the cabinet system

Once a policy initiative has been formulated, and business has started to work its way through the cabinet system, an important series of stages has to be negotiated. In the process which ends with the taking of a decision, material must be (i) collected, (ii) interpreted, (iii) distributed and (iv) prioritised within the cabinet system's tight timetable. In theory, at each of these apparently mundane stages there is scope for shaping policy by altering, facilitating or hindering its flow through the cabinet system. Each is therefore reviewed in this section.

Stages one and *two*, collection and interpretation of material, comprise tasks usually undertaken by secretariat officials in liaison with their departmental counterparts. The standard procedure is for departments to send papers for cabinet in draft form. They are then reproduced in the secretariat, and minor presentational changes are made. By contrast, papers for cabinet committees are usually produced in final form by the sponsoring department. However, all copies are always handed to the secretariat, which is responsible for their distribution and security. It gives each paper a number, and records its multiple destinations. From this point onwards, these are cabinet system papers. Even originating departments must apply to the secretariat for additional copies, and all papers are expected to be returned to the secretariat when no longer needed.

On the face of it, there are clear opportunities here to affect the progress of policy. On the one hand, the timing of a policy's movement through the cabinet system can be altered. On the other, the interpretative function could allow marginal alterations to be made to proposals put before cabinet or its committees. Both tasks are fulfilled by secretariat officials. Moreover, possibilities for intervention in at least one of these areas have been enhanced in recent years, as the secretariat has increased its surveillance of standards of clarity required of material entering the system. However, the secretariat's work in regard to these tasks is largely routine, and the expectation is that departments will know that they have to comply with the conditions for entering material into the cabinet system, and will therefore do so. Much is achieved through informal liaison. These tasks are also driven by time pressures and external forces. The opportunity to intervene significantly, should anyone wish to seize it, is therefore strictly limited.

Stage three, distribution of papers within the cabinet system, centres on the question of who should see what. For each committee, the committee clerk produces a standard distribution list. To a degree this is a routine matter, partly determined by membership of cabinet and its committees. However, because it is not always clear who, outside these groups, should receive papers, some discretion is created. Problems arise notably in relation to committee papers. The rules state that all departments which have an interest in an issue should receive papers relevant to it. However, in cases of doubt cabinet and committee secretaries often need to take decisions about distribution on the basis of a 'need to know' criterion. In highly sensitive areas, this criterion is strictly, and often restrictively, applied.

Accepted distribution procedures apply to both cabinet and committee papers. Distribution of cabinet papers is limited to cabinet ministers, who are entitled to show relevant parts to immediate advisers concerned with policy formulation. In actual fact, when cabinet papers arrive in ministers' private offices, they are usually seen not only by the principal private secretary but also by the permanent secretary. Non-cabinet ministers are shown relevant sections of cabinet papers. Outside the accepted circle of cabinet members, the exact circulation of cabinet papers is a matter for the cabinet secretary to decide, in consultation with the prime minister if absolutely necessary. Only very rarely is it necessary for such consultation actually to take place.

Ministerial cabinet committee papers go as a matter of routine to all committee members. Beyond this, it is the job of each committee secretary to decide who should receive papers. They are often sent to the chief whip and the law officers. Beyond this distribution is usually determined on the basis of perceived departmental concerns. At the margin judgement can inevitably be rather arbitrary. At interview, cabinet ministers often stated that their lack of access to full committee papers diminishes the collective nature of cabinet government. They also felt that matters about which they have a collective, rather than a departmental, interest may be determined in committee without their knowledge.

The range of papers that a minister actually sees is determined partly by members of his or her private office. It is standard practice for a minister to be informed about cabinet committee business in which he or she has not been directly involved, but which develops important implications for his or her department. Members of ministerial committees do not see official cabinet committee papers until the officials complete their deliberations, although those officials are usually working within terms of reference set by their ministerial counterparts. The matter of who has seen what can occasionally be the cause of public rows. Much of the Scott inquiry into arms sales to Iraq turned on this very point.

Some papers have a decidedly restricted circulation. Information gathered by the security services comes into this category. If made available at all, such information is usually distributed only to selected members of cabinet's defence and overseas policy (OPD) committee. Distribution of papers generated by *ad hoc* committees may also be very limited. Some documents are designated 'CMO', for circulation to concerned ministers only (Ponting, 1986a: 116), and do not usually go beyond committee members. In these instances, only one copy is made available per minister, and can only be seen in his or her private office. The CMO designation has become more common since the mid-1980s. In recent years there has, however, also been movement in the opposite direction, through extension of the types of personnel who are given access to papers and meetings. Notable in this regard are members of the PMPU, some special ministerial advisers and, during its existence from 1970 to 1983, some members of the CPRS (Blackstone and Plowden, 1988: 43–5).

Stage four, prioritisation of business, is one of the most important tasks undertaken within the cabinet system, for time resources are among the most precious in that system. It actually comprises two main activities: timetabling, which is essentially a medium- and long-term activity, and agenda management, which is decidedly short term.

The scope for individual initiative in timetabling business within the cabinet system is limited by the inevitable momentum generated by normal business flows, and by the requirements of the parliamentary timetable. Some items require an immediate response, and thereby secure priority, but most issues make steady progress to points at which they can be settled. However, the work of the cabinet system is not entirely conditioned by 'natural' flows of business. Indeed, secretariat officials take great pains to impose some measure of control on the system's timetable by engaging in forward planning. Several committees meet on a regular basis to organise future business, and are attended by the cabinet secretary and officials from the secretariat and the Prime Minister's Office. A key meeting takes place under the cabinet secretary each Thursday afternoon to finalise arrangements for cabinet and committee business over the coming three weeks, and occasionally to take a 'forward look' at matters likely to be in the pipeline over the next three to six months (Donoughue, 1987: 27–8; Seldon, 1990: 110).

The 'forward look' procedure, introduced in 1973, enables secretariat officials to discover from departments what is likely to be coming forward, and to inform them about the likely timing of future business. This helps to avoid log-jams, and to ensure that materials are ready on time. The procedure has been developed in recent years by the introduction of computers and networked facilities, which enhance officials' ability to plot and oversee the 'rolling programme' of business over the months ahead. This planning innovation was not simply sensible. It was also significant, for it helped to strengthen the secretariat's ability to influence and control the organisation and flow of business from departments. Cabinet Office staff are no longer obliged simply to respond to the momentum of business fed into the cabinet system by departments. They can at least partially orchestrate it.

Those in advantageous positions within this process are the prime minister and his or her staff, some committee chairs, and members of the secretariat. An important, if negative, part can be played by the government's law officers, who by raising questions about the legality of a proposal may slow its progress, or even require it to be re-examined. Party whips can have a similar effect if they report negative reactions on the part of backbenchers (Parkinson, 1992: 120). The Treasury may retard proposals or cause them to be altered on financial grounds.

Agenda management is a more short-term, tactical matter. Again, this activity has a potential impact on policy. Prioritising items on a cabinet or committee agenda generates an opportunity to facilitate or hamper consideration of a proposal. Agendas are determined by the cabinet secretariat in conjunction with committee chairs (the prime minister and senior ministers). A further contribution made by members of the secretariat at this point is provision of a handling brief for each cabinet and committee meeting. A handling brief is a guidance note to a committee chair. It is drawn up by the member of the secretariat who is secretary to the committee, or in the case of cabinet, by the cabinet secretary, often in consultation with departmental officials. Departments are never shown these briefs, though they may be informed about some of the issues contained in them, so that their minister is able adequately to respond to them. Handling briefs indicate how far an issue has progressed, remaining points of contention, and matters which need to be addressed and on which a decision needs to be taken by cabinet or committee.

A proposal which has negotiated each of these stages will reach a formal point of decision in either cabinet committee or cabinet: in essence, *stage five* in the process of handling business. The dynamic of a committee is determined partly by the business before it, partly by membership and partly by the chair (who, in turn, may be influenced by the secretariat's handling brief). Many accounts concentrate solely or predominantly on this point, but it is in fact only one of many in the process of handling business, and not necessarily the only significant one.

Management of cabinet system outputs

Once a decision has been taken, four main stages remain to be negotiated. They are (i) recording the decision, (ii) distributing records of it, (iii) formulating consequences which emanate from it and (iv) monitoring its implementation. Each stage is reviewed in this section.

Stages one and *two*, recording and distributing the minutes and conclusions of cabinet and committee meetings, are cabinet secretariat tasks. Cabinet deliberations are recorded in longhand both by the cabinet secretary and by two members of the secretariat. The cabinet secretary takes notes on the full meeting. The secretariat officials take alternate notes according to the business in hand. A member of the economic secretariat records discussion of economic business, a member of the defence and overseas secretariat records debate of foreign affairs. Once an official's item is concluded, he or she leaves the meeting to dictate his or her notes. The cabinet secretary drafts the cabinet conclusions on the basis of his own notes and those dictated by the secretariat officials. Committee minutes are drafted in a similar fashion by the committee secretary, assisted by other members of the relevant secretariat. Cabinet conclusions and committee minutes follow a standard format, covering the matter at issue, the main points of discussion, and, most importantly, decisions reached and directions for action.

Conventionally, the directive parts of cabinet conclusions and committee minutes are written on the basis of summaries from the chair. However, on occasions when such a summary is either not made or is imprecise, officials need to make what they can of the outcome of the discussion which took place. Although Crossman believed that Wilson (1976: 56) rewrote minutes and conclusions, this almost certainly did not happen. These documents have to be produced within 24 hours, and are hardly ever submitted to the chair for approval in advance of circulation. Compilation of conclusions and minutes is undertaken almost wholly within the secretariat and only on very rare occasions, when there is doubt as to what was decided, will the prime minister or any other committee chair be consulted. Indeed, most experienced prime ministers are likely to be adept at finding ways of intervening at a much earlier stage in the policy process (or indeed at shaping the process itself).

Cabinet conclusions are circulated to the Queen, Prince Charles, all members of the cabinet and senior members of the cabinet secretariat. A small number of others receive cabinet conclusions, or sometimes extracts from them, on a 'need to know' basis. Cabinet committee minutes go as a matter of routine to all committee members, and to all cabinet ministers. Wider distribution is again on a 'need to know' basis. Occasionally, when matters of great sensitivity are involved, a confidential annexe is attached to cabinet conclusions or committee minutes, and circulated to only a few cabinet or committee members. This practice is long established.

Stage three, formulating consequences which flow from decisions taken, is again a secretariat task. Procedures are covered partly by those covering the drafting of cabinet conclusions and committee minutes (which are authoritative directives from the centre to the rest of government). If an item is likely to result in legislation, it will be drawn back into the cabinet system through the legislation network centring on LG committee (see Chapter 5).

Stage four, monitoring the implementation of decisions, is a task which is not undertaken on a systematic basis by any member of the central executive. According to Daalder (1964: 244–5), during the late 1940s and early 1950s the Cabinet Office was charged with drawing the attention of departments to omissions in the execution of cabinet decisions. It is clear from Morrison's (1964: 26) account of the same period that secretariat officials used to circulate periodic reports on the implementation of decisions. Nowadays this is not done. Only a specific cabinet or cabinet committee request could provoke a monitoring exercise.

Change since 1974

Since 1974 gradual changes in links and processes have taken place. Informal facilitative links have become more focused on cabinet system institutions. The potential to initiate policy at cabinet system level has been expanded by creation of the PMPU, and concentration of more functions in the system. Business flows in the cabinet system have become more regulated and planned by the secretariat. These seemingly marginal changes constitute some enhancement of the power potential of cabinet system institutions.

One apparently contrary trend must also be addressed. In the course of our period, and particularly since 1979, the amount of activity undertaken by cabinet and its committees has declined. This decline is reflected in the progressive fall in the annual number of cabinet and, in particular, cabinet committee meetings discussed in Chapter 2. It is reinforced by the present tendency to timetable committee meetings for only one hour instead of the hour-and-a-half that used to be common practice. The trend is explained in a number of ways. More matters of a minor nature are being determined in or between departments, leaving the cabinet system more free to determine big, cross-departmental issues. Material is more refined before it reaches the cabinet system, allowing for more speedy treatment within the system. Partly this development reflects the more onerous preconditions which have to be fulfilled before an item can be submitted to cabinet or its committees (see Chapter 3). There has also been a significant growth in ministerial correspondence. Matters are increasingly determined by some ministers serving on the same committee, and then reported by letter to other committee members. In addition, committees have been encouraged to be more decisive and less discursive. Decisions are now less likely to be put off or referred upwards. Furthermore, business is now better planned and managed, and handling briefs are more pointed. Finally, 16 years of Conservative government may bear some of the explanatory burden. Sustained ministerial familiarity with the cabinet system and its ways of operating may have eased decision-making and provoked shifts away from formal structures into semi-formal and informal ones.

Conclusion

The links and processes examined in this chapter are key aspects of the cabinet system. Facilitative links predominantly involve officials, though ministers often tap into them to find out what is going on. The pattern of advantage generated by them varies a great deal. Similarly, processes of business management are chiefly managed by officials. Systems of selection and refinement in the cabinet system have been developed progressively to ensure that matters are settled at the lowest possible level. The key aim is to ensure that business is increasingly refined until it reaches a point of decision and despatch. In part, this is a response to administrative necessity, and an attempt to avoid overload and ensure smooth handling of business.

Although the content of material entering the cabinet system is determined largely in and between departments, the passage of material through the system is very much the preserve of cabinet system actors. Business flows have a natural momentum, but on occasion their speed and direction can be altered. Selectivity is reflected not only in the handling of material, but also in individuals who are drawn into the process. Both aspects are potentially open to exploitation. Over the years, however, routines and standard procedures have become established. These serve to limit and channel opportunities for individual initiative. Relatively few actors are advantaged by holding positions at strategic points in the cabinet system policy process. Notable among them are the prime minister, committee chairs, the cabinet secretary, and top officials in the secretariats. It does not follow that opportunities available to them are exploited. Much depends on the attitudes of individuals occupying these positions. Officials' attitudes are especially conditioned by the established values and practices of the cabinet system, which emphasise the need to ensure that matters are in a fit state for effective ministerial consideration (see Chapter 3). The central aim of secretariat officials is to achieve a smooth flow of business and full involvement of all relevant departmental interests.

Nevertheless, in the politics of any established institution the ability to manipulate machinery and means whereby decisions are reached is an important aspect of power potential. Deciding where, how and among whom matters are to be determined is the very essence of practical politics. The potential to exploit this power, while constrained by routines, accepted ways of working and time pressures, is concentrated at the very centre of the cabinet system. The prime minister, those who advise him or her, and committee chairs are most privileged. The scope for individual initiative on the part of other senior-ranking ministers is less substantial than is sometimes thought. The power potential of officials is substantial, but also heavily constrained by the restricted number of opportunity points, the very clear framework within which business is handled in the cabinet system, and civil servants' fixed attitudes towards their job.

A clear shift to a leaner and smoother process of handling business has taken place during our period. It can be interpreted in one of two ways. One interpretation is that the cabinet system has been strengthened by the more precise focus which now characterises much of its work. The other is that it has ceded some elements of control to departments. However, these interpretations are not mutually exclusive. Furthermore cabinet, its committees and the secretariats are only part of a wider cabinet system. In our next chapter we examine significant recent expansion of other elements of the system.

5

□

Networks and tasks

In the British system of government, policy initiative and formation are traditionally held to be departmental responsibilities. This view is substantially correct, but on its own it does not fully capture the division of responsibility between distinct parts of the state. In fact, the cabinet system is also the focal point for management of some of the key tasks of government. All of these tasks are crucial to the functioning of the state. Their location at its core indicates the range and extent of the contemporary cabinet system. Around each of these management tasks stable networks of individuals have formed. In this chapter, we analyse the main networks which centre on the cabinet system. Many of them reach out to other parts of the government machine and draw in actors from departments and elsewhere, but their cores are securely located in the cabinet system. As before, our central interest is power potential.

Network theory and the cabinet system

Network theory holds that the basic analytical units in any political system are not individuals or formal organisations, but the 'positions or roles occupied by social actors and the relations or connections between these positions' (Knoke, 1990: 7). Its primary concerns are twofold. First, it focuses on the external features or structure of a network, such as its scope, membership and distinctiveness from other networks. Second, it investigates the internal features or character of a network, as revealed by its internal relations. In the latter case, the minimum aim is to distinguish key positions by the extent to which they control scarce resources, such as information, staff and finance (Knoke, 1990: 8–9). The central contention is that relationships within a network reveal actual or potential influence, and therefore have important consequences for individual units, the political system as a whole, and products of the system such as policy decisions (Knoke and Kuklinski, 1982: 13).

Derived from network theory, the concept of policy network has been applied to a series of policy areas and issues. Industrial policy (Wright, 1988), central–local relations (Rhodes, 1988) and youth employment policy (Marsh, 1992) are examples. It has generated typologies of networks distinguished by membership, degree of integration, and internal resource distribution (Marsh and Rhodes, 1992: 14). Our approach is both more particular, and more modest. Our area of analysis is not policy sectors or issues (the latter are the concern of Part 2), but the main tasks which are concentrated in the cabinet system, and the distinct network of positions which relates to each. We seek to identify central network positions, and to analyse changes in the structure and character of each network in the period since 1974.

In evaluating the structure of a network, we investigate two features: membership and distinctiveness. Some networks are small and exclusive. Others are large and open. In assessing the internal character of a network, we seek to isolate key positions best able to shape the tasks undertaken by it. In each case, we construct a network diagram which reveals in its shaded central area the core of the network. Finally, we are also keen to identify positions common to more than one network, and therefore influential in work undertaken in the cabinet system as a whole.

This focus on tasks and positions is central to our approach. In total, we examine eight management tasks which are focused on the cabinet system. Many have become a cabinet system concern only since 1916. Indeed, most of these tasks have only been securely located in the cabinet system during the post-war period, and all have witnessed substantial development both in the past 50 years and during our 20-year period. Each is the preserve of a relatively distinct network. The eight tasks involve management above the level of department of:

- domestic policy;
- overseas policy;
- European Union policy;
- national security information and policy;
- government legislation;
- the government's political support base;
- the civil service and machinery of government; and
- government presentation.

One further task in which the cabinet system is implicated is management of public finances. However, as this task is centred not on the central executive but on the Treasury, we do not investigate it in this chapter. It is instead addressed in Chapter 6, where management of the government's legislative programme is also covered in more detail. Both tasks are unusual because they are managed by means of established and highly regularised annual policy cycles. They also stand alone in setting the parameters (in terms of time and money) within which all other government activity must take place.

Aspects of management of the government's political support base which are subject to variation by party are analysed in Chapter 7. Elements that are common to both governing parties are investigated in this chapter.

In examining the eight distinct networks formed around our eight key tasks, we pay most attention to the situation in 1995, though we are also concerned to state how the functions and membership of each network have changed in the period since 1974. The networks which we analyse centre on tasks which are almost certain to remain the preserve of the cabinet system. All involve significant matters which are either cross–departmental and/or central to overall government strategy. From time to time during out period other management tasks and associated networks have been centred within the cabinet system. Here we only analyse those eight networks which are well established features of the cabinet system.

Management of domestic policy

There is a crucial divide within the cabinet system between domestic and overseas policy. Business flows in each sphere are handled by separate networks, which together provide a key structural underpinning for cabinet system operations. The domestic policy network (Figure 5.1) is the more extensive of the two. Its key task is to oversee flows of business on the domestic side of cabinet system operations. At ministerial level it centres on the economic and domestic policy (EDP) committee of cabinet, which has 13 members and is chaired by the prime minister. Also central to the network are EDH, the ministerial committee on home and social affairs, and EDC, the ministerial committee on competitiveness. Both are extremely large committees comprising almost the entire cabinet. Only the prime minister and defence and foreign secretaries are not among the 21 members of EDH, which is chaired by the lord president of the council. These three plus the lord chancellor and the chief whip are also absent from EDC, which is chaired by the deputy prime minister and covers most aspects of industrial and economic regeneration policy. At official level the network centres on staff from the economic and home and social affairs secretariats, which are coordinated by the deputy secretary in charge of economic affairs. EDP is pre-eminent in the hierarchy of domestic cabinet committees, and tends to operate as a formal sub-cabinet.

The domestic policy network stretches from the Cabinet Office and Prime Minister's Office to encompass all domestic departments of state, and a broad range of cabinet committees. In July 1995, 10 (13 in May 1992) out of 19 (26) ministerial standing committees and sub-committees were economic and domestic, and were serviced by the economic and home and social affairs secretariats. Three other committees – legislation (FLG and LG) and Northern Ireland (NI) – were also serviced by these two secretariats, but were isolated because they handled a separate area of activity.

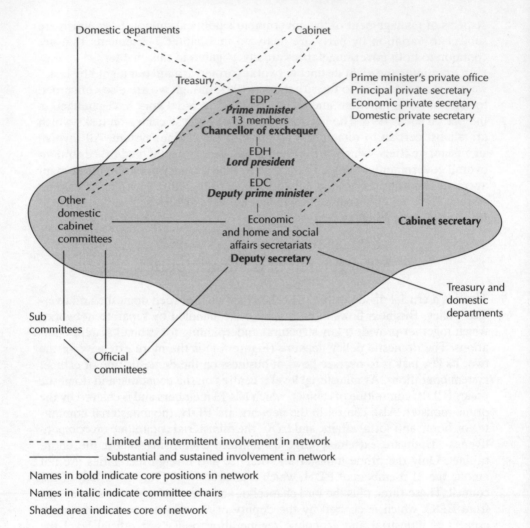

Figure 5.1 The domestic policy network.

Key positions within this network are held by the prime minister, who chairs EDP, the lord president who chairs EDH and the deputy prime minister who chairs EDC and a number of other domestic committees, the chancellor of the exchequer, the cabinet secretary and leading officials in the two secretariats which service the network. The deputy secretary in the economic affairs secretariat, who oversees the work of both secretariats, occupies a pivotal coordinating role. The Treasury is drawn into the network on a consistent basis. All other domestic departments are drawn in from time to time. Ministers who sit on key committees, notably EDP, play important secondary roles. Private secretaries from the prime minister's private office are frequently drawn into the network as, on occasion, are members of the PMPU.

Since 1974 the cohesion of the domestic policy network has increased substantially. During the Wilson administration of 1974–6, three major domestic committees covered economic policy, home affairs and social services (Castle, 1980: 105). Under Callaghan, and in the early part of the Thatcher adminstration, this threefold division was consolidated into a split between economic and home affairs policy. During the Thatcher years, the home and social affairs secretariat became subordinate to the economic affairs secretariat, and the deputy secretary in charge of the latter became the effective coordinator of both (Seldon, 1990: 108). The enhanced status of the economic affairs secretariat seems to have been consequent upon abolition of the CPRS in 1983, and delegation of some of its *ad hoc* analytical work to that secretariat (Seldon, 1990: 107). Integration of the two secretariats was later reflected, under Major, in creation of EDP, an overarching ministerial committee covering both economic and domestic policy. In July 1995 steps were taken to increase coordination of economic regeneration and industrial policy through creation of EDC committee, which took responsibility for the work previously undertaken by standing ministerial committees EDI (industry, consumers), EDI(P) (public sector pay), EDR (urban regeneration), and EDS (science and technology). The result has been to streamline and integrate further the domestic network, and to make the system both more focused on key central actors, and slightly less fragmented.

Management of overseas policy

The overseas policy network (Figure 5.2) is the counterpart of the domestic policy network. Its task is to oversee business flows in the defence and overseas spheres of cabinet system operations. It centres at ministerial level on the defence and overseas policy (OPD) committee of cabinet, which has a membership of eight and is chaired by the prime minister. At official level, the network centres on staff from the defence and overseas secretariat, which is headed by a deputy secretary. OPD is pre-eminent in the hierarchy of overseas cabinet committees and, though small, tends like EDP to operate as a formal sub-cabinet.

The overseas policy network stretches from the Cabinet Office and Prime Minister's Office to encompass the two major overseas departments of state, the FCO and MoD, plus the DTI, which has important inward investment responsibilities. The JIC is also drawn in from time to time. This network is therefore less extensive than the domestic policy network, and contains a smaller range of cabinet committees. In July 1995, only two (six in May 1992) of 19 (26) ministerial standing committees and sub-committees were primarily concerned with overseas matters. The main servicing of these was provided by the defence and overseas secretariat.

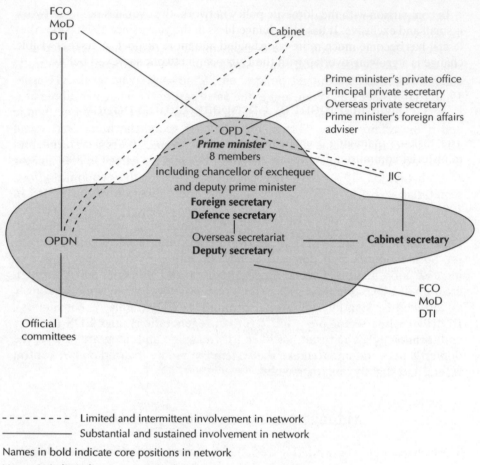

Figure 5.2 The overseas policy network.

Key positions in this network are held by the prime minister, foreign secretary, defence secretary, cabinet secretary and leading officials in the defence and overseas secretariat. The deputy secretary in this secretariat has an important coordinating role. The FCO and MoD are frequently drawn into the network. The DTI is drawn in rather less frequently. The chancellor of the exchequer and the attorney general are both members of OPD, and play important secondary roles. The creation of the position of deputy prime minister in July 1995 placed its incumbent, Michael Heseltine, in a potentially important strategic position within this network through membership of both key committees. Private secretaries from the prime minister's private office, and the prime minister's foreign affairs adviser, are drawn into the network from time to time.

In comparison with the domestic policy network, the overseas policy network is small and exclusive. It has also changed less in the years since 1974. Nevertheless, it has become much more coordinated and more distinct. A further visible change is a growing overlap with the European network surveyed below.

Management of European Union policy

The task of managing European Union (EU) policy focuses on one key ministerial committee, European questions (OPD(E)) chaired by the foreign

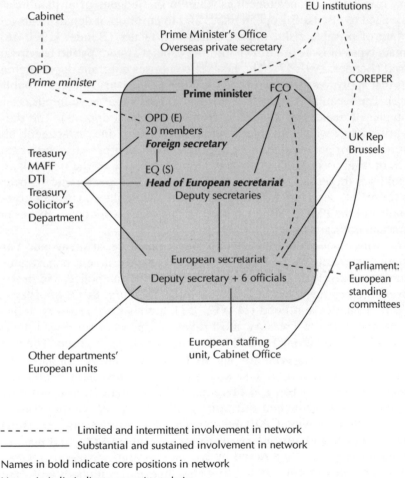

-------- Limited and intermittent involvement in network
———————— Substantial and sustained involvement in network

Names in bold indicate core positions in network

Names in italic indicate committee chairs

Shaded area indicates core of network

Figure 5.3 The European policy network.

secretary, on its shadowing official committee (EQ(S)), and on the European secretariat in the Cabinet Office. These two committees now oversee most aspects of EU policy. A separate ministerial committee (OPDSE) dealing with European security (and chaired by the prime minister) was shown in the May 1992 list of cabinet committees, but had been abolished by November 1994. The European secretariat coordinates EU policy across Whitehall. Together, these are the elements which form the core of this network (Figure 5.3, p. 87).

The European secretariat comprises seven senior staff. In some of its work it is assisted by the European staffing unit in the senior and public appointments group of the Cabinet Office, which has a senior staff of four. One committee clerk services OPD(E) and EQ(S). This secretariat plays a proactive role, and convenes meetings when in the judgement of its officials there is a need to discuss European issues and to ensure that departments are fully aware of possible risks, opportunities and tactics (Bender, 1991: 16). Three main types of issue are drawn into the cabinet system by the European secretariat (Bender, 1991: 17). The first set comprises constant departmental interests that apply to a range of proposals (such as Treasury interest in public spending). The second set comprises horizontal issues that have implications for a number of departments (such as frontier control proposals). The third set comprises issues which fall chiefly within the ambit of one department, but are nevertheless of potential interest to others (such as proposals which raise questions of legal precedent). Also drawn into the centre of the network are personnel from the Prime Minister's Office. There, European policy is overseen by the private secretary for overseas affairs, and might also be monitored by a member of the PMPU, although most of that unit's work concentrates on economic and domestic policy.

This network reaches domestically into government departments and Parliament, and externally to the EU in Brussels. The government departments which have most involvement in management of European policy, and probably provide the key members of EQ(S), are the Treasury, FCO, Ministry of Agriculture, Fisheries and Food (MAFF), DTI and also the Treasury Solicitor's Department. In the Treasury, most relevant aspects of European policy are handled by EU divisions I and II in the overseas finance group. The staff comprise four senior civil servants. The FCO has separate EU departments for internal and external affairs. One assistant under secretary heads both departments. MAFF has two EU divisions within its agricultural commodities, trade and food production directorate. One deals with coordination of common agricultural policy (CAP) matters. The other manages links between the UK Parliament and various EU institutions. The MAFF legal advisers division handles legal matters raised by EU membership. Finally, the Treasury Solicitor's Department has a European division of three senior staff, which coordinates legal advice across Whitehall on aspects of European law and the conduct of litigation before the European Court of Justice (ECJ). Other departments are brought into the work of this network as necessary.

Some, notably the Department for Education and Employment (DfEE), Department of the Environment (DoE), Northern Ireland Office (NIO), and Department of Transport (DTp), have well-established coordinating units on European affairs which are responsible for achieving a coherent approach across the department. Most other departments have sections dealing with aspects of European business (Cabinet Office, 1994b). The parliamentary link is supervised by the Cabinet Office, which is responsible for ensuring that the relevant scrutiny committee in both Houses is kept informed of any European Commission proposals, plus the government's view on them. This gives Parliament the opportunity to express its position before a final decision is taken in Brussels (Bender, 1991: 19).

This network links into the EU mainly through the office of the British permanent representative (UKRep) in Brussels. This is an overseas post of the FCO, with a large proportion of its staff on secondment from other departments. It is engaged not only in carrying out instructions, but also in helping to formulate them. To this end members of its staff usually attend Cabinet Office meetings, and its head has a weekly meeting with top officials in the secretariat (Bender, 1991: 18).

Coordination of the network in this sphere is rather different from that which takes place elsewhere, for two main reasons. The first is that much EU business is highly specialised and technical, and is therefore often handled in a web of official committees. The second is that business flows in this sphere are often unorthodox. Community business usually moves through UKRep to the FCO for distribution to departments, although on occasion liaison is direct. Moreover, if the issue is one of broad policy, or concerns a range of departments, liaison must also involve the European secretariat. The secretariat then coordinates departmental responses through its official committees. In this operation, the committee of deputy secretaries which shadows OPD(E) – EQ(S) – plays a crucial role. It meets several times a week, and is chaired by the head of the European secretariat (Edwards, 1992: 84–5). Once a British line has been set, it is fed back to UKRep Brussels office for discussion in the committee of permanent representatives (COREPER) from all EU member states (James, 1992: 57–8). The volume of business which now flows into the cabinet system from the EU is substantial. At the start of the 1990s the Cabinet Office chaired 200 meetings a year on EC issues, and circulated over 300 papers (Bender, 1991: 16).

As Britain has been a member of the EU only since 1973, most developments in this sphere fall within our period. Two opposed patterns are visible. One is gradual centralisation of the lines of broad policy making in the Cabinet Office, and in particular in the European secretariat. This reflects the enormous growth in European business over the period and, more pertinently, the increasing tendency of this business to involve more than one department. This has served to enhance the core positions in the network. The second major development since 1973 works in the opposite direction. It is reinforcement of departmental autonomy through integration of European business in the existing departmental structure of government. Thus, although cabinet system actors have been provided with new coordinating mechanisms which stretch across the whole of Whitehall, departments have also been able to exploit European links and alliances to their own advantage. This has enhanced departmental points at the rim of the network on matters that fall clearly within departmental spheres. The result is a segmented pattern of policy making. Issues of high political salience or substantial interdepartmental significance tend to be coordinated by cabinet system actors. Other matters tend to be left to departmental specialists (Armstrong and Bulmer, 1995).

This network is large and relatively open. On a permanent basis, key figures in it are the foreign secretary and members of the European secretariat. The prime minister also plays a central, but intermittent, role in the network. Since 1974, the growth of EC/EU policy competence has caused the network to expand greatly to encompass most government departments. It now reaches across most of Whitehall, and into the EU policy process. During our period it has thus become one of the major coordinating networks at the heart of British government. As such, it has been an important element of centralisation of policy making in the central executive.

Management of national security information and policy

The task of managing national security information and policy centres formally on the prime minister, who has final responsibility for the security services, and chairs the ministerial committee on the intelligence services (IS). Membership of this committee is very restricted. Under Major in July 1995, it was limited to the deputy prime minister, foreign secretary, chancellor of the exchequer, home secretary and defence secretary. The lord president of the council and attorney general were invited to attend as appropriate (Cabinet Office, 1995c). The committee is serviced by the joint intelligence secretariat. These are the core elements of the national security information and policy network (Figure 5.4).

This network is the smallest and most exclusive in British central government. Outside the core of senior ministers who are members of IS, cabinet ministers are involved only on a 'need to know' basis. IS discussions and conclusions are hardly ever considered in cabinet (Wilson, 1976: 167). However since 1994 a committee of privy councillors has exercised some oversight functions regarding the security services. The network manages three main tasks: assessment and transmission of security and intelligence information to ministers; management of intelligence activities and the security services; and collection of information. Most of this work is undertaken by officials.

Assessment and transmission of information are coordinated by the JIC. This was first established in 1936 and was brought into the Cabinet Office in

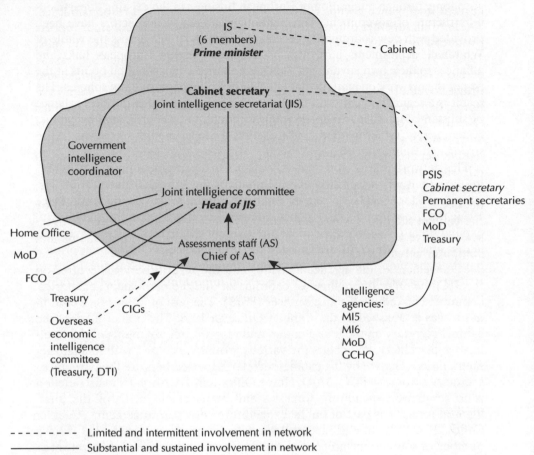

IS -
(6 members)
Prime minister   - - - Cabinet

- - - **Cabinet secretary** - - - - - - - -
Joint intelligence secretariat (JIS)

Government
intelligence
coordinator

PSIS
Cabinet secretary
Permanent secretaries
FCO
MoD
Treasury

Joint intelligence committee
Head of JIS

Home Office

MoD

FCO

Assessments staff (AS)
Chief of AS

Treasury

CIGs

Overseas
economic
intelligence
committee
(Treasury, DTI)

Intelligence
agencies:
MI5
MI6
MoD
GCHQ

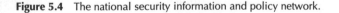

- - - - - - - -   Limited and intermittent involvement in network
———————   Substantial and sustained involvement in network

Names in bold indicate core positions in network

Names in italic indicate committee chairs

Shaded area indicates core of network

Figure 5.4 The national security information and policy network.

1957 (see Chapter 1). It now usually meets on a weekly basis. The JIC is supported by an assessments staff and the joint intelligence secretariat. Both are located in the Cabinet Office. JIC members are senior officials in the FCO, MoD and Treasury, heads of the three main intelligence agencies (the security service (MI5), the secret intelligence service (MI6) and GCHQ, Cheltenham), the government's intelligence coordinator, and the chief of the assessments staff. Officials from the Home Office attend as required. The JIC is chaired by the head of the joint intelligence secretariat, who has direct access to the prime minister. It has a number of sub-committees or current intelligence groups (CIGs), with specific territorial responsibilities. These bring together officials from relevant departments to consider reports produced by the assessments staff prior to consideration by the JIC (Franks, 1983: 95). The JIC also receives information from the cabinet's overseas economic intelligence committee, which is chaired by a Treasury official and draws together information on economic intelligence from the main economic departments and other sources, assesses it and distributes its findings (Norton-Taylor, 1988). The JIC fulfils two functions. It coordinates, directs and reviews the work of the intelligence services. It also provides intelligence reports in the form of a weekly 'Red Book', which is distributed to ministers and officials on a 'need to know' basis (Cabinet Office, 1993: 11, 23–4). The JIC is the key collection and transmission point within the intelligence network. There is also an official committee on security, chaired by the cabinet secretary, which is serviced by various sub-committees. It oversees positive vetting of personnel and security of property, documents and computer networks (Gill, 1994: 176).

Management of intelligence activities and the security services centres on the JIC, the office of intelligence coordinator and the permanent secretaries' committee on the intelligence services (PSIS). The post of intelligence coordinator was established in the Cabinet Office in 1968. The holder advises the cabinet secretary on the coordination and resource requirements of the intelligence machinery, and chairs the various groups concerned with its management. PSIS is chaired by the cabinet secretary. Its members are the permanent secretaries from the FCO, MoD, Home Office and Treasury. Its main function is to scrutinise expenditure forecasts and management plans of the intelligence agencies as part of public expenditure survey arrangements (Cabinet Office, 1993: 17). Intelligence and security information is collected from a number of sources, including diplomatic reports, telegrams and secret intelligence material amassed by the three main intelligence agencies and the defence intelligence staff within the MoD.

Since 1974 the national security network has become both more centred on and more coordinated within the cabinet system. In 1983, following publication of the Franks report on the Falklands war, the chair of the JIC passed from the FCO to the Cabinet Office. Initially, this position was combined with that of intelligence coordinator, but since 1985 the two posts have been separated (Cabinet Office, 1993: 12). In recent years, lines of responsibility within the Cabinet Office have been tightened. The former intelligence and security secretariat has been placed more clearly within the ambit of the JIC, and clearer lines of responsibility have been established.

This network is small and closed. It is, in fact, the most exclusive in Whitehall and is largely dominated by specialists who are officials, not ministers. Alongside the prime minister, key figures in it are the cabinet secretary and the head of the joint intelligence secretariat. During our period the network has been focused ever more clearly on the cabinet system.

Management of government legislation

The task of managing the government's legislative programme is conducted on medium- and long-term bases. In each case, the network of individuals at the core is largely the same (Figure 5.5). Indeed, under some administrations, the two tasks have been undertaken by a single ministerial committee (and attendant sub-committees). More commonly, the tasks are divided between two committees. Lists of committees published by the Major government in 1992, 1994 and 1995 contained a ministerial committee on legislation (LG), and a separate ministerial committee on the queen's speeches and future legislation (FLG). Each was chaired, as is usually the case, by the leader of the House of Commons (lord president of the council). Membership of FLG was more restricted than was that of LG, the chief difference being that the Scottish and Welsh (but not Northern Ireland) secretaries were members of LG, but not of

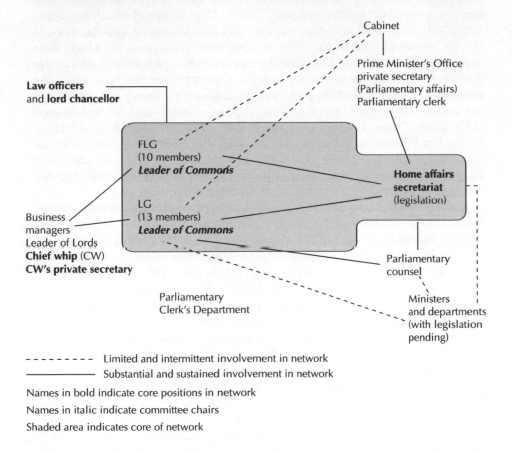

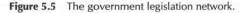

Figure 5.5 The government legislation network.

FLG. Government chief whips in both Houses were members of both committees. The home and social affairs secretariat services both committees.

Core members of this network at ministerial level divide into two main groups. One is the government's business managers. The other is the government's law officers (see Chapter 2). Formally, the prime minister is not a member of the network, though matters concerning the activities of the LG arm of the network are frequently made known to the prime minister and cabinet through the report on forthcoming parliamentary business which begins every regular meeting of cabinet. Core officials include members of the Cabinet Office's home and social affairs secretariat. This secretariat has a staff of six under an under secretary, though not all are consistently involved in this network. Officials from this secretariat are the key actors when it comes to distribution of information within the network. The chief whip's private secretary is also usually an important figure. He is the government's chief communication link with the opposition on parliamentary business, and also liaises closely with the Parliamentary Clerks' Department (Griffith and Ryle, 1989: 300). Individual ministers and their officials are drawn into the work of the LG committee network when it deals with legislation on which their department has the lead. Expertise is at a premium in this sphere, and brings parliamentary counsel to the fore at the drafting stage. In June 1995, the parliamentary counsel office contained 33 draftsmen, directly accountable to the leader of the House of Commons (Rippon, 1992: 7) and funded through the Cabinet Office. In 1990, a further 10 parliamentary counsel were located in the Lord Advocate's Department to deal with Scottish legislation (Miers and Page, 1990: 50). Many papers for consideration by LG, and especially FLG, are prepared by secretariat officials. The result is that information and advisory resources are concentrated at the core of the network.

During the period since 1974 there have been very few changes to the structure and character of this network. Some have argued that there has been a slight shift in the nature of tasks undertaken, with the result that nowadays less attention is paid to vetting government bills, and more to managing the government's programme (Rippon, 1992). It is also clear that the workload borne by this network increased in the late 1980s. As a consequence, membership of the network has been marginally expanded to include more parliamentary counsel. Beyond this, change has been slight.

This is a small, specialised and relatively closed network. Key positions are held by the leader of the House of Commons, and officials dealing with legislation matters in the home and social affairs secretariat. Important roles are also played by the chief whip and his private secretary, the leader of the House of Lords, the law officers and the lord chancellor. Much of the work of this network is undertaken by officials with expertise that no minister possesses. Even on the ministerial side, tasks are specialised and therefore largely exclusive. Management of government legislation is discussed at greater length in Chapter 6.

Management of the government's political support base

A further specialised task which is substantially centred on personnel within the cabinet system is management of party support in Parliament and, to a lesser extent, in the country. Here the prime minister, as party leader in both the Conservative and Labour Parties, is the focal point of the network. Also centrally involved are the government's business managers, especially the whips' office, and, in the Conservative Party, the party chairman who provides the main link to Conservative Central Office and the party in the country. When Labour is in government, formal links to the mass party are more numerous and are not channelled through one individual (see Chapter 7). From the prime minister's staff only the prime minister's parliamentary private secretary (PPS)

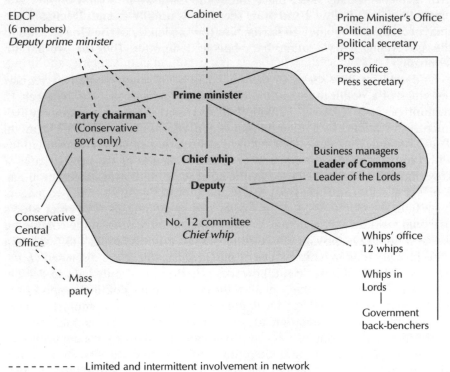

- - - - - - - - - Limited and intermittent involvement in network
—————————— Substantial and sustained involvement in network

Names in bold indicate core positions in network

Names in italic indicate committee chairs

Shaded area indicates core of network

Figure 5.6   The government's political support base network.

and political office are involved. Civil servants are not usually members of this network (Figure 5.6). However, although the tradition that officials leave cabinet or other formal meetings when overtly party political business is discussed continues to be respected, a few civil servants are now being drawn into some aspects of this party political network.

The key members of this network are not formally constituted in a cabinet committee, but are drawn together in a series of meetings which take place each week in parliamentary session. Under Thatcher and Major, a Monday morning meeting, chaired by the prime minister, has usually been held in Downing Street to review the political situation and plan the week ahead. This meeting is followed by a debriefing session at Conservative Central Office, chaired by the party chairman. On Wednesday mornings the chief whip chairs a meeting of whips to plan management of the following week's parliamentary business (Parkinson, 1992: 121). A further meeting to finalise arrangements usually takes place under the chief whip in the evening. The prime minister's political and press secretaries usually attend. Decisions are then presented to cabinet, to Parliament (by the leader of the House), and to the governing party's main back-bench committee (by the whips) on Thursdays.

Under Major, this series of meetings has been supplemented by regular meetings of a political committee of about 20 individuals. The Number 12 committee, as it is known in Whitehall, is reported to meet extremely frequently in session: at 9 a.m. on Mondays and Wednesdays and at 8.20 a.m. on Tuesdays and Thursdays. Its function is to oversee cabinet system relations with the parliamentary party, and to consider aspects of the presentation of government policy. It is chaired by the chief whip, and brings together ministers, some senior officials from the Prime Minister's Office, party managers from both the Commons and the Lords, and party officials. The chief whip's personal assistant acts as minute taker. One unusual feature of the committee is that it brings two private secretaries from the Prime Minister's Office into a semi-formal arena in which issues of party management are discussed (*Independent*, 3.1.95). It is not clear, however, whether they contribute to debate. Questions concerning management of the government's political support base are likely to be discussed in EDCP, the ministerial standing committee on the coordination and presentation of government policy. This committee was established in the spring of 1995 and was chaired initially by the chancellor of the Duchy of Lancaster, and, after July 1995, by the deputy prime minister. This committee brings together the government's business managers, including the chief whip and the party chairman. It is said to meet almost on a daily basis.

The central linkage between cabinet system actors and the parliamentary party is through the whips. Although there are differences in whipping between the Conservative and Labour Parties, the similarities are a great deal more striking. In both parties, the whips preside over what former chief whip

Francis Pym calls 'a highly elaborate communications network' (King and Sloman, 1973: 106). At its apex stands the chief whip, who always has excellent access to the prime minister. Interconnecting doors link Number 10 to Number 12 Downing Street, where the chief whip has his official residence (Jones, 1985a: 75). He is likely to see the prime minister on a daily basis (Redmayne, 1972: 76). The chief whip is an important cabinet system actor. Because he is extensively drawn into business at cabinet system level, his deputy effectively takes charge of day-to-day management of the parliamentary party. For this reason he also holds a key position in the network. He is assisted by 12 further whips. Each individual whip has area responsibilities, and looks after some 30 MPs from a particular region of the country. Each also has a subject specialism, relates to the ministerial team in the relevant government department, and attends on one or more of the 30 or so party back-bench subject and area committees. Whips' departmental affiliations are rotated on an annual basis. In addition, each develops *ad hoc* back-bench contacts by means of virtually permanent attendance in Parliament (Redmayne, 1972: 75). A whip is assigned to cover every debate on the floor of the House, and in a bill committee. The whips operate as intelligence gatherers and talent spotters (Parkinson, 1992: 120). They are a disciplining agent on behalf of the executive, an organising presence seeking to ensure successful completion of the government's parliamentary business, and a communication channel from the back-benches into the heart of the cabinet system. Their principal weapons are patronage and favours ranging from the promise of office to the placement of members on overseas delegations and select committees. Before any ministerial reshuffle, the chief whip is consulted. *Ad hoc* relationships also characterise this network. Austin Mitchell (1982: 173) notes that the wise prime minister always has additional lines of communication and intelligence. In the 1960s, George Wigg performed this function for Wilson. In the 1970s, Callaghan similarly relied on James Wellbeloved. In the early 1980s, but not later in the decade (Clark, 1993), Thatcher took parliamentary advice from her PPS, Ian Gow ('Supergrass'). Other key members of the central executive also have independent links into party back-benches. Contacts between the cabinet system and the governing party in the country run through rather different channels in the Conservative and Labour Parties, and are therefore analysed in Chapter 7.

It is hard to identify change in the character of this network during the period since 1974, because management of the government's support base is deeply affected by contingent factors, notably size of government majority and party in office. However, the links between ministers and governing party back-benchers have been augmented and extended significantly over the period (see Chapter 7). These links have also become more regularised, and drawn more centrally into the cabinet system. Towards the end of Thatcher's period in office, cabinet occasionally held a session at the end of the weekly Thursday meeting to hear information about the general political situation.

Under Major, this became a regular event in which cabinet was not simply informed, but also encouraged, to discuss fully matters raised. The creation of the Number 12 committee, and the emergence and consolidation of EDCP are further developments of the party management function.

This network has always focused on a small party leadership group. Key positions in it are held by the prime minister, chief whip and deputy chief whip, who oversees the main information channel with the parliamentary party. Also involved are the leaders of both Houses. In recent years the network has become increasingly open and extended, as the party management function has become both more difficult and more pressing. Because the network is party political, it is not centred on a formal cabinet committee. However, creation of the Number 12 and EDCP committees has generated new oversight mechanisms within this sphere.

Management of the civil service and machinery of government

The task of managing the civil service and machinery of government centres at ministerial level on the positions of prime minister, as minister responsible for the civil service and machinery of government, chancellor of the Duchy of Lancaster, as head of OPS and minister in charge of the civil service (under the deputy prime minister and the prime minister), and a Treasury minister, the paymaster general who, under the chancellor of the exchequer, has responsibility for civil service pay. On the official side, the key positions are those of cabinet secretary, as head of the home civil service, permanent secretary to the OPS, officials in the economic affairs secretariat, and the deputy secretary in charge of the civil service management and pay division in the Treasury. Below this top level, most of the personnel engaged in the network are senior officials drawn from the OPS divisions dealing with civil service matters, efficiency and machinery of government and the civil service management and pay division in the Treasury (Figure 5.7 *see* opposite page). Matters raised by this network are sometimes discussed at the weekly meeting of permanent secretaries (see Chapter 4).

The tasks of this network are fairly self-explanatory. The Cabinet Office machinery of government division is charged with providing policy advice on a series of organisational questions, including allocation of functions between departments. Other divisions within the OPS are responsible for the training, standards, restructuring and evaluation of civil service activities. The Treasury division generates policy on management issues, pay, personnel policy and various organisational matters.

The network is not centred on a standing ministerial committee. In Major's 1992 committee list (Cabinet Office, 1992b) there was a committee dealing with civil service pay. A similar committee existed under the Thatcher administration (Hennessy, 1986: 27). This committee has since been abolished, and did not

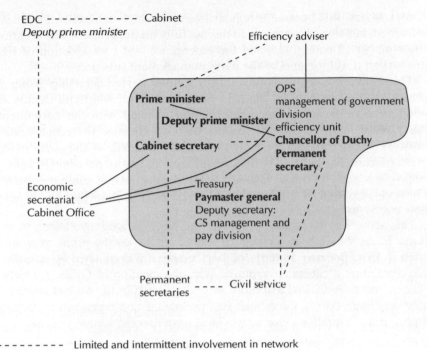

EDC ------------ Cabinet
Deputy prime minister

Efficiency adviser

Prime minister

Deputy prime minister

Cabinet secretary

OPS
management of government
division
efficiency unit
Chancellor of Duchy
Permanent
secretary

Economic
secretariat
Cabinet Office

Treasury
Paymaster general
Deputy secretary:
CS management and
pay division

Permanent ____ Civil service
secretaries

--------- Limited and intermittent involvement in network

————————— Substantial and sustained involvement in network

Names in bold indicate core positions in network

Names in italic indicate committee chairs

Shaded area indicates core of network

Figure 5.7 The civil service and machinery of government network.

feature in the 1994 or 1995 lists (Cabinet Office, 1994b). Of course, matters concerning the civil service may be drawn into other standing committees, such as the ministerial committee on competitiveness (EDC) which as part of its terms of reference handles public sector pay. However, the network does not have a regular cabinet system location which consistently draws in other cabinet ministers. Rather, its main strands are contained within cabinet system agencies, and at ministerial level are firmly placed within the prime ministerial domain.

This concentration and centralisation of the network in cabinet system organisations is a clear trend over the period since 1974, and especially since 1979. A further aspect of change in the network has been the gathering of existing functions more tightly towards its centre. Notably, abolition of the CSD in 1981 led to incorporation of its personnel and management functions in the Cabinet Office. (Other functions returned to the Treasury, from whence they had come when the CSD was established in 1968.) A further change has been an expansion in the range of tasks placed within the network, many of which involve greater oversight of and intervention in the work of departments. Most important among these have been responsibilities for the overall efficiency of government. In 1979 an efficiency unit was created in the Cabinet Office under Sir Derek (now Lord) Rayner who oversaw short-term 'scrutinies' of aspects of government activity. Over time, further initiatives, such as the FMI and Next Steps programmes, were developed (see Chapter 2). The 1991 Citizen's Charter initiative further extended cabinet system activities. Each of these new tasks enhanced cabinet system actors' opportunities to oversee the activities of departments. At each stage, the requirements placed upon departments grew and were often supplemented by a series of monitoring mechanisms. Following launch of the Next Steps initiative, for example, all departments were required to put a specified amount of internal operations out to tender. This initiative arose within and is being monitored by cabinet system organisations.

This network is potentially very large, and has expanded significantly in recent years. It has always been focused, to a large extent, on the prime minister, but often in an *ad hoc* way. In terms of membership it is dominated by officials; it is not centred on a cabinet committee. With the creation of OPSS, the network became more regularised and more securely located in the cabinet system. It is now very much part of the cabinet system domain, and represents an important aspect of the centralising tendency evident under recent administrations.

Management of government presentation

The task of managing government presentation centres on EDCP, the standing ministerial committee on the coordination and presentation of government policy, and on the Number 10 press office. This office has a staff of 10, and is headed by the prime minister's (or chief) press secretary. Other members of the network are the most senior information officers working in the press offices of Whitehall departments, and the Central Office of Information (COI) (Franklin, 1994: 91). Until recently, this was a fairly self-contained network, though the chief press secretary has always liaised closely with the prime minister on a daily basis, and departmental press secretaries have always liaised equally closely with their respective ministers (Figure 5.8). In the mid-1990s the network has become slightly less contained, as a result of Major's creation of the Number 12 and EDCP committees.

The traditional forum in which this network is brought together is a weekly meeting of information officers. This takes place every Monday at 5 p.m. in conference room D of the Cabinet Office, and is chaired by the prime minister's press secretary. Its central function is to coordinate the management of government presentation, particularly over the coming week (Franklin, 1994: 91). The main channel through which government information officers release information to the outside world is the parliamentary lobby of some 220 accredited journalists. Members of the lobby are briefed twice daily by the

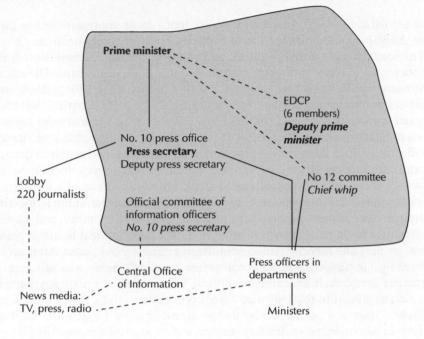

Figure 5.8 The government presentation network.

chief press secretary, at around 11 a.m. in Downing Street and 4 p.m. in the House of Commons (Cockerell, Hennessy and Walker, 1985: 44–5). A great deal of briefing also takes place on an *ad hoc* basis by telephone, over lunch, in corridors and so on (Ingham, 1991).

A new dimension has been added to the network by creation of the Number 12 committee under the chairmanship of the chief whip and of EDCP under the chairmanship of the deputy prime minister. Currently, both the chief press secretary and his deputy sit on the Number 12 committee. This committee liaises closely with EDCP, which attempts to coordinate presentation of the government's case across all departments. Prior to the creation of EDCP, the Number 12 committee's normal practice was to invite ministers to attend its meetings on days on which they had an important announcement to make. Ministers were usually accompanied by their special advisers and directors of information. The aim was to generate an early warning system with regard to announcements which were likely to be contentious (*Independent*, 3.1.95). EDCP is likely to have assumed many of these functions.

The main changes in the structure and character of this network since 1974 are that it has become both more coordinated and more centralised. The rise to prominence of Bernard Ingham, chief press secretary from 1979 to 1990, and head of government information services from 1989 to 1990 (Harris, 1990: 170), was one important source of change. Unlike many of his predecessors Ingham was a regular presence at the weekly meeting of information officers. He took a detailed interest in the work of government departments, and required departmental information officers by the Wednesday of each week to inform the Downing Street press office of intended dealings with the media during the week to come. This information generated the agenda for the Monday meeting of information officers. Ingham also required loyalty to his office and agenda (rather than to those of departments) and took a close interest in the appointment, training and career development of government presentation staff across Whitehall. He also created sub-committees to handle news management in particular areas, such as economic policy. The centralisation of government news management in the Downing Street press office which took place in the Thatcher years was reinforced by technological change. In 1989 the COI installed an electronic news delivery service, which allowed the Downing Street press office both to collect press releases from departments and to feed them into newspaper offices and press agencies with great efficiency (Franklin, 1994: 98). The departure of Ingham in 1990 led to a reversion to the practice whereby whereby the head of the government information service is not a member of the Prime Minister's Office (Devereau, 1992), though the centralisation of the service which took place under him remained under his two immediate successors, Gus O'Donnell and Christopher Meyer. Creation of the Number 12 and EDCP committees brought management of government presentation into a clear cabinet system arena, and ensured that it was more closely coordinated with related matters such as management of the political support base.

Despite reaching out to ministers and the media this network is relatively small in membership. The Number 12 and EDCP committees impose new oversight mechanisms on the network. However a central focus remains the prime minister's press office. Key positions are held by the prime minister and chief press secretary. Since July 1995, the deputy prime minister has also been key. In recent years, the network has become increasingly coordinated and regularised. A further major change witnessed in the years 1974–95 has been a strengthening of central positions in the network.

Key cabinet system positions

Having investigated the main networks involved in management of the eight key tasks which face the cabinet system, we now bring our analysis together by assessing positions which are privileged by membership of more than one network.

An initial point relates to the first two networks analysed in this chapter, domestic and overseas policy. These are especially important because they oversee the major business flows within the cabinet system, and divide its operations substantially into two spheres. In recent years these key networks have become increasingly separate. The divide they impose on cabinet system activity is significant. As has already been noted, in July 1995, of 19 ministerial committees and sub-committees 12 fell into the category either of domestic or of overseas policy: 10 were domestic, two were overseas. There were therefore only seven residual committees, of which only two were serviced by other secretariats. They were European questions (OPD(E)), and the intelligence services (IS).

The domestic–overseas divide structures much cabinet system activity. Very few individuals straddle it. Indeed, only Treasury ministers play a substantial part in both networks, being formal members of all of the combined total of 12 domestic and overseas committees (and of 17 of the full total of 19 ministerial standing committees). The two committees which did not have Treasury representation in July 1995 were EDCP, the ministerial committee dealing with the coordination and presentation of policy, and OPD(T), the ministerial sub-committee on terrorism. The degree of separation between the two networks is further revealed by committee memberships in the domestic sphere, only two of which – EDE and EDH(D) – involve overseas departments. Within this sphere, the representation of other departments is variable. The three territorial ministries are strongly represented. Of the 10 domestic committees Scotland is represented on eight, Wales on eight and Northern Ireland on six.

The relative closure of these two important cabinet networks is further revealed by the small number of individuals who are members of both. In July 1995, at ministerial level only the deputy prime minister (who sat on eight of the relevant 12 standing committees), the chancellor of the exchequer (eight), the president of the Board of Trade (eight) and the home secretary (six) were significantly drawn into the work of both networks. The foreign secretary was on both overseas committees, and one domestic committee. He was also on four of seven residual committees which are outside the two main networks. In July 1995, even the prime minister was a member of only one domestic committee and the two overseas committees. He did, however, chair each committee of which he was a member, and was in an important strategic position as chairman of the important and overarching domestic committee, EDP. He also chaired two of our seven residual committees. Prime ministerial practice is, however, variable. When Thatcher was prime minister she chaired at least four standing committees in the domestic field (Hennessy, 1986: 27). At official level, staff from the Prime Minister's Office join the prime minister in having access to both networks, as do the cabinet secretary and, to a lesser

Table 5.1   Core positions in eight cabinet system networks, 1995.

	PM	CS	DPM	LH	FS	CW
Domestic policy	X	X	X	X		
Overseas policy	X	X			X	
EU policy	X				X	
National security policy	X	X				
Government legislation				X		X
Government political support	X			X		X
CS and MG	X	X	X			
Government presentation	X			X		

Others

Domestic policy	chancellor of the exchequer, heads of the economic and home and social affairs secretariats
Overseas policy	defence secretary, head of the overseas secretariat
EU policy	head of the European secretariat
National security policy	head of joint intelligence secretariat
Government legislation	lord chancellor, law officers, leader of the House of Lords, head of home and social affairs secretariat (legislation), chief whip's private secretary
Government political support	deputy chief whip, party chairman
CS and MG	paymaster general, ministerial head and permanent secretary to OPS, deputy secretary, Treasury
Government presentation	chief press secretary

PM: prime minister; CS: cabinet secretary; DPM: deputy prime minister; LH: leader of the House of Commons; FS: foreign secretary; CW: chief whip.

extent, the deputy secretaries in charge of the economic and overseas and defence secretariats. Few others manage this feat.

Central positions in these two key policy networks are thus held ministerially by the prime minister, the few ministers (notably from the Treasury) who straddle both networks and chairs of important ministerial committees. Since July 1995 the deputy prime minister has also been in a key position. On the official side, core positions are held by a very small group who are in a position to survey policy management across both networks. This group is restricted to the cabinet secretary, the deputy and under secretaries in charge of the overseas and defence and economic affairs secretariats, and a few members of the Prime Minister's Office. These two groups of ministers and officials are the only ones to have full access to information about activities in both networks. Subsidiary positions are held by other chairs of ministerial committees, and by leading officials within each of the two main policy sectors. This group comprises senior members of the economic, home and social affairs, and overseas and defence secretariats. Other officials have restricted access to one of the main policy networks. This group comprises senior departmental officials who are drawn into the work of a network either through provision of memoranda for consideration in committee or as participants in or, occasionally, chairs of official committees which mirror ministerial committees and prepare business for them. Really central positions are thus held by a handful of leading ministers, the cabinet secretary and privileged members of the prime minister's private office. Members of the major secretariats are also in key positions to facilitate policy management and oversee their respective networks.

We can develop this analysis by identifying individuals who are core players in each of our networks. Table 5.1 presents the full list. It reveals that only six individuals are core members of more than one network, and that only four are core members of more than two. The prime minister is a core member of seven networks. The cabinet secretary is a core member of four, and is the only official to be a core member of more than one network. This analysis does not comprise a 'total picture' of key cabinet system positions, for individuals who regularly participate in networks without being core members of them may nevertheless be important players. Other ministers are members of a number of networks, and thereby keep in close contact with developments within them. Nevertheless, by focusing on core players we are able to demonstrate that there is a high degree of fragmentation in the cabinet system. The networks we have identified are important contributors to that fragmentation.

Throughout our period attempts have been made to overcome this fragmentation. Often such attempts have taken the form of the appointment of a senior minister to chair cabinet committees and help to coordinate government activities. Under Wilson, Edward Short fulfilled this function as did William Whitelaw under Thatcher and John Wakeham under both Thatcher and Major. In 1994 David Hunt, as chancellor of the Duchy of Lancaster and ministerial head of OPSS, was given the task of chairing six ministerial cabinet committees and of overseeing government policy in the domestic sphere. In spring 1995 Hunt was given the chairmanship of the new cabinet committee EDCP with a remit to manage the coordination and presentation of government policy. In July 1995 this increasingly regularised oversight function was extended further with the appointment of Michael Heseltine as deputy prime minister. Heseltine is a member of 14 out of 19 standing committees spanning all major spheres of government policy. He has inherited all of his predecessor's coordination responsibilities in the domestic sphere and has added to them membership of key overseas committees. This gives Heseltine access to both the domestic and overseas networks and places him in a strong position to coordinate government policy and oversee its presentation. This potentially powerful position partially reflects the particular political circumstances surrounding the Conservative leadership election of July 1995. However, there is also a degree of administrative logic to the changes which have been made, as trends during our period indicate.

A further point revealed by our analysis is the marginal position of traditional collective arenas in each of our networks. In not one network is cabinet in any sense central to activity, though very occasionally it may, of course, become an important player in some (but not all) networks. In one or two networks even cabinet committees are not central. Some networks tend to be highly exclusive.

Since 1974 the number and range of networks centred on the cabinet system has changed at the margin as from time to time tasks have been drawn within the central executive, sometimes on a temporary basis. The most notable change has concerned the management of science and technology policy which was an important growth area in cabinet system activity for nearly all of our period. Following the creation of a Cabinet Office science and technology group under Heath in the early 1970s (Gummett, 1991), a free-standing secretariat emerged in 1983. It also took on the functions of a small information technology secretariat which had been set up in 1981 (Cunningham and Nicholson, 1991: 32). The secretariat's activities expanded substantially during the mid-1980s, under active leadership and an interested prime minister (Seldon, 1990: 107). A standing cabinet committee on science and technology seems to have been created in 1986 (Cunningham and Nicholson, 1991: 35). In April 1992 cabinet system activity in this sphere was developed further by creation of an office of science and technology within OPSS, which gradually gathered together almost all remaining science functions located in departments. This progressive centralisation of science functions in the Cabinet Office was abruptly reversed in July 1995 as part of the changes which saw Michael Heseltine become deputy prime minister. Science and technology functions and the 94 associated staff were transferred to the DTI, and that department's competition and deregulation division with its staff complement of 69 was brought into the Cabinet Office.

During our period, our networks have almost uniformly become more coordinated, more regularised and more focused on the cabinet system. Almost every one has seen its centre of gravity shift closer to the centre. This in itself represents an extension of the power potential of cabinet system actors. The power potential of key positions has also been enhanced. The prime minister's power potential has been increased in all networks within which he or she is core. The power potential of the cabinet secretary has been extended in the sphere of civil service and machinery of government. In 1994, the ministerial head of OPSS became an important individual at the heart of the cabinet system. In 1995 this role was subsumed and augmented by the deputy prime minister. However, it must be remembered that the power potential of all core actors relies crucially on lines of communication which are managed by secondary actors. For this and many other reasons, power potential may not be realised.

6

□

Time and money

Many problems faced by the British central executive are the product of scarce resources. Two in particular are in pressingly short supply: time and money. The pressure of time upon individual ministerial workloads is now well documented (Headey, 1974: 32–7). Less extensively noted is the collective dimension to time pressures at the centre of British government. On the one hand, a regularised timetable – much of it set by the routines of Parliament – structures the annual, weekly and even daily timetable of central executive actors. On the other, much government policy requires legislative enactment and has to be accommodated within a restrictive parliamentary timetable (Quinlan, 1994: 27). The constraint placed by these timetables on executive activity is real, and often substantial. Also at the forefront of many accounts of the British state is its perpetual struggle to raise money and distribute it between spending programmes. This is, of course, a problem faced by all contemporary governments. It too places a major constraint on central government action. Management of these scarce resources is a major source of conflict within the cabinet system.

In this chapter, we begin by describing the annual, weekly and daily timetables which structure central executive activity. Fixed dates in the cabinet system calendar impose deadlines which must be met. They therefore have an important structuring effect on cabinet system operations. We next move to analyse the established policy routines which the British central state has developed to manage time and money. Organisation of the legislative programme, and mechanisms for both raising and allocating public money, have evolved into highly institutionalised processes. In each case, short- and long-term procedures have been developed which create frameworks within which policy making takes place. These frameworks are not entirely rigid, but they do shape and restrict the potential for policy making in other policy areas. Shortage of money or parliamentary time serves greatly to limit policy initiative. Although the frameworks are well established, they are also subject to adjustment from time to time. Each generates a balance of advantage and

107

disadvantage for individual actors, and imposes a bias and momentum on the policy process.

In our analysis of the three main policy processes devised to manage time and money, we look at the nature of each process and highlight change in the period since 1974. In line with the approach taken in Chapter 5, participants in the networks created around the three policy processes are identified. In this chapter, however, in three summary tables a distinction is drawn between central and marginal actors in terms of (i) those organising and initiating the process, (ii) those subsequently brought into the process, often by these actors, and (iii) those merely consulted by members of the network. By these criteria, we indicate the core membership of each network and the pattern of advantage within it. While each process is characterised by established procedures and routines, we also note the key shaping points in each annual cycle at which opportunities for the exercise of individual initiative are greatest.

Timetables

Before investigating the policy processes devised to manage time and money within the cabinet system, it is important to describe the annual, monthly and daily timetables of the central executive. These timetables serve to structure all activity within the British cabinet system.

The annual timetable

The annual timetable (Table 6.1) is structured chiefly by the routines of Parliament, to which the executive is formally accountable, and also by the routines of British party politics and the major international organisations of which Britain is a member. The central parliamentary cycle which is discussed in this section is that of a normal session, by which we mean one which is not extended or contracted by the timing of a general election. Although in each of these sections on cabinet system timetables we focus on the procedures of the House of Commons, it should not be forgotten that similar procedures in the House of Lords also have an impact on cabinet system operations. The other routines which are discussed here are also those of a normal political year.

The central impact of the parliamentary year on the cabinet system derives from the pattern of parliamentary sittings. In a normal year, the House of Commons goes into recess four times, for periods of about three weeks at Christmas, one week each at Easter and spring bank holiday, and two to three months in the summer. The House does not sit on bank holidays and other public holidays (Griffith and Ryle, 1989: 184). This parliamentary cycle has a major impact on cabinet system operations. When Parliament is in recess, or

Table 6.1 The annual timetable of the cabinet system during a normal parliamentary session.

Early November	Opening of Parliament
	Queen's speech
Late November	Budget
Early December	European Council
December–January	Three-week parliamentary Christmas recess
March/April	One-week parliamentary Easter recess
Late May	One-week parliamentary spring bank holiday recess
Late May/June	G7 Economic Summit
June	European Council
Late July/early August–mid-October	Two/three-month parliamentary summer recess
End September–mid-October	Party conference season
Mid-October	Brief parliamentary resumption for one or two weeks

simply adjourned for a public holiday, the activities of the entire system tend to run down and less business passes through it. Cabinet usually only meets in its regular Thursday morning slot when Parliament is in session, as one of its chief reasons for meeting on a regular basis is to consider business to go before Parliament the following week. Cabinet committees also meet less frequently in parliamentary recess and may not meet at all. In the main summer recess, ministers take holidays, and the activity of the entire cabinet system diminishes. In order to ensure that the system continues to tick over effectively, and in particular that any media interest is properly handled, a ministerial rota is drawn up to 'mind the shop'. This has two main dimensions. Within departments, junior ministers rotate holiday cover. Within the cabinet system as a whole, an attempt is made to ensure that sufficient senior ministers are always on hand to deal with any questions that may arise (usually in the media). Civil servants' holidays are also coordinated to ensure that core cover is maintained. The importance of this pattern of cabinet system activity is that it can in itself either impose delays on the progress of business through the system, or mean that material which does pass through the system in parliamentary recess is subjected to less intensive scrutiny than takes place at other times of the year.

Key dates in the parliamentary calendar serve to complicate the part of the political year when Parliament is in session. Of particular note are the two classic set-piece executive policy announcements, the queen's speech and the budget. From the start of our period until 1992, the chancellor used to present a tax budget to the House of Commons in late March or April, and to make a separate autumn statement of public expenditure projections at the end of November. However, when in 1993 the budget was moved from March/April to late November, the autumn statement was incorporated in a single, 'unified' budget announcement combining taxation and spending proposals. The impact of this change on the cabinet system's annual calendar was minimal, as the tax side of the budget is determined almost exclusively from within the

Treasury, and requires almost no cabinet system involvement (see below). Of far more importance in shaping the routine of the cabinet system are the queen's speech, which opens a parliamentary session and is made at the start of November, and the public spending element of the budget (or old autumn statement), which is announced at the end of November. Both impose important constraints on cabinet system actors, who must adhere to a very strict timetable imposed by evident deadline dates (see below).

The cabinet system's annual timetable is structured further by party political activity and international summitry. Party political activity reaches its height in October, when the major party conferences take place. The Liberal Democrats usually hold their party conference at the end of September. The Labour and Conservative Parties meet in the first and second weeks of October. Conference season is a period when ministers' attention is strongly focused on party political matters, with the result that some policy questions acquire an inflated importance and others are temporarily eclipsed. International summitry does not always follow a regular pattern. However, meetings of the European Council are now an established feature of June and December, and G7 Economic Summit meetings take place every late May or June. Each of these summits involves the prime minister and other senior ministers, and temporarily skews the activity of the cabinet system. Before an international summit, extensive preparation and briefing of senior ministers takes place. On return from a summit the prime minister always makes an early statement to the House of Commons. A weekend summit is usually reported to the House on the following Monday afternoon.

The weekly timetable

Like the annual timetable, the weekly timetable is structured chiefly by parliamentary routine. Out of session, the pattern described in Table 6.2 does not apply fully. The weekly timetable is also structured by the timetable of the lead individual in the cabinet system, the prime minister.

It can be seen from Table 6.2 that when Parliament is in session the weekly timetable of the cabinet system is heavily influenced by parliamentary procedure, and in particular by its implications for the prime minister's timetable. The routine of prime minister's questions in the House of Commons on Tuesday and Thursday afternoons does not merely expose the prime minister to 15 minutes' scrutiny; it also requires substantial preparation for an event which almost all prime ministers view with apprehension (Wilson, 1976: 132). More generally, it means that Tuesdays and Thursdays are regular cabinet system days on which the prime minister is committed to cabinet system activity. In other parts of the central executive, parliamentary procedure has a marked impact on Wednesdays and Thursdays, as business for the coming week is finalised. When parliamentary cooperation has been agreed by the

Table 6.2 The weekly timetable* of the cabinet system during a normal parliamentary session.

Monday	Morning: Party political meeting at Number 10
	17.00: Meeting of government information officers
Tuesday	Morning: Cabinet committees (and possibly cabinet itself)
	Afternoon: Cabinet committees
	13.00–15.00: Briefing of prime minister for prime minister's questions
	15.15–15.30: Prime minister's questions in the House of Commons
	18.30: Prime ministerial audience with the Queen
Wednesday	Morning: Permanent secretaries' meeting (chaired by cabinet secretary)
	Morning: Government whips' meeting at 12 Downing Street
	Afternoon: Meeting of government chief whip and business managers at
	12 Downing Street; liaison with opposition whips
Thursday	Early morning: Cabinet committees
	10.30–12.30: Cabinet
	Afternoon: Cabinet committees
	13.00–15.00: Briefing of prime minister for prime minister's questions
	15.15–15.30: Prime minister's questions in the House of Commons
	15.30: Announcement of government business for the week ahead
	Afternoon: Meetings of back-bench parliamentary groups
	'Forward look' meeting in Cabinet Office

*Some timings are approximate.

two main front benches, negotiations take place through what are commonly known as the 'usual channels' (Griffith and Ryle, 1989: 298–300), and details of the coming week's business are considered first at a meeting of government whips drawn together by the chief whip each Wednesday morning, and then by government and opposition business managers each Wednesday afternoon. The programme is subsequently agreed by cabinet on Thursday morning and reported to Parliament on Thursday afternoon. The cycle is complete when on Thursday evening a junior whip reports arrangements to back-bench committee meetings, and the chief whip makes himself available thereafter to clarify points of contention.

Other regular aspects of the cabinet system's weekly timetable are the processing of business through cabinet and its committees, liaison meetings across Whitehall which bring together information officers on a Monday and permanent secretaries on a Wednesday, and a liaison meeting with the party both in Parliament and in the country on a Monday. This latter meeting is a Conservative innovation dating from the early Thatcher years (see Chapter 7). Its main point is to discuss general political strategy. Matters relating to the coming week in Parliament are often also on the agenda. The 'forward look' meeting, which takes place regularly on a Thursday afternoon in the Cabinet Office, is chaired by the cabinet secretary, and reviews progress of business through the cabinet system during the week ahead and beyond (see Chapter 5).

The prime minister's weekly Tuesday evening audience with the Queen, which lasts for about 45 minutes, takes precedence over all other domestic business. Only if either individual is out of the country does it not take place.

The daily timetable

Finally, a daily routine also structures the activities of the cabinet system. When Parliament is in session, one aspect of this is ministerial questions in the House of Commons. These are taken for 45 minutes each afternoon on Mondays to Thursdays. Major departments reach the top of the ministerial question rota about once every three to four weeks, and always on the same day of the week. Only on these days are questions about these departments likely to be reached on the order paper (Griffith and Ryle, 1989: 254). Other elements of the daily routine are regular briefings of the media on the part of the chief press secretary, and the red boxes which ministers pore over late at night. In session, the Major government's Number 12 committee met virtually every working day: at 9 a.m. on Mondays and Wednesdays and at 8.20 a.m. on Tuesdays and Thursdays. It was subsequently supplemented by EDCP (see Chapter 5). Further discussion of the prime ministerial day in the 1970s can be found in accounts by Wilson (1976: 83–8) and Donoughue (1988).

Change since 1974

Together, the three timetables described in this section comprise the framework within which all cabinet system activity takes place. Their importance is that they structure and inadvertently shape outcomes in that system. They also provide some indication of the time constraints within which cabinet system actors are forced to operate.

Change in cabinet system timetables since 1974 has been slight. The annual timetable has been affected by the switch to a November budget and by the rise of international summitry. However, as has already been noted the alteration to Britain's budget arrangements has so far had limited impact on the cabinet system, despite a slight increase in cabinet and cabinet committee involvement in spending decisions (see below). International summitry and European Union meetings have had more important consequences for operation of the system (Lee, 1995). They require the prime minister and other senior ministers, notably the chancellor of the exchequer and foreign secretary, to be out of the country on a regular basis, and increase the amount of routine preparation and briefing demanded of cabinet system actors. When Thatcher was prime minister her entourage often included the cabinet secretary, thereby extending the strain on cabinet system resources. This practice has been curtailed by the current cabinet secretary, Sir Robin Butler. The weekly timetable has been affected by the development of a political meeting at Number 10 on Monday mornings and by the emergence of the 'forward look' meeting in the Cabinet Office on Thursday afternoons, both of which have enhanced coordination within and outside the central executive. The daily timetable has been altered by the recent emergence of the Number 12 and EDCP committees, which have sought to improve cohesion in the Conservative Party and presentation of the government's case.

Processes developed to manage shortage of parliamentary time

Time constraints on the cabinet system are generated not simply by the routine timetables within which it operates, but also by limits on parliamentary time. It must, of course, be noted that not all executive initiative requires legislative enactment. Some foreign policy can be conducted by treaty or lesser form of international agreement. Much domestic policy can be developed under the rubric of existing legislation by means of statutory instruments, ministerial orders or yet more *ad hoc* arrangements. However, substantial policy change generally involves new legislation, and must compete for time in the government's legislative programme.

The parliamentary phase is only one in a series of phases in the legislative process. Hogwood (1987: 104) notes that the full cycle has three main phases: pre-parliamentary, when bills are prepared for presentation to Parliament; parliamentary, when they are debated by the two Houses; and administrative, when if duly enacted they are implemented. However, the central parliamentary phase imposes a constraint on the whole cycle, for it is here that time is most limited, and demands are most excessive. It operates as a bottleneck in the legislative process.

Parliamentary time is not only limited. It is also largely fixed. Each session usually consists of around 170 sitting days (Griffith and Ryle, 1989: 182–3). However, not all of this time is available to the executive. Instead, by convention time must be allowed for non-government business, such as debate of opposition motions and private members' bills. The exact time granted to each of these purposes varies marginally from session to session. However, since 1985, 20 days per session have been reserved for opposition debates, with three of these days being allocated to the second-largest opposition party (currently the Liberal Democrats) (Borthwick, 1988: 60). Private members' business also has to be accommodated.

The impact of these provisions is not insignificant. The 20 days per session reserved for opposition business amount to some 12 per cent of the entire session. Furthermore, from analysis of the 1984–5 and 1985–6 parliamentary sessions, Borthwick (1988: 57) calculates that some 7 per cent of time on the floor of the House of Commons is accounted for by discussion of private members' bills and motions. In total, around 20 per cent of time on the floor of the House of Commons is thus out of the executive's control. This places severe constraints on a government's ability to introduce new legislation, and makes the task of establishing priorities yet more difficult. Consequently, parliamentary time is one of the most scarce and contested resources in government. The activities involved in organising and allocating this scarce resource are located firmly within the cabinet system.

Organising the legislative timetable

Many factors shape the executive's organisation of the legislative timetable. These range from matters of routine to considerations of strategic and tactical advantage. They can be listed as follows:

- likely length of Parliament;
- routine matters;
- availability of legislation;
- manifesto commitments; and
- strategic and tactical consideration.

The first and most basic consideration for any government is the *likely length of the Parliament*. This depends chiefly on the size and reliability of its majority. Provided that this is a 'working majority', and likely to remain so for the foreseeable future, a government can turn its thoughts to tentative planning of the timetable of a full Parliament. Government majorities in the period 1945–92 are shown in Table 7.1.

Detailed planning, however, really spans a 22-month period leading up to and covering each annual session of Parliament (Rippon, 1992: 115). Within the schedule which they develop, government business managers have to find time for a series of *routine matters*. These are not to be confused with the parliamentary time allocated to opposition and private members' business, which is an entirely separate matter. Government time must be found for many matters which are strictly routine, and bear little or no relation to policy change. These include regular business items such as general debates, adjournment debates at the end of each day and before each parliamentary recess, and ministers' (including prime minister's) question time. In addition, there are items of regular and recurring legislation that need to be accommodated in government time, including the Appropriation and Enabling Acts and the Finance Bill. The latter alone usually requires about 15 days of House of Commons time (Miers and Page, 1990: 34). Moreover, as a legacy of parliamentary distrust of the crown in former times there are some 11 laws which must be re-enacted each year, and require government time. One example is the Consolidated Fund Acts, which must be put before the Commons before money to pay the costs of government can be authorised (Van Mechelen and Rose, 1986: 28). So great is the pressure exerted by these various claims that Borthwick (1988: 57) calculates that only around 28 per cent of total parliamentary time, or about 42 days on average per session (Miers and Page, 1990: 34), is available for new government legislation. If secondary legislation is also taken into account, the total rises to nearly 40 per cent.

The third factor which shapes executive organisation of the legislative timetable is *availability of legislation*. This is unlikely to be a problem for a government which has held office for some time previously. Indeed, for such a government the problem is likely to be the precise reverse, with far too much potential legislation already in the pipeline. However, for a government which gains office after a lengthy period in opposition it can be significant (Wilson, 1976: 129). It takes parliamentary counsel six months or more to draft legislation. Despite the established practice that prior to a general election civil servants prepare alternative programmes, detailed bills are not usually ready for immediate presentation to Parliament. It is thus often necessary to find initiatives which do not require legislation to fill the first months of a new Parliament. This problem was particularly acute for the incoming Thatcher government in 1979, and precipitated the decision to establish a new system of select committees, a proposal which needed to be discussed by the House but did not require legislation.

A fourth factor is *manifesto commitments*. Although only a small proportion of legislation comes from this source, it can nevertheless act as a determining factor in the shaping of legislation, notably in the early year or two of a Parliament. Rose (1984: 65) estimates that the Conservative government of 1970–4 enacted around 80 per cent of its manifesto commitments, and that the subsequent Labour governments of 1974–9 (which spent much of their period of office in a minority in the House of Commons) enacted 54 per cent of theirs. He nevertheless concludes that manifesto pledges form 'a very small part of the legislative activities of any government' (Rose, 1984: 72). Between 1970 and 1974, only 8 per cent of government bills could be traced to the manifesto. Between 1974 and 1979, the figure was slightly higher at 13 per cent. Although the figure may have increased further since 1979, it remains clear that most of any government's legislative initiative is attributable to other sources: the internal Whitehall policy process, the initiative of outside bodies, international treaty requirements, implementation of EU directives and force of circumstance (Rippon, 1992: 164).

A final factor is *strategic and tactical consideration*. Governments tend to be deeply influenced in their policy initiatives by the electoral cycle, and seek as much as possible to table difficult or unpopular legislation early in it (Lawson, 1993: 814). Such legislation therefore tends to be introduced during the first years of a Parliament. Highly controversial measures introduced in the session following the 1987 general election included bills to provide for reform of the rates and introduction of a community charge, creation of a national curriculum, abolition of the Inner London Education Authority, privatisation of water utilities, further contracting-out of local authority services and further restrictions on trade union closed shops at the workplace.

Nature of the legislative process

The process whereby a government's legislative programme is set is complex. It involves selecting priorities and organising the business programme over the short (week), medium (session) and long (Parliament) terms. A reasonably closed network of individuals centred on the cabinet system manages each of these tasks.

It was shown in Chapter 5 that planning and supervision of the government's legislative programme and management of parliamentary business are centred on two of the cabinet's standing ministerial committees: LG and FLG (sometimes referred to as Q or the queen's speech committee). Both committees are chaired by a senior cabinet minister involved in management of government business, usually the leader of the House of Commons. They are always serviced by the home and social affairs secretariat in the Cabinet Office. The group of people brought into this network was shown in Figure 5.6.

Provided that a government has both a clear and reliable majority, and a strong sense of purpose, *long-term* planning of the legislative programme begins as soon as it takes office. At the start of a Parliament, the government's business managers draw up a draft plan of manifesto items which are likely to require legislation and attempt to establish a rough order of priority for their introduction into Parliament. The key individuals here are the chief whip, leader of the House of Commons (who often liaises with the leader of the House of Lords), prime minister, and other cabinet ministers who are given legislative responsibilities essentially on an *ad hoc* basis. Even in the favourable circumstances of a very large government majority (such as were won by the Attlee government in 1945 and by the Thatcher governments in 1983 and 1987), long-term planning has to be tentative, for new demands on parliamentary time are bound to arise during any government's term in office. Nevertheless, most governments attempt to generate at least a loose framework within which both medium- and short-term planning can take place.

In the *medium term*, FLG is at the centre of operations. It considers and works on the government's proposed legislative programme in advance of each parliamentary session. From departments it receives demands for parliamentary time for proposed legislation on which ministers have already consulted their colleagues, or for which formal approval has been given by the appropriate cabinet committee. The task of FLG is to select from these demands the elements which will make up the queen's speech in November. In essence, its task is discriminatory. Since the 1960s FLG has worked on the basis of including around 30–35 bills in the speech. At least double that number of bids is regularly submitted (Miers and Page, 1990: 35). Headey (1974: 49) claims that as many as 300 bids for legislative time are sometimes made. Selection necessarily involves a good deal of negotiation and representation on the part of ministers. By the time of the queen's speech, government business managers have a detailed calendar of the legislative timetable for the coming session of Parliament. This calendar identifies both bills which the government will seek to pass through Parliament, and an outline of the likely timing of their passage. During the course of the session, the calendar may of course be disrupted, sometimes significantly.

There is now an established cycle whereby medium-term planning takes place. It begins soon after the parliamentary session has been opened by the Queen in November, in order to give ministers an opportunity to make early representations, and parliamentary counsel time to draft bills. Submissions to FLG are organised by the home and social affairs secretariat. In January, a letter is sent to ministers requesting their list of proposed bills placed in order of priority, and with some indication of the urgency and potential degree of controversy involved in each (Miers and Page, 1990: 35). At roughly the same time, a skeletal timetable for the coming parliamentary session is worked out, usually by the leader of the House of Commons and the chief whip. This covers the likely timing of routine and non-government business, and indicates the time left for new legislation (Bradshaw and Pring, 1973: 30–1). The aim is to gain some notion of the shape of the next session's programme by the beginning of the calendar year. Together, the skeletal timetable and bids for legislative time form the raw material for consideration by FLG, which makes legislative priorities and presents them to cabinet for formal approval, usually during the Easter recess (Rippon, 1992: 9). It is normally only at this point that parliamentary counsel are instructed to begin drafting bills (Rippon, 1992: 115). Thereafter, from May to September, FLG meets to finalise the draft queen's speech, which is presented to cabinet in October/November.

After the queen's speech has been presented to Parliament management of the legislative programme centres on LG committee, the home and social affairs secretariat and the offices of the leaders of both Houses. Their aim is to ensure that major bills reach second reading by Christmas, so as to avoid crowding later stages of the parliamentary session (Rippon, 1992: 165). They regulate the flow of instructions to the parliamentary counsel office, and review progress in the preparation of bills. If a bill relates to one of the government's major policy commitments its progress in draft may also be monitored by the relevant cabinet committee (Miers and Page, 1990: 40; Rush, 1984: 47). LG also approves alterations to the programme, such as inclusion of bills not contained in the queen's speech.

Short-term planning is conditioned by both long- and medium-term plans. These play an important part in generating a framework within which the legislative programme is organised on a week-to-week basis. In addition, standing commitments feed into the deliberations of government business managers. However, there can also be a strictly tactical element to short-term planning. Such planning is organised around the skeletal sessional timetable drawn up by the chief whip and leader of the House of Commons.

Short-term planning is handled chiefly by LG and members of the home and social affairs secretariat and staff from the office of the leaders of both Houses. Informal contacts between the leaders of both Houses, their respective chief whips and their opposition counterparts through the 'usual channels' are also important. In the short term, LG has a number of functions, although these tend to vary across administrations. Its most established task is to examine bills and important statutory instruments in detail before they are presented to Parliament, in order to ensure that they conform to the government's objectives, are adequately drafted, and are in keeping with the rules of parliamentary procedure. The committee also monitors the progress of a bill during its subsequent parliamentary stages. In fulfilling these tasks, LG gives consideration to a number of tactical matters, such as whether a bill should be introduced initially into the Lords or Commons, what concessions might be made if there is unanticipated back-bench pressure and what the government's attitude should be to private members' bills (Miers and Page, 1990: 37–8).

Really short-term planning tends to be handled not by LG, but by the whips' office and the offices of the leaders of both Houses. Within the framework established by the queen's speech and the timetable drawn up at the beginning of each session, the chief whip works out the business of each sitting on a weekly basis, often liaising with ministers. In this task he is assisted by his deputy and by his private secretary. Together, these three individuals constitute the government half of the 'usual channels'. Since the post was established by Lloyd George in 1919, there have only been three private secretaries: Sir Charles Harris until 1961, Sir Alfred (Freddie) Warren to 1978 and Murdo Maclean thereafter. The importance of the chief whip's private secretary was noted by Crossman (1976: 23): 'Freddie [Warren] and the Clerks at the Table between them run the Government's legislative programme for the day, the week and for the whole session'. Others have confirmed this assessment. On occasion, mechanisms of parliamentary co-operation between government and opposition front benches break down, thereby making short-term planning more difficult and precarious. One such occasion was initiated by the Labour Party in December 1993, and curtailed in April 1994.

The nature and disposition of the legislative process network are shown in Table 6.3. The disposition of advantage in the network lies with government business managers, who are however severely constrained by the shaping factors outlined in this section.

Table 6.3 Nature and disposition of the legislative process network.

Central organising participants:
> Leader of the House of Commons
> Leader of the House of Commons' private secretary
> Chief whip
> Chief whip's private secretary
> Members of the home and social affairs secretariat
> Leader of the House of Lords
> Chief whip, House of Lords

Those drawn into the process:
> Prime minister
> Prime minister's PPS
> Prime minister's private secretary (parliamentary business)
> Deputy chief whip
> Scottish secretary
> Welsh secretary
> Junior ministers from the Treasury, FCO and Home Office
> Lord chancellor
> Attorney general
> Solicitor general
> Lord advocate
> Parliamentary draftsmen
> Cabinet ministers collectively and individually when departments have legislation before LG

Those consulted by those organising and drawn in:
> Party back-benchers
> Party chairman (in the case of the Conservative Party)*
> Opposition business managers
> Speaker's office

Key shaping points in the legislative process:
> At the beginning of a Parliament
> At the beginning of each parliamentary session
> January (when the programme is being outlined in draft)
> Period leading up to spring cabinet
> May–July (when detailed drafting of the queen's speech takes place)

*The lists of ministerial standing committees published by the Major government since July 1994 indicate that the Conservative Party chairman, who is also minister without portfolio, is a full member of FLG and therefore a rather more significant actor than is shown by our listing here of Conservative Party chairman. The involvement of the Conservative Party chairman in the cabinet system varies greatly (see Chapter 7).

Change since 1974

The legislative process has changed little in the period since 1974. More precise and specific manifestos have evidently facilitated executive planning of business across a Parliament, though this trend was established before 1974 (Rallings, 1987: 4). In a rather uneven fashion, consultation with the parliamentary party has increased over the period (see Chapter 7). There have also been periodic attempts to amalgamate FLG and LG to form a single legislation committee. Both Callaghan (Wilson, 1976: 129), and Thatcher from 1981 to about 1984 (Miers and Page, 1990: 33–4), took this step. Finally, over the period legislation committee has become increasingly concerned with management of the parliamentary programme, and has spent less time vetting the form and substance of legislation (Miers and Page, 1990: 66). However, the main feature of the legislative process is its stability, with a slight trend towards a more systematic, broad-brush and organised approach.

Processes developed to manage shortage of money

Money is a basic resource of the state. Established procedures have been developed to manage its acquisition, through taxation, and its expenditure. Although both processes are centred on the Treasury, at significant points they engage the cabinet system and constitute two of the most important routine tasks performed by it. More importantly, they limit and shape opportunities for development of other policy initiatives, and thus form a key part of the constraining framework within which all cabinet system personnel are obliged to operate.

Traditionally, both tax and spending proposals were presented to Parliament at the same time in the annual budget statement. In line with the recommendations of the 1961 Plowden report on the planning of public spending, a separate public expenditure white paper has been published annually since 1963 (Thain and Wright, 1992: 3). For 30 years the two processes were thereby separated into distinct time sequences, with tax changes being announced in the March budget and, from 1977, expenditure changes in the autumn statement (Treasury, 1992: paras 5 and 6). From 1993, however, the two procedures have been drawn together, and are announced in the single 'unified' budget statement made to the House of Commons in November. However, while there is now considerable potential to integrate the two processes, they have initially remained largely separate (Treasury, 1992; Dilnot and Robson, 1993). Although there is some evidence that they are gradually becoming more fused, we have maintained this separation in our analysis, as the current level of integration is small. Our outline of the two cycles relates to the new framework adopted from 1993 onwards.

Raising money

For many decades, an annual budget has been the regular mechanism for raising money. Occasionally revenue changes, in the form of mini-budgets, may be introduced at other times in the annual cycle. Between 1974 and 1979 chancellor Healey introduced a series of budgets and mini-budgets. The two 1974 elections obliged him to read two budget statements to the House of Commons in that year, and the change of government in 1979 caused his 'care and maintenance' budget of 3 April to be followed by a full Howe budget on 12 June (Browning, 1986: 121). Healey also introduced mini-budgets to deal with economic crisis. In 1994, chancellor Clarke was obliged to make two successive budget statements when his projected value added tax (VAT) changes were defeated in the House. However, these instances are relatively unusual. For most of our period, the ritual of an annual budget has been strictly adhered to, only being disrupted at the end of it by the 1993 switch to a November budget. The annual budget is the regular point around which planning of revenue changes operates.

A number of factors shape the tax budget (Robinson and Sandford, 1983). The general economic situation is surveyed by the Treasury, and forms the basis for its forecast of economic prospects. Evidently, public revenues are likely to fall in recession and rise in periods of buoyancy and economic growth. However, it is not only economic considerations which shape a budget. Political factors are also important. Most governments take a distinctive line on taxation, seeking either to change its overall level or to alter its balance. An example is the attempt both to cut the overall tax burden and to effect a switch from direct to indirect taxation made by the Conservative governments which first took office in 1979 (Johnson, 1991: 141–3). The latter attempt has been a good deal more successful than the former.

A budget, then, is very much a political act. Like many such acts it is deeply affected by a series of other factors, many of which are economic. Perhaps chief among shaping factors is the pattern of past budgetary decisions. Rose and Karran (1987: 161) note that 'the inertia of established tax laws accounts for 97.9 per cent of revenue in the average year'. The tax budget, like the expenditure one, is characteristically incremental (Wildavsky, 1975). The room for manoeuvre and innovation in any one year is, therefore, generally held to be slight. However, significant changes are made from time to time, examples in our period being the virtual doubling of VAT in 1979, and the lowering of the top rate of income tax from 60 per cent to 40 per cent in 1988. Taken together, these and other tax changes implemented since 1979 have radically altered the structure of the tax system, and its distributive effects (Wilkinson, 1993).

The budget-making process

The process whereby a revenue budget is made can be divided into a series of phases. These are outlined in Table 6.4, which covers both the pre-1993 and post-1993 time sequences. Preparatory moves are made almost as soon as the previous budget has been presented by the chancellor, such that the budget

Table 6.4 The tax budget cycle.

December/January (April/May)*	Budget framework sketched by Treasury
January–March (May–July)	Broad revenue calculations made Tax options run through Treasury computer
April/May (September)	Detailed option papers produced by Treasury, IR and C&E officials
April–July (September–December)	Treasury receives representations from lobbyists Treasury hearings for 'accredited' lobbyists
June/July (October/November)	'Budget starters' listed and sorted
July (December)	Economic and tax strategy papers produced
July/September (January)	Chevening meeting of Treasury ministers and officials to determine main thrust of budget
October (February)	Broad shape of budget set Prime minister informed of budget strategy Chancellor presents paper to cabinet on state of the economy
October/November (February/March)	Presentational matters brought to top of agenda
November (March)	'Red Book' printed Saturday before budget Cabinet informed of budget contents at special Tuesday cabinet Budget announced to House of Commons by chancellor on Tuesday afternoon

*The first month cited refers to the post-1993 cycle. The month cited in brackets refers to the pre-1993 cycle.

cycle effectively occupies an entire year. As increasingly detailed plans are drawn up, negotiations are simultaneously conducted both with ministers and with a range of outside interests. In the final phase of budget preparation the Treasury team has traditionally gone into purdah, enabling the chancellor to unveil a largely secret package in his budget speech. However, in 1993, chancellor Clarke went into rather less purdah than had his predecessors. In this section our dates refer to a November budget, though Table 6.4 provides dates for both the old and new regimes.

Preparatory moves are made in the Treasury public finance division at the end of the calendar year. During the winter and early spring, broad revenue calculations are made, and tax options are run through the Treasury's economic model. At this stage, officials are said to list every possible tax change. The list is constantly updated in the period leading up to the budget (Hogwood, 1987: 152). Soon after Easter, Treasury, Inland Revenue (IR) and Customs and Excise (C&E) officials are able to produce detailed option papers. Officials from the Bank of England also play a part in developing both general strategy and some detailed proposals. Option papers list alternative measures that would meet the government's revenue requirements in line with its tax aims.

After Easter, lobbying by outside pressure groups begins in earnest. It continues throughout the summer. Lobbying is so intense that a schedule of representations is drawn up to enumerate the many proposals requiring decision (Rose and Karran, 1987: 155). Lipsey (1983) puts the number at 400 or more. Miller (1990: 86) claims that in 1986 2000 letters and briefs were received, and that in 1985 (an especially difficult year) the Treasury dealt with 12 000 representations. Lawson (1993: 317) is content to note that 'an enormous number' of representations are received by the Treasury, the most important of which are allowed an oral hearing. Notably privileged delegations tend to come from the TUC under a Labour government, and the CBI under a Conservative government (Young and Sloman, 1984: 73). Lawson asked his officials to construct a matrix showing which groups favoured which changes. Only those gaining substantial support would be subjected to examination.

From this mass of proposals, the main task for officials is to *clarify detailed options*. By early summer, officials have a series of 'budget starters'. These are option papers, papers covering technical questions, outside submissions and ideas put forward by Treasury ministers, cabinet colleagues and officials. In June/July, these 'starters' are sifted, analysed and divided into 'major' (expensive) and 'minor' (inexpensive) measures. Treasury officials and junior ministers usually conduct these tasks. In July, officials prepare two detailed papers. One is written by the government's chief economic adviser, and covers the state of the economy and the medium term financial strategy (MTFS). The other is produced by the tax policy division of the Treasury and examines tax strategy, outlining the various options available. It is at this point that the first drafts of the chancellor's budget speech begin to be produced by officials and advisers.

These two papers form the basis for the next stage in the process, *determining the strategy*. The key point in this stage is a weekend meeting in late July or early September usually held at Chevening (the foreign secretary's official residence). It is attended by the entire Treasury team of ministers, special advisers, the chief economic adviser, Treasury permanent secretaries, the head of the Treasury tax policy division and the chairmen of IR and C&E (Lawson, 1993: 318). The chancellor's PPS attends as note taker. On occasion, other Treasury and IR officials may attend. At this meeting, provisional decisions about total tax take are reached, as well as fairly firm decisions about the types of taxation to be used.

After the Chevening meeting, detailed official papers are produced. The Treasury's financial secretary chairs meetings dealing with Inland Revenue matters. Its minister of state (paymaster general) chairs those dealing with Customs and Excise. Key decisions emanating from these official committees are taken in weekly overview meetings chaired by the chancellor. Participants are for the most part those who attended the Chevening meeting: this group forms the core of the process from mid-summer onwards. However, other officials are called in for specific items. The final shape of the budget is usually determined some five to six weeks before budget day. It is usually around this time that the prime minister is informed of budget strategy.

Political consultation also takes place in the period after the Chevening meeting. Meetings are held with back-benchers in the governing party, at which the chancellor and other Treasury ministers listen to representations but avoid giving any inkling of their budget plans. In mid-October, the chancellor presents a paper to cabinet on the state of the economy. At this cabinet he does not say anything about the budget, but it is expected that ministers will make suggestions, and that the chancellor will note them.

In the final weeks of the budget cycle, attention turns to *presentational matters*. Budget day is always a Tuesday. The *Financial Statement and Budget Report* (or 'Red Book'), which accompanies the budget speech, is usually printed on the previous Saturday. The final version of the budget speech is placed before the prime minister for comments, and is then unveiled to

Table 6.5 Nature and disposition of the tax budget process network.

Central organising participants:
   Chancellor of the exchequer
   Treasury ministers (notably the financial secretary and the minister of state (paymaster general))
   Treasury permanent secretaries
   Chief economic adviser to the Treasury
   Head of Treasury tax divisions
   Other senior Treasury officials

Those drawn into the process:
   Chairs of IR and C&E
   Chief secretary to the Treasury (minister)
   Economic secretary to the Treasury (minister)
   Chancellor's PPS
   Other Treasury officials
   Treasury special advisers
   Prime minister
   Treasury press secretary (for information purposes)

Those consulted by those organising and drawn in:
   Cabinet
   Governing party back-benchers
   Departments (especially if affected)
   Outside pressure groups (who make representations)

Key shaping points in the tax budget cycle:
   December/January (start of the cycle)
   April/May (production of option papers)
   April–July (some lobbyists)
   June/July ('budget starters')
   July (economic and tax strategy papers)
   July/September (Chevening meeting)
   October (meeting with prime minister)

cabinet on the Tuesday morning, by which time it is far too late to make changes. The budget speech is read to the House of Commons on the Tuesday afternoon. The finance bill is then published, and debated both on the floor of the House of Commons and in standing committee (Hogwood, 1987: 152).

In this cycle the key period in which decisions are taken lasts for just a few months. It runs from the preparation of position papers at the start of the summer, through the Chevening meeting at the end of July, to final drafting of the budget speech in mid-October. After that point, few changes are made.

This network is very much Treasury-centred. It is both exclusive and secretive. It has limited prime ministerial engagement, though clearly there is scope for such involvement at crucial points in the central two-month decision period. It has very limited cabinet involvement: as Lawson (1993: 322) notes, the budget 'is not determined collectively'. As if to confirm cabinet's lack of input into budget making, budget details are never recorded in cabinet conclusions (Wilson, 1976: 59). Main participants in this network are serviced solely by the Treasury. The revenue budget contains a key set of policies, and sets the framework for a vast amount of government activity. Despite this, it hardly engages cabinet or even the cabinet system at all. The nature and disposition of the tax budget process network are shown in Table 6.5.

Change since 1974

Several major alterations have been made to the tax budget cycle in the period since 1974. An attempt to enhance consultation with ministers by means of a general cabinet discussion prior to the budget cabinet was instituted by the Callaghan government in 1977 (Barnett, 1982: 114). This practice was not initially maintained by the Thatcher government, but following the furore which surrounded the 1981 budget ministerial consultation procedures were restored. They have been partnered by wider modes of consultation among governing party back-benchers. Although consultation is now more extensive, it is hard to judge whether it is real or merely a new aspect of party management: much of it takes place after key decisions have been reached. The period has also witnessed an increase in coordination between Treasury ministers and officials. Institution of the Chevening meeting by Howe in 1982 was an important development in this regard. Towards the end of the period Lamont introduced a system of 'wise men' to advise the chancellor on overall government economic policy (including tax policy) and created the 'unified' November budget (Treasury, 1992). Clarke partially undermined the tradition of purdah. Overall, the budget-making process has become increasingly organised, slightly more open, and more sophisticated in terms of the statistical base on which it operates.

Spending money

Government expenditure has grown markedly during the course of the twentieth century (Hogwood, 1992: 38–44). Throughout the period covered by this study, public spending has consistently consumed more than 40 per cent of gross domestic product (GDP) (see Table 1.2). Even a series of governments committed to cutting spending and rolling back the state has had no more than a marginal impact on the continuing growth of public spending totals. The Thatcher governments only managed to cut public spending in real terms in 1987 and 1988. Moreover only in the mid 1980s did they manage to reduce the proportion of GDP which it consumed from 54 per cent in 1982 to 44 per cent in 1988. In the recession-bound early 1990s, even that figure rose again to about 50 per cent.

Like revenue budget decisions, public spending decisions are made on an annual basis. Two conditioning factors are particularly important in all spending rounds. The first is economic and political circumstance. The second is the historic pattern of spending decisions, which strongly influences the pattern of spending in any given round. Just as most of the tax take is secured by means of old taxes, so the vast bulk of the spending round is determined by old expenditure decisions. It is a conventional view that, in any given year, only about 2.5 per cent of total spending can be reallocated between programmes (Heclo and Wildavsky, 1981: 24–5). This very small percentage figure should not, however, mask significant changes that can be made between programmes over time, and within programmes in perhaps shorter periods of time. In the nine years from 1979 to 1988, for example, real increases of 64, 63 and 37 per cent were registered in the employment, home office and health spending programmes, respectively, while housing and trade and industry suffered reductions of 79 and 68 per cent (Burch and Wood, 1990: 118).

The public expenditure process

The form of the current public expenditure process can be traced to the 1961 Plowden reforms (see above). Prior to these, expenditure was organised on an annual basis, and announced as part of the budget statement. The new system inaugurated by Plowden was designed to ensure longer-term planning of public spending (Treasury, 1992). A five-year forward look was initially selected, though this was eventually reduced in practice to three years. On the basis of a medium term assessment (MTA), which forecast economic development, spending decisions were to be related to estimated available resources. Planning was to be done in real terms, by focusing on inputs as measured in volume rather than cash figures. This was a resource planning system, not one centred on expenditure control.

The momentum generated by the Plowden system, combined with rapid and increasing inflation, led to a breakdown in expenditure control in the early 1970s. Actual spending overshot planned levels by an average of 5 per cent in each of the early years of the decade, and reached a peak overshoot of 8 per cent in 1974–5 (Wright, 1980: 101). A series of reforms was duly enacted which effected a complete shift in the structure and disposition of the public expenditure system (Treasury, 1976).

First, from 1975 the annual expenditure review was tightened across the entire public sector, reflecting increased central intervention in the affairs of local government in particular (Pliatzky, 1984: 138; Rhodes, 1988: 74). Secondly, in 1976 cash limits were introduced for year one of the survey (though planning was still undertaken in volume terms for the remaining years). Thirdly, the MTA was abandoned in the mid-1970s, and in 1981 the MTFS was introduced. The MTFS subjected expenditure, money supply and public-sector borrowing to strict monetary targets in an attempt to impose a strait-jacket on the entire process of public expenditure planning through cash control of the main monetary aggregates. Shortly thereafter, a shift to cash planning was made (Treasury, 1981). From 1981–2, all annual reviews of expenditure were conducted in cash terms. Since March 1982, they have been published in this form. This latter reform was the turning point in development of the Treasury's public expenditure survey (PES), which is the central feature of the public expenditure process (Thain and Wright, 1992). It was supplemented by occasional institution of the 'star chamber', which first sat in October 1981 (Jenkins, 1985) and was subsequently convened in the 1983–7 annual spending rounds (Thain and Wright, 1994: 5). This was an *ad hoc* ministerial committee, chaired in its early years by William Whitelaw (deputy prime minister), which acted as a court of appeal at the very end of the spending round. Fourthly, in 1992 the 'new control total' (NCT) was introduced. The NCT imposes top–down limits of aggregate public spending for each of the three survey years. Allocations within the NCT are considered and decided by a new cabinet committee, EDX, chaired by the chancellor, which makes final recommendations to cabinet. EDX is a very different committee from the star chamber. It is a standing committee which does not act as a court of appeal, but attempts to determine allocations between departments (Thain and Wright, 1994: 55–6).

The 1992 reforms and the creation of EDX could be important innovations. They have diminished the importance of bilateral negotiations, and increased the role of a cabinet committee and cabinet in determining outcomes. They have also enhanced the Treasury's pivotal position in the expenditure process by making the chancellor, as chair of EDX, more central to it. In July 1995 EDX membership comprised the chancellor of the exchequer, deputy prime minister, home secretary, president of the Board of Trade, lord president of the council, chief secretary to the Treasury and lord privy seal. Three aspects of this membership are noteworthy. One is that

Table 6.6 The public expenditure cycle.

Phase 1: Setting targets
January/February
Treasury post-mortem on previous round. Treasury begins work on *Guidelines* for the next round. Target for overall spending (NCT) set in last year's round reviewed

March/April
Draft guidelines for the coming round agreed by departments and possibly approved by EDX committee or even cabinet

May/June
Departmental ministers bid to chief secretary for additional resources. Treasury and departmental officials clear the ground for bid negotiations between chief secretary and ministers

July
Cabinet confirms NCT figures for coming year as set out in the previous year's round and charges the chief secretary with reaching agreements within that total and clarifying points of difference in readiness for meetings of EDX

Phase 2: Settling bids
August/September
Ministerial bilateral discussions between chief secretary and individual ministers. Some matters are settled. Others are honed for consideration by EDX

September/October
EDX settles outstanding bids, and works out package of spending decisions within the overall NCT limit established in July

Late October/November
Cabinet meets to discuss EDX's proposals and to resolve any outstanding matters

Phase 3: Formal decision and presentation
November
Cabinet meets to endorse final proposals

Late November/December
Spending proposals announced by the chancellor to the House of Commons in unified budget statement

Source: Thain and Wright (1992), updated.

two of seven members of EDX are Treasury ministers, thereby giving the Treasury a dominance it did not possess in the star chamber. The second is that no big spending ministers sit on EDX. The third is that many individuals are members of EDX not because of the department they represent, but because they are themselves key members of the government. The list of people who sat on EDX in July 1995 was Clarke, Heseltine, Howard, Lang, Newton, Waldegrave and Cranborne.

The set annual procedure (Table 6.6) runs from the start of the calendar year to its finish, its highlight being the chancellor's statement on public spending, which is now delivered as part of the unified budget in November.

At this time, projections of public spending over the next three years are made. The process has three main phases: setting targets; settling bids; and formal decision and presentation.

The process of *setting targets* begins almost as soon as one expenditure round has been announced in the budget statement. At the start of the calendar year Treasury officials conduct a post-mortem on the previous year's spending round. Similar exercises are undertaken in spending departments. Treasury officials also begin work on *Guidelines* for the forthcoming PES, working within the limits set by the MTFS. In March/April, draft *Guidelines* are agreed by spending departments. These may be considered by EDX (as happened in 1994) before being approved by cabinet. Treasury and departmental officials revise and agree baseline expenditures for the next three years. In June, spending ministers submit bids for additional resources to the chief secretary. A period of 'shadow boxing' (Thain and Wright, 1990: 52) ensues, as Treasury and departmental officials prepare the ground for bid negotiations between the chief secretary and ministers. At the same time, officials in the Treasury's public expenditure division work with the chief secretary to prepare papers for a late June/early July cabinet meeting, at which confirmation of the Treasury target for the next three spending rounds is secured.

The process of *settling bids* then ensues, as the chief secretary and individual spending ministers bargain over departmental allocations within the agreed spending total. This process lasts from July to September. It used to begin with an aggregate overshoot, and the aim of Treasury officials was to reduce the overshoot by as much as possible. Most departments usually settled early, leaving only a few outstanding bids. However, creation of the NCT in 1992 imposed a fixed top–down aggregate on the entire spending round and eliminated the initial aggregate overshoot. It also made negotiations at this stage less final, and somewhat altered the role of the chief secretary, who is now more concerned to gather information for consideration by EDX. The result is that some of the process of settling differences is now the responsibility of that committee.

A process of tidying up is triggered in September, and lasts through October. Its aim is to secure agreed spending totals for those remaining departments which have not yet settled. In the past, before EDX had been created, it sometimes first involved the prime minister in laying down the law by memorandum. Some departments used to settle at this stage. Ministers from those which did not engaged in further, hectic bilaterals with the chief secretary, who could as a last resort call on the prime minister to back him up. At the end of this process, all departments had settled. Some may have managed to exceed their notional Treasury spending totals, thereby pushing the entire spending round over budget. It was during this stage that the star chamber was sometimes convened in the 1980s. In the 1990s, the process was substantially altered by the creation of EDX. A fixed aggregate for the spending

Table 6.7 Nature and disposition of the expenditure process network.

Central organising participants:
    Chancellor of the exchequer
    Chief secretary to the Treasury
    Second permanent secretary to the Treasury (public expenditure)
    Officials from Treasury expenditure divisions
    Departmental finance officers and divisions

Those drawn into the process:
    Prime minister
    Members of EDX (since 1992)
    Ministers collectively in cabinet
    Departmental ministers
    Departmental officials

Those consulted by those organising and drawn in:
    Executive agencies (by their sponsor departments)
    Public corporations (on an *ad hoc* basis)
    Local authorities and associations (on an *ad hoc* basis)
    Major interest groups (on occasion)

Key shaping points in the expenditure cycle:
    March (cabinet approval of draft *Guidelines*)
    June ('shadow boxing')
    July (cabinet)
    July/August (ministerial bilaterals)
    September/October (meetings of EDX and cabinet)

---

round now means that the final total is less likely to be pushed over target. EDX is expected to present a package of proposals within the overall limit of the NCT, and to settle any outstanding departmental allocations (Thain and Wright, 1994: 56). In late October, cabinet considers EDX's proposals and settles any outstanding matters. This may involve the informal intervention of the prime minister, as happened in 1993.

Formal decision and presentation take place in November. Cabinet formally agrees the package, and the chancellor then presents the annual public spending projections to the House of Commons as part of his budget statement. (Until 1993 a separate autumn statement was made.) In January of the following year departmental plans are published in separate volumes, incorporating any changes made since the chancellor's statement.

Only a small range of individuals and institutions is involved in the public expenditure process (Table 6.7). It is, moreover, very much an insider process. Central organising functions are undertaken by the Treasury's public expenditure divisions, which operate under the chief secretary. The chancellor has, since 1992, been more involved as chair of EDX. On the departmental side, principal finance officers and their divisions play key roles. These two ministers and a small number of officials constitute the prime movers in the annual drama, though there is much more ministerial involvement in the expenditure cycle than in the budgetary one. Many institutions – such as Parliament, local authorities, public corporations and pressure groups – are only drawn into the process indirectly through the intermediary of their sponsoring spending ministry. Parliament is only drawn in when central decisions have been taken. There are, then, clear structural biases in this process. They reinforce the exclusive nature of the British public expenditure process.

Change since 1974

Many of the changes that have affected this network since 1974 have already been discussed in detail. They include coordination of public spending across the whole range of government activity; moves from volume to cash limits and then to cash planning; introduction of the MTFS strait-jacket; introduction of the NCT and EDX committee. It is worth extracting from these a number of general points. One is that the position of the Treasury has been strengthened since 1974, in large part as a result of the move to cash controls. Despite this, public expenditure has continued to grow. The creation of EDX in 1992 is actually a recognition of failure in this regard. A second is that ministerial involvement has also increased during the period, first as bilateral negotiations have become a more critical feature of the annual expenditure round, and secondly as the 1992 reforms have through EDX brought senior ministers to the heart of the public expenditure process, and given cabinet a larger role at the end of it. A third is that there has been a decline in the role and participation of external interests. The most visible losers in this regard have been local authorities and their associations, which have found themselves brought within central procedures to which they make no more than minimal input.

It is important to note the unintended consequences of changes made to public expenditure processes. In the mid-1970s the use of volume figures, coupled with an over-optimistic MTA, contributed to spending overshoots. In 1976 cash figures were introduced to tighten control. Subsequently, the MTFS imposed severe monetary and borrowing constraints on the whole process. These changes altered the disposition of the process from one designed to plan expenditure growth to a financial control system more overtly designed to limit it. These innovations had their own unintended outcomes. Cash limits produced unplanned underspending on some programmes. Moreover, the practice of dealing with the residue of outstanding bids through bilateral bargaining contributed to a tendency to exceed the spending target approved by cabinet in July. It was for this reason that the 1992 reforms were introduced. They aim to prevent slippage by imposing an overall total earlier in the cycle. Although it is too early to judge the exact effect of these new procedures, they are certain to generate their own logic and unintended consequences.

Conclusion

Shortages of time and money are major sources of conflict in the cabinet system: at interview many ministers made this point. Decisions about the allocation of legislative time and of spending between departments are frequent sources of dissension. These shortages also severely constrain the opportunities available to cabinet system actors. Furthermore, mechanisms developed to manage them often shape outcomes, sometimes in unintended or unforeseen ways. They are an important and often neglected part of the framework which shapes actors' opportunities and behaviour.

Timetables impose a general constraint on all cabinet system activity. The prime minister's personal timetable is one of the determining factors of the cabinet system timetable, but it is difficult to argue that he or she is notably advantaged by this. Rather, cabinet system timetables are set chiefly by the core needs of the central executive, and have their own internal logic. These timetables are policed, but in no clear sense set, by cabinet system officials. They structure the activities of parts of the government machine which lie well outside the cabinet system itself. Indeed, whenever departmental business moves within cabinet system range it is likely to be required to conform to cabinet system timetables.

The processes which have been developed to manage time and money constraints have a number of common features. Although each involves the taking of big decisions which have an impact on all cabinet system activity, each is managed by a small core network of organising participants. Within the framework of established procedures these individuals have the greatest potential to set the terms of debate and to shape options. Other actors are not as central to the process, but tend to be drawn into it. They have the potential to intervene, and to alter the line of policy development set by those at the very core. The prime minister has this status in all three networks. Cabinet ministers have it collectively in the legislation and expenditure networks. Their involvement in the expenditure process has only recently been enhanced. The key shaping points in each process are both few in number, and constrained by time pressures. Core organising actors are most advantaged at many of these points.

Each network is highly self-contained. Even the revenue budget and public expenditure networks did not cohere or even overlap very much until recently. In terms of opportunity in these areas, the Treasury remains unusually advantaged for a government department, having substantial control over development of both the revenue budget and the public expenditure processes. Even creation of EDX has not yet significantly changed this. The result is that of these three process networks, only the legislative one centres fully on the cabinet system. A further point to be made about all three processes is that they are often strongly inertial. In large part, policy in each tends to be determined by underlying factors, such as the nature of the parliamentary timetable and financial decisions taken in earlier years. The scope of action for decision takers is correspondingly reduced. Nevertheless, Howe, Lawson and Lamont all changed tax structures significantly; public expenditure has frequently been substantially altered in the run-up to general elections; and over a long period of Conservative government important cumulative shifts in government priorities have been made.

Change in our period has been variable. The increasingly regular demands of international (including EU) relations have complicated the overall timetable within which the cabinet system works. The legislative process has only changed slightly. The process for raising finance has become more regularised, and involves marginally more consultation, though both the network and the process still remain firmly located within the Treasury. The public spending process has changed most substantially. Serial attempts to improve public expenditure controls have provoked shifts in the disposition of both the network and the process, culminating in the 1992 reforms and creation of EDX. This has increased opportunities available to cabinet system actors. Despite this, the general theme is gradual consolidation. Attempts to develop greater coherence and coordination in the allocation of time and money have extended the power potential of cabinet system actors, but only marginally.

7

□

Parties and individuals

To this point, abiding features of the cabinet system have been our central interest. Even the links and networks investigated in earlier chapters are relatively fixed and stable aspects of the central executive. Although change does occur, each is substantially institutionalised. Together, these features provide a reasonably secure framework within which individuals act.

To develop a more complete analysis of the cabinet system it is also necessary to investigate less constant factors. Many such factors, with variability ranging from low to high, impinge on central executive operations. In this chapter, we investigate only two: party and the individual. Party is a factor of middle-range variability. Its impact on cabinet system operations varies according to the nature of the governing party, and the reliability of its party political support in the House of Commons. For all of the period since 1974 (and for most of the period since creation of the modern cabinet system in 1916) only two parties, Conservative and Labour, have been in a position to form a government and fill ministerial posts within the central executive. We make a number of points about the differential impact on the cabinet system of these two parties. Our second factor, the individual, is subject to far more extensive variability, as many individuals have worked in the cabinet system during our period 1974–95. More importantly, this factor is impossible to model because the precise impact of the individual on cabinet system operations depends at least in part on personal qualities about which universal statements cannot be made. We limit our remarks in this chapter to exploration of some of the general ways in which individuals affect cabinet system operations, and to identification of some of the factors which shape and facilitate individual initiative in the system. In Part 2 we seek, through case studies, to assess the impact of particular individuals (and, indeed, other contingent factors) on cabinet system operations.

In line with the approach adopted in earlier chapters, we consider the impact of parties on the distribution of power potential within the cabinet system. We also seek to determine the pattern of change in party impact on the central executive since 1974. We do not seek to do either of these things with reference to the individual, as in this regard general statements cannot be made.

Party

The impact of party on operation of the cabinet system can be explored at three main levels. The first is party character. This is a long-term factor, which tends to remain reasonably fixed over time. Two main aspects of the distinct characters of the Conservative and Labour Parties impinge directly on cabinet system operations. One is their differing structures. The other is their differing philosophies about how the cabinet system should operate and how leadership should be exercised in government. The second main level of exploration is ways in which parties formulate a programme for government, normally a manifesto, which later serves as part of the policy framework within which the cabinet system operates. This is a medium-term factor, which can only be substantially changed over a reasonably long period. The third level is the nature of a governing party's support base at a given moment in time. This factor operates largely independently of party character, and is short term in nature. It is determined by such matters as size of majority and unity of parliamentary party. We explore all three of these main dimensions, and subsidiary aspects of them, in relation to the Conservative and Labour Parties. The fact that Labour was only in power for five years at the start of our period, and that the Conservatives have been in power for the subsequent 16 years, imposes some limitations on our analysis.

Party character

The characters of the Conservative and Labour Parties are different. In the Conservative Party, more power is concentrated in the leader and focused on the parliamentary party than is the case in the Labour Party, where power is comparatively dispersed among members of the leadership group and a significant role is given to the extra-parliamentary party. These different characteristics have an impact on cabinet system operations. They are the product of the distinct histories of the parties and can be explored by focusing initially on their origins and traditions.

The Conservative Party was the first of the two major parties to emerge as a structured national political unit. It was already in existence as a parliamentary party prior to expansion of the franchise in the mid-nineteenth century and, indeed, prior to development of modern notions of party democracy. The key external event in persuading the Conservative parliamentary leadership to create a mass party organisation was the Reform Act 1867, which extended voting rights to working-class men in boroughs. The leadership reacted by creating a Central Office and a National Union of Conservative and Constitutional Associations (Coleman, 1988: 144–5). By 1872 these were established as the main Conservative organisations in the country (Blake, 1985: 145–6). Their function was to organise the Conservative vote, not to represent mass Conservative opinion in Parliament. Power over appointments, policy and strategy was retained by the parliamentary party and its leadership, to whom the mass party was seen as an appendage or 'handmaiden' (McKenzie, 1963: 146). This formal concentration of power in the parliamentary leadership has remained characteristic of the party ever since, the mass party holding a secondary and subsidiary position focused on political education and getting the Conservative vote out at elections (McKenzie, 1963: 185).

By contrast, the Labour Party was created outside Parliament in 1899 as the Labour Representation Committee, and was initially concerned to represent the interests of trade unions (Beer, 1965). The parliamentary party emerged from this body in the early 1900s, and in alliance with various socialist societies and trade unions formed the modern Labour Party. The nature of the alliance ensured that power was distributed beyond the confines of the Parliamentary Labour Party (PLP), and that the mass party and its trade union support base were allowed an explicit role in policy making. The party constitution adopted in 1918 gave formal recognition to this power distribution (Beer, 1965: 126), by allocating significant positions to the party conference and its national executive committee (NEC). The three main elements of the party – PLP, constituency parties and affiliated organisations, and trade unions – were all drawn into these core structures. At the centre of elite–mass Labour Party relations is the NEC, which comprises representatives of all main elements within the party. The leader and deputy leader are ex-officio members. The result is that in a formal sense power in the Labour Party is deconcentrated in ways that have no parallel in the Conservative Party.

These differences in origin, and the distinctive party structures to which they have given rise, have clear consequences for the operation of ministerial personnel in the cabinet system. In the Conservative Party, formal concentration of power in the leader, while not preventing a wider distribution in practice (Norton and Aughey, 1981; Pinto-Duschinsky, 1972), is formidable. Current arrangements are that the leader is responsible for general strategy, policy development and appointment both of top officials in Conservative Central Office and the front-bench team in government and opposition. Powers of patronage and command placed in the hands of a Conservative prime minister are therefore substantial, although in practice they need to be exercised sensitively to balance opinion groupings and interests within the party (Alderman and Cross, 1985; Burch, 1995: 108). In Conservative governments, the key personnel with responsibility for managing and liaising with both the parliamentary and the mass party (notably the chief whip and the party chairman) are appointed by the prime minister as party leader. They are drawn into the cabinet system directly. The party chairman usually holds a ministerial post and is often a cabinet member. Party chairmen who are not cabinet ministers tend to participate in cabinet and cabinet committee meetings as the need arises. The chief whip attends cabinet and cabinet committee meetings (see Chapter 2). These party functionaries keep in close contact with the prime minister. The result is that sub-sections of the Conservative Party are brought directly into the cabinet system, and relate chiefly to the prime minister as party leader. Consequently, the position of prime minister in Conservative governments is relatively strong.

The power of a Labour prime minister is more constrained, and party lines of command are less centred on his person. Unlike his Conservative counterpart, the Labour leader does not appoint the party's general secretary nor, as a consequence, does he have any direct control over the party organisation. Its leadership is not drawn directly into the cabinet system. In addition, within the parliamentary party the chief whip is elected by Labour MPs, and not appointed by the party leader. The formal distribution of power in the party also means that a Labour prime minister is likely to find himself confronted by colleagues who have independent support bases within it. In Wilson's 1974–6 cabinet, for example, eight ministers were also members of the NEC, as were five in Callaghan's cabinets of 1976–9. Thus, although party concerns are brought into the cabinet system, they are not under the direct control of the prime minister but instead link formally into elements of the mass party. Furthermore, some bodies within the party have a degree of formal status which constrains the activities of the ministerial team in general. From time to time, Labour's link with the trade unions has prompted formal relations to be established between a Labour cabinet and the trade union movement. Ministerial membership of the NEC also has a constraining effect on cabinet system operations. In sum, power is much less concentrated in a Labour cabinet than in a Conservative one. More ministers relate to power bases outside the scope of prime ministerial influence, and key elements of the mass party outside Parliament are more closely drawn into the cabinet system.

These variations in party power structure reflect distinct philosophies about how the cabinet system should operate. These philosophies in turn find expression in the attitude of ministers towards leadership and collective action within the cabinet system. When interviewed, Conservative ministers tended to accept more readily the status and authority of the prime minister, and were likely to see themselves as serving his or her wishes and objectives. This partly reflects the philosophy of organisation associated with the Conservative Party, which places enormous emphasis on the power and responsibility of the leader (often spelt with a capital 'L'). The party looks to that individual for leadership, and has a tendency to judge its own success in terms of the performance of the leader. Such an organisational philosophy inevitably enhances his or her profile. Provided that the leader is held to be doing a good job (an important proviso), he or she is able to exercise substantial power in the party.

If things go wrong, the leader naturally attracts the bulk of the blame. By contrast, Labour ministers tended to lay greater stress on limits on the leader, to emphasise the collective role of the leadership group, and to be aware of the need for it to be sensitive to wider party interests. The principle of prime ministerial leadership was less readily accepted, and collective discussion, based on some notion of 'collegiality' (Ingle, 1987: 118), was seen as an essential feature of the way in which the cabinet system ought to operate.

Similar differences emerged when use of cabinet committees was discussed. Conservative ministers tended to seek efficiency in cabinet procedures. Labour ministers placed a premium on responsiveness and accountability. Conservative ministers were more likely to view the cabinet committee system as not only necessary, but also beneficial. By contrast, Labour ministers considered extensive use of cabinet committees to be largely unavoidable, but nevertheless believed it to be a worrying development.

Since 1974 the main alteration in cabinet–party relations has been an increase in coordination of party activities from within the cabinet system. This development has been particularly evident at the parliamentary level, notably within the Conservative Party. In addition to the Monday morning meeting between the prime minister, government business managers and party chairman described in Chapter 5, other regularised ways of bringing party concerns into the heart of the cabinet system have been developed. Such changes have taken place progressively under the leaderships of Heath, Thatcher and Major. Major's Number 12 and EDCP committees are the most thorough attempts to manage the parliamentary party (see Chapter 5). These changes reflect the important shift in the leader's power base which resulted from granting the parliamentary party the power in 1965 to elect, and in 1975 to dismiss, the leader (Burch, 1983: 408). Each of the last three Conservative prime ministers has been concerned to facilitate lines of communication between both themselves and the parliamentary party and ministers and the parliamentary party. Under Thatcher, ministers increasingly fed proposed legislation or bills recently introduced to the House of Commons through the relevant party committee in an attempt to gauge probable back-bench reaction. Some ministers, such as Whitelaw when home secretary and Hurd when foreign secretary, developed the practice of meeting their relevant back-bench committee officers and other interested Conservative MPs on a regular, almost weekly, basis. This practice of back-bench consultation has continued under Major's premiership, and was extended following the so-called 'September crisis' of 1992 when, having withdrawn sterling from the exchange rate mechanism (ERM), the government was faced with a number of divisive issues such as ratification of the Maastricht treaty and the pit closures programme (see Chapter 8). More frequent meetings between the prime minister and the executive of the 1922 committee also now take place.

Similar developments were witnessed under Labour in the 1970s. When the party was in government from 1974 to 1976 some ministers chose to keep in close contact with the relevant party back-bench committee, but this did not become standard practice until the Lib–Lab pact was formed in 1977. As this introduced new mechanisms for consulting Liberal MPs on matters coming before the House (Marsh, 1990), Labour party managers made it standard practice for ministers to consult Labour Party subject groups about pending legislation (Kaufman, 1980: 106). Links outside the PLP were also strengthened by means of the Labour Party–TUC liaison committee, established before and during the Wilson and Callaghan governments of the 1970s. This brought a number of ministers into direct and formal contact with the trade unions by means of three types of linkage. Joint meetings of cabinet and the NEC were held. More regularly, meetings of a liaison committee consisting of cabinet ministers nominated by the prime minister and executive members nominated by the NEC took place. More informally, a 'high-level liaison committee' consisting of leading ministers and NEC members met at 9.30 a.m. every Tuesday morning, government commitments permitting (Wilson, 1976: 164–5). Since Labour last formed a government, a number of constitutional reforms have been enacted within the party. In 1980, for example, PLP standing orders were changed to state that the first cabinet formed by an incoming Labour prime minister must include the 18 elected members of the shadow cabinet (Griffith and Ryle, 1989: 21). This provision was clearly intended to give the PLP greater control over a Labour executive. However, the precise impact that this and other reforms will have on cabinet system operations cannot be assessed until Labour is returned to power.

Regularisation of cabinet system contact with the mass party has also taken place, though to a lesser extent. The main changes at this level also relate to the Conservative Party for, as was noted above, elite–mass contact in the Labour Party has always been significant and regularised. On the Conservative side a number of changes have been made. Heath was the first party leader to attend the annual conference of the National Union in full (Burch, 1980: 170). Under Thatcher, it became standard practice for relevant ministers to attend not only the annual conference but also the central council and subconferences of the National Union. Kelly (1989) argues that attendance at this series of party meetings has made Conservative ministers more aware of, and hence more prone to influence by, the opinions of party activists.

Party programmes

A further source of party impact on cabinet system operations derives from party programmes, which set the broad framework of policy within which cabinet system actors are obliged to operate. Often these programmes take the form of an election manifesto. In both the Conservative and Labour Parties the leadership is highly influential in developing the party programme and in writing the manifesto. Equally, each elite must take account of party opinion. Furthermore, in both parties that opinion is likely to be more influential when the party is in opposition. However, development of policy is again more formalised in the Labour than in the Conservative Party, and requires the involvement of various sections of the party.

Clause V of the Labour Party constitution gives formal policy-making roles not simply to the party leadership, but also to the annual conference and NEC. The party 'programme' consists of those party conference decisions passed by majorities of more than two-thirds. It is on these that the parliamentary committee of the PLP and the NEC, meeting jointly, are supposed to draw when compiling the election manifesto. However, the leadership is not wholly constrained by Clause V. Not only does it decide which items from the 'programme' shall be included in the manifesto, it is also able to define policy on issues which are not covered by conference resolutions (Wilson, 1976: 158). The result is that the party leadership shapes the content of the manifesto substantially, within reasonably broad parameters set by the NEC and annual conference.

No equivalent mechanisms constrain the Conservative Party leadership. In theory, the drafting of the manifesto is solely the responsibility of the party leader. In practice, he or she involves in the process other members of the leadership team, aides, advisers and perhaps individuals thought to represent key strands of party opinion. There is, however, no set format whereby this is done, and the leader has substantial discretion in approaching the task. When what became the 1983, 1987 and 1992 manifestos were drafted, control was firmly embedded in the cabinet system under the auspices of the prime minister and a committee of senior ministerial colleagues and party aides, though party opinion was consulted informally. Each of these manifestos was coordinated and often drafted by the PMPU (Kavanagh, 1981; Butler and Kavanagh, 1992: 92–3).

Since 1974 changing modes of producing a manifesto have been most evident on the Conservative side. Under Heath, the Conservatives began to produce more detailed manifestos, thereby conforming to established Labour practice. Under Thatcher, the Conservatives altered the status of the manifesto by adopting the argument that once elected to office a party is mandated to implement its programme. This view is traditionally found on the left in politics. In the Thatcher period, it was used to justify the pursuit of certain policy goals, and to limit argument about the content of policy by focusing attention on its implementation. Most recently, under John Smith and Tony Blair as leaders, Labour has adopted new procedures which have given more responsibility for policy initiative to the members of the leadership team, plus six subject area policy commissions, the NEC and a 100-strong policy forum, before proposals are put before the annual conference for approval. As these practices have been developed while the party has been in opposition, it remains to be seen what impact they might have upon the party's programme in government.

Reliability of the support base

Reliability of a governing party's support base in the House of Commons has an independent impact on cabinet system operations. Two factors are particularly important in this regard: size and discipline of governing majority. Each conditions operation of the cabinet system. Although there are differences in the way in which Conservative and Labour governments manage their support base, similarities are more striking.

Size of majority is an obvious source of either opportunity for or constraint on party leadership. For Callaghan, the absence of a reliable majority during his period as prime minister was the most demanding of all requirements upon his time and that of his cabinet colleagues. By the same token, the large majorities enjoyed by the Thatcher governments gave them a great deal of freedom to pursue policies even against the opposition of significant groups of party back-benchers. The full extent of this freedom was revealed most clearly after the Major government was returned in April 1992 with a majority of only 21, and struggled to get elements of its programme through the Commons. In November 1994, the government's majority was technically wiped out by withdrawal of the party whip from Conservative rebels, thereby increasing the government's difficulties in getting its programme through the House. The whip was restored to the rebels in April 1995. Government majorities for the period 1945–92 are given in Table 7.1.

A second factor which affects reliability of the government's support base is the discipline of its parliamentary majority. Norton (1975, 1980, 1985) shows that since 1970 in particular party cohesion in the voting lobbies has declined.

Table 7.1 Government majority on election, 1945–92.

Election	Prime minister	Majority*
1945	Attlee (L)	146
1950	Attlee (L)	5
1951	Churchill (C)	17
1955	Eden (C)	58
1959	Macmillan (C)	100
1964	Wilson (L)	4
1966	Wilson (L)	96
1970	Heath (C)	30
1974F	Wilson (L)	−33
1974O	Wilson (L)	3
1979	Thatcher (C)	43
1983	Thatcher (C)	144
1987	Thatcher (C)	102
1992	Major (C)	21

Source: Butler and Butler (1994: 216–19).

*Over all other parties.

Against him, Rose (1983) argues that the decline in terms of sheer voting records is actually not significant. However, this is to miss the point that a great deal more pre-emptive action now has to be taken by the executive to manage its parliamentary support base. Decline in parliamentary party cohesion, which is common to the Conservative and Labour Parties, appears to reflect change in the social composition of the House of Commons, examples being the rise of the professional politician (King, 1981) and the decline in numbers of MPs drawn from traditional Conservative and Labour backgrounds (Burch and Moran, 1985; Baker, Gamble and Ludlam, 1992).

Whereas size of majority reveals no secular trend in our period 1974–95, discipline of majority has altered markedly. Majorities which prior to 1970 could be taken for granted are now much more uncertain. One result has been the increased attention now paid to back-bench concerns discussed above.

The individual

The impact of the individual on the operations of the central executive is both highly variable and extremely difficult to model. Here we limit our analysis to consideration of the role played by individuals in setting the tone of an administration, and to evaluation of the conditions which help to shape and facilitate individual action. This allows us at the end of the chapter to consider in a general sense the scope for individual initiative in the cabinet system. This dimension is explored at length and in detail by means of case-study analysis in Part 2.

Tone of administration

One important contribution of individuals to cabinet system operations is in setting the general tone of an administration. This tone helps to condition the functioning of parts of the central executive (and of other parts of the government machine) for the lifetime of that administration. Its impact should not be exaggerated. On the one hand, the 'mood of the times' can also condition the functioning of an administration. The mood of post-war reconstruction influenced the workings of the Attlee administration. The planning vogue played a similar role in the 1960s. On the other, and far more importantly, the cabinet system comprises a set of mature institutions with deeply-rooted ways of doing things which are seldom significantly disrupted by any one administration. Nevertheless, each administration does have a discernible tone which contributes to its mode of operating.

That tone is generated by predominant individuals, and is therefore a function of leadership (Hermann, 1986: 174–5). Within the British cabinet system, there is no formal presumption about who should provide policy leadership in government (King, 1991: 33–4). There are, however, established expectations about who should give direction to the central executive. In conventional terms the task of leadership lies in the hands of party politicians: the prime minister, and members of his or her cabinet. It is their responsibility to provide overall direction either individually or collectively (McEldowney, 1994: 74). This does not mean that all policy initiatives come from ministers. The scale of business is too large, and the size of the ministerial element in government too small, for this to be so. Nor does it imply that ministerial involvement determines policy development. Policy making, because it is cumulative and seldom determined at any one point, is certain to reflect the contributions of many actors, including civil servants and others alongside ministers. It also reflects external pressures and forces. However, the initiative in providing general direction to policy is widely expected to lie in the ministerial domain.

At least four clear departures from this expectation of ministerial lead may be identified. First, there are some areas of policy making from which ministers are likely to be excluded because they lack expertise. These especially concern technical questions about which ministers lack the knowledge necessary to make a useful contribution. Secondly, there are some matters on which ministerial involvement is likely to be discouraged, notably those which directly affect the interests of other state personnel, such as officials. In the past, civil servants' pay and conditions have come into this category (Donoughue, 1987: 181–2). A third exception is when ministers fail to exercise leadership and direction. In the absence of a clear ministerial lead, decisions still have to be reached and business conducted. In such situations, other factors shape policy development and the opportunity, indeed the necessity, for civil servants to play a more significant role is enhanced. Finally, there are situations in which business is given no persistent strategic direction by any particular set of personnel. In these circumstances, it is very often the case that the existing momentum of administration takes over as accepted ways of doing things are pursued. This, however, does not mean that business makes entirely its 'own' way through the cabinet system. Rather, it means that multiple minor interventions, by ministers and civil servants, set its passage.

Despite the fact that these exceptions apply not only to a great deal of routine business, but also to some which is very important, the established expectation is that leadership in the cabinet system is exercised by ministers. Thus a key task in evaluating the tone of an administration is to isolate patterns of leadership. We seek in a fairly rough-and-ready way to capture the tone of post-war administrations by modelling two main aspects of leadership: prime ministerial style and mode of cabinet system relations among top personnel. These two elements are closely interlinked, but they can be separated for purposes of analysis and exposition. In modelling both elements of leadership, and in thereby capturing the tone of post-war administrations, we acknowledge that our categorisations are subjective and thus open to challenge. Our judgements may be compared with those reached by others (Andeweg,

Table 7.2 Prime ministerial style, 1945–95.

	Objective setting	Intervention
Thatcher	H	H
Wilson I	M	H
Heath	H	M
Macmillan	M	M
Callaghan	M	M
Attlee	L	M
Churchill	L	M
Eden	L	M
Wilson II	M	L
Major	L	M
Douglas-Home	L	L

Wilson I = 1964–70; Wilson II = 1974–6. H = high (across all departments); M = medium (across some departments); L = low (across few or no departments).

1993; James, 1994: 623–6). We investigate all 11 post-war administrations because they give us a more substantial sample than the four administrations which fall within our period. Wilson's two administrations (1964–70 and 1974–6) are treated separately because they are distinct.

We take prime ministerial style as the first dimension of the predominant tone of an administration because the prime minister is potentially the most significant determinant of it, and is certainly more important in this regard than are equivalent figures in other west European cabinets (Müller, Philipp and Gerlich, 1993: 240). In attempting to model prime ministerial style, we exploit James Barber's (1992) analysis of American presidential leadership styles, which are labelled active or passive according to the amount of effort an incumbent is held to put into the job. In applying this distinction to British prime ministers we use two criteria: (i) extent of intervention in the work of departments, and (ii) role played in setting policy objectives. In each case, we are dealing in matters of degree. No prime minister can be entirely dominant on either dimension. None in the modern period has been entirely passive in either regard. Nevertheless, there are distinct differences in prime ministerial style. Five main categories of prime ministerial style emerge from our analysis. In the 1945–95 period, Thatcher emerges as the most active prime minister, and Douglas-Home as the most passive (Table 7.2).

The second dimension of tone derives from the mode of cabinet system relations adopted by an administration. This may be set more by the prime minister than by any other single individual, but it will never be wholly determined by any one person (Hermann, 1986). Instead, the predominant mode is likely to be influenced both by a number of key individuals and by a range of other factors, such as institutional structures and traditions, and

144

external circumstance. Cabinet system relations within the Thatcher and Major governments could have been very different had their majorities and wider circumstances been switched. The main modes which we isolate are (i) singular, (ii) oligarchic, and (iii) collective. Opportunities for individual initiative differ under each.

Singular leadership is self-explanatory. Although the prime minister is most likely to set the overall tone of an administration, in particular policy spheres it is possible for other cabinet ministers, or even on occasion prominent officials, to play the lead role. Such a style of leadership emphasises the attributes of the individual leader, with decisiveness, determination, robustness and stamina at a premium.

Oligarchic leadership is that provided by a small and relatively stable elite group. Usually this group comprises senior ministers and the prime minister, who may or may not be dominant. Within the group, the role of officials and other advisers can be substantial, depending in large part on prime ministerial taste. Although the exact constellation of individuals involved is likely to alter from issue to issue, on key matters a solid core will usually be consulted. Within an oligarchy, relations tend to be informal and secretive. The aspects of individual character that are emphasised are discretion, trustworthiness and a willingness to share power and to compromise within the group.

Collective leadership is the traditional view of how the cabinet system ought to – and on some accounts does – work. In conventional accounts the relevant collectivity is the cabinet, and the implication of the collective approach is that its members are fully informed about issues before them, and fully consulted and involved in determining policy. This is an ideal model which bears little relation to contemporary governing practice. Indeed, in view of the burden and specialised nature of business flowing through the modern cabinet system, there are bound to be limits on information, consultation and involvement. These make it impossible to attain the collective ideal. However, some governments may try harder than others to maintain a collective approach. Officials do not feature as members of the collectivity in traditional accounts. It is, however, clearly possible by moving outside the formal structure of cabinet and its ministerial committees to construct an analysis of collective government which embraces both ministers and high-ranking officials. The individual characteristics highlighted are those that are conducive to compromise and consensus. They include persuasiveness and the ability to master information and articulate arguments in a convincing manner.

Applying these three categories to all 11 post-war administrations (Wilson again counts twice), we find that two (Eden, Thatcher) are predominantly singular, two (Callaghan, Major) are predominantly oligarchic, and the rest range between oligarchic and collective. It is easiest to capture this dimension of cabinet system relations in a figure which also has prime ministerial style as one of its axes (Figure 7.1). It provides us with a crude summary of the tones of all 11 post-war administrations.

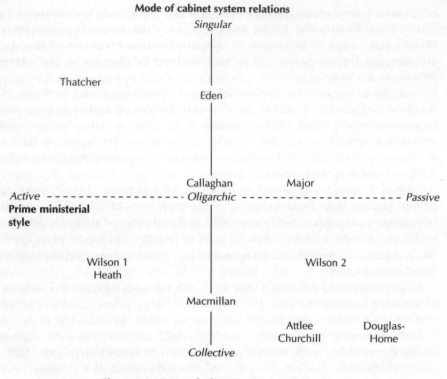

Figure 7.1 Tones of administrations, 1945–95.

In Figure 7.1 the classic form of collective cabinet government is in the bottom right-hand corner, and the form of prime ministerial government which Crossman (1963) alleged had replaced it in the post-war period is in the top left-hand corner. Our figure shows that neither tone has ever been fully realised in the post-war period. Instead, the tones of post-war administrations have been a great deal more complex and varied.

Conditions which enhance opportunities for individual impact

Within the context generated by the tone of an administration, it is possible to isolate conditions which are likely to enhance opportunities for individual impact in the cabinet system. Predominant in this regard are situations which generate a break in established patterns of doing things.

Certain types of policy issue expand the scope for individual initiative because they require a radical adaptation of or alteration to existing procedures. Two types may be noted: crises and novel issues. By their nature, crises arise unexpectedly, require relatively fast and speedy resolution and are often driven by external events and pressures. Crisis issues characteristically involve adaptation or bypassing of normal procedures, shortened timescales and continual extemporisation to take account of changes in the external environment. Such issues are likely both to extend opportunities for individual initiative, because the individual is less constrained, and to limit them severely, because of the sheer force of external events and pressures. Novel issues comprise a significant departure from existing policy norms, and a substantial rethink of existing ways of doing things. By breaking with the previous trend of policy they open up substantial opportunities for individual initiative and direction. Sometimes novel policies arise because of changes in the general perception of policy priorities to which the central state then adapts. An example is the creation of the DoE in 1970, following growth in environmental concern during the 1960s. Sometimes new initiatives arise from within the central state itself. These sorts of changes often take place outside the established institutional framework, and provide considerable opportunity for innovation.

Major changes in personnel can also open up opportunities for individual initiative. Examples are changes of government or prime minister. In addition, changes in the external environment to which the state has to respond provide enhanced opportunities for individual initiative, as new ways are adopted for dealing with change. An example is Britain's entry to the EEC in 1973, which generated institutional innovations within the cabinet system (Edwards, 1992).

Personal skills and resources

A final set of factors which affects individual impact on cabinet system operations and about which some general remarks can be made is personal skills and resources. Within the context generated by factors already discussed, opportunities from time to time open up for individuals. Whether they are successfully exploited depends on a wide range of factors. Here we survey some of those which relate to the individual.

Individual motivation is an appropriate starting point. Some may have limited expectations and ambitions about the position they hold, desiring merely to fulfil minimum demands required of them. Others will be more motivated, and are thereby likely to have a bigger impact on policy making. Of course, individual expectations are often themselves shaped by institutional factors. As we have seen, civil servants are expected to play a limited role in policy initiation, and in the absence of ministerial lead will normally pursue and develop existing lines of policy. Ministers are expected to innovate. At ministerial level, Headey (1974: 66–8) in the early 1970s distinguished a small group of 'minimalists' who concentrated solely on fulfilling the most basic tasks required by their jobs. These he defines as legitimating decisions, clearing in-trays, fighting cabinet battles and parliamentary trouble-shooting. Most other ministers (44 of his sample of 50) were found to be far more active in seeking to initiate and develop policy, and to intervene in the work of their departments.

Assuming that the right opportunities arise, and that an individual is willing and motivated to seize them, the next step is to consider factors that can affect an individual's ability to act and to have some impact. In addition to the institutional resources available to the individual the key factors are a compound of acquired skills and innate personal characteristics, which are inherently difficult to capture in any kind of general model. However, three elements can be isolated: knowledge, concentration of effort and certain personal attributes.

Two types of knowledge are especially pertinent. Knowledge about the content of an issue under discussion is particularly necessary in specialist and technical areas. This point was emphasised by both ministers and civil servants in Headey's (1974: 211) survey. In addition, knowledge about the machinery of government and how best to exploit it can be crucial. This might be encapsulated in the phrase 'good political judgement', which comprises knowledge of how best to act and judgement concerning the potential practicality and political sensitivity of proposals. This is the kind of knowledge often in short supply when party politicians first enter government. Few understand the inner workings of the government machine, or ways in which they can exploit it to best advantage. They are likely to spend the first few months in post discovering, rather than altering, the rudiments of the system (Clark, 1993).

Concentration of effort is essential if an individual is to act and to have an impact. No one individual can cover the whole range of business handled in the cabinet system. According to Headey (1974: 279), ministerial allocation of his or her own time is likely to be the 'single most important' decision taken in office. The same principle can be applied to top civil service and advisory personnel. The effective individual is, therefore, likely to be someone who has the ability to be highly selective in concentrating personal resources. Success is likely to reflect an ability to develop well-defined objectives, to concentrate energy on them, and to delegate less central tasks to others. In the case of ministers, Headey (1974: 206) concludes that those who select key issues to concentrate on, and allocate their time accordingly, 'greatly improve their prospects of making a significant contribution to policy'.

Knowledge and concentration of effort are shaped by other, more personal, attributes. Most ministers and top civil servants work at least 60 hours a week (Dean, 1978; Drewry and Butcher, 1991). Ministers, in particular, are subject to scrutiny and a good deal of criticism by the media, Parliament and their own party. The demands of the job are onerous and stressful (Barnett, 1982: 16–19). An essential requirement for the effective actor is, therefore, a robust constitution. Energy and stamina are key prerequisites. Thatcher, for example, required only four to five hours of sleep a night (Thomson, 1989: 204). Callaghan tended to pace himself, and to restore his energy by cat-napping in the afternoon (Donoughue, 1987). Illness or physical weakness are clear disadvantages. Churchill's energy and concentration levels are said to have declined markedly from 1944 following a series of attacks of pneumonia. This situation was exacerbated by a mild stroke in 1949, and by a major one (when prime minister) in June 1953. Effectively for his last two years in office Churchill was incapable of anything more than sporadic intervention in affairs (Moran, 1968). In Attlee's cabinet Ernest Bevin was often incapacitated by heart trouble, Sir Stafford Cripps' concentration level was severely impaired by insomnia, and even Attlee was brought low by a duodenal ulcer during the crucial split over prescription charges in 1951 (L'Etang, 1969: 140–4). Eden suffered from recurrent fevers, and had what amounted to a nervous break-down during the Suez crisis in 1956 (James, 1987). Wilson slowed down mark-edly in his third and fourth terms (1974–6), giving the first indications of the severe illness that was to plague his later years. In Thatcher's cabinets at least one minister, John Moore, was incapacitated by a viral infection at a critical moment in development of health care policy for which he was responsible (see Chapter 8). Under Major, John Patten, secretary of state for education, was seriously ill during a period of difficulty over implementation of the national curriculum. A robust constitution naturally needs to be com-plemented by a robust attitude towards the business of government and rela-tions with others. Indeed, the two elements are almost certainly interrelated. An effective actor must be temperamentally capable of reaching decisions quickly. Vacillation or delay can lead to loss of opportunity. Decisiveness is likely to partner other personality traits of the successful actor, such as 'self-confidence and a degree of ruthlessness' (Headey, 1974: 212).

In sum, the ability of an individual to exert influence if the right opportunity arises, and if he or she is minded and willing to act, is greatly assisted if he or she knows what to do and how to do it, and if he or she has the physical and personal attributes to facilitate success. In this sphere it is hard to identify any change during our period. However, the increasing intrusion of the media has, if anything, increased the pressure on individuals at the top. Such intrusion has also meant that illnesses which could be kept largely hidden in the 1950s, and possibly even the 1960s, would now be exposed to substantial coverage, thereby making resignation more likely.

Scope for individual initiative

In analysing the role of the individual, our central concern has been to identify factors which are likely to affect the extent to which a particular actor might exploit available opportunities. As such, we have focused chiefly on the scope for individual initiative which exists in the cabinet system.

We take an institutional approach to understanding the role of the individual (see Introduction). This enables us to avoid either of the extreme positions which state on the one hand that the individual is the key determinant of political outcomes, and on the other that structural factors are decisively important. We maintain that individuals occupying positions and having access to resources in the cabinet system operate in structured situations within which constantly shifting opportunities for significant action arise. The key task is to identify the conditions under which individual action can be significant. This analytical focus emphasises contingency without losing sight of structural factors.

Within the cabinet system opportunities for individual initiative have already been shown to be substantial. They are, however, never entirely unconstrained. Individuals operate within an established institutional framework which shapes their attitudes, preferences and strategies. Issues tend to move down pathways on which a critical point or choice of route is periodically reached. It is notably at these critical points in the development of an issue that the moment for individuals to contribute arises. The individual tends, therefore, to have a fleeting opportunity to act, and may or may not take advantage of it (Clarke, 1992: 7). Individuals are also capable of manipulating the opportunity structure which confronts them, and may do so very successfully. The essence of decisive intervention in the cabinet system policy process thus lies in both conditioning and exploiting limited 'political breathing space' within constraints established by broader, more contextual factors. The logic of this line of analysis can be expressed in the form of three linked equations:

Position + Resources + Circumstance = Opportunity
Opportunity + Willingness to exploit + Ability to do so = Usage
Usage + Impact on outcome = Power

These three equations provide a summary of the conditions under which power can be exercised by individuals. In drawing lessons from our case studies in Chapter 9, we seek to isolate actual exercises of power by individuals through application of an institutional approach. This enables us to distinguish, first, instances of individual initiative and, secondly, the significance of these instances judged in terms of their impact on policy outcomes.

Conclusion

We have sought in this chapter to investigate two of the more important variable factors which affect the workings of the cabinet system. We have argued that party is a significant variable, and that the different characters of the two main governing parties have consequences for the way in which the cabinet system operates. In the Conservative Party, the position of leader is more prominent than is the case in the Labour Party. Other effects, such as media presentation of the leader, may of course be similar in the two cases, but the point remains that party has a differential impact on the two parties' experience in government. Further aspects of party power structures also have consequences for cabinet system operations. In many ways, the power potential of individual ministers is influenced by party. It is worth noting that this element of our analysis qualifies Robert McKenzie's (1963: 635) contention that the power structures of both governing parties in Britain have been similarly shaped by the requirements of cabinet and parliamentary government. McKenzie's argument is not wrong, but it does underestimate the extent to which the relationship which he investigates is reciprocal. Parties have also shaped British cabinet government.

We do not believe that generalisations about power potential can be made with respect to the individual, as much depends on available opportunities and the extent to which responses are conditioned by wider institutional and contextual factors. In Part 2 we address the role of the individual in the cabinet system by means of case-study analysis.

Part Two

8

□

Case studies of the cabinet system at work

Thus far, we have been chiefly concerned to analyse aspects of the cabinet system which are relatively constant and about which meaningful generalisations can be made. In Part 1, our analysis of the distribution of advantage within the cabinet system was therefore conducted in terms of power potential. Now, in Part 2, we engage in case-study analysis of the cabinet system at work, which enables us to examine real instances of the exercise of power within that system. In addition to demonstrating how the system described in Part 1 actually operates in practice, Part 2 thus makes an analytical advance. It allows us to incorporate highly contingent factors in our analysis. The 14 cases presented in this chapter are all drawn from our period 1974–95. Each is analysed individually here, and more extensively and comparatively in Chapter 9.

Case study analysis

The value of case studies is threefold. They provide insights into the actual working of the cabinet system. They enable us to bring variable factors such as issue, circumstance and individual initiative within our analysis. They allow us to pay some attention to factors shaping the means by which power potential is transformed into actual power within the cabinet system. However, because it is focused on the particular, case-study analysis also raises problems about generalising from specific events. For this reason, it is essential to adopt an analytical approach which can be generalised across cases, thereby allowing broad lessons to be drawn from them.

The approach we adopt in analysing our cases is to follow a clear sequence relating to the way in which an issue is processed by the cabinet system. By following the sequence of treatment of an issue, we are able to draw lessons about cabinet system processes and procedures. This is the central aim of this part of the book. Although each of our 14 cases is interesting and revealing in its own right, each has been selected not on its own intrinsic merits but for the light it throws on cabinet system operations. Our sequence comprises the following main stages: origins; entry into the government machine; entry into the cabinet system; treatment within the cabinet system; exit from the cabinet system.

Parts of this sequence are more important than others. The origins of an issue are chiefly of interest to us because of the initial orientation they give to an issue, and to the way in which it is handled in the cabinet system. Similarly, entry points into the government machine or cabinet system (which can be identical) affect the way in which an issue is initially perceived and addressed, and are therefore potentially very important. By contrast, the exit point of an issue from the cabinet system is of comparatively limited interest. From our point of view, it marks completion of cabinet system treatment of an issue, though we do acknowledge that the issue may return to the cabinet system in another guise at a later date. Most important of all to us is treatment of an issue within the cabinet system. Occasionally in our analyses, issues move into and out of the cabinet system more than once.

Origins

The origins of an issue are the source from which it chiefly arose. We isolate five main sources of issues entering the cabinet system: inherited; consequential on policy change elsewhere; generated within the party; generated within the state; and generated externally.

Inherited issues may derive either from a previous administration of the same party as that which is currently in government, or from a previous administration of the opposition party. Many policy issues pursue a largely continuous existence across administrations. Issues which are consequential on policy change elsewhere derive from an unexpected trend of policy in a different policy sphere. Many policies have unintended consequences, some of which spill into other policy domains and require action on the part of new sets of actors. Issues which are generated within the party may derive from a number of sources. A party's general election manifesto is an important source of policy initiative, but party conference (notably in the case of the Labour Party), other mass party organs (again mainly in the case of Labour), and back-bench committees may also develop new policy initiatives. Issues which are generated within the state may trace their origins either to politicians or to officials, or to a combination of the two. When politicians are the primary source of policy initiative it can be difficult to distinguish party origins from state origins. Issues which are generated externally can be further divided between those which have domestic origins, and those which have overseas origins. Domestic sources of policy initiative include pressure group activity and the more amorphous trend of public opinion. Overseas sources include EU policy initiative, the actions of foreign governments and agencies, and the actions of foreign interests of other kinds (such as multinational corporations). It is quite possible for an issue to originate from more than one of these sources, although one may predominate. The source of an issue affects not only its content, but also the manner in which it is handled in the cabinet system.

Entry into the government machine and/or cabinet system

All issues, whatever their origins, enter the government machine at a specific point. Sometimes an issue may enter the cabinet system directly without having first been processed by another part of the government machine. On other occasions, an issue is initially addressed by a government department before moving into the cabinet system.

Our main interest is state of play at entry into the cabinet system. In investigating this, we attempt to identify who sought first to address the issue, and how that person or (more usually) group of people initially viewed it. Here we consider whether the issue had to be dealt with by cabinet system actors, whether they had a clear solution in mind, and whether they viewed it as high, medium or low priority. There is an element of difficulty involved in judging each of these matters. We hold that cabinet system actors are required to act when they have a legal or treaty obligation, or when they are faced with an evident political crisis. We hold further that a clear solution should be precise and detailed. For us, a general idea of ways forward does not count as having a solution in mind. We hold finally that a high priority issue is one which is recognised by almost all key cabinet system actors to require immediate action; that a medium priority issue is one which is high priority for only a sub-section of key cabinet system actors; and that a low priority issue is one which is not seen as requiring immediate attention by a significant number of key cabinet system actors. Again, entry and initial handling affect not only the content of an issue, but also the manner in which it is handled subsequently.

Treatment within the cabinet system

Examination of the way in which an issue is handled within the cabinet system is our core interest. In each case, we present a compressed narrative from which we subsequently draw a number of lessons.

Exit from the cabinet system

Having analysed treatment of an issue within the cabinet system, we close each narrative with a brief statement of the means by which the issue left the system. Just as many different entry points are possible, so an issue may leave the cabinet system by a number of routes. The final decision on it may take place in cabinet, in committee or elsewhere. The issue may then move into a government department, into Parliament, or directly into an implementing agency. Alternatively, the issue may make no further progress once it has left the cabinet system. We do not analyse the progress of issues once they have left the cabinet system because our interest lies in how the cabinet system works, and not in the issues themselves.

Analysis

Once the main lines of a case have been established, we conclude with an analytical section which draws out the main lessons to be learned from it. We present a short account of factors which mainly determined the outcome of the case, and then focus on three main elements.

The first is key shaping points. We define a key shaping point as a moment when an issue: changed direction; was significantly progressed or retarded; had an option (or options) selected or filtered out of it; was refined by a choice being made between a number of alternatives; or reached a point of final decision. Although precise definition is difficult, identified in these terms many key shaping points become obvious and uncontentious when case material is analysed. Frequently, points at which formal decisions are taken are not key. Cabinet, for instance, often does little more than ratify decisions taken elsewhere, though it may do more than this. The second element is key actors. We attempt to distinguish core actors from peripheral ones by identifying the following classes of actor: initiating; organising; full participant; or merely consulted on an *ad hoc* basis. We are also interested in identifying actors who possess, and exercise, a veto. The third element is what the case reveals about operation of the cabinet system. Here we look at a series of aspects: pathways taken through the cabinet system; the role of procedure; the role of internal versus external factors; the impact of party; and the skill and importance of particular individuals. The analysis of the cases is taken further in Chapter 9 where we attempt to generalise across all 14 case studies, and draw lessons from them about cabinet system operations and the role of the individual in the play of power within that system.

Our 14 cases

Our 14 cases all fall within our chosen period of 1974–95. Five are drawn from the 1974–9 period of Labour government. Eight come from the following 16 years of Conservative government. One (Trident) was continuous across one Labour and one Conservative government. The cases span the administrations of four prime ministers: Wilson, Callaghan, Thatcher and Major. In selecting our cases, we have sought to secure reasonable representation of all four administrations. We have also sought to cover a wide range of policy areas in an attempt to illustrate as many aspects as possible of the cabinet system at work.

The cases are presented chronologically in terms of appearance on the cabinet system agenda. They are:

- the industry white paper, 1974;
- reform of section 2 of the Official Secrets Act 1911, 1974–9;
- direct elections to the European Assembly, 1974–7;
- Chrysler UK, 1975;
- the IMF crisis, 1976;
- Trident, 1977–82;
- the employment bill, 1979–80;
- the Falkland Islands, 1979–82;
- community charge, 1984–6;
- sterling's entry into the ERM, 1985–90;
- the Next Steps report, 1986–8;
- the NHS review, 1988–9;
- council tax, 1990–1; and
- pit closures, 1991–2.

These 14 cases have been selected from an initial list of more than 30 which we judged capable of sustaining detailed analysis on the basis of material available on the public record. The fact that no more than 14 cases are analysed here reflects in part pressures of space, but also our belief both that our chosen cases do not overlap in the lessons they provide about the cabinet system at work, and that between them they illuminate a very broad swathe of cabinet system operations. Our 14 cases also form a large enough sample to allow some generalisations about cabinet system operations to be made.

Our use of material in the public domain means that each of our cases revolves around an issue of high policy and considerable political salience. We thus face the problem that analysis of high-profile cases focuses on the exceptional, and thereby exaggerates non-routine processes. Against this, we maintain that most routine issues are settled at a lower level than the cabinet system itself and only marginally engage that system (if at all), that many routine processes have already been investigated at length in Part 1, and that even in exceptional situations cabinet system routines are in fact revealed. The fact that routines are important in shaping outcomes even in cases of high political salience reinforces our argument about the importance of routines and procedures in the cabinet system. Although our range of cases is limited, it is not therefore unbalanced.

The industry white paper, 1974

Origins

The 1974 industry white paper had party origins, being developed by the Labour Party in opposition between 1970 and 1974. The industrial policy which was agreed at this time had two main elements. One was a proposal to create a National Enterprise Board (NEB), which would channel investment funds into industry and bring into public ownership prominent companies occupying key positions in the British economy. The other was a system of planning agreements negotiated jointly by major firms, government and trade unions, which would provide a framework for securing investment and industrial democracy at the workplace (Butler and Kavanagh, 1974: 19). These policies were endorsed at the 1973 Labour Party conference. Labour's manifesto for the February 1974 general election subsequently contained a commitment to introduce an Industry Act featuring both the NEB and planning agreements (Labour Party, 1974: 10–11).

The main driving force behind policy development in opposition was the left wing of the Labour Party, which worked chiefly through the party's national executive committee (NEC) and home policy sub-committee. The leadership group was, however, deeply split on the issue. Most members were either lukewarm or hostile to the full package of proposals (Healey, 1990: 368–70; Wilson, 1979: 30–1). The proposals' main supporter within the leadership group was Tony Benn, chair of the NEC's home policy sub-committee in opposition.

Although Labour won the February 1974 general election, it did not secure a majority in the House of Commons. Another general election was thus certain to take place before long. The central aim of prime minister Harold Wilson was therefore to buy time to improve the government's standing by ensuring that some of the major policies Labour had put to the country were worked out in detail before the next election. Ministers were expected to spend the next few months turning election commitments into detailed white papers (Wilson, 1979: 13–14).

Entry into and treatment within the government machine

A queen's speech was duly written, approved by cabinet and presented to the House of Commons on 12 March 1974. It contained a commitment to produce an industry bill. The task of generating the white paper which would form the basis of the bill was devolved to the Department of Industry (DoI) under Tony Benn (industry secretary). His two junior ministers, Eric Heffer (minister of state) and Michael Meacher (parliamentary under secretary), were also from the left of the party, and were strong supporters of the party's industrial policy.

In the DoI, a white paper drafting committee was formed under Heffer's chairmanship. The other members of the committee were Meacher, Alan Lord (deputy secretary and principal finance officer), Ron Dearing (under secretary), Stuart Holland (Sussex University) and Benn's political advisers Francis Cripps and Francès Morrell (Heffer, 1991: 151). The drafting committee was mirrored and serviced by a team of officials under Lord and Dearing (Part, 1990: 172). No civil servants from outside the DoI were involved. All non-civil service members of the committee were from the left of the Labour Party, and had been closely involved in policy formulation in opposition. Meetings were held three or four times a week, and the group consulted regularly with David Lea from the TUC (Castle, 1980: 84).

Drafting took until the beginning of June. However, long before the committee's work was done the allegedly radical nature of its deliberations brought negative reactions from elsewhere in Whitehall, notably the Treasury and other parts of the DoI. Benn and his team of ministers and political advisers (especially Morrell and Cripps) thought that DoI civil servants were sabotaging their proposals by dragging their feet (Benn, 1989: 152). Indeed, as early as 14 March 1974, when Benn discussed matters with his senior civil servants, he felt that some of them, and in particular Sir Anthony Part (permanent secretary), had reservations about the proposed policy (Benn, 1989: 121). Part (1990: 172) denies this, arguing that throughout he was simply concerned to ensure that proposals contained in a white paper were both practical and constitutional. By June, substantial concern was building up in Whitehall among senior civil servants and senior ministers that the DoI exercise was likely to produce a more radical policy than was either feasible or desirable.

Benn reacted to the growing ministerial and official opposition to his policy by attempting to mobilise Labour Party and TUC opinion. On 20 May 1974, at a meeting of the cabinet–TUC liaison committee, he presented a paper which argued that 100 firms would initially be involved in planning agreements, that the NEB would be empowered to purchase key sectors of manufacturing industry, and that government aid to industry would be channelled through planning agreements. The paper seems to have reflected thinking in Heffer's committee. Castle (1980: 103n) notes that Benn's proposals were 'much more specific than the manifesto'. Benn later, on 10 June, persuaded the NEC's home policy sub-committee to release the paper to the press, causing a furore. Newspaper comments were hostile. Wilson and other ministers felt that Benn was trying to pre-empt cabinet decisions. Castle (1980: 109n) believed Benn's approach to constitute a clear breach of collective responsibility. Around this time, Benn also made a number of speeches which were judged by some to be antagonistic towards private-sector industry. The Prime Minister's Office became increasingly worried about Benn's tactics, and Wilson made efforts to restrain his statements and public appearances (Benn, 1989: 154, 168). The CBI also reacted against the policy. Cabinet ministers who were opposed to the policy were able to use Benn's tactics as an excuse to clip his wings, helping thereby to retard and obscure the main line of policy development.

Nevertheless, in the DoI policy development continued. By the end of April at the latest, it had been decided that Heffer's committee was drafting not a white paper, but a green one: a paper for discussion rather than action. This change in approach had not been approved by Number 10 or the Cabinet Office. A first draft was ready by the end of May. However, Meacher, Cripps and Morrell felt that its language was not sufficiently radical and changed it, much to the displeasure of Heffer (1991: 154). This draft was discussed at a meeting on 11 June chaired by Benn and attended by Part, Peter Carey (second permanent secretary, DoI) and all the members of the drafting committee. Part and Carey objected to the language of the paper as 'too polemical for Whitehall', and liable to discourage inward investment by multinational corporations. It was agreed that sections on planning agreements would be redrafted by officials and that Meacher, Dearing, Cripps and Morrell would look again at sections on the NEB (Benn, 1989: 172). The redraft was completed and agreed within the DoI on Monday 17 June. Later that week it was sent to the Cabinet Office, and circulated to ministers.

Entry into and treatment within the cabinet system

When this issue entered the cabinet system, ministers did not need to act in the sense that they had no legal or treaty obligation. However, because it was a manifesto commitment, and because of the situation of the minority Labour government, the issue was medium priority. A clear solution had already been fixed in outline.

Wilson was aware that the issue could prove problematic, and had taken steps to ensure that the DoI document would be thoroughly examined within the cabinet system. Under the chairmanship of Edward Short (lord president of the council), he had already created a cabinet committee on industrial development (ID) to examine the draft 'green' paper. After the first meeting, and immediately following the leak on 11 June of Benn's paper to the cabinet–TUC liaison committee (Castle, 1980: 109n), Wilson appointed himself chairman of the committee and made James Callaghan (foreign secretary) a member (*The Times*, 13.6.74). Callaghan was known to be concerned about the NEB proposals. At this point, the prime minister had taken over policy handling. Wilson made it clear to Benn that he was not happy to receive a green paper which was likely to encourage discussion, when what he was seeking was a white paper with firm and agreed proposals for action (Benn, 1989: 177). He considered the draft to be 'sloppy', 'half-baked' and 'polemical' (Wilson, 1979: 33).

ID met to discuss the draft paper in detail on Friday 28 June 1974, following a 21-vote Commons defeat the previous Friday on a Conservative censure motion on the government's industrial policy. Wilson chaired the meeting and, according to Heffer (1991: 154), took the paper into his own hands, stating that it should be rewritten. Wilson, Callaghan, Denis Healey (chancellor of the exchequer), Anthony Crosland (environment secretary), Shirley Williams (secretary of state for prices and consumer protection) and Harold Lever (chancellor of the Duchy of Lancaster) spoke against parts of the draft and the style in which it was expressed. Peter Shore (trade secretary) and William Ross (Scottish secretary) spoke in favour of the draft. At the end of the meeting Wilson laid down the procedure that was to be followed. He himself undertook to circulate a paper which would come back to the committee for discussion in about a week. Thereafter, the draft would go to an official committee which would report to a small group of ministers. The result of this group's deliberations would then be reported to ID, and would go from there to cabinet (Benn, 1989: 187).

This procedure seems to have been followed. ID met on 9 July to discuss the paper circulated by Wilson, which had been drafted by Bernard Donoughue (head of the PMPU) and members of the PMPU (Donoughue, 1987: 54). The paper had only been circulated at the very last moment. Benn received his copy at 10 p.m. the previous day and considered it to be 'disastrous'. The meeting lasted for four hours. It was agreed that aircraft, shipbuilding and ports should be handled under separate powers, and that the proposals should not contain a list of companies which might be drawn into public ownership (Benn, 1989: 193–4).

At this point, the matter was delegated to an official committee reporting to a group of senior ministers under Wilson. Michael Foot (employment secretary) took charge of most of the final drafting (Wilson, 1979: 33). The Treasury was especially active in pressing for removal of any hint of compulsion in negotiating planning agreements with companies. It also felt that the NEB should be largely limited to administering existing state assets, rather than acquiring new ones. On 31 July, the draft was taken to ID (Benn, 1989: 210). The committee agreed that the NEB's proposed acquisition powers should be limited, that for at least the next year regional aid should not be channelled through planning agreements, and that any industrial acquisition would be by specific Act of Parliament, except in circumstances of compelling urgency, when a statutory instrument could be used (Castle, 1980: 162).

At the end of the week, on Friday 2 August, a special three-and-a-half-hour cabinet meeting was held to consider the draft. Castle (1980: 167) states that Benn had very little support. It was agreed that regional development grants would not be part of the planning agreement process. On this point, Benn asked for his dissent to be recorded in the cabinet minutes. It was also agreed that acquisitions by the NEB would be voluntary except in compelling circumstances (Benn, 1989: 212–13). The document was then again redrafted in Number 10 and the Cabinet Office, and sent to the DoI by Sir John Hunt (cabinet secretary) on 5 August, with a note saying the prime minister had read the new draft, and did not feel that a drafting committee was required as no further changes were necessary (Benn, 1989: 215).

Exit from the cabinet system

On 15 August, the white paper was published. It marked a clear dilution of the proposals contained in the DoI's draft green paper. In particular, companies would not be required to enter a planning agreement, financial assistance flowing from planning agreements was to be additional rather than conditional, planning agreements were to be bipartite (government–business) rather than tripartite (government–business–trade union) with an expectation that unions would be consulted by management, the extent of public ownership was circumscribed, NEB acquisition powers were only to be exercised through agreement, and any substantial acquisition was to require legislation (Department of Industry, 1974). After Labour had won the October 1974 general election with a majority of four seats, it introduced an industry bill to the Commons in February 1975. When Benn was replaced by Eric Varley as industry secretary in June 1975, the bill's contents were diluted further. The Industry Act was passed in November 1975. The NEB was subsequently established, and a single planning agreement was negotiated with the National Coal Board.

Analysis

The outcome of this case was greatly influenced by party and political factors. The nature of the policy developed in opposition, the manifesto commitment, divisions within the party leadership over the issue and the constraints of minority government all played a significant part in shaping the way in which the issue was handled.

The first key shaping point in development of this issue was the agenda-setting effect of policy making in opposition, which resulted in a manifesto commitment. At the DoI, Heffer's drafting committee of March to May, and the redrafting which took place in early June, were key. The leak of Benn's paper at about this time marginally retarded progress of the issue. Within the cabinet system the ID meeting of 28 June, when Wilson formally brought control of policy redrafting into the cabinet system, resulted in a significant shift in policy content. Serial redrafting by the PMPU, the official committee, and finally the Cabinet Office resulted in substantial dilution of the initial policy. This shift was then formally agreed at ID meetings on 9 and 31 July. The final decision point was cabinet on 2 August 1974.

Key actors changed as the policy developed. In the first stage of clarification, the initiative lay with ministers and officials in the lead department,

Industry. Key participants here were Benn and especially Heffer, plus the members of his drafting committee. Others, notably Lea, were drawn in on a consultative basis. From the beginning a bias was built into the process by Wilson's choice of ministerial personnel, which made it likely that the departmental exercise would produce a fairly radical document. This initial bias was further accentuated by the membership of the drafting committee. However, the apparently radical nature of what was being hatched meant that others, through leaks and rumours, were drawn into the process as a kind of Greek chorus commenting on the action and mouthing disapproval. This chorus included the prime minister and his staff, and senior ministers and officials from other departments (as well as from the DoI). The opposition and the press hovered in the background. Key actors within the cabinet system were Wilson, Foot, Treasury representatives and Hunt. The PMPU and the official committee, which between them did much of the redrafting, were also important. These actors blatantly hijacked policy development. They did so through careful use of cabinet system machinery, with the result that the emphasis and contents of the DoI's draft were altered substantially. This exercise was only successful because the prime minister was able to rely on the active support of nearly all other senior ministers.

The case provides a number of lessons about cabinet system operations. On the face of it, this issue took entirely orthodox pathways through the cabinet system and is a classic example of collective cabinet government in action. The lead department generated raw material for discussion in the cabinet system, committees deliberated, and cabinet itself was involved at the end of the process. However, what is significant about this issue is the way in which the cabinet system was used to bring policy that had gone astray back into line. Procedure did not so much constrain in this case as generate opportunities for policy change. Wilson's exploitation of opportunities available through manipulation of cabinet system machinery was masterful. Yet he could only do this because Benn was isolated, and did not have significant support at either top ministerial or official level.

The role of party in this case was important. As was shown in Chapter 7, party–cabinet system links are both more formalised and more extensive in the Labour Party than in the Conservative Party. Especially interesting in this case was the operation of the cabinet–TUC liaison committee, and the attempt by Benn to galvanise party opinion through the NEC and its home policy sub-committee. A further party political dimension was generated by the government's minority position in the House of Commons. This completely coloured the process of policy making, and was a crucial determinant of Wilson's paramount aim to produce proposals that would form the basis not of an immediate parliamentary test, but of a future election platform. An essential part of this strategy was to keep the party united, and not to provide the opposition with ammunition with which to mount an effective attack. Such matters of political strategy were crucial to the outcome of the case.

The role of the individual has already been analysed, particularly with regard to Wilson. However, it is worth noting the aspect of the convention of collective responsibility revealed by this case, which evidently holds that ministers should not only speak with one voice once they have agreed a line, but also remain silent until they have agreed a line.

Reform of section 2 of the Official Secrets Act 1911, 1974–9

Origins

Reform of section 2 of the Official Secrets Act 1911 (OSA) had dual origins, being both an inherited policy issue and a manifesto commitment developed through internal party machinery. The latter dimension was probably the more important in locating it on the Labour government's agenda in 1974.

The issue can be traced to the series of quasi-constitutional issues which appeared on the public agenda in the 1970s. In 1968 the Fulton report began to develop one of two main lines of criticism of section 2, when it called for more openness in government. This may be labelled the positive critique. It prompted the Wilson government to publish the 1969 white paper, *Information and the Public Interest* (Civil Service Department, 1969), but no concrete action resulted. The reform agenda was thus taken over by the Conservatives, who in the 1970 general election campaign promised more openness in government. The Heath government duly established a series of inquiries, one of which, the Franks Commission, was given the task of investigating section 2 of the OSA. It reported in 1972. However, Franks looked chiefly not at the positive question of openness in government, but at the more negative question of the nature of criminal offences specified by the Act. In this concern, the Commission was responding to two celebrated court cases of the early 1970s, each of which had failed to secure a conviction under section 2 (Kellner and Crowther-Hunt, 1980: 265). Franks proposed a more limited – and also more effective – law. Again, however, no action was taken.

The result was that the chance to return reform of the OSA to the political agenda fell again to Labour. By an almost unnoticed route, the positive side of the question – open government – found its way into the Labour Party manifesto of October 1974. The key event was publication in the summer of 1974 of a Transport House sub-committee discussion paper, 'People and the Media', which floated the idea of increased public access, as of right, to official information (Kellner and Crowther-Hunt, 1980: 266). In office Harold Wilson did, this time, take steps to act on the manifesto commitment derived from this idea, and reform of the OSA became a matter of government concern.

Two lines of debate thus emerged around calls for reform of the OSA. One was the essentially negative desire – expressed by Franks – to remould section 2 into an efficient piece of legislation. The other was the more positive desire – contained in the Labour Party manifesto – to restrict section 2 in the cause of open government. At times, the two issues became fused in reform debates, and in ministerial and official initiatives. They are nevertheless separate.

Entry into and treatment by the government machine

The issue entered the government machine through the Home Office. Home secretary Roy Jenkins decided to address the positive issue of open government by studying for himself recent American reform in the field. He travelled to Washington in January 1975 in the company of several senior officials, including the permanent secretary to the Home Office, Sir Arthur Peterson. In Washington, the Home Office party heard at first hand the objections of Justice Department and FBI officials to the workings of the American Act (*The Times*, 29.6.78). Despite his liberal commitments, Jenkins returned to Britain unimpressed by open government American-style, which he described as 'costly, cumbersome and legalistic' (Kellner and Crowther-Hunt, 1980: 267). Yet again, reform of the OSA was apparently going nowhere. Donoughue (1987: 122) claims that the PMPU helped to keep the issue on the government's agenda, but it was chiefly pressure from the Labour Party which kept it alive in 1975.

Entry into and treatment by the cabinet system

Reform of the OSA appears to have entered the cabinet system in October 1975, when it was made the preserve of MISC 89 (Donoughue, 1987: 122). At point of entry ministers were not required to act, they had no solution in mind, and they viewed the issue as low priority. MISC 89 was almost certainly chaired by Wilson. It decided first to place reform of the OSA in the queen's speech of 1975, second to look for simpler ways than the American to open government, and thirdly to split the reform agenda into two for further consideration. Criminal aspects of the OSA (the negative dimension) were placed under the auspices of the Home Office. The question of liberalising publication of official documents (the positive dimension) was made a CSD responsibility. However, by the time reports on these matters were received by cabinet system actors, Callaghan had replaced Wilson as prime minister (in April 1976), and MISC 89 had been relabelled GEN 29 (Kellner and Crowther-Hunt, 1980: 266–7).

Callaghan was a natural sceptic and opponent of OSA reform (Kellner and Crowther-Hunt, 1980: 266). His first action as prime minister was thus to order all reform activity to stop. However, he was forced to reverse his initial decision when *New Society* on 17 June 1976 carried a spectacular and evidently accurate leak of cabinet discussion of child benefit changes. As it was clearly impossible to prosecute, Callaghan and a number of equally sceptical senior civil servants were persuaded of the need to create an efficient and effective law. The issue was back on the agenda.

GEN 29 was set to work under Callaghan's chairmanship (Kellner and Crowther-Hunt, 1980: 268). At the same time, a committee of privy councillors under Lord Houghton was established to investigate procedures for handling cabinet documents (*The Times*, 23.11.76). However, little progress had been made by September 1976, when Jenkins resigned his cabinet seat and Merlyn Rees replaced him as home secretary.

The new minister was quickly provided by permanent secretary Peterson with a blueprint for OSA reform. At about the same time, Callaghan also received the report of Houghton's group of privy councillors, which recommended a tightening of procedures for handling cabinet documents. Rees duly made a statement to the Commons on 22 November 1976 regarding reform of section 2 of the OSA. This statement clearly represented something of a compromise within government. Liberals could point to an increase on Franks in the sphere of cabinet documents and economic affairs. Here a less onerous regime was to be instituted. Sceptics could content themselves with the fact that Rees had announced tighter restrictions than recommended by Franks in the spheres of foreign, defence and security policy. Here a new classification, 'Defence and International: Confidential', was to be created (*The Times*, 23.11.76). In all, the new system represented minimal change, but it did seem both more liberal and also more effective than the old. As Rees put it (with perhaps unintended candour), the blunderbuss was to be replaced by an Armalite rifle.

Only at this point did detailed reformist activity begin, as officials from the Home Office, Cabinet Office and CSD started to draft a white paper. It is probable that they formed the nucleus of an official cabinet committee. The bulk of the work on replacement of section 2 was undertaken by Anthony Langdon, under secretary in the criminal justice department of the Home Office. Also closely involved were Anthony Brennan and Neil Cairncross, both deputy secretaries in the Home Office. Responsibility for advising ministers about foreign experience of freedom of information and open government rested with CSD officials. Most important among these were John Moor, deputy secretary in charge of the CSD's personnel management group, and Alan Duke, assistant secretary in charge of security affairs. The secretary of GEN 29 was William McIndoe, a Cabinet Office deputy secretary (*The Times*, 29.6.78), who is also likely to have chaired any official grouping.

Members of GEN 29 after Jenkins' replacement by Rees in September 1976, and David Owen's promotion to foreign secretary following the death of Anthony Crosland in February 1977, were Callaghan, who chaired the committee, Rees, Denis Healey (chancellor of the exchequer), Owen, Fred Peart (lord privy seal), Michael Foot (lord president of the council), Fred Mulley (defence secretary), Lord Elwyn Jones (lord chancellor), Shirley Williams (education secretary), Edmund Dell (trade secretary) and Samuel Silkin (attorney general) (*The Times*, 17.7.78). Throughout, GEN 29 experienced great difficulty in drafting an official information bill for presentation to Parliament in the 1977–8 session. In particular, ministers found it hard to know where to draw the line in foreign affairs and defence matters. Beyond this, several ministers had serious doubts about the whole enterprise, questioning the sincerity of reforming efforts which claimed to be liberal, but which could turn out to be anything but that.

Nevertheless, the committee was forced to stick to its task by external factors. One was media interest in reform efforts, spearheaded by Peter Hennessy of *The Times*, and the rather diffuse public concern which it helped to generate. Rather more pressing were two other factors. First, the Lib–Lab pact, which the government had agreed on disappearance of its parliamentary majority in spring 1977, was premised in part on reform of the OSA (Steel, 1980: 64). Secondly, Labour's NEC was conducting a parallel analysis of OSA reform, and exerting pressure on the government to take significant action in the sphere of open government (*The Times*, 29.6.77).

The NEC working party was chaired by Eric Heffer. Taking an idea from Frances Morrell, special adviser to Tony Benn (energy secretary), the working party commissioned the drafting of an access to information bill modelled on American, Swedish, Danish and Dutch experience. The product was a 'dummy' 19-clause bill drafted by Joseph Jacob, law lecturer at LSE. This would generate far wider access, and cut the 30-year rule for release of cabinet papers to two years. The central intention was to provide an incoming Labour government with a ready-made statute which could be enacted before civil servants had a chance to water it down (*The Times*, 29.6.77).

The reaction of GEN 29 to these various pressures was prevarication. Early on, the committee rejected the freedom of information approach to open government, purportedly on cost grounds. However, it is clear that both ministerial and official objections went deeper. Within ministerial ranks there seem to have been few champions of freedom of information (Donoughue, 1987: 122). Within official ranks, natural caution in this sphere was reinforced by the experience Peterson had heard about in Washington, when accompanying Jenkins in January 1975. GEN 29 thus took the decision to pursue greater openness in government through publication of more consultative documents and green papers. A statement from Number 10 was issued to this effect in June 1977. However, a leaked letter sent by Sir Douglas Allen, head of the home civil service, to all permanent secretaries indicated that even voluntary 'openness' was to be interpreted restrictively (*Sunday Times*, 25.9.77).

Further prevarication was revealed in the autumn. An October 1977 meeting of GEN 29 was faced with the decision whether to publish a white paper as a means of testing parliamentary opinion, or to proceed directly to a bill. The latter route was said to be favoured by Callaghan, who was attracted by the prospect of an effective secrets law (*The Times*, 26.9.77). In the event, the queen's speech of 1977, unlike that of 1975, did not contain a commitment to introduction of reformist legislation during the coming session. Instead, it promised the white paper which would appease Labour proponents of reform, and indicate to Liberals that the government continued to think seriously about an official information bill. The reason for continued delay was that ministers and officials were embroiled in a dispute about categories of infor-mation to be protected by criminal sanctions (*The Times*, 21.10.77).

Such blatant lack of progress could not be allowed to continue for ever. Eventually, the government was forced by the series of pressures which it faced to come up with some sort of initiative. These pressures manifested themselves in a hostile reception given to Rees in April 1978 by the home affairs group of Labour back-benchers, and by the NEC study group chaired by Heffer. Again the issue was back on the agenda. At a meeting of GEN 29 held on 25 May 1978, ministers decided to support further study of foreign freedom of information experience. Foot was particularly concerned that the government should not be seen to break a manifesto commitment. At this meeting, GEN 29 decided to publish a white paper. Its text was endorsed in cabinet on 22 June with only minor amendments. Here, Benn spoke in favour of freedom of information and was supported by Williams, Owen and William Rodgers (transport secretary). However, Callaghan and Rees took the con-trary view, and no commitment was made (Benn, 1990: 314–15).

When the long-overdue white paper was finally released on 19 July 1978, it (unsurprisingly) described foreign arrangements as costly, cumbersome and inimical to good government, and stuck to the minimalist line which had been deployed for the previous few years. It also made a commitment to further study. A disclosure statute was ruled out, and in a speech to the House of Commons Callaghan stated that the cabinet was now unable to take the position contained in the October 1974 manifesto. The white paper insisted on refining criminal sanctions before moving any further in the direction of open government (*The Times*, 29.6.78). Hennessy's request for background papers relating to the white paper was met with the reply that there were none (Kellner and Crowther-Hunt, 1980: 269).

The issue returned to cabinet on 28 September 1978, when the question of inclusion in the queen's speech was addressed. Again opinion was divided, and it was decided to reconvene GEN 29 (which had not met since publication of the white paper) to discuss the issue (Benn, 1990: 349–50). It seems likely that the shadowing official committee was in fact reactivated to prepare stud-ies of foreign experience, as promised in the white paper. The key meeting was, however, that of the future legislation committee, FLQ, chaired by Foot. In October 1978, FLQ decided against inclusion of an official information bill in the speech on the grounds that it was far too dangerous. The sense that the cabinet line could not be held had recently been reinforced by demands at the Labour Party conference for a freedom of information bill, and by pressure both from the campaigning group Justice and from Lord Scarman in a letter published in *The Times* on 11 October (*The Times*, 12.10.78). Proposals to reform the OSA were therefore included in the queen's speech delivered on 1 November 1978, but no definite undertaking to legislate was given.

Ministerial or official relief that the issue had successfully been postponed again was, however, tempered (if only slightly) by the luck of Liberal MP

Clement Freud in topping the ballot for introduction of private members' bills. At the end of 1978, he chose to introduce an official information bill giving public access to government papers, and repealing section 2 of the OSA. It was clearly inspired by the American Act. The government could not oppose the bill, and it got through a second reading. In committee, however, the bill was successfully stalled by the mass of papers prepared by civil servants (Benn, 1990: 445–6). GEN 29 duly reconvened, and met on 23 January and 21 February 1979 (Benn, 1990: 445, 462). It had a new member, Tony Benn, who had been added by Callaghan in October 1978 when, as Benn (1990: 445) put it, he was 'trying to be friendly'.

The new member made no difference to the outcome. At cabinet on 15 March 1979, Callaghan stated his boredom with the subject, Rees spoke against the Freud bill, Foot sought some action from the government, Peter Shore (environment secretary) made principled objections to the bill, Owen spoke against Freud but in favour of reform, and Benn spoke in support of Freud (Benn, 1990: 472–3). Freud's official information bill was never enacted.

Exit from the cabinet system

Reform of the OSA effectively left the cabinet system with the change of government in May 1979. The first Thatcher government chose not to pursue the matter with any vigour.

Analysis

The outcome of this case was determined chiefly by a combination of inertia and internal opposition, which together ensured that reform of the OSA was kept successfully from happening for an entire parliamentary session. This was in spite of a manifesto commitment, party support, coalition support and a measure of public pressure.

Key shaping points were nearly all negative. The issue was repeatedly returned to the political agenda by external factors, but each time the cabinet system succeeded in ensuring that little came of it. The main shaping points were Rees' 'minimal change' announcement (November 1976), the GEN 29 decisions to pursue greater openness through consultation documents and green papers (June 1977), to put a commitment to a white paper rather than a bill in the 1977 queen's speech (October 1977), to commission further foreign studies (May 1978) and finally to publish a white paper (June 1978), and the decision of FLQ to put no more than a very weak proposal in the 1978 queen's speech. In this case no final decision point was reached, and the issue was effectively halted in the cabinet system. One important reform option, a right to information, was selected out of consideration at an early stage.

Key actors were mainly officials from the Home Office, CSD and Cabinet Office. Although Wilson took the initiative in bringing the matter forward, key initiating actors were the officials who formulated studies and options for deliberation by ministers. Notable among these were Peterson and the official groups under Langdon and Moor. Civil service caution was shared by the two key initiators on the ministerial side, Rees and Callaghan. Key organising actors were drawn from within the cabinet system. Callaghan, Wilson and officials from the cabinet secretariat all played important roles. Other ministers were drawn in, notably through meetings of GEN 29, though progress was marginal because GEN 29 was split between liberals and minimalists. Lack of enthusiasm on the part of Callaghan and Rees was critical, for it robbed the issue of the policy drive required to overcome the natural caution and conservatism of officials. In essence, these two ministers exercised a veto through indifference.

The issue reveals a number of aspects of cabinet system operations. Pathways through the system were mainly orthodox. Procedure was used effectively to retard the issue, which became enmeshed in a wealth of detail. The roles of internal and external factors were very clear. Party was a particularly important external factor in keeping the issue on the agenda. Internal resistance to reform was, however, stronger. Individuals played important parts in generating this resistance, but their roles should not be exaggerated. So great was the scepticism of ministers, and even more of key officials, that OSA reform was an unlikely occurrence under almost any plausible late 1970s scenario. Lack of policy drive is the outstanding feature of this case.

This is, then, a case of a series of non-decision points at which external reforming pressures were successfully deflected by a cautious and sceptical government machine. Within that machine, ministerial and official opinion seem to have coincided remarkably regularly. The result is that crude conspiracy theories which attempt to lay the blame at the door of the British civil service have to be discarded. By the same token, attempts to identify a crucial obstructive individual – such as Callaghan – also appear implausible. Failure to reform the OSA in the 1970s was the product of a much broader, and very powerful, group of forces.

Direct elections to the European Assembly, 1974–7

Origins

The origins of direct elections to the European Assembly were chiefly external, and partly inherited. They can be traced to Britain's accession to the European Economic Community (EEC) on 1 January 1973, when it became bound by the Community's founding treaties. Article 138 (3) of the 1957 Treaty of Rome contained provision for a system of direct elections to the European Assembly (later Parliament) by a uniform procedure across the Community.

By 1973 little progress towards this goal had been made. A European Assembly existed, but membership of it was by nomination, not election. However, chiefly for reasons relating to French domestic politics, pressure to bring EEC practice in line with the provisions of the Treaty of Rome soon developed (George, 1990: 118). At the inaugural European Council meeting held in Paris in December 1974, direct elections were therefore placed on the agenda by the French president, Valéry Giscard d'Estaing, and received broad support. Only the British position was unclear. Prime minister Harold Wilson agreed to the principle of direct election, but reserved full approval until after his renegotiation of British membership had been approved by the British people in a referendum (Wilson, 1979: 97). Industry secretary Tony Benn (1990: 36) notes that this early decision was taken by Wilson without consulting cabinet. It seems likely that Wilson backed Giscard's initiative in the hope of securing French support for his renegotiation of Britain's budgetary contribution (George, 1990: 118).

Once the June 1975 referendum had delivered a majority of two to one in favour of Britain's continued membership of the Community, ministers were thus forced to think seriously about direct elections and the position they would take in future European debate of the issue. In the period since the December European Council, the European Assembly had itself issued draft proposals for direct election in January 1975.

Entry into and treatment by the cabinet system

It is not clear how or when the issue entered the cabinet system. It is possible that work on position papers, coordinated by the European secretariat in the Cabinet Office, started as soon as Wilson had given his agreement in principle in Paris in December 1974. Alternatively, it may not have been until after the June 1975 referendum that serious work began. At point of entry, policy makers were required to act, but they viewed the issue as low priority and had no clear solution in mind.

The first major paper on direct elections was presented to cabinet on 18 November 1975 (Benn, 1989: 462). This was probably prepared by officials from the Home Office and FCO, which were the lead departments in later stages of policy development. It may have drawn on work undertaken by British officials serving on an EEC working group set up by European foreign ministers following a reaffirmation of intent by EEC heads of government at the Brussels European Council of July 1975.

No decisions were taken at the November 1975 cabinet, and it was clearly without cabinet authorisation that Wilson agreed to direct elections to the European Assembly at the Rome European Council of 1–2 December 1975. Benn (1989: 473), now energy secretary, claims that his first knowledge of this policy development came from the nine o'clock news. Following this European Council, preparatory work at the EEC level was remitted to the Council of Ministers (Foreign Affairs), which set up a further working group. It did not begin work until April 1976.

The government was now faced with a developing European policy agenda, to which it was forced to respond. It issued a green paper in February 1976. This had three parts. The first analysed the existing state of play. The second listed questions which would need to be decided at European level. Most issues were in fact located at this level. The third listed questions which would need to be decided by the British Parliament. Chief among these was the electoral system to be used for a European Assembly.

Direct elections next came before cabinet on 12 March 1976, when foreign secretary James Callaghan urged colleagues to make some kind of response to direct election proposals emanating from the Council of Ministers. Despite some dissent within cabinet, the decision was taken to respond positively (Benn, 1989: 516–17). Opening a debate in the House of Commons on 29 March, Callaghan stated that the government was prepared to propose the setting up of a select committee to consider the issue of direct elections. The committee was finally agreed by the House on 17 May, and had its first meeting the following day. It eventually produced three reports in June, August and November 1976. The first favoured an Assembly of between 350 and 425 seats to be elected in May or June 1978 with a fixed term of either four or five years. The committee thought that an optional dual mandate (whereby individuals could be elected to both the British Parliament and the European Assembly) should be allowed. The second report recommended that at least the first set of elections to the European Assembly be conducted on a first-past-the-post (FPP) basis. The third noted that urgent progress needed to be made.

By July 1976 a 410-seat European Assembly had been negotiated by representatives of the nine member states, and simultaneous elections were planned to take place throughout the EEC in May or June 1978. Callaghan, now prime minister, agreed at the September 1976 European Council to do all he could to ensure that direct elections were held in May–June 1978. The fact that

Britain was to hold its first EEC presidency in the first half of 1977 made it particularly important for Callaghan to demonstrate the European commitment of his government. He also seemed to feel that Britain had something of an obligation to join its European partners in using proportional representation (PR) for European Assembly elections. Outside the government, the Labour Party conference and NEC voted decisively against direct elections in the closing months of 1976.

A commitment to introduce legislation on direct elections in the 1976–7 session was nevertheless included in the queen's speech of November 1976, but little progress was made. Although the Commons select committee had stated in its third report that a bill would need to be introduced to Parliament by the start of 1977 if the spring 1978 deadline for elections were to be met, ministers showed either no desire or no ability to conform to this timetable.

It is not clear where work on the issue took place. Bill drafting could have been departmental, in which case it would have taken place in the Home Office and FCO. Alternatively, it could have taken place in an official committee within the cabinet system, in which case the Home Office and FCO would have been lead departments and the European secretariat would have played a large part. The latter alternative seems the more plausible.

On 25 February 1977 the issue went to a special cabinet, which debated direct elections for a full morning, and for half an hour after lunch, without coming to a decision. Some ministers, including Michael Foot (leader of the House) and Benn, declared themselves to be against the European Assembly in principle. The issue had, indeed, been a major point of contention in the 1975 referendum, when some Labour ministers had campaigned for a No vote. Others accepted the principle, but would not agree to PR. In essence, cabinet was divided between die-hards like Foot and Benn, and pragmatists who sought a policy which could be sold to the Labour Party (Benn, 1990: 49; Owen, 1992: 276). Callaghan was evidently in the latter camp, and affirmed his 'best endeavours' to meet his commitment to his European partners (*The Times*, 26.2.77).

During the following month, pressure on the government mounted. Against background threats that the NEC might call a special Labour Party conference on the issue, and that the Conservative Party might use the issue to intensify parliamentary pressure on the government, cabinet met on 17 March 1977 purportedly to discuss direct elections (*The Times*, 17.3.77). However, as Merlyn Rees (home secretary) and his officials had not yet drafted the long-awaited white paper, no decision could be taken (*The Times*, 18.3.77). Thus, no bill had been introduced to Parliament when the government, now in a minority position in the House of Commons, found itself faced with a Conservative vote of confidence, due for debate on 23 March 1977.

This vote was the trigger for negotiation of the Lib–Lab pact, which lasted from March 1977 to July 1978 (Steel, 1980), and through it for increased progress on the direct elections issue. A central Liberal demand made during secret negotiations conducted by Callaghan, Foot and the Liberal leader David Steel between 7 and 23 March 1977 was that the long-promised European Assembly elections bill both contain a commitment to proportional representation, and receive priority in the government's legislative timetable (Steel, 1980: 37; Marsh, 1990: 293). When a special cabinet met on 23 March it had the choice of either endorsing this arrangement, or of rejecting it and thereby courting certain defeat in the House. It was judged by foreign secretary David Owen (1992: 290) to be 20–4 in favour of the pact. The no confidence motion was defeated in the House of Commons by 322 votes to 298.

The Lib–Lab pact meant that there was now an extra dimension to cabinet system treatment of the direct elections issue. The pact had two main features: a set of policy objectives, and a mechanism for cooperation between the Labour and Liberal front-benches comprising both direct contact, chiefly on a one-to-one basis, and a consultative committee of Labour and Liberal leaders (Marsh, 1990: 299). A central policy objective such as PR for direct elections to the European Assembly was therefore expected to be developed in a cooperative fashion by the two party leaderships. Cabinet was thus yet further constrained.

A 'consultative' white paper (appropriately) published by Rees on 1 April 1977 set out four options: (i) an FPP system, (ii) a regional list PR system, (iii) a single-transferable-vote (STV) PR system, and (iv) a combination of any one of these three with a compulsory dual mandate which would make membership of the House of Commons an essential condition for membership of the European Assembly. Northern Ireland was recognised to be a special case, to which STV would apply. However, when Rees finally put a draft bill before cabinet on 21 April 1977, it was drafted on the basis of FPP. This evidently made a mockery of the consultative white paper, and also conflicted with the quasi-obligation felt by Callaghan to adopt PR. It probably represented an attempt to win Labour Party support. Now, however, the government also needed to maintain Liberal Party support, which was very strongly premised on PR. Callaghan thus told ministers that he had given the Liberals his word on PR, and threatened resignation if they did not back him (Benn, 1990: 116). Foot, Benn, Peter Shore (environment secretary) and Stan Orme (social security secretary) spoke against the principle of direct elections, and sought a free vote in the House (Benn, 1990: 117). At the end of a lengthy discussion, no decision was taken. One week later, on 28 April 1977, cabinet was also devoted almost entirely to direct elections. The Rees draft bill had now been rewritten on the basis of a regional list PR system. Again Callaghan threatened resignation. Again no decision was taken (Benn, 1990: 121).

Instead, the issue began to drift out of cabinet system control. Callaghan was under strong and conflicting pressure from the Liberals and dissenting ministers within his own cabinet. By May 1977, this latter group had swollen to six members: Foot, Benn, Shore, Orme, John Silkin (agriculture secretary) and Albert Booth (employment secretary). Some of these ministers were thought to be prepared to resign rather than vote for direct elections (*The Times*, 6.6.77). Furthermore, Callaghan faced problems in the wider Labour Party. At a meeting of the TUC–Labour Party liaison committee on 23 May, direct elections were discussed. At a meeting of the NEC on 25 May, Callaghan stated that division on the issue of direct elections could wreck the Labour Party (*The Times*, 26.5.77).

On 13 June 1977, within the framework of the Lib–Lab pact, Callaghan showed a draft bill to Steel (1980: 54). At least nine individual contacts between Liberal MPs and Labour ministers took place over the following two days in June, when the issue was before cabinet. However, at a meeting of the Lib–Lab consultative committee on 15 June, the Liberals rejected the government's proposals (Steel, 1980: 55–7). At five subsequent meetings they maintained pressure on the government until, on 26 June, Callaghan accepted the Liberal approach, and at the same time agreed to allow all members of the Parliamentary Labour Party (PLP) (including ministers) a free vote on the issue. For a measure contained in the queen's speech for the session, the move was unprecedented (Marsh, 1990: 299).

To sustain the Lib–Lab pact, the bill that was presented to the House of Commons in June 1977 thus indicated a government preference for a regional list PR system for European Assembly elections. To prevent a cabinet revolt, a free vote was taken on the second reading of the European Assembly elections bill on 7 July 1977. Although the vote on the principle of direct elections was passed by 394 votes to 147, there were six cabinet ministers and 26 junior ministers among the No votes. Only 40 per cent of the PLP had voted for the bill, which passed on opposition votes.

As the bill could not complete its passage in the 1976–7 session of Parliament, it was reintroduced in the next session. A further successful vote on principle was held on 24 November 1977, dissident ministers (and more than half of the PLP) this time abstaining on a three-line whip. A subsequent vote on method of election was held on 13 December 1977. In a free vote, the government was defeated by 319 votes to 222 on its proposal that a regional list PR system be adopted, 147 Labour members voting against the government. For Britain, FPP was chosen. In Northern Ireland, STV was felt to be the only appropriate system (*The Times*, 14.12.77).

Exit from the cabinet system

Community-wide European Assembly elections could not now be arranged for the target date of May–June 1978. The first direct elections were instead held in June 1979. Only in Britain did they not embody some form of PR.

Analysis

Direct elections to the European Assembly was a policy issue which was determined chiefly by external factors. It had been inherited by the Labour government in 1974, and its chief character was the displeasure with which ministers viewed it. In no sense was this a policy which the Labour government itself sought to pursue. It was impelled by its European commitments and, later, by the conditions of the Lib–Lab pact, to do so. In the event, the outcome of the case was determined by this external drive, and by the firm desire of the British House of Commons, including a substantial minority of Labour MPs, not to allow a PR system to be adopted for nationwide elections in Britain.

Key shaping points relate initially to prime ministerial initiative: the commitments made by Wilson at the European Councils of December 1974 and December 1975, and by Callaghan at the European Council of September 1976. Yet none of these moves was definitive, for on 26 June 1977 cabinet ministers secured free votes on both the issue of principle and the issue of detail, and thereby released themselves from earlier prime ministerial commitments. This more than any other shaping point determined the precise outcome of the issue. Final decisions were taken in Parliament on 24 November and 13 December 1977. By these points, the issue had been substantially diluted.

Key initiating actors were Wilson, Callaghan, Rees and Home Office and FCO officials. With members of the European secretariat, they were also key organising actors. Yet these central actors were not able either to maintain the initiative or to control the passage of the issue, both of which were from time to time taken over by other actors within cabinet, in the Liberal Party and in the EEC. Foot played a pivotal role in mediating between cabinet factions. Although Callaghan threatened resignation on at least two occasions, he neither carried out his threat, nor secured much from it.

The issue reveals unusual aspects of the cabinet system. Lack of central control over its passage meant that it took an extremely unorthodox course through the system. Direct elections were debated at length in cabinet, the classic central forum of British cabinet government. They were also considered both in innovatory institutional procedures created by the Lib–Lab pact, and in the very traditional setting of the floor of the House of Commons. In the House, a special committee was created to consider the issue. The result of such broad discussion was that even policy options – such as method of election – which had been narrowed down were reopened and reconsidered. Throughout, policy making was thus highly inclusive, partly because a key constitutional issue was at stake, but more importantly because on pragmatic grounds of party unity and Lib–Lab pact maintenance Callaghan could not afford to adopt an exclusive strategy. The procedure the government was forced to adopt shaped significantly the development and outcome of policy.

Party was an important factor, in terms of relations both with the Liberals and with Labour back-benchers.

This, then, is in one sense a case of ministerial veto of prime ministerial initiative. The veto was applied through cabinet itself, but it relied for at least part of its effectiveness on a broad Labour Party coalition. In these circumstances, only by means of reliance on cross-party support was Callaghan able to see his policy through to partial (and delayed) completion. In another sense, it is a case of a heavily constrained British polity responding in a reactive fashion to decisions taken externally to it.

Chrysler UK, 1975

Origins

At the end of 1975, Harold Wilson's Labour government faced a crisis in the British car industry. Although a number of reports had indicated that the industry was in difficulty the crisis, when it came, was unexpected and almost entirely of external generation. It concerned Chrysler UK (CUK), threatened with abrupt closure by its American parent, Chrysler Corporation (CC).

Reports detailing problems in the industry came from a number of sources. A CPRS report, *The Future of the British Car Industry*, presented to cabinet on 9 October 1975, argued that annual over-production in the British vehicle industry as a result of a worldwide decline in demand following the 1973 oil crisis stood at some 400 000 units. At the time, CUK's production was 365 000 units (Wilks, 1984: 127). Prior to the crisis, CC itself had also indicated that CUK faced particular problems. To consider government policy towards the car industry a cabinet committee, MISC 59, chaired by the prime minister, had already been set up before the crisis broke (Dell, 1992: 2).

The government thus had a general awareness of problems both in the British car industry and at CUK, but was nevertheless unprepared for the announcement made by CC at the end of October 1975 (Expenditure Committee, 1976: ch.4). On 29 October John Riccardo (CC chairman), in reporting worldwide CC losses of $231.8 million for the first nine months of 1975, identified CUK as a major loss-maker, and implied that corrective action would be taken. Any threat to CUK would clearly be problematic for the British government. CUK employed 26 000 at plants in Linwood (near Glasgow), Coventry and Stoke, and a similar number of jobs were dependent on it (Dell, 1992: 3). It had also negotiated a lucrative contract with the Shah to supply car kits to Iran, thereby making it an important contributor to Britain's balance of payments (Dell, 1992: 5–6).

Entry into and treatment by the cabinet system

At the time of its emergence, the CUK crisis was high priority and certainly obliged ministers to act. However, they neither understood the precise nature of the problem, nor perceived a solution to it. A government review of industrial policy which was close to completion was to conclude that in future government aid would be given only to industries that had 'a real prospect' (Granada Television, 1976: 49). Beyond this, ministers were feeling their way.

Although the CUK issue was briefly picked up by the DoI, it moved so quickly into the cabinet system that it was really a cabinet system matter from the start. On 30 October, Eric Varley (industry secretary) wrote to CC asking it to clarify its intentions. In response to Varley's letter on 3 November, CC

179

executives flew to London to discuss CUK's future at a two-hour meeting with ministers. The meeting, held at Chequers, included on the Chrysler side Riccardo, Eugene Cafiero (CC president), Gwain Gillespie (CC executive vice-president Europe), W. W. Larsen (CC vice-president public affairs), Gilbert Hunt (CUK chairman), Don Lander (CUK managing director) and Sir Eric Roll (chairman of S G Warburg, CUK's merchant bank; CUK board member; ex-permanent secretary to the Department of Economic Affairs). The government side included Wilson, Varley, Edmund Dell (paymaster general), Sir John Hunt (cabinet secretary), Sir Peter Carey (second permanent secretary to the DoI), Sir Kenneth Berrill (CPRS head) and Kenneth Stowe (prime minister's principal private secretary) (Dell, 1992: 2; Expenditure Committee, 1976: 60–1).

At this meeting, CC issued what was in effect an ultimatum, described by Wilson (1979: 197) as 'blackmail'. For US tax reasons, it would liquidate CUK by 1 January, and pull out of Britain by March 1976 (Wilks, 1984: 128). If the government wanted CC to stay it would have to cover nearly all costs. Alternatively, the government could have CUK for nothing. The government was thus faced with three unpalatable options: liquidation, permanent subsidy of CUK or nationalisation. As soon as the meeting was over, the issue was referred to MISC 59 (Dell, 1992: 2). Under Wilson's chairmanship the members were Denis Healey (chancellor of the exchequer), James Callaghan (foreign secretary), Michael Foot (employment secretary), William Ross (Scottish secretary), Peter Shore (trade secretary), Varley, Harold Lever (chancellor of the Duchy of Lancaster) and Dell (Granada Television, 1976: 49).

On 4 November a team of officials led by Richard Bullock (deputy secretary, DoI, in charge of the motor vehicles division) met a CUK team headed by Hunt, Lander and Roll (Granada Television, 1976: 49). Later, MISC 59 discussed the issue (Castle, 1980: 545). It took a hard line on the CC ultimatum, agreed that options should be explored by a team of DoI officials under Bullock, and appointed a negotiating team under Varley and Dell (Wilks, 1984: 128–9). Varley, plus officials, met Riccardo that afternoon, and agreed that the government should be given time to examine the options (Dell, 1992: 5). Riccardo departed for Detroit saying 'the ball is now in the government's court' (Granada Television, 1976: 49).

Much activity now took place in MISC 59. On 6 November in a paper to the committee, Varley argued against nationalisation, but in favour of a phased closure of CUK over 12 months, with costs being shared equally by CC and the British government. He was also in favour of immediate publication of the CPRS report, as a means of substantiating the genuine problems of the British motor industry. In a paper, Ross argued that the government must save Linwood. Treasury ministers took an even harder line than Varley, arguing against nationalisation and against phased closure (Dell, 1992: 6–7). The committee concluded that the government could not save CUK but that it should attempt to preserve the Iranian contract, possibly through transfer to British

Leyland (BL). It agreed that Lever should go to Iran immediately to explore this option (Dell, 1992: 7). On 11 November, an oral report which reflected the hard line of MISC 59 was made to cabinet. Benn (1989: 460) reports that 'Harold Wilson said it [CUK] wasn't a lame duck, it was a dead duck'. On 12 November Varley, in a paper to MISC 59 which noted that CC's position was unchanged, again took a hard line on the government's response. The general view of the meeting was also against compromise with CC (Dell, 1992: 8).

Riccardo returned to Britain on 17 November for a second phase of meetings with the British government. Present on the government side were Varley, Dell, Gerald Kaufman (minister of state, DoI), Berrill, Sir Antony Part (permanent secretary to the DoI), DoI and Treasury officials and, for the first time, Ross and his officials (Expenditure Committee, 1976: 68). Varley told Riccardo that the government would not nationalise CUK, and that it was only willing to provide limited financial aid under sections 7 and 8 of the Industry Act 1975 (Wilks, 1984: 133). Riccardo created opportunities for further development of the issue with a new proposal which soon became known as scheme B (Dell, 1992: 9). The government should nationalise CUK and pay the cost of the envisaged 11 000 redundancies. CC would manage the company under contract. The new company was predicted to break even after losses of £40 million in the first two years.

After the meeting of 17 November, the CPRS submitted a new paper to ministers. It presented a hierarchy of options: allow CUK to close and transfer the Iranian contract to BL; keep the Stoke plant for the Iranian contract; keep Linwood for the Iranian contract (Dell, 1992: 10). At MISC 59 on 20 November, Varley continued to argue for closure, and was supported by Dell and Lever. Ross argued for scheme B. The committee concluded that negotiations with CC should continue. Varley therefore wrote to Riccardo on 21 November to explore options further. He received a reply from Roll, dated 24 November, which confirmed the CC view that some compromise on the basis of scheme B was possible.

Before cabinet on 25 November, Wilson met Varley and Ross. Ross insisted that he would resign if Linwood was closed (Donoughue, 1994: 78). At cabinet, Varley presented a hardline paper which made four key recommendations: no nationalisation; introduce import restrictions on cars; announce a redundancy scheme; publish the CPRS report. Ross again expressed his support for scheme B. Cabinet agreed to extend negotiations with CC (Dell, 1992: 14). Once the meeting had finished, Wilson lunched with Bruce Millan (minister of state, Scottish Office), and discovered that his position was the same as that of Ross. Should Linwood close, Wilson was therefore faced with two ministerial resignations from the Scottish Office, and great difficulty in finding a credible secretary of state (Donoughue, 1994: 78). At a time of substantial Scottish National Party (SNP) advance in Scotland, this was not a pleasant prospect. That day, Wilson therefore wrote a memorandum to Varley stating that Millan should attend all future meetings with Riccardo, so that he could see for himself the full measure of Riccardo's intransigence (Dell, 1992: 14). He also instructed Hunt to tell officials in the DoI that rapid closure of Chrysler must be prevented. In addition, he asked Bernard Donoughue (head of the PMPU) to attend future top-level meetings on Chrysler as his representative, chiefly to 'save Ross' (Donoughue, 1994: 78–9). During the next few days, Wilson's agenda was dominated by the Rome European Council of 1–2 December.

A third round of meetings duly took place. On 26 November, Varley, Kaufman, Ross, Millan and Dell, plus eight officials, met eight CC representatives (including Riccardo and Roll). A new CC offer, known as scheme B financial, was on the table. It consisted of two options. The government could nationalise CUK, in which case CC would contribute £35 million. Alternatively, CC could retain a 20 per cent equity stake in a publicly owned CUK, and contribute £13 million (Dell, 1992: 15; Expenditure Committee, 1976: 68). On 27 November, before cabinet, Varley, Dell and Millan met Riccardo to discuss the matter further (Dell, 1992: 17). The issue again went to cabinet later that day. Millan, attending in place of Ross who was in Scotland (Expenditure Committee, 1976: 68), argued strongly in favour of rescue. Cabinet remained sceptical of scheme B, but decided to continue negotiations with CC against the wishes of Varley and the DoI. After cabinet, the government and CC agreed to commission an independent investigation of scheme B by government auditors Coopers and Lybrand (C&L). C&L concluded on 2 December that scheme B was not viable. Also at this time, Varley and Foot met leading trade unionists on 1 December, Foot wrote a paper on the job implications of closure, and Varley and his officials wrote a further hardline paper for cabinet on 2 December (Dell, 1992: 18–20).

At cabinet on 4 December, Varley argued on the basis of the C&L report that scheme B was not viable, and again stated his preference for closure. Ross again insisted that Linwood must be saved. Cabinet was in fact about to reject the renewed CC offer, when Wilson asked Lever for his opinion (Granada Television, 1976: 23). To this point little more than a marginal participant in the saga, Lever stated that the papers did not provide sufficient basis for judgement, and that the government's negotiators had not probed far enough. Scheme B, he thought, might be viable. Wilson therefore asked Lever to look at the papers, and report back the next day (Castle, 1980: 579–80; Dell, 1992: 21).

Lever duly presented his findings to a special cabinet on 5 December. He concluded that scheme B was not in fact viable (Dell, 1992: 22), but proposed that the government call CC's bluff by offering to meet a slimmed-down CUK's forecast loss of £40 million over the first two years of operations, and also offering to share with CC any further losses (or profits) over the first four years. Ross backed the proposal because it would save Linwood. Foot supported it because redundancies would be minimalised. Shore saw in it a means of avoiding import controls, which were already attracting international opposition. Even Healey appeared to be in favour, largely on cost grounds (Wilks,

1984: 139). After a lengthy and heated argument, cabinet agreed that Lever should join the negotiating team to put this deal to CC.

That evening, and on the following day, 6 December (a Saturday), the negotiating team of Varley, Lever, Ross, Dell and officials met CC at the start of the fourth and final round of meetings (Granada Television, 1976: 52; Dell, 1992: 23–6). Riccardo accepted the principle of the loss-sharing proposal, but objected to the detail: £40 million was not enough (Wilks, 1984: 141). The British team disagreed about what cabinet had actually agreed to offer CC. CC, pushing at an opening door, also asked for a government-guaranteed loan of £35 million from Finance for Industry, and an unsecured £55 million government loan to finance the development of new models. Varley and Dell remained in favour of closure (Donoughue, 1994: 80).

On the morning of 8 December MISC 59 met to discuss the size of the government's loss-sharing offer. Varley argued that the grant should be £40 million in the first year, plus no more than £5 million (half of losses up to £10 million) in each of the agreed four years, making a maximum government commitment of £60 million. However, the committee agreed to Lever's proposal of a maximum grant of £72.5 million. In the afternoon, further negotiations took place, and CC agreed to the £72.5 million figure. It also offered to invest £10–12 million to enable its new C6 Alpine model, then built in France, to be assembled at Ryton. Lever immediately welcomed this. In the evening, MISC 59 discussed whether to grant the £55 million loan without a written guarantee from CC. It accepted Lever's compromise that £28 million should be with a written guarantee, and £27 million without (Granada Television, 1976: 52).

In the early morning of 11 December, Riccardo met the negotiating team and reluctantly agreed to guarantee £28 million of the loan. At 9.30 a.m., in cabinet, Wilson announced that CC was likely to accept the deal, but full discussion was postponed to a special cabinet the next day (Granada Television, 1976: 53). In MISC 59 later that day, a majority, including Wilson, favoured the rescue scheme. Varley did not, and reserved the right to state his opposition in full cabinet. The Treasury was divided, Healey being in favour and Dell against (Dell, 1992: 81).

Varley was reported to be considering resignation on 12 December, but after seeing Wilson before the special cabinet agreed to remain in office. A large meeting at the DoI secured final agreement in principle, leaving detailed drafting to be undertaken over the weekend of 12–15 December (Expenditure Committee, 1976: 75). In cabinet that same day, Varley argued against the deal and was supported by Roy Jenkins (home secretary), Roy Mason (defence secretary), Fred Mulley (education secretary), Shirley Williams (prices and consumer protection secretary), Reg Prentice (overseas development secretary) and Dell. Others, including Healey, Foot, Anthony Crosland (environment secretary), Shore, Lever and Ross, argued for it (Granada Television, 1976: 53; Wilks, 1984: 145). Wilson summed up by registering cabinet's acceptance of the deal (Castle, 1980: 610).

Exit from the cabinet system

The special cabinet's decision was announced by Varley to the House of Commons on 16 December. The government's contingent liabilities in respect of CUK were then put by him at £162.5 million (Expenditure Committee, 1976: 8). The final agreement between the British government, CC and CUK was signed on 5 January 1976.

Analysis

The outcome of this case was determined chiefly by the political pressures which the British government felt, and which CC was able to exploit. The final decision to save CUK was at odds with the government's own position on industrial support adopted in early November. Indeed, from the start, most participants recognised that there was no economic rationale for anything other than closure. This view was consistently expressed by the DoI team. However, for political reasons a pattern of negotiation was sustained until it produced a compromise solution. In effect, attention shifted from the economic merits of the case to political considerations. Crucial to this shift was the position of the two Scottish ministers. The outcome of the case was also shaped by time pressures, with decisions being taken in a constrained, six-week period.

There were a number of key shaping points in development of the issue. The first was CC's ultimatum of 3 November. The second was CC's announcement of scheme B on 17 November. The third was the clear expression of opposition from the Scottish ministers, and the series of pro-compromise manoeuvres on which Wilson embarked from 25 November. The fourth was CC's announcement of scheme B financial on 26 November. The fifth was Lever's intervention in cabinet on 4 December, and his subsequent inclusion in the negotiating team. The sixth was agreement in MISC 59 on 11 December. The seventh was the special cabinet on 12 December, which finally endorsed the deal. On the government side, the most important shaping points were the events of 25 November, and the meeting of 4 December. Final decisions were taken partly in cabinet committee, and partly in informal arenas. Policy was substantially made in the cabinet system.

Key initiating actors were the Riccardo and Varley teams. Other members of the government's negotiating team also subsequently took important initiatives. Key here were Dell and Treasury officials, Ross, Millan and Scottish Office officials, and Lever. All set terms of debate to which others had to respond. The main organising actors were Wilson and his cabinet system advisers and officials. These key actors drew in other central participants, such as those members of MISC 59 and cabinet not on the negotiating team. CPRS officials played a significant part in advising ministers. Other senior officials and advisers were even involved in negotiations.

The case reveals a number of aspects of cabinet system operations. At one level, it took orthodox routes through the system, being handled chiefly in cabinet committee and frequently being discussed in full cabinet. However, because the issue was based on negotiation within severe time constraints, at another level less orthodox and more flexible procedures were followed. Negotiating teams of both ministers and officials worked on details which were fed through formal cabinet and committee for discussion and approval. In a very unorthodox manner, the issue was at the last moment removed from the control of the lead department, the DoI, and placed in the hands of Lever. In consequence, Varley nearly resigned. The role of procedure was not constraining until towards the end of the case. Until 5 December, the government's chief objective was simply to keep CC talking, and in this sense cabinet procedures were positively helpful. When, on 5 December, the government moved into finalising the deal, procedures may well have been frustrating for Lever in particular. There is, however, no indication that the outcome of the case was thereby altered. External factors were clearly key in placing the issue on the political agenda. Thereafter, they kept pressure on the government, but internal factors also came into play, mediated by the Scottish ministers in particular. They, if anyone, exercised an effective veto. Wilson, conscious of the need to maintain the unity of his government, skilfully engineered the opportunity for an acceptable compromise.

The IMF crisis, 1976

Origins

In autumn 1976, a run on the pound obliged the British government to secure a loan from the International Monetary Fund (IMF). The difficulties facing the Callaghan government at this time were partly inherited, and partly a consequence of earlier policy decisions: sterling's weakness reflected deep-seated economic problems. The pound's problems on international money markets generated a strong external dimension to the issue.

The scale of Britain's economic problems was reflected in late 1975 figures for inflation of 23 per cent, a public sector borrowing requirement (PSBR) of around £12 billion, and a growing balance of payments deficit. In January 1976, the Wilson government had attempted to control public finances by making significant expenditure cuts (Donoughue, 1987: 85). The successor Callaghan government was deeply constrained by a Commons majority of only three seats, a fractious parliamentary party, and the necessity to maintain trade union support for a voluntary prices and incomes policy. In international financial markets and the US Treasury Department, the British government was seen as profligate. These factors meant that ministers' and officials' freedom of manoveure was severely limited.

Entry into and treatment within the government machine

In early 1976, the Treasury and Bank of England were both deeply divided about exchange rate policy (Dell, 1991: 179–80). In the Treasury, the predominant view was that sterling was overvalued at just over $2. A float to around $1.90 could engender export-led growth for the beleaguered British economy. Certainly the value of the pound should not be allowed to appreciate. Thus, when on 3 March 1976 the pound began to rise on international markets, the Bank of England surreptitiously intervened to sell sterling. Two days later, a prearranged quarter-point cut in interest rates to 9 per cent further weakened sterling. Quite coincidentally, other holders of sterling also sold at this time. The effect of all these moves was to precipitate a run on the pound. It is unclear whether the Treasury and Bank were deliberately pursuing a secret policy of controlled devaluation, or whether they simply acted inadvertently and unintentionally (Burk and Cairncross, 1992: 29; *Contemporary Record*, 1989: 42; Fay and Young, 1978: 10–11). The crisis of confidence was not helped by the sudden resignation of Harold Wilson on 16 March, and his subsequent replacement as prime minister by James Callaghan.

By June 1976 sterling had fallen to $1.71. In order to defend the currency, chancellor of the exchequer Denis Healey on 7 June raised a six-month standby loan of $5.3 billion from international bankers for use against any run on sterling. The US Treasury insisted on the time limit, and the condition that Britain apply to the IMF if it could not repay the loan at the end of six months (Burk and Cairncross, 1992: 44; Fay and Young, 1978: 8).

On 21 July, cabinet agreed further expenditure cuts of £1 billion for the year 1977–8, plus a 2 per cent surcharge on employers' national insurance contributions. The government also secured TUC agreement to a 4.5 per cent pay norm. The markets were briefly reassured, but the pound came under pressure once more in the late summer. Initially, the Bank of England intervened to support sterling, but on 9 September Healey instructed it to stop. Over $1.6 billion of the standby loan had already been spent (Callaghan, 1987: 436). The following day, interest rates were raised from 11.5 per cent to 13 per cent.

Entry into and treatment within the cabinet system

The issue was discussed at a meeting of the cabinet's economic policy (EY) committee on 23 September, and can be said to have entered the cabinet system at this point. Healey told colleagues that he expected to have to apply for an IMF loan (Burk and Cairncross, 1992: 55), but only to cover the amount of standby money which had already been used (Fay and Young, 1978: 19). He stated that he intended to explore this option at a forthcoming IMF conference in Manila. This was the perceived solution to the government's problem at the issue's point of entry into the cabinet system. Ministers had to act, and gave the issue high priority.

However, on 28 September the pound fell to $1.64, and Healey cancelled his trip in order to deal with the crisis. On the following day, with Callaghan's agreement (Burk and Cairncross, 1992: 57), he announced Britain's application to the IMF (Dell, 1991: 236). The pound continued to experience difficulty. Consequently, on 7 October, Healey raised interest rates to 15 per cent (Benn, 1989: 620). Callaghan initially refused to support this increase, but changed his mind after Healey effectively threatened to resign (Healey, 1990: 430–1). The decision to raise interest rates was endorsed by EY committee on the morning of the announcement (Burk and Cairncross, 1992: 61).

At this point, policy development broke into two strands. The first was pursued largely by the prime minister. Callaghan felt that the markets, in a quite uninformed way, were dictating policy and might bring down the government. Independently of the Treasury, he sought to create political breathing space by developing a way of funding the sterling balances. As sterling was still a reserve currency, money lodged by governments in London was often removed at short notice, increasing sterling's instability. Callaghan sought to use his contacts with world leaders to arrange a safety net which could be used whenever the movement of reserve funds placed pressure on the pound (Fay and Young, 1978: 24). He launched his policy on 30 September in telephone calls to West German Chancellor Helmut Schmidt, US President Gerald Ford and US Secretary of State Henry Kissinger. On 9 October, Callaghan met Schmidt. Unbeknown to the overseas finance division of the Treasury, Sir John Hunt (cabinet secretary) was then sent to Bonn to talk further.

To international leaders, Callaghan emphasised the dire political implications of draconian IMF terms for Britain. By the end of October the US, French and German leaders seemed sympathetic. In early November, Ed Yeo (deputy director of the US Treasury) visited Schmidt to persuade him not to do anything that might undermine the IMF initiative. Yeo found that Schmidt was not willing to act unilaterally to help the British (Fay and Young, 1978: 28). Callaghan now tried to gain the support of President Ford. He sent Harold Lever (chancellor of the Duchy of Lancaster and prime minister's adviser on financial policy) to Washington on 14 November to press the idea that a safety net agreement should be announced simultaneously with the IMF loan agreement, to allow the government to maintain elements of an expansionary policy. The aim was to exploit a division of opinion between the US State and Treasury Departments over how best to handle the UK problem. The tactic failed. The US government agreed with the principle of a safety net for sterling, but insisted (in line with the US Treasury position) that the IMF terms be agreed first (Burk and Cairncross, 1992: 82; Callaghan, 1987: 433).

While initiatives were taking place at prime ministerial level, the second strand of policy development centred on a team of Treasury and Bank of England officials under Douglas Wass (permanent secretary to the Treasury), involved in negotiating a loan with a six-man IMF team under Alan Whittome (head of the IMF's European department). The IMF team arrived in London on 1 November (Fay and Young, 1978: 26). As Treasury officials were divided about both the need for a loan and the exact conditions which ought to be attached to it, progress was slow (Dell, 1991: 248). Whittome met Healey on 4 November. The two teams met in full for the first time on 10 November, and on at least five occasions over the next fortnight (*Contemporary Record*, 1989: 44; Fay and Young, 1978: 34). Each meeting was exploratory, seeking merely to clarify options.

At cabinet level during the first two weeks of November, discussion of possible conditions for an IMF loan was confined to the 11 ministers on EY committee, who met on three occasions to discuss the matter (Benn, 1989: 636–8; Dell, 1991: 254). At the end of an almost wholly separate exercise, on 11 November cabinet endorsed the cuts contained in the annual public expenditure white paper, but left open the possibility of further cuts (Barnett, 1982: 101–3). On 18 November, Callaghan reported the IMF situation to cabinet for the first time. He asked ministers to submit papers for discussion (Callaghan, 1987: 435). At least 14 papers were submitted (Burk and Cairncross, 1992: 96). On 19 November, full negotiations between the Treasury and IMF teams opened (Burk and Cairncross, 1992: 83). The IMF sought tough terms, including a £4 billion reduction in the PSBR (estimated at about £10.5 billion) over two years, plus tighter controls over money and credit (Fay and Young, 1978: 27).

Informal discussions now took place between ministers. On the night of 22 November, the day before the first full IMF cabinet, two separate groups met informally to survey their positions. A social–democratic group drawn together by Shirley Williams (education secretary) included Lever, David Ennals (health and social services secretary), Roy Hattersley (secretary of state for consumer protection) and William Rodgers (transport secretary). It had the tacit support of the absent Anthony Crosland (foreign secretary). All were opposed to further large-scale public spending cuts. A left-wing group brought together Michael Foot (lord president of the council), Tony Benn (energy secretary), Peter Shore (environment secretary), Albert Booth (employment secretary) and Stan Orme (social security secretary). This group was also opposed to further cuts, and favoured import controls (Crosland, 1982: 376; Dell, 1991: 258–9). In cabinet on 23 November, Healey presented the Treasury's proposals: a package of £1.5 billion in cuts, including a £500 million sale of British Petroleum (BP) shares (Benn, 1989: 652). At this point he had only two firm supporters in cabinet, Edmund Dell (trade secretary) and Reg Prentice (secretary of state for overseas development). Discussion of the IMF issue in the following cabinet, on 25 November, was limited. Fuller discussion of all papers submitted was put off until the next week (Burk and Cairncross, 1992: 89). Cabinet, at this stage, contained a centre–left majority against a deflationary package. Without the prime minister's clear support, the chancellor and the Treasury package were vulnerable.

Callaghan's position at this stage is open to interpretation. He says that for some time he had privately supported the loan package, provided that the PSBR cut was restricted to £1 billion (Callaghan, 1987: 433–4; Donoughue, 1987: 97). Others believe that he was yet to be convinced (Dell, 1991: 258, 277–8). As Callaghan's main concern was to hold the government together, he accepted the need to let ministers discuss the issue at length (Dell, 1991: 262). He also recognised the pivotal position of Crosland (Callaghan, 1987: 434), with whom he discussed the matter on 30 November at a European council meeting. There they met Schmidt, who made it clear that he was not willing to intervene with the IMF to secure better terms. On the flight back to London Callaghan told Crosland that at the decisive cabinet he would support Healey (Callaghan, 1987: 438).

When cabinet next met on 1 December, the start of the meeting was delayed from 10 a.m. to 10.30 a.m. (Benn, 1989: 661) because of the unexpected and secret arrival of Johannes Witteveen (IMF managing director), who was on a one-day visit to Callaghan and Healey (Burk and Cairncross, 1992: 92–3). After a short and heated exchange, he was asked to await the end of the day's cabinet, which considered the papers that had been submitted (Benn, 1989: 664–5). Discussion centred on a scheme to act on imports as a means of reducing the PSBR, and thus avoid spending cuts. All alternative proposals were subjected to close scrutiny and found wanting, but no decisions were taken (Benn, 1989: 662–9). After cabinet, Callaghan was persuaded by Witteveen that the loan could be granted only on stringent conditions (Fay and Young, 1978: 32). Witteveen sought a £2 billion cut in spending for 1977–8. Healey stated that only cuts of £1 billion could be contemplated (Healey, 1990: 431). That evening Crosland met Hattersley, Lever and Williams. Lever stated that he would support Healey. Williams also appeared to be shifting. Crosland informed Callaghan of his support that evening (Crosland, 1982: 380–1; Burk and Cairncross, 1992: 100). Opposition to the Treasury package was crumbling.

Cabinet, on 2 December, was decisive. Healey outlined his proposals once more and stated that, with cabinet backing, he would put them to the IMF team. Callaghan finally declared in favour of the chancellor (Callaghan, 1987: 440; Benn, 1989: 673). Crosland and a series of ministers then did likewise. A total of 15 ministers favoured the package, five were against and three expressed reservations (Benn, 1989: 674–8). Cabinet authorised the chancellor to offer the IMF a £1 billion reduction in the PSBR in 1977–8, followed by £1.5 billion in 1978–9, plus £500 million in BP share sales. He was also authorised to test the idea of import deposits with the IMF team (Benn, 1989: 678–9). Cabinet had accepted the position it had previously rejected on 23 November (Burk and Cairncross, 1992: 102). No minister resigned.

On 3 December Healey met the IMF team to put the cabinet's offer. Negotiations collapsed when the IMF team insisted on tighter conditions, and returned to Washington. However, within two days it was back in London with a more flexible position (Callaghan, 1987: 440–1), which appears to have comprised a slightly larger PSBR cut than Callaghan had sought (Benn, 1989: 685). Cabinet now began the task of agreeing the package of cuts at a special meeting on the afternoon of Monday 6 December, at its regular meeting and a further evening meeting on 7 December, and at its regular meeting on 9 December (Benn, 1989: 686; Barnett, 1982: 106). A draft letter of intent (containing loan conditions) was finalised by the Treasury and PMPU over the weekend of 10–13 December (Donoughue, 1987: 98), and put before cabinet on 14 December.

Exit from the cabinet system

Healey announced details of the letter, and of the government's package, to the House of Commons on 15 December. The PSBR was to be cut by £3.5 billion over two years (including the BP sale), domestic credit expansion was to be restricted, and import deposits were ruled out (Burk and Cairncross, 1992: 107). The chancellor formally announced the safety net agreement in the House on 11 January 1977 (Fay and Young, 1978: 45).

Analysis

The outcome of the IMF crisis was determined chiefly by external factors, in the context of which cabinet system actors sought to find, or create, political breathing space. When the standby facility negotiated in July failed to bolster sterling, the issue shifted from whether to seek a loan, to possible terms. On both matters the government found itself with little room for manoeuvre. Even detailed policy making was largely driven externally. The result was a package of expenditure cuts which the overwhelming majority of cabinet members had neither sought nor foreseen in September.

External constraints meant that key shaping points in policy development were not so much formal decisions as the wider factors which conditioned them. Loss of control over currency movements in March, the terms of the standby loan in July and continuing lack of international confidence in the British economy were all important. Within this broad context, key shaping points were the decision on 23 September to apply for a loan, Callaghan's international lobbying which brought the political dimension of the crisis into play, Callaghan's decision to back Healey, Crosland's shift, the cabinet on 1 December which ruled out the main alternatives, the meeting with Witteveen immediately thereafter, and the cabinet on 2 December when a final decision was taken and the Treasury's original proposals were endorsed. The final decision point was therefore cabinet. By this point, the initial solution envisaged by Healey had been expanded, in reaction to deepening of the sterling crisis.

Key actors were Callaghan, Healey, Lever, Crosland, officials in the Treasury and Bank of England plus a number of external individuals. The key initiating actors were both external and internal to British government. Externally, currency market judgements pushed the issue on to the agenda. US Treasury officials made sure that it stayed there. Internally, Healey and Treasury officials controlled (and possibly mismanaged) early development of the issue. They also supplied most serious information and options on which decisions were reached, and conducted negotiations with the IMF team. Other key actors, notably Callaghan and Lever, attempted to expand the area of discretion available by moving outside the Treasury ambit, but their initiative failed to weaken the Treasury's hold on the issue. In late stages of policy development, cabinet held nine full meetings, but this was chiefly an exercise in collective learning and in coming to terms with the inevitable.

A number of lessons about cabinet system operations are revealed. The issue took highly orthodox pathways through the system. Indeed, on the face of it this is a classic example of collective cabinet decision making. However, the fact that cabinet was brought into debate at a very late stage when the issue had already gained a high degree of momentum and pressure for a settlement was increasing by the day rather undermines this perception. Procedure was not particularly constraining in this case. The major constraints were external, and the main impact of British government procedures was to retard policy development slightly as Callaghan struggled to secure cabinet endorsement of a decision which was in many ways programmed from outside. Party operated as a contextual constraint, but had little direct impact on policy development.

The role of the individual was more significant. Indeed, the skill with which the cabinet system was used by Callaghan to ensure ministerial compliance to a major policy adjustment is a key feature of the case. His aim, once he had grasped what was going on, was to maximise his limited freedom of manoveure, and to limit the extent of any damage. His pursuit of the sterling balances issue could be seen as a diversion, but it did help to soften pressure from the US Treasury and may, in consequence, have contributed to a more generous settlement on the part of the IMF than was originally on offer. The case also reveals the difficult position of a chancellor who does not have prime ministerial backing and, conversely, the strength of these two figures in alliance. Nevertheless, the prime minister was brought in at a relatively late stage of policy making and, on an issue crucial to the survival of his government, found himself excluded from some central areas of policy making. In sum, the case reveals the important influence of external factors on domestic economic policy development. Within such a context, opportunities for cabinet system actors to exert influence are severely constrained.

Trident, 1977–82

Origins

Britain's decision to purchase the Trident nuclear weapons system from the United States in 1982 is a classic case of policy-making continuity. As all accounts make clear, the decision of the first Thatcher government was consistent with decisions taken by each of its predecessors since 1945 (see in particular Malone, 1984: ch.5; Hennessy, 1986: ch.4; Greenaway, Smith and Street, 1992: ch.9). The manner in which the Thatcher government took its decision was also consistent with procedures adopted by most predecessor administrations. This is therefore very much a case of an inherited policy issue being managed in well-established ways.

Because policy making in the nuclear defence sphere has been so continuous, the background to this case is important. It may be traced to the 1947 decision of a small group of senior ministers in the Attlee government to develop a nuclear weapons programme. This decision has not been questioned by any subsequent government. Instead, all successor administrations – or, more usually, small groups of senior ministers and officials within them – have grappled with problems of modernising the British nuclear deterrent (Greenaway et al., 1992). In 1957, Britain began to develop a new generation of nuclear weapons, known as Blue Streak. Blue Streak was, however, cancelled in 1960 and Britain instead negotiated purchase of the US Skybolt system (Defence Committee, 1981: xxxix). When, in November 1962, Skybolt was in turn cancelled by the US, British prime minister Harold Macmillan at Nassau in December 1962 negotiated a very favourable purchase of the successor Polaris system from President John F. Kennedy. Britain's four-boat Polaris fleet, delivered on time and below budget, was operational by the late 1960s, but beginning to look ineffective by the early 1970s.

At this point the Heath government had the choice either of replacing Polaris with the successor US Poseidon system, or of upgrading it by means of what became known as the Chevaline project. For three main reasons, it favoured Chevaline (Greenaway et al., 1992: 187). The first was perceived cost savings. The second was that the US was already working on a further generation of nuclear weapons which could soon supersede Poseidon. The third was that a decision to upgrade Polaris would be less visible, and therefore less controversial, than a decision to buy a new generation of nuclear weapons. In fact, no final decision had been taken when the Heath government was defeated in the February 1974 general election. The decision to proceed with Chevaline was thus duly taken by five senior members of the minority Labour government which succeeded it. The decision may have been communicated to the cabinet's defence and overseas policy committee (Hennessy, 1986: 151).

On re-election to office in October 1974, Harold Wilson took the decision to cabinet. It was discussed there on 20 November 1974, and although debate was fairly wide ranging it was not (and could not be) based on detailed knowledge. Having attempted to square the decision to proceed with Chevaline with Labour's October 1974 manifesto renunciation of 'any intention of moving to a new generation of nuclear weapons', Wilson listened to the first few ministerial comments and then left to unveil a plaque to Churchill. Ted Short (lord president of the council) took the chair (Benn, 1989: 268). Barbara Castle (1980: 228) records that Wilson 'took himself off, looking pleased with himself, as well he might'. The decision to develop Chevaline was not announced to Parliament until 24 January 1980, by which time the Conservatives were in office (Cockerell *et al.*, 1984: 112).

Within three years, the issue of modernisation was again on the agenda. Discussion of the issue was well aired among specialist commentators on defence issues. Options for replacing Polaris, rather than merely upgrading it, became central to debate. MoD officials were almost certainly already thinking along similar lines, and at some point in 1977 'discreetly approached the Callaghan government to suggest that the problem merited consideration' (Malone, 1984: 106). The Treasury was also concerned about the increasing cost over-runs of the Chevaline project. Thus, in 1977, the idea of replacing Polaris had become a live option in government circles. It eventually resulted in the decision to purchase Trident from the US.

Entry into and treatment by the government machine

It is impossible to say how this issue developed departmentally within the British government system. Elements of that system which deal with nuclear weapons are notoriously secretive. However, it is clear that a small group of nuclear weapons insiders had been considering the issue for some time – possibly months, possibly years – before James Callaghan was approached in 1977. Central to this group will have been the MoD's chief scientific adviser, leading MoD officials and possibly also leading FCO officials. The chiefs of staff are likely to have been aware of developments. The cabinet secretary and a small number of individuals in the defence and overseas secretariat of the Cabinet Office would also probably have known of the policy initiative prior to the approach to Callaghan. However, if any such individuals were involved, they will themselves have been committed insiders.

Entry into and treatment by the cabinet system

Although the precise timing of entry of the issue into the cabinet system is therefore unclear it is best to date it at late 1977, when Callaghan responded to the request from the MoD by reconvening a ministerial group of four to consider strategic nuclear defence policy. This had been established by Wilson in 1974 (Owen, 1992: 380), and was in line with almost all previous governments' practice (Hennessy, 1986: ch.4). The group, which was not given a GEN number and therefore did not form part of the formal set of cabinet system committees, comprised Callaghan, Denis Healey (chancellor of the exchequer), David Owen (foreign secretary) and Fred Mulley (defence secretary) (Hennessy, 1979). It is unclear how frequently the committee met, but evident that it did so 'in conditions of exceptional secrecy' (Malone, 1984: 37). It was probably serviced on an informal basis by members of the Cabinet Office's defence and overseas secretariat, and by MoD and FCO officials. At entry into the cabinet system the nature of the problem was clear, but the solution was not. The issue was medium priority, but policy makers were not required to act.

The initial question exercising the ministerial group was whether to cancel the Chevaline project because of the 'scandalous' cost escalation which was taking place (Owen, 1992: 380). For varied reasons, it was decided not to do this. Nevertheless, the group did embark on sustained consideration of means by which the Polaris system might be replaced, and Chevaline superseded. Owen (1992: 381) reports that the MoD was in favour of the state-of-the-art technology embodied in the Trident system currently being developed by the US. He himself was in favour of the allegedly cheaper land-based cruise missile system, and used his own private office policy unit to develop arguments for what was known as the 'minimum credible deterrent'.

One of the reasons for convening the ministerial group of four was to provide 'ministerial approval' for studies which officials wanted to undertake (Hennessy, 1979). In January 1978, two Whitehall working parties were commissioned to look into possible replacements for Polaris. One, headed by Sir Anthony Duff (deputy secretary in the FCO), was asked to investigate the political and military implications of competing options. The other, headed by Professor Sir Ronald Mason (chief scientific adviser to the MoD), was asked to investigate possible delivery systems. The driving force on both working parties was said to be Michael Quinlan (deputy secretary in the MoD) (Hennessy, 1986: 153). The joint product of these two working parties was the Duff–Mason report, delivered to the ministerial group on 7 December 1978 'at virtually no notice' (Owen, 1987: 147). It recommended replacement of Polaris by Trident.

Debate within the group was now focused by the forthcoming Guadeloupe summit of 5–6 January 1979, at which Callaghan was to discuss matters nuclear with President Carter, President Giscard d'Estaing and Chancellor Schmidt (Owen, 1992: 380). The British insider group of four met on 21 December 1978 to brief Callaghan in advance of Guadeloupe. It discussed the Duff–Mason report, which favoured Trident, and a 38-page paper by Owen, which argued for minimum credible deterrence. At a second briefing meeting on 2 January 1979 it was decided that Callaghan would ask Carter whether Britain would be allowed to purchase Trident from the US, should it seek to do so at some future point in time (Callaghan, 1987: 553). Carter's response at the summit was favourable, and it was agreed that two British officials – Mason and Clive Rose (deputy secretary in the Cabinet Office) – would travel to Washington to discuss technical and financial aspects with their American counterparts (Callaghan, 1987: 556).

Hennessy (1986: 153) states that the Callaghan government – or the group of four within it – had taken the decision to buy Trident by the time the government fell in spring 1979. However, it is doubtful whether this was in fact the case, as both Callaghan (1987: 558) and Owen (1992: 403) emphatically deny it. What seems more likely is that by this time a consensus had emerged in both the MoD and FCO, and possibly also in the ministerial group of four, that a successor to Polaris would have to be bought, and that it should be submarine-based (thereby ruling out the cruise option favoured by Owen) (Greenaway *et al.*, 1992: 191). Even so, there may have been some residual dissent from this view within the MoD. The House of Commons defence select committee in its 1981 report implied as much when it stated that it had 'reason to believe that there is more than one view on this [the purchase of Trident] in the Ministry' (Defence Committee, 1981: lxii). What is nevertheless clear is that the Labour government left office without having chosen a successor to Polaris.

Policy development therefore passed to the incoming Thatcher government. Callaghan took unusual steps to preserve policy continuity in this decidedly atypical sphere. First, on 27 March 1979, on the eve of the confidence motion which brought his government down, he set out in a letter to Carter his understanding of the discussion at Guadeloupe, so that the matter would be on record. Secondly, on 4 May 1979, the day on which he left Downing Street for the last time, he wrote a final minute authorising his Conservative successor, Margaret Thatcher, to see both his correspondence with Carter on the issue and the Duff–Mason report of December 1978 (Callaghan, 1987: 557).

Thatcher quickly established her own insider group of five. In addition to the prime minister it comprised William Whitelaw (home secretary and deputy prime minister), Lord Carrington (foreign secretary), Sir Geoffrey Howe (chancellor of the exchequer) and Francis Pym (defence secretary). It was recorded as MISC 7 (Hennessy, 1986: 154), and unlike its Labour predecessor was therefore serviced as a normal cabinet committee. The practical difference may in fact have been slight. The new government embarked on fresh discussions with the Carter administration. In July 1979, Pym had exploratory discussions with his opposite number, Dr Harold Brown. By the end of September 1979 the ministerial group had come to the view that purchasing Trident from the Americans was the most promising option (Thatcher, 1993: 244). The group also considered purchasing Poseidon missiles from the US, and ways of upgrading Polaris, but decided against these options on cost grounds (Defence Committee, 1981: xliii). On 6 December 1979, the group took the decision to buy Trident. Thatcher (1993: 245) writes that this decision 'was later confirmed by Cabinet', though the level of debate was probably no greater than in Wilson's time as prime minister. A positive communiqué was issued after a Carter–Thatcher summit in Washington on 18 December 1979 (Defence Committee, 1981: xxxviii), and terms were formally finalised by Thatcher when she met US Defence Secretary Brown in Downing Street on 2 June 1980. A great deal of negotiation at official level must have preceded this meeting. The policy was announced to the House of Commons by Pym on 15 July 1980, and outlined in a 'Defence Open Government Document'.

In fact, the Trident purchase had not quite been fully decided. Issues concerning numbers of submarines and warheads remained to be determined, and were known to be significantly dependent on an expected US decision to move from the smaller Trident C4 to the larger Trident D5 system. The US upgrade was in fact made once Ronald Reagan had become president, and was announced on 2 October 1981. As Britain had negotiated purchase of C4, it was faced with the danger of being left with obsolete technology once again. Thatcher's inner group – which now included Sir John Nott in place of Pym as defence secretary – therefore reconvened in November 1981, and further UK-US discussions took place (Malone, 1984: 120). As there was considerable dissent in the ministerial group from Thatcher's view that Britain should seek to purchase not C4 but the more expensive D5, a further and fuller discussion based on a presentation (presumably by the MoD) was staged in January 1982. It seems likely that officials took the same view as Thatcher. The ministerial group duly endorsed her line. The decision was confirmed by cabinet later in the month, and a message was sent to Reagan on 1 February 1982 (Thatcher, 1993: 247). The terms which Reagan offered the British were unusually advantageous. Thatcher (1993: 248) was 'delighted', and authorised Nott to announce the purchase to the House of Commons on 11 March 1982.

Exit from the cabinet system

Once the purchase of Trident had been confirmed, an implementation phase was entered which saw the cost of Trident, like that of many of its predecessors, move beyond initial estimates to reach more than £10 billion.

Analysis

The outcome of this case was strongly influenced by the underlying continuity of policy making in this sphere, revealed most clearly in the unique steps taken by Callaghan to inform his successor of the details of policy development during his administration. The outcome was also heavily influenced by technological drive and bureaucratic momentum. Nevertheless, there was a decision to be taken, and it did allow for a fresh assessment of options within a very narrow set of parameters. Although Britain was clearly not going to abandon its nuclear defence capability at any point in the period 1977–82, its policy makers did have to decide what to do about an increasingly obsolete Polaris force. The decisions to switch from upgrade through Chevaline to the new generation of Trident nuclear weapons, and subsequently to buy D5 rather than C4, were therefore real rather than fully programmed from the start. They were, however, decisively shaped by the official consensus which seems to have emerged by May 1979 at the latest, and by the very good relations established between the two British prime ministers and American presidents involved in the case.

The first key shaping point was the mid-1977 decision – taken primarily in the MoD, but also influenced by Treasury concerns – to consider replacement options for Polaris. The second was Callaghan's agreement in January 1978 to create the Duff and Mason working groups, which within a year or so had generated an official consensus that Britain should replace Polaris with a submarine-based force. The third was the successful Callaghan–Carter meeting discussion in January 1979, which confirmed the willingness of the US to sell Trident to the UK, and set the tone for all subsequent UK–US negotiations discussions. The fourth was the decision in early autumn 1979 to buy Trident. The fifth was the January 1982 decision to buy D5 rather than C4. This decision was taken in cabinet committee, and was largely consistent with the official consensus which had emerged by 1979.

Key initiating actors were officials. Centrally important were the MoD's chief scientific adviser and leading officials in the MoD, FCO and the defence and overseas secretariat of the Cabinet Office. These individuals led policy development, though both prime ministers and cabinet secretaries were clearly critical in allowing them to do so. The same group of officials also constituted the main organising actors, as they drew into the policy process the various ministerial teams under both governments. Few other cabinet system actors were significantly drawn in to the process.

The case is of course atypical, but it nevertheless reveals a great deal about cabinet system operations. This issue took a highly unusual route through the cabinet system, until 1979 being discussed in a small and secretive unofficial group of ministers, and after that being discussed in an equally small, secretive and official group of ministers. In each case, the same leading ministers were involved. Other members of cabinet were effectively excluded from decision making, and cabinet itself genuinely did act merely as a rubber stamp in this sphere. On the official side, the number of participants was stable and restricted, with a small group of only marginally changing members directing policy. Perhaps 50 officials in total had access to information relating to nuclear defence policy (McIntosh, 1990: 122). The very great continuity of nuclear insiders is a key feature of this case. Their policy preferences remained paramount across governments of different political complexions.

Formal procedure was not constraining in this case, as almost no formal procedures were observed. By contrast, semi-formal procedures were highly significant in contributing to a situation in which ministers were presented with a single option, and effectively prevented from pursuing alternatives to it. External factors were also significant in shaping the outcome of the case, as successive US nuclear upgrades established new contexts to which British policy makers sought to respond. The role of the individual cannot really be highlighted, as the chief feature of this case is the tightly knit group of insiders which operated fairly collectively to produce an agreed outcome. Maverick proposals, like that of Owen, got nowhere. There was some room for prime ministerial initiative in negotiations with US presidents, but this too was largely programmed by the official consensus which had emerged by 1979. Party concerns failed to affect policy development, despite the Labour government's manifesto commitment.

This case thus reveals in very stark terms the limits on cabinet system policy-making competence. The initiative was taken by officials, not ministers, and the case was subsequently driven by the consensus which developed among them. The group which controlled policy was always small, secretive, closed and largely unaccountable. This is a case of expertise and secrecy placing very severe limits on cabinet system power.

The employment bill, 1979–80

Origins

The employment bill of 1979–80 had primarily party origins. In opposition in the 1970s, two main strands of Conservative thinking fed into it. An economic policy document, 'Implementing our Strategy', written by Chris Patten at the CRD, took a 'cautious and pragmatic' line on trade union reform (Howe, 1994: 105). A report written by Conservative advisers John Hoskyns and Norman Strauss, under the auspices of shadow chancellor Sir Geoffrey Howe and shadow industry spokesman Sir Keith Joseph, took a more radical line (Howe, 1994: 104). This 'Stepping Stones' report was presented to Thatcher on 17 November 1977, and strongly endorsed by her (Ranelagh, 1992: 219–20). However, when the two reports were discussed by the shadow cabinet on 30 January 1978, the gradualist line of shadow employment spokesman James Prior prevailed (Howe, 1994: 106). 'Stepping Stones' was remitted for further consideration by a group chaired by William Whitelaw. Caution was thus the Conservatives' watchword, and only Prior was allowed to make speeches on trade union reform.

This position was subsequently changed slightly. First, in summer 1978, other shadow spokesmen were permitted to speak on trade union matters. Howe (1994: 106) made two radical speeches. Secondly, during the 1978–9 'winter of discontent', a convergence of Conservative (and other) thinking around the more radical themes of 'Stepping Stones' took place. Yet when Margaret Thatcher set out the party's thinking on trade union reform in a party political broadcast on 15 January 1979, she listed essentially gradualist proposals, and did not follow the 'Stepping Stones' prescription of radicalising public debate (Howe, 1994: 107). Similarly, the 1979 Conservative manifesto was also gradualist in emphasis, limiting itself to piecemeal reform of trade union activity: a review of trade union immunities; the right of appeal and compensation for those made redundant by operation of a closed shop; public money for trade union ballots.

In developing an opposition policy on trade union reform Prior, as employment spokesman, thus prevailed over his radical shadow cabinet critics. The fact that Thatcher was herself disposed towards caution at this time clearly reinforced his position. 'In the battle for the election manifesto,' writes Stephenson (1980: 63), 'Prior won.' Furthermore, it was on this agenda (and no other) that Prior agreed to act when appointed secretary of state for employment in May 1979.

Entry into and treatment by the government machine

The employment bill entered the government machine with Prior's appointment to the Department of Employment (DEmp), and was initially developed chiefly there. From the start, however, cabinet system actors were kept informed of progress. As early as 14 May 1979, Prior wrote to Thatcher outlining his plans for trade union reform. The two met to discuss tactics on 6 June 1979. A cabinet paper containing outline proposals was then submitted by Prior two weeks later. In all essentials, the paper conformed very closely to the position taken in the manifesto and, indeed, to what eventually became the 1980 Act (Thatcher, 1993: 98–9). Its key aim was to change attitudes by means of a graduated attack on trade union power which did not invite set-piece confrontation.

The central executive took a sporadic interest in trade union reform during the summer and autumn of 1979. On 12 September 1979, Thatcher chaired a meeting with Prior, chancellor Howe and other colleagues to plan strategy (Thatcher, 1993: 100). That Prior did not have the unqualified support of a united cabinet was evident from statements made both in private and in public. A hostile speech given by Howe on the eve of the 1979 TUC conference was only the most evident example of this (Prior, 1986: 157).

Nevertheless, in the main this issue in its early stages was the preserve of the DEmp. A draft bill was drawn up by ministers and officials during the late summer and autumn of 1979. They had extensive – often almost daily – contact with Harry Urwin, deputy general secretary of the Transport and General Workers' Union (TGWU), and an acknowledged representative of the TUC (Stephenson, 1980: 68). They also kept in touch with the CBI. Detailed policy making in government thus conformed very much to the traditional consultative approach to industrial relations adopted by both major parties in the post-war period. Both the TUC and the CBI were consulted and given ample access to a secretary of state who was temperamentally inclined towards the consensual tradition of Conservative trade union relations, and to a department which remained very much neocorporatist in orientation.

Entry into and treatment by the cabinet system

It is hard to date precisely the moment when the employment bill entered the cabinet system. In a sense, it had been present in the system ever since the Conservative election victory of May 1979. However, it seems that most central executive discussion of the issue during the remaining months of 1979 was conducted either in Thatcher–Prior meetings, or just occasionally in larger *ad hoc* groups. It may have been considered – possibly in some detail – by the cabinet's economic (or E) committee during this period, and would certainly have been debated by this committee before first reading in the Commons. It must also have passed through legislation committee before being presented to Parliament in December 1979. However, it seems likely that substantial cabinet system involvement did not take place until late 1979, when the bill was already in draft. At this point, the issue was medium priority. Policy makers had a solution, but did not have to act.

An important context in which drafters of the employment bill operated was an imminent House of Lords ruling on a Court of Appeal judgement made in December 1978 with regard to secondary picketing. As both Prior (1986: 158) and Thatcher (1993: 102) recognised, there was always the possibility that the House of Lords ruling in *Express Newspapers* v *MacShane* might restrict trade union immunities, and thereby do some of the new government's work for it. Legislation in the sphere of secondary picketing might not even be necessary.

In this context, the employment bill was presented to Parliament and had its first reading on 7 December 1979. It had four main aims, each of which was consistent with manifesto commitments: to require unions to hold pre-strike ballots, to limit secondary picketing, to restrict the closed shop, and to undermine coercive trade union recruitment. It seems likely that the bill was discussed in cabinet in late November, where agreement was reached to draw the sting of trade union hostility by getting most parliamentary debate out of the way before Christmas (*The Times*, 1.12.79). Second reading was therefore set for 19 December.

However, on 13 December the law lords made their ruling in the *MacShane* case, overturning Lord Denning's earlier decision in the Court of Appeal to restrict trade union immunities in the sphere of secondary picketing. The courts, it was now clear, would not do any of the government's intended work for it. The law lords' judgement reopened debate on the employment bill, for it raised the possibility of revision of Prior's list of measures. Indeed, Prior himself acknowledged that he had acted throughout on the understanding that an additional clause might be required were the law lords' judgement to prove unfavourable to the government cause. In his speech opening the second reading debate, he therefore stated that further measures for inclusion in the bill were being considered.

A yet more important factor in broadening debate was, however, a national steel strike called – on the night of the employment bill's first reading – for 2 January 1980. Its immediate effect was to take the issue out of orthodox procedures contained within the cabinet system, and to open it up to debate in wider arena, notably the parliamentary party. During January, Conservative MPs' anger at government inability to halt the steel strike, and in particular at the spread of mass secondary picketing to private firms, raised the profile of the employment bill within the central executive. At issue was the revision recognised by all Conservative ministers – including Prior – to be required by the law lords' ruling on picketing of December 1979. Disagreement centred on the immunity, if any, that was to be given to secondary action, and the timing of any changes that might be made (Thatcher, 1993: 103–4). Prior favoured minimalist and gradualist change. He faced trenchant and formidable opponents in Thatcher, Joseph (industry secretary) and Howe (1994: 165).

Prior took the initiative on 30 January 1980, announcing that new proposals on secondary action would be put into the employment bill at committee stage in the House of Commons, and that full consultation on his cautious proposals for change would be conducted. On the same day, he requested a meeting with Thatcher to discuss the situation (Thatcher, 1993: 104). Meanwhile the battle in the party, notably in Parliament, continued to intensify. By the start of February, leading Thatcherite back-bencher, George Gardiner, was orchestrating Conservative back-bench attacks on Prior. A critical early day motion tabled by Conservative MP Tony Marlow on 4 February, and signed by almost 100 of his colleagues, did not attract much apparent ire from the whips. Strident attacks on Prior in the Conservative press even appeared to have Thatcher's tacit support.

Prior and his officials continued to work on a consultative paper, which they hoped to publish in the early part of February. However, when its contents were released to E committee on 6 February 1980 they provoked substantial disagreement. Present at this meeting were Thatcher, Prior, Howe, Whitelaw (home secretary), Michael Heseltine (environment secretary), Lord Hailsham (lord chancellor), Joseph, Peter Walker (agriculture secretary), John Nott (trade secretary), John Biffen (chief secretary), Sir Angus Maude (paymaster general), Sir Ian Percival (solicitor general) and Norman St John Stevas (chancellor of the Duchy of Lancaster) (*The Times*, 7.2.80). Prior's cautious and minimalist line was not overturned in committee, but nor was it endorsed. Instead, he was instructed to return to E committee with a full list of possible reform options, including extreme ones (*The Times*, 13.2.80). Although the issue went to cabinet on 7 February, little debate of it seems to have taken place there.

At this point, Thatcher was clearly becoming increasingly frustrated by Prior's actions. Howe (1994: 165) was also an important figure in developing the attack on Prior. On 5 February Thatcher and Prior held meetings with CBI representatives and private steel makers. To Thatcher, the attitude of the CBI was complacent, while the pleas of the private steel makers provided her with evidence of the difficulties faced by entrepreneurs on the front line in industrial disputes (Thatcher, 1993: 105–6). She was evidently now determined to increase the pressure on Prior for more radical action.

Prior was not, however, to be shaken from his approach. He responded by broadening his campaign into a widespread programme of persuasion. On 7 February, against the advice of both his own officials and Bernard Ingham (prime minister's chief press secretary), he set out his position in an interview on the BBC radio programme, *The World at One*. On the same day, he defended his line at a meeting of the 1922 committee of Conservative back-benchers. On 12 February, in advance of the next day's meeting of E committee, he engaged in intensive lobbying of ministerial colleagues. Having already secured the support of Gilmour and Walker, and arranged a meeting with Hailsham, he fixed additional meetings with Whitelaw, Peter Thorneycroft (party chairman), St John Stevas and Heseltine, and spoke with Lord

Carrington (foreign secretary) by telephone. This strategy was devised by Prior in consultation with his wife, Jane, who then took the responsibility of developing it with Prior's political advisers and diary secretary at the DEmp (Prior, 1986: 164). Throughout February, Prior also launched a series of private initiatives to bring the steel strike to an end, and recreate a climate of industrial peace for debate of his bill (Stephenson, 1980: 71).

Prior was not, however, the only senior minister to go on the offensive at this time. On 9 February, Howe again made an inconvenient speech which had not been checked with him. It is said to have been prepared with the help of John Hoskyns (head of the PMPU), and with the encouragement of the prime minister (Stephenson, 1980: 73). At prime minister's questions in the House of Commons on 12 February, Thatcher firmly endorsed a Conservative MP's statement that tough action was required in the trade union sphere. Again, hostile leaders appeared in the Conservative-inclined press (cf. *The Times*, 9.2.80).

On the morning of the crucial E committee meeting of 13 February, *The Times* (13.2.80) estimated that seven ministers were backing Prior, and that two were inclined to back him. They were Hailsham, Walker, Carrington, Sir Ian Gilmour (lord privy seal), Francis Pym (defence secretary), Nicholas Edwards (Welsh secretary) and Sir George Younger (Scottish secretary), plus St John Stevas and Mark Carlisle (education secretary). Against him were said to be eight ministers, plus two thought likely to swing against him. They were Thatcher, Howe, Joseph, Biffen, Maude, David Howell (energy secretary), Sir Humphrey Atkins (Northern Ireland secretary) and Patrick Jenkin (health and social security secretary), plus Heseltine and Whitelaw. The one genuinely undecided member of the committee was thought to be Nott (though both Prior (1986: 162) and Thatcher (1993: 104) clearly believed he was on Thatcher's side throughout). E committee was split down the middle.

In the event, Prior's line prevailed with only minor qualifications. If defeated, Prior would have resigned. It seems likely that this threat was understood, at least implicitly, by a meeting which was 'touch and go' (Prior, 1986: 164). Howe (1994: 166) writes that Prior succeeded in getting his own way 'with threats of his own resignation if his step-by-step line did not prevail'. It was agreed that a new clause to curb secondary action would be inserted into the employment bill at either committee or report stage. A consultative document was to be published the following week, and a full review of secondary action launched by the DEmp. Although the language was tougher than Prior might have wanted, the essence of the proposal was his. It involved taking the law 'back to Denning', that is, back to the position taken by the Court of Appeal in the *MacShane* case. Only immunities extended to the trade union movement by Labour government legislation of 1974 and 1976 were thus to be withdrawn. Immunities granted in 1906 were not to be tackled. The desire of some ministers to 'seize the hour' and enact punitive legislation was not to be met (*The Times*, 14.2.80).

Exit from the cabinet system

Cabinet on 14 February formally endorsed the decision reached by E committee, and gave Prior permission to publish his proposals on 19 February. Again he had prevailed over Thatcher. The bill left the cabinet system and returned to Parliament. It passed into law in the summer of 1980.

Analysis

The outcome of this case was determined internally as a result of the power play between two strands of opinion within the Conservative government. One strand was represented by Prior, the other by Thatcher. Ultimately, the former prevailed. Development of the issue was also shaped by external factors, but these were secondary and served either to open up opportunities for the protagonists or as forces to be mobilised in support. This is, then, a case of successful ministerial defence of a departmental line which faced attack from both inside and outside the cabinet system. Prior's victory was the product of his canvassing of support within E committee, and of his success in keeping a threat to resign alive at the crucial meeting on 13 February (Prior, 1986: 164; Young, 1991: 196). It is a good illustration of the extent of ministerial power, and of concomitant limits on prime ministerial power. Prior could always call on strong and highly supportive departmental resources in his battle with Thatcher. She, by contrast, was forced to rely on *ad hoc* support lines, ranging from ministerial allies to the PMPU and Conservative backbenchers.

Key shaping points stretch back to the opposition period. Thatcher's decisions to allow Prior to retain the employment portfolio in 1975 and 1979 were crucial to this case. Many battles over the eventual line to be taken in the 1979 manifesto were also important. In government, Thatcher was unable to undermine the logic of the position she had already taken by sending Prior to the DEmp. A series of negative decision points – not to alter the line taken by Prior – was the outcome. The chief positive decision point was Prior's victory on 13 February 1980. The issue was determined in the formal setting of E committee, and remained largely consistent with Prior's initial policy line. It went to full cabinet for formal endorsement.

Key actors were Prior and officials in the DEmp, and Thatcher and Howe backed by their advisers. The main initiating actors were Prior and his team. Others addressed proposals formulated by them. Thatcher's team attempted to seize the initiative, but without success. The same two sets of actors organised passage of the issue through the cabinet system. Others were drawn in by them. While in theory the prime minister could have applied a veto, such action would have risked provoking Prior's resignation. Thatcher, still a very inexperienced premier in a relatively weak position in her cabinet, simply could not take that risk. In the end, it was Prior who applied a veto. His 'back me or sack me' challenge to his colleagues proved effective.

The employment bill reveals a number of features of cabinet system operations. It was initially developed within the DEmp, where a highly consultative style prevailed. The issue which entered the cabinet system was thus in some ways out of joint with the prevailing ethos of the new Conservative administration. Nevertheless, throughout the issue seems to have passed through orthodox channels, ending its cabinet system journey with endorsement in full cabinet. Formal procedures affected the outcome of the case by constraining Thatcher to operate within the conventions of collective cabinet government. External factors were also important in opening the issue up for reconsideration while it was passing through the cabinet system. Crucial in this regard were the law lords' ruling and the steel strike. Together, they enabled hostile individuals within the cabinet system to broaden the issue, using a variety of tactics to do so. Notable among these was the use of Conservative back-benchers and the Conservative press to put pressure on Prior. On the side of Thatcher and Howe, a key role was played by Hoskyns. In opposition, Thatcher 'set Hoskyns on to Prior' (Cosgrave, 1985: 37). In government, she relied on him to provide a critique of the Prior line. Beyond this, the ministerial arena was a reasonably open forum for debate and lobbying. It was also extremely large: E committee contained almost the entire cabinet. Here, the two sides were evenly matched.

The Falkland Islands, 1979–82

Origins

On 2 April 1982, Argentina invaded the Falkland Islands and triggered a brief war with Britain. In this case study we do not investigate cabinet system activity during the war itself, but look instead at British government treatment of the issue in the three years leading up to war, beginning with the election of Margaret Thatcher's first Conservative government in May 1979.

The issue was very much inherited by the Thatcher government. As a legacy of empire, Britain exercised sovereignty over a group of islands in the south Atlantic to which Argentina had, for some time, laid claim. Over the years, a number of unsuccessful attempts to negotiate a peaceful settlement had been made, but without success. Three aspects of policy during the pre-Thatcher period are relevant to what happened after 1979. First, the 'islanders' veto' was an established feature of British government perceptions of the issue, in that the received wisdom was that any proposed solution had to be 'acceptable' to the islanders. None was. This government line was frequently reinforced by a vigorous pro-Falklands parliamentary and media lobby (Franks, 1983: paras 22, 23). Secondly, consequent failure to make progress in negotiations over sovereignty meant that Argentina had gradually become less and less patient, increasingly with the backing of other elements of international opinion, such as the United Nations. Time was therefore beginning to run out for the British. Thirdly, because the issue remained 'alive', it had been continually kept under review by previous administrations. The departments most involved were the FCO, which was lead department, and the MoD. However, when necessary, the issue had been brought into the cabinet system either at the level of the JIC, which conducted assessments of the situation on more or less an annual basis, or at the level of the Prime Minister's Office, or in cabinet or cabinet committee. The issue had thus been persistently, if at times intermittently, on the cabinet system agenda in years prior to 1979.

Entry into and treatment within the government machine

When the Conservatives entered office in May 1979, FCO officials immediately raised the issue of the Falkland Islands with Lord Carrington (foreign secretary) and Nicholas Ridley (minister of state, FCO). Ridley was the minister with most immediate responsibility for the Falklands. Officials stated that Argentina was pressing for progress (Carrington, 1989: 351), and presented ministers with a full range of options. Thereafter, during June and July, Ridley visited Argentina and the Falklands to sound out views. On his return he emphasised the need to act, but with due respect to the wishes of the islanders

(Franks, 1983: paras 71–2). Clearly, as a new initiative was being proposed, other colleagues would need to be involved.

Consequently, following the summer break, on 20 September Carrington sent a minute to Thatcher and other members of the cabinet's defence and overseas policy (OD) committee seeking permission for negotiations to take place on a 'leaseback' arrangement under which formal sovereignty would pass to Argentina, but British administration of the islands would continue (Carrington, 1989: 354–5). Thatcher was reluctant to assent to this proposal, and stated that a decision would need to await a meeting of OD (Dillon, 1989: 22, 25). On 12 October, Carrington therefore circulated a minute asking that the issue be placed on the OD agenda for the following week. Thatcher preferred to postpone discussion until the Rhodesia question had been settled (Franks, 1983: paras 75–6). Neither she nor any other member of OD seemed enthusiastic to pursue the FCO proposal (Dillon, 1989: 24). In November the JIC carried out its periodic review, and concluded that the Argentines were likely to become more 'forceful' if they perceived that the British government was not willing to negotiate seriously on sovereignty.

Entry into and treatment within the cabinet system

Only on 29 January 1980 did OD consider Carrington's September and October minutes. At this point of entry into the cabinet system, ministers were not required to act; they did have a solution, but they viewed the issue as low priority. OD agreed to a resumption of talks with Argentina, but only after obtaining agreement to do so from the Falkland Islands Joint Councils (Franks, 1983: paras 77–8). The islanders in fact agreed to the resumption, and talks took place in New York in April. The British government now began to pursue in earnest the leaseback option, and the policy line was fully endorsed by OD in July (Franks, 1983: para. 80). Thatcher says that she disliked this proposal, but that she and Ridley agreed that it should be explored subject to the islanders having the final word. In any case, it was the only realistic option left. As Thatcher (1993: 175) notes, the alternative to negotiation was a 'Fortress Falklands' strategy, comprising investment in the islands' economy, and provision of a new runway capable of taking long-haul aircraft. Throughout, this was ruled out on cost grounds by both the prime minister and the Treasury.

Further progress was made at a meeting of OD on 7 November 1980, when it was agreed that Ridley would visit the Falklands to test support for lease-back. However, island opinion turned out to be divided, with a substantial minority against and the majority undecided (Franks, 1983: para. 81). On 2 December, when Ridley revealed to Parliament that leaseback was being considered, he thus made a point of saying that any settlement would have to be endorsed by both the islanders and Parliament. Despite these assurances, his statement was given a very hostile reception. In OD on 3 December, and in cabinet the following day, ministers considered the parliamentary reaction and the views of the islanders, but no action was agreed (Franks, 1983: para. 82). The negative drift of policy was compounded when, on 6 January 1981, the Islands Councils rejected Ridley's proposals, and urged that further talks should seek Argentine agreement to freeze the sovereignty dispute for a specified period of time (Franks, 1983: para. 83). Following this announcement, OD met on 29 January 1981 to consider a memorandum submitted by Carrington, and to review the situation. The meeting accepted the FCO line that the islanders' rejection of leaseback should not end negotiations, but that instead they should be kept going in the hope that in time the islanders would come to see 'the need to explore' such a solution (Franks, 1983: para. 84).

At this point, the issue became largely suspended. In February 1981, further talks were held with Argentina, but no progress was made. On 13 March 1981 Carrington sent a minute to Thatcher and other members of OD reporting that Argentina had rejected the freeze proposal. He saw little point in further talks until the islanders had cleared their own minds on the issue. Significantly, he noted that if they refused to change their position contingency plans for supply and defence of the islands might have to be made (Franks, 1983: para. 86). By mid-1981, further progress on talks awaited the outcome of autumn elections to the Islands Councils. The hope was that these would signal a change of view. In June and July both the FCO and the JIC reviewed the situation, and concluded that Argentina still wished to proceed by peaceful means, though military leaders were becoming less patient (Dillon, 1989: 30–1).

Failure to agree leaseback meant that at this point there were really only two remaining initiatives open to the British government. It could either prepare contingency plans for military action and response, or it could develop a public education strategy aimed at altering opinion in the UK and on the islands about the merits of leaseback. Contingency plans for military action were reviewed in detail by the FCO and by the chiefs of staff in the MoD (Carrington, 1989: 359), but were not taken beyond these departments (Dillon, 1989: 33–4). The option of a public education campaign was raised by Ridley on 20 July 1981 in a memo to Carrington recommending that the issue be brought before OD in September (Franks, 1983: para. 96). On 7 September, Carrington rejected this advice on the grounds that a campaign would not be agreed by colleagues and, in any case, would be counter-productive (Carrington, 1989: 358; Franks, 1993: para. 99). Carrington therefore decided not to put the matter before OD, though he minuted the prime minister and members of the committee on 14 September, raising the possibility of military contingency plans (Franks, 1983: para. 100). In the event, then, neither of the options open to the British government was pursued.

In September 1981, Richard Luce replaced Ridley as responsible minister in the FCO. In October, elections to the Islands Councils produced a hardening of islanders' attitudes on sovereignty. The leaseback option was now effectively dead. Having failed to develop alternative options, the government was at this point without a feasible policy (Franks, 1983: para. 104).

At much the same time, the government's commitment to the islands became open to question as a result of an MoD decision to remove the survey and support ship HMS *Endurance* from the south Atlantic. In June 1981, Carrington pressed John Nott (defence secretary) to keep the vessel *in situ*, so as not to send misleading signals to Argentina and the Falklands about the government's resolve. The decision was not reversed, and was announced to Parliament on 30 June 1981 (Franks, 1983: para. 114). The removal of *Endurance* led to speculation in the British and Argentine media and the British Parliament that Britain was abandoning the Falklands. Fully 150 MPs signed a motion critical of the action. In January 1982, Carrington wrote again to Nott about HMS *Endurance* but, supported by the prime minister, Nott refused to reverse his decision (Franks, 1983: para. 117). On 17 February Carrington threatened to take the issue to OD, once talks with the Argentines had been completed at the end of the month. In the event, he did not do so (Dillon, 1989: 37).

Meanwhile, important changes were taking place in Argentina. On 22 December 1981, General Galtieri became president with the support of the Navy, the most bellicose of the Argentine services on the Falklands issue (Carrington, 1989: 365). This change greatly increased the likelihood of military action. Argentina again pushed for negotiations on sovereignty. The British government refused to discuss this issue, but made it clear that it would like to have talks in any case. On 15 February 1982, against the background of open speculation in the Argentine press about the possibility of invasion (Franks, 1983: para. 129), Carrington sent a minute to OD members proposing that the issue be discussed in March. Thatcher commented in response that it must be made clear to the Argentines that the wishes of the islanders were paramount (Franks, 1983: para. 133). At the end of February, talks in New York produced an agreement to set up a working party of ministers from both sides to resolve the issue or discuss it for one year.

Desultory consideration of the issue continued on the British side. On 3 March, Thatcher, having seen a cable from the British ambassador in Argentina, noted the need to develop contingency plans (Thatcher, 1993: 177). However, she concluded that any further discussion should be shelved, as Carrington was expected to bring the issue before OD in the 'fairly near future' (Franks, 1983: 152). Intelligence reviews suggested that an Argentinean invasion was unlikely to take place immediately, though such an event was possible within a year. No contingency plans were made. On 5 March, an FCO meeting was held to review the situation, and it was agreed that a draft paper would be prepared for OD 'fairly soon'. The paper would review initiatives that might be taken if talks broke down (Franks, 1983: para. 148). For the first time, Carrington was informed of the previous Labour government's action in 1977 when, in response to a threat of Argentine naval intervention, one submarine and two frigates were sent to the area, though the Argentines were not told of their presence. This precedent was not pursued.

Events outside the control of the British government now began to dictate policy development. On 19 March, an 'underhand provocation' took place. Argentine citizens occupied South Georgia, an island falling within the Falklands protectorate. A gradual breakdown of relations followed as the mobilisation of Argentine forces became more evident. On 24 March Carrington sent a minute to Thatcher and other members of OD, having last reported to them on the matter some five weeks previously. He recommended that OD meet to discuss the possibility of Argentine action, and to consider possible British responses to it (Franks, 1983: para. 187). On the following day, Carrington reported the situation in South Georgia to cabinet and secured agreement that the withdrawal of *Endurance* might need to be reconsidered (Franks, 1983: para. 194). This was the first time that the Falklands issue had been raised in cabinet since December 1980. On 28 and 29 March, Carrington and Thatcher discussed the deteriorating situation. On 31 March, with an Argentinian deployment clearly heading for the islands, Thatcher, FCO ministers, Nott and military and other officials held a meeting which decided that if necessary a seaborne task force could be launched. Carrington was on an official visit to Israel and missed this meeting. On 1 April, at 9.30 a.m., cabinet met and thereafter a meeting of OD was convened to discuss military plans (Thatcher, 1993: 180). This was the first time that OD had discussed the issue since January 1981. Cabinet met again the next morning and evening, and decided to send a task force (Thatcher, 1993: 181). The next day Argentina invaded the Falkland Islands.

Exit from the cabinet system

The issue did not leave the cabinet system at this point, but was delegated to a war cabinet which oversaw policy until the surrender of the Argentine invasion force on 14 June 1982. In the intervening period, Carrington and two other FCO ministers resigned on 6 April.

Analysis

The factors which mainly determined the outcome of this case – war with Argentina – were a series of clear failures in cabinet system operations. Policy development was consistently neglected, to the extent that it virtually stopped, and alternatives were ruled out to the point where the British government was effectively left without a policy. Although the potential dangers of policy change elsewhere, in the form of MoD defence cuts, were appreciated by the FCO, no effective way of dealing with them was developed. The central problem was that for a long and crucial period the matter failed to make it on to the cabinet system agenda for collective discussion. The result was a major failure of policy comprehension, coordination and direction (Young, 1991: 258, 262).

Key points in policy development were negative and covert. There were few overt decision points. Acceptance of the islanders' veto limited the chances of developing alternative lines of policy on the sovereignty issue. Equally, other alternatives were ruled out, or only marginally explored on grounds of either financial or political viability. For these reasons policy was allowed to drift. The one key, overt decision point was the OD meeting in July 1980 which agreed to pursue leaseback. This, however, was a false start which led nowhere. The case is characterised by missed opportunities, which meant that policy was increasingly responsive, driven and towards the end dictated by external factors. These more than anything else determined its outcome. No final decision point was ever reached.

The key initiating actors were FCO ministers, notably Carrington and Ridley, and officials. These actors also organised development of the issue, with Luce taking over from Ridley in September 1981. However, their policy making was at times lackadaisical, and often frustrated by Thatcher and to a lesser extent Nott and other members of OD. The activities of these core players were shaped by a number of individuals external to British government, including members of the Islands Councils, supporters of the islanders in Parliament and the media, and officials and military personnel in Argentina.

A number of aspects of cabinet system operations are revealed. The issue clearly failed to take the correct pathways through the system. It was not given sufficient priority to make it on to the cabinet system agenda, chiefly because meetings of the relevant committee were not called. This negative gatekeeping function meant that cabinet system machinery was hardly brought into play. Cabinet first discussed the issue fully 18 months after the Thatcher government entered office. OD discussed it a mere four times in three years. Procedural failings were also substantial in this case. Issues deemed to be of higher priority – such as Rhodesia – kept it off the agenda. The system also had difficulty in comprehending, interpreting and coordinating intelligence information in a changing foreign policy situation. Varied signals coming into London conditioned ministerial and official perceptions, and contributed to a situation in which the government was taken off guard by the Argentine invasion. The party dimension to this issue was small but significant. The Falklands lobby in the Conservative Party placed important constraints on ministerial manoeuvre. The role of the individual was also significant. Carrington, the FCO and the defence and overseas affairs secretariat of the Cabinet Office failed to push the matter with sufficient energy. Thatcher exploited her ability to keep the issue off the cabinet system's agenda, but found that having failed to address it she became a prisoner of factors beyond her sphere of influence.

Community charge, 1984–6

Origins

Community charge (or poll tax) was the system of local taxation chosen in the mid-1980s to replace the rates. This case examines the formulation of the community charge up to its endorsement by the cabinet in January 1986. Rates reform was generated largely by party and external factors. It was a low priority in the 1979 Conservative manifesto (Conservative Party, 1979: 14), and was the subject of two DoE reviews in the early 1980s (Department of the Environment, 1981; 1983). Both supported retention of the rates. By August 1983, reform had thus been subjected to searching scrutiny, and rejected with cabinet endorsement. The issue was off the agenda (Howe, 1994: 520). It was returned to it by business and Conservative Party pressure. When a series of motions calling for abolition of the rates was submitted to the 1984 Conservative Party conference by constituency parties, Patrick Jenkin (environment secretary), under whom the 1983 review had been completed, felt required to respond. On Sunday 2 September 1984 he met prime minister Margaret Thatcher at Chequers. Although Thatcher (1993: 644, 646) was reluctant to allow him to promise a new inquiry into local government finance, she eventually stated that he could submit an outline paper to cabinet committee to gauge ministers' response (Crick and Van Klaveren, 1991: 401). Jenkin's initiative thus brought the issue back into currency.

Entry into and treatment within the cabinet system

Policy makers had no solution to rates reform when it entered the government machine for the third time in the 1980s. They were not required to act, and viewed the issue as medium priority. Jenkin's paper was discussed at two cabinet committee meetings during September 1984. On 27 September 1984, at a meeting at Number 10 chaired by Thatcher, Jenkin and Kenneth Baker (minister of state, DoE) presented the arguments for a fresh review. Of the other five ministers present only Nigel Lawson (chancellor of the exchequer) was openly hostile (Baker, 1993: 114). The meeting agreed to proceed, though William Whitelaw (deputy prime minister) and Thatcher insisted that the initiative should be referred to as a 'study', as they could not feasibly establish another review. The decision was announced by Jenkin at the Conservative Party conference in October, and later that month a cabinet standing committee on local government finance – E(LF) – was established with the prime minister in the chair. Most senior cabinet ministers on the home policy side were members, as were John Wakeham (chief whip) and John Gummer (party chairman) (Baker, 1993: 114, 122). However, E(LF) initially played little part in policy development, which was left to study teams in the DoE.

213

Treatment within the relevant government department

In the DoE, responsibility for the study was placed under Baker, who delegated the work to William Waldegrave (parliamentary under secretary). The study was conducted by two groups selected by Baker, Waldegrave and Terry Heiser (deputy secretary in charge of local government finance). One was a group of officials under Heiser. It included Anthony Mayer (assistant secretary), who had day-to-day responsibility for the work of the group, and principals Roger Bright, Jill Rutter (seconded from the Treasury), Don Brereton (seconded from the Department of Health and Social Security) and John Smith and David Lewis (in-house economists). These individuals were later joined by Peter Owen (under secretary). All were high-flyers chosen for their ability to find a solution to a problem. The second group was a body of outside assessors. Headed by Lord Rothschild, a former head of the CPRS, it comprised Leonard Hoffman QC, Professor Tom Wilson and Professor Christopher Foster (Crick and Van Klaveren, 1991: 403; Thatcher, 1993: 646). Only Foster brought expertise to the problem, having explored the idea of a poll tax or per capita charge in a book on local government finance (Foster *et al.*, 1980). Other departments (Treasury, Social Security, Scottish and Welsh Offices, Education, Transport) (Baker, 1993: 121) were occasionally consulted, as were the PMPU and advisers at Number 10. Some ministers and officials were informally canvassed by Waldegrave and Baker (Baker, 1993: 122; Ridley, 1991a: 124). Michael Ancram (minister of state, Scottish Office) was involved from February 1985 onwards (Channel Four, 1993). Despite this, the study was almost wholly contained in the DoE, and representatives of other departments were consulted on its initiative.

The group of DoE officials began its work in October 1984. The assessors were appointed in November. Most detailed work was in fact undertaken by Waldegrave and the official group, and then discussed with the assessors. Initially, study participants were asked to examine both the structure and financing of local government, with the aim of increasing local authorities' accountability to their electors. A key conditioning factor in the exercise was the fact that many who benefited from local government services did not pay rates: only 50 per cent of voters and one-third of adults in fact did so. By taxing more electors, an important constraint on high-spending local authorities would be created. This perception of the nature of the problem greatly affected the choices which were made subsequently.

By the end of December, study participants had agreed that non-domestic rates, paid mainly by business, should be fixed nationally (Butler, Adonis and Travers, 1994: 55). Proposals for reforming the local tax system were examined concurrently. The available options were clear, having been outlined in both previous reviews. Initially, a local sales tax was considered and rejected, partly because of its impact on inflation. Next, a local income tax was considered to be unacceptable on grounds that it would be too complex and, as a direct tax, would be contrary to government policy. Also by the end of

December, these two alternatives had thus been rejected, and the groups' attention focused on the only remaining option, some form of per capita tax, to be used as a supplement to the rates (Butler *et al.*, 1994: 56).

By early 1985, a per capita tax was thus fast becoming the favoured option (Crick and Van Klaveren, 1991: 405). As it would be a highly visible tax, with a wide incidence, it was felt most able to meet the accountability criterion. However, within the group of assessors Hoffman and Wilson were opposed to the idea, feeling that a per capita tax would be too regressive (Wilson, 1991: 579). Hoffman, who favoured reform of the rating system, had his views printed and circulated to Number 10 and the relevant ministers and officials (though not to Jenkin). By then, however, the idea of a per capita tax had substantial momentum. In March, with Baker's backing, Waldegrave and the official group dropped the two-tax idea, having become convinced of the need to replace the rates with a straight per capita tax.

A further factor which helped to shape policy development was the early 1985 revaluation of Scottish rates, which resulted in average increases of 20 per cent in the valuation of domestic properties. Especially hard hit were wealthy, Conservative-voting areas. The strong feelings of Tory activists in Scotland were relayed to Thatcher (1993: 647), and more directly to White-law, who had 'one of the most uncomfortable experiences of his political career' when he was badly heckled at a party reception in Scotland (Crick and Van Klaveren, 1991: 409).

Finally, the study group exercise was shaped by the knowledge that results were to be presented to Thatcher at a Chequers meeting scheduled from early 1985 for Sunday 31 March. Increasingly, the attention of Waldegrave and the study groups focused on the task of presentation. An outline of current think-ing was given to Jenkin on 3 February, and to Sir Robert Armstrong (cabinet secretary) later in the month. A week before the Chequers meeting, a full dress rehearsal was given to Jenkin (Channel Four, 1993). In the wider party, the discontent of Scottish Conservatives was expressed very forcefully in the weeks immediately prior to the Chequers meeting. Whitelaw, usually an im-portant and influential voice for caution, thus became sympathetic to pro-posals to reform the rates. The impact of the revaluation also convinced George Younger (Scottish secretary) and the other Scottish ministers that the rates had to go, and Thatcher and others of the need to avoid the similar revaluation in England and Wales which could not, feasibly, be long delayed (Young, 1991: 532). It was thus with a sense of a need to do something that ministers met at Chequers on 31 March 1985.

Re-entry into and treatment within the cabinet system

At Chequers, Thatcher and eight other cabinet ministers were in attendance. Gummer, the Conservative party chairman, was present, as were Younger and Ancram. Lawson did not attend, but instead sent Peter Rees (chief secretary) with a brief to speak against any change. On the official side, only Heiser, Mayer and members of the cabinet secretariat were present. Rothschild also attended. The presentation, including a slide show and visuals, lasted five hours. Baker (1993: 122) put the case against the rates, and Waldegrave presented the alternatives. A per capita tax was advanced as the most promising of several means of increasing local government accountability. Other measures included annual local government elections, and unitary authorities. A per capita tax was strongly supported by the Scottish ministers (Butler et al., 1994: 74). Although Thatcher took some persuading, in the end she was won over (Channel Four, 1993; Thatcher, 1993: 648; Young, 1991: 533). Despite the misgivings of the Treasury and home secretary Leon Brittan, the meeting agreed that a per capita tax represented the best way forward (Baker, 1993: 123). The proposal that there should be a single, national, uniform business rate was also accepted (Thatcher, 1993: 648). Other proposals were shelved.

The decision to proceed with a per capita tax was thus effectively taken at Chequers outside formal cabinet system structures (Lawson, 1993: 571). Now, with the prime minister behind it, Baker began to take control of detailed policy development. However, although Younger and Thatcher declared in favour of reform at the Scottish Conservative Party conference in early May (Butler et al., 1994: 80), the tax was not fully accepted by ministers. Lawson and the Treasury were opposed, as were Brittan, Michael Heseltine (defence secretary) and Peter Walker (energy secretary). The latter two were not, however, drawn into key discussions (Walker, 1991: 186). In April Lawson met Waldegrave and later Thatcher to put his reservations. For the first post-Chequers meeting of E(LF), chaired by Thatcher on 20 May, he prepared a detailed memorandum. In it, he argued that a per capita tax would be 'unworkable and politically catastrophic', and proposed that the rates be maintained and that central government take from local authorities the financing of education (Lawson, 1993: 573–4). About 12 ministers were present at the meeting. Apart from Lawson, supported by Rees, Brittan was opposed to a per capita tax, and Lord Gowrie (chancellor of the Duchy of Lancaster) was lukewarm. The meeting agreed that both the per capita proposal and Lawson's alternative should be developed (Thatcher, 1993: 650), though the Lawson option was not the main runner. In effect, this meeting brought the Chequers decision into the formal cabinet system machinery, and endorsed it.

After the May meeting, E(LF) seems to have been engaged in examining technical details of the proposed tax, though most of this work was contained within the DoE and managed by Baker, Waldegrave and their officials. Outside experts from the LSE and Institute of Fiscal Studies were asked to provide advice on the possible impact of the tax (Butler et al., 1994: 81; Watkins, 1992: 57). In the same month, the group of assessors was dissolved. Of its members, only Foster remained supportive of the idea of a per capita tax. Rothschild's position was ambiguous. During the first week of September Jenkin was dismissed and replaced as environment secretary by Baker, with Waldegrave promoted to replace him as minister of state. Apart from working out the details of the tax, two major issues remained to be resolved: whether the tax should operate as a supplement to the rates or should replace them altogether, and if it did replace them whether there should be a phasing-in period or not. The matter of what the tax should be called also had to be decided.

In August 1985, during the summer break, Lawson's alternative proposal was circulated to a limited number of ministers but failed to win much support (Thatcher, 1993: 650). Opposition to a per capita tax thus made no headway. At a meeting of E(LF) on 23 September Lawson, supported by John Mac-Gregor (new chief secretary), again voiced objections. The meeting was inconclusive, and a further meeting of the committee took place on 3 October, partly to determine what Baker should say to the Conservative Party conference. At this meeting, it was decided that the new tax would be called 'community charge', and it was formally approved as the main replacement for the rates. Either at this meeting or at an earlier one in September, it was agreed that the new tax would be introduced at a stroke in Scotland one year earlier than in England and Wales, where it would be levied alongside rates for between three and 10 years depending on the local authority. About a dozen ministers were present at these meetings.

These many proposals were drawn together in the form of a draft green paper, which was submitted to E(LF) on 12 December. On 31 December Baker visited Chequers to discuss the draft with Thatcher. She insisted that during the transitional stage any increase would fall on the community charge, and not on the residual rates element (Thatcher, 1993: 651). Duly amended, the document was placed before cabinet for the first time on 9 January 1986. However, the attention of the meeting was concentrated on Heseltine's walk-out over the Westland affair. Following his dramatic exit, and a quick change of ministers in mid-session, cabinet devoted only 15 minutes to the issue. The most substantial reform in local government taxation since 1601 was thus agreed by cabinet almost 'on the nod'.

Exit from the cabinet system

On 28 January 1986, the green paper was published and a statement was made by Baker to the House of Commons. Community charge was scheduled to replace domestic rates, though matters such as the length of phasing-in and whether there should be a system of banding remained to be determined before legislation was passed in 1987 for Scotland, and in 1988 for England and Wales. Community charge came fully on stream in 1989 in Scotland, and in 1990 in the rest of Britain. In 1992 it was abolished.

Analysis

The factors which mainly determined the outcome of this case were party pressure for something to be done about the rates, and the procedures used by the study groups to arrive at a per capita tax. The study groups' method comprised serial assessment of possible options according to the criteria of accountability and fit with other elements of government policy. In conducting this assessment they began with the most feasible option and, when it was found wanting, moved to the next option. By this process of elimination, they arrived at the possibility of a per capita tax only when all other options had been rejected. They thereby alighted on a tax which all previous reviews had dismissed as the least credible option. The activities of the groups were also shaped by time pressures, notably the Chequers deadline, and by presentation considerations. Once their solution had emerged, and was sold to key policy makers, it proved impossible to stop. In this context, Thatcher's conversion was crucial, for once committed she refused to be moved on the principle of a per capita tax.

The key shaping points in development of the issue were Jenkin's decision on 2 September 1984 to reopen the issue of rates reform, the decision to move on 27 September to establish the study group exercise, the decision in October 1984 to adopt accountability as the main criterion for judging reform proposals, the choice in October of the membership of the study groups and their subsequent decision on method of procedure, the negative response to revaluation in Scotland, the Chequers meeting on 31 March 1985 when Thatcher and others were sold and bought community charge in principle, the meeting of E(LF) on 20 May 1985 which formally endorsed what had been decided at Chequers, and the September/October 1985 meeting of E(LF) at which community charge was formally approved as the main replacement for the rates. Of these points the most critical was the Chequers meeting, although its outcome was significantly shaped by the method used and the skills deployed by the study groups. The final decision was taken in E(LF), and merely confirmed in full cabinet.

Key actors were Jenkin, Baker, Waldegrave and the members of both study groups, notably the official one. Latterly, Thatcher was also key. These were the full participants. Others, notably the Scottish ministers and other members of E(LF), were essentially partial participants. The key initiators were Jenkin, Baker, Waldegrave and members of the study groups. Baker, Waldegrave and officials organised much of the passage of the issue through the cabinet system, and were substantially aided by the drive that Thatcher gave to the issue after the Chequers meeting. Initially, there was little consultation with other departments, and none with outside agencies and experts, such as local government tax administrators. Subsequently, relevant home departments were more substantially involved through the formal mechanism of E(LF). The process thus became more collective in its later stages, but a full collective assessment of community charge was never undertaken.

The case reveals a number of aspects of cabinet system operations. This issue took orthodox pathways through the system, and was not affected by procedures used within it. However, procedures used before the issue reached the cabinet system were critical to policy development, and illustrate the extent to which a lead department can set the parameters of cabinet system debate, at least in terms of detailed proposals and supporting information. Party was an important influence in this case, for it generated and sustained pressure for policy change. The greatest individual influence within the cabinet system was Thatcher, although others had already decisively shaped policy development before she was fully drawn in. Her determination to push the matter through the system was largely shared by other senior ministers. The one key dissenter was Lawson, who was unable to apply a Treasury veto in an area outside of its immediate responsibility because he had the support of neither the prime minister nor a coalition of senior ministers.

Sterling's entry into the ERM, 1985–90

Origins

The origins of sterling's entry into the exchange rate mechanism (ERM) of the European monetary system (EMS) date from the late 1970s: the decision to establish the ERM within the EMS was taken at the Bremen EEC summit of July 1978. At this time, Britain declined to participate. The ERM was therefore launched without sterling on 12 March 1979. In choosing to stay out, James Callaghan's Labour government was reflecting both the official view of policy makers in the Treasury and Bank of England and that of most British economists. The Conservative Party, by contrast, condemned the Callaghan government's decision.

However, although this issue was thus partly inherited by the Thatcher government which took office in May 1979, the main drive which subsequently kept it on the political agenda was external. The success of the ERM in the 1980s, and the determination of EC leaders to intensify exchange rate linkages across the Community, ensured that Britain was always faced with the issue of joining. Sterling's volatile performance on the foreign exchanges in the early 1980s generated a further element of external drive towards ERM membership. The first Thatcher government considered ERM entry on taking office, but decided against (Ridley, 1991a: 169). The policy line was then reconsidered by Margaret Thatcher, key ministers and the governor of the Bank of England at meetings held in October 1979, March 1980 and January 1982 (Thatcher, 1993: 691–2). It was also briefly considered at chancellor Sir Geoffrey Howe's pre-budget Chevening meeting in January 1983 (Howe, 1994: 275–6). On each occasion, all agreed that sterling should only join the ERM when the time was right, and almost all – with the notable exception of the FCO – considered that that time had not yet been reached. This broad consensus was not breached until Thatcher's second term.

The breach happened when a third factor came into play. The effective abandonment of the government's early monetarist experiment at the start of Nigel Lawson's chancellorship in June 1983 left policy makers without a monetary anchor, and substantially increased the attraction of ERM membership as an alternative means of securing monetary policy.

These, then, were the origins of this issue. Their complexity ensured that although ERM membership was on the political agenda from 1978 onwards, it was not really a live issue for policy makers until the mid-1980s.

Entry into and treatment by the government machine

The issue of ERM membership did not exactly enter the government machine in the mid-1980s, for it had long been on policy makers' agendas. Instead, at the start of 1985, it changed from being a rather distant and unfocused aspiration to being a leading political issue. A key figure in provoking this transformation was Lawson, who by January 1985 (at the latest) had become a firm advocate of ERM entry. The abandonment of monetarism was central to the enthusiasm with which he pursued ERM membership; two sterling crises, in July 1984 and January 1985 (when the pound fell almost to parity with the dollar), exposed the precarious situation in which he now found himself (Smith, 1992: 48–50). Using the time for reflection offered by the Christmas/New Year break of 1984–5, Lawson (1993: 485) came to the conclusion that it was time to think seriously about ERM membership.

For a while, the prevailing Treasury view remained contrary. At the Bank of England the governor, Robin Leigh-Pemberton, supported entry, but some key officials were opposed. Thatcher was considered by Lawson (1993: 484–5) to be against entry, but not determinedly so. Her central objections were well known: that you cannot 'buck the market', and that closer European ties were undesirable.

An appropriate moment appeared to be reached in January 1985. Sterling's instability on the foreign exchanges required Lawson to raise interest rates several times. On 11 January, he therefore called a meeting of Treasury colleagues and officials and for the first time asked them to examine seriously the possibility of sterling's entry into the ERM. Among those present were Ian Stewart (economic secretary), Sir Peter Middleton (permanent secretary) and Sir Terence Burns (government chief economic adviser), all of whom opposed entry (Lawson, 1993: 486). Indeed, the Treasury view remained at best agnostic, but, as chancellor, Lawson (1993: 486) was able to insist that his chosen policy line be followed. To this point under Lawson's chancellorship, the issue of sterling's entry into the ERM was essentially a Treasury matter.

Entry into and treatment by the cabinet system

The issue entered the cabinet system proper when Thatcher took an interest in it. Prompted by sterling's alarming experience on the foreign exchanges, she did so very soon after Lawson had convened his meeting in the Treasury. On 28 January 1985, Thatcher told Lawson that she had discussed with Dutch prime minister Ruud Lubbers the possibility of sterling's entry into the ERM, and that she would like him to look into it (Lawson, 1993: 487). The issue was now very clearly on the cabinet system agenda. Policy makers did not have to act, a clear solution (entry) was available, and the issue was medium priority.

Activity at this point was substantial. A Thatcher–Lawson meeting on 3 February 1985 discussed the issue. It was followed by a further Treasury meeting on 8 February, and by a Downing Street seminar on the ERM on 13 February. Present at the seminar were Thatcher, Howe (now foreign secretary), Lawson and a Treasury team, Leigh-Pemberton and a Bank of England team and John Redwood (head of the PMPU). A notable absentee was Sir Alan Walters, economic adviser to the prime minister and a known sceptic on the issue. The seminar concluded that sterling entry to the ERM was a good idea in principle, but that the time was (still) not yet right to join (Lawson, 1993: 488–9). The issue was put on hold.

For a number of reasons, it was revived in late summer 1985. Chief among these were Lawson's continuing commitment to the cause (made evident in a meeting with Thatcher at the end of August), and conclusion of the G5 Plaza Agreement on 21 September, which signalled international action to reduce the value of the dollar. At a debriefing meeting with Lawson, Thatcher was sufficiently persuaded of the desirability of managed exchange rates to offer Lawson a second seminar on ERM membership on 30 September (Lawson, 1993: 493).

This second seminar was attended by about a dozen people. Lawson brought with him Stewart, Middleton, Burns and Frank Cassell (another leading official). Leigh-Pemberton was accompanied by Kit McMahon (deputy governor), Eddie George (executive director in charge of monetary policy) and Anthony Loehnis (executive director in charge of overseas operations). Thatcher was accompanied by Brian Griffiths (new head of the PMPU) and by a private secretary, David Norgrove, who took notes. Howe was also present. Walters, again, was absent in the US. His sceptical influence on Thatcher was nevertheless evident, for she responded to Lawson's paper in favour of sterling's ERM entry by announcing that she was still not persuaded, and that she would therefore circulate a list of questions which could form the agenda for a subsequent meeting to which a wider group of ministers would be invited. Lawson claims to have had the full support of the Treasury team, the Bank of England team and Howe at this seminar (Lawson, 1993: 494–6). Howe (1994: 449) does not dissent from this view.

A ministerial meeting was duly convened on 13 November 1985 to discuss the list of 23 questions circulated in advance by Thatcher (Lawson, 1993: 496). It turned out to be the key moment in delaying sterling's ERM entry for five years. Present on this occasion were Thatcher, Lawson, Howe, William Whitelaw (deputy prime minister), Norman Tebbit (party chairman), Sir Leon Brittan (trade and industry secretary), John Biffen (leader of the House of Commons) and John Wakeham (chief whip), as well as Middleton and Burns from the Treasury, Leigh-Pemberton and George from the Bank, and Griffiths from the PMPU. Thatcher's private secretary attended to take notes. Walters was again absent – because not invited – though he had sent his comments in a letter to Thatcher (Lawson, 1993: 497–8). Lawson, seeking to build as wide a coalition as possible in favour of entry, had both coordinated a Treasury–Bank joint effort and lobbied ministerial colleagues. The meeting quickly fell in line behind him: Howe spoke in favour of joining, as did Brittan and (according to Lawson and Howe) Tebbit. As expected, Biffen spoke against. Whitelaw joined the emergent consensus. When it was clear to

Thatcher that she was in a minority in a hand-picked gathering she played the only card left to her, prime ministerial veto, and announced that ERM entry, if it were to happen, would take place without her. The meeting came to an abrupt end (Lawson, 1993: 499; Howe, 1994: 449–50). Many participants believed the influence on Thatcher of 'a distant professor' (Howe, 1994: 450) – Walters – to have been crucial.

Thatcher's intervention was decisive. Lawson next raised the issue with her in autumn 1986, when sterling was again plunging on the foreign exchanges, but was told that a policy shift could not be contemplated until after the next general election (Thompson, 1995). To the extent that he could, Lawson therefore took matters into his own hands and from March 1987 adopted a policy of shadowing the Deutschmark at a level of DM3 (Lawson, 1993: 682–3). Thatcher (1993: 701–2) claims to have had no knowledge of this informal policy. However, Thompson (1995) points out that her economic private secretary received Treasury market reports on a daily basis, making Lawson's assertion that he concealed nothing from her more plausible. At Thatcher's insistence, the policy was discontinued in March 1988 (Thatcher, 1993: 702–3).

Once the 1987 general election had been won, Lawson again raised the issue of ERM entry with Thatcher on 27 July 1987. She vehemently attacked the ERM, and told Lawson that she would not discuss the matter again with him that year. He insisted that it was too important to drop (Lawson, 1993: 732). By this point, as the memoirs of Thatcher, Lawson and Howe make clear, the ERM had become the focal point of a blatant power struggle at the heart of the British cabinet system. On one side was Thatcher, reinforced in her conviction (but not her power base) by Walters. On the other were Lawson and Howe, both of whom were committed to sterling's entry.

The external drive which sustained the issue for much of the 1980s soon returned it to the top of the political agenda. At the Hanover EC summit in June 1988, an agreement to investigate means of attaining economic and monetary union (EMU) was reached. The resultant Delors report of April 1989, which set out stages for attainment of EMU, again focused attention on the anomalous position of sterling. By this time, City of London opinion was also deeply concerned about precisely this issue. Lawson and Howe thus began to work together to defeat Thatcher's ERM veto. Even before publication of the Delors report, they had started to plan tactics, meeting without officials three times between mid-March and end April 1989 (Howe, 1994: 577). They also arranged an Anglo–Dutch mini-summit on 29 April 1989 in an attempt to exploit Thatcher's liking for Dutch prime minister Lubbers in the cause of ERM entry. The attempt failed (Howe, 1994: 577–8; Lawson, 1993: 913–16). When Lawson raised the topic at his next bilateral with Thatcher on 3 May she told him never to speak of it again: 'I must prevail' (Lawson, 1993: 917–18).

Thatcher's two senior ministers thus began to prepare the ground for the Madrid EC summit, due to open on 26 June 1989. On Howe's initiative they worked on a joint minute to Thatcher specifying conditions for sterling entry. A draft was produced in the Treasury, and was then jointly honed by Tim Lankester (senior Treasury official) and John Kerr (senior FCO official). The final draft was discussed by Lawson and Howe after dinner on 13 June 1989, and the resultant 12-page minute was sent to Thatcher on 14 June, with a request that she meet her two ministers to discuss it. She eventually did so on 20 June having, on the previous day, held a meeting of all her Number 10 advisers (including Walters and Griffiths) to talk the matter through. At the meeting with Lawson and Howe Thatcher resisted any move towards conditions for sterling entry. However, the very next day, on the advice of Walters, she responded with a set of counter-conditions, drafted by Charles Powell (foreign desk private secretary at Number 10). These conditions were so stringent as to rule out the possibility of sterling entry. On 23 June, Lawson and Howe thus sent a further minute to Number 10 requesting another meeting, which eventually took place on 25 June. During this 'nasty little meeting' (Thatcher, 1993: 712), at which no officials were present, both ministers threatened to resign unless Thatcher agreed to their conditions for entry. Although the meeting broke up with the matter still unresolved (Howe, 1993: 578–80; Lawson, 1993: 928–33), at the Madrid summit itself Thatcher announced a set of conditions which were held to indicate a move towards sterling entry, and thereby undercut any possibility of joint resignations by Lawson and Howe (Howe, 1994: 583; Lawson, 1993: 934).

Within four months, both ministers were nevertheless gone from their posts. Thatcher moved Howe from the Foreign Office on 24 July, and received Lawson's resignation on 26 October. Lawson went because he objected to the excessive influence of Walters at Number 10. Walters himself subsequently resigned within hours. By the end of October 1989, John Major was chancellor and Douglas Hurd had been appointed foreign secretary. Awkwardly for Thatcher, each was committed to ERM membership (Anderson, 1991: 132).

The issue was raised frequently at Thatcher–Major weekly bilateral discussions in spring 1990 (Thatcher, 1993: 719). On 13 June, Thatcher eventually told Major that she would not resist sterling joining the ERM (Thatcher, 1993: 722), leaving only the matter of timing to be settled. At around this time, she also enlarged the circle of advisers considering these matters, bringing in her own firm supporter Nicholas Ridley (trade and industry secretary) (Thatcher, 1993: 726). In July 1990, however, Ridley was forced to resign following publication of anti-German remarks in the *Spectator*. Major and Hurd were now able to argue that it was important for Britain to restore confidence in its approach to the EC by joining the ERM. As Thatcher could not afford a single further resignation (Thatcher, 1993: 722), and could not therefore risk the veto threat again, sterling's ERM entry became only a matter of time.

Thatcher (1993: 723) resisted Major's wish to go into the ERM in July 1990 but finally, in October, allowed government policy to fall in line with what had become an economic orthodoxy shared by financiers, businessmen, politicians and academics alike. On 4 October, Major and his Treasury officials, and George (now deputy governor of the Bank of England) and his officials, approached Thatcher to discuss preparations for entry by the end of the year. Thatcher in fact sanctioned entry for the very next day (Thompson, 1995). She also set some of the conditions of entry, including what some at the time believed – and certainly turned out – to be an unsustainable rate of 2.95 against the Deutschmark (Thatcher, 1993: 718–23).

Exit from the cabinet system

Entry to the ERM was announced by Major on 5 October, and took effect on 8 October 1990. On 16 September 1992, sterling was forced out of the ERM by intense currency speculation.

Analysis

The outcome of this case was determined mainly by the strong external drive which sustained it from start to finish. Although the issue was riven with individual conflict, and its implementation thereby delayed for some five years, sterling did eventually join the ERM. Thatcher could not buck the economic and political forces driving the issue. Yet she did play a significant role in stalling policy development, thereby ensuring that the circumstances of entry were significantly altered due to change in the value of sterling.

Within the context of increasing external pressures, key shaping points were the initial EC decision to establish the ERM in July 1978, Lawson's instruction to his Treasury officials to work on the issue in January 1985, the subsequent conversion of officials in the Treasury and Bank of England, Thatcher's veto in November 1985, her acceptance of the 'Madrid conditions' in June 1989, and the removal of her veto in principle in June 1990 and in practice in October 1990. The final decision was taken in an informal arena, and was consistent with Lawson's initial intent.

Key actors were broadly the members of the inner group which considered this issue: relevant personnel from the prime minister's side, the Treasury and the Bank of England. Key initiating actors came from the Treasury, the Bank and, later, the FCO. Notable among them were Lawson and Howe – later Major and Hurd – and their officials. These individuals repeatedly succeeded in returning the issue to the agenda. However, key organising actors were the prime minister and her aides, who chose not to facilitate passage of the issue but to stall it. Only a very small group of other actors was drawn in. Thatcher was the only person to exercise a veto. Although she delayed progress significantly, she did not prevent entry.

The case reveals unusual aspects of cabinet system operations. It took a highly unorthodox route through the system, never being discussed in formal cabinet or cabinet committee. Instead, it was managed by very small groups of high-ranking individuals (often officials), and excluded all other members of the cabinet system. In this sense, it was very close to Callaghan's use of the so-called economic 'seminar' in the late 1970s (Donoughue, 1987: 101), and demonstrates that his attempt to incorporate exchange-rate policy into the prime ministerial domain was continued by Thatcher. The small numbers involved, the close involvement of officials and the confidentiality surrounding their deliberations are typical of the way in which currency questions are handled in government. The sensitive and confidential nature of the issue also meant that party pressures hardly impinged upon policy development. Formal procedures were not constraining in this case, as they were entirely bypassed. By contrast, informal procedures were exploited by Thatcher to stall sterling entry to the ERM for five years. In addition, the small respite in ministerial schedules provided by the Christmas break was important in providing Lawson with time to satisfy himself of the case for entry. The role of the individual in exploiting the opportunities allowed by external factors also looms large. Lawson was crucial in convincing a sceptical Treasury of the merits of ERM entry. With Howe, he sustained a remarkable battle with Thatcher. She in turn, under the influence of Walters, exercised a clear veto. Yet, given the forces stacked against her, this was not a form of power which she could employ indefinitely. In the end, she was obliged to give way.

The Next Steps report, 1986–8

Origins

The proposals for civil service reform embodied in the February 1988 Next Steps report were generated within the state. Indeed, they were developed at its very core by senior civil servants. They were also consequential on previous policy change, being prompted by dissatisfaction with earlier attempts to increase civil service efficiency. These included the Rayner reviews of the early Thatcher years, and the Financial Management Initiative (FMI) of 1982, both of which concentrated on developing better management practices within government departments (see Chapter 2). By 1985 the scope and pace of these reforms were prompting concern among senior civil servants. The feeling was that officials at middle management levels were being frustrated (Flynn, Gray and Jenkins, 1990: 162; Greer, 1994: 9), that changes in management attitudes were limited (Fry, 1988: 430), that delegation of responsibilities had not gone far enough (Public Accounts Committee, 1987: 5), and that incentives were restricted by the unified nature of the civil service pay structure. A final aspect of the origins of this set of reforms was a standing Conservative commitment, expressed in manifestos and ministerial speeches, to value for money in the public sector. There was also, therefore, a party element to the background of the case, but it was very marginal. The case is unusual, in that throughout its development it was almost wholly contained within the cabinet system.

Entry into and treatment within the cabinet system

This was not a case on which policy makers had to act, it did not have a single solution when it entered the cabinet system, and it had a low priority on the political agenda. The initiative in launching a review of civil service practices was taken by Sir Robin Ibbs, head of the prime minister's efficiency unit (PMEU), who was particularly concerned about the limited impact of previous reforms (Flynn *et al.*, 1990: 162; Metcalfe and Richards, 1990: 228). He first began to register concern in the autumn of 1985, but it was not until summer 1986 that his discontent 'crystallized into a plan of action' (Hennessy, 1990: 622). Ibbs' misgivings were given some support in October 1986, when the National Audit Office published an investigation of 12 departments' experience of the FMI. This proposed that more responsibility for resource control be delegated to line managers (Public Accounts Committee, 1987: 5). A similar proposal on delegated budgeting emerged from the Wilson report commissioned by the Treasury, and completed in 1986. Ibbs' speculative thinking was made known to prime minister Margaret Thatcher, and on 3 November 1986, in response to a request from Thatcher (Flynn *et al.*, 1990: 162), he launched a review of existing programmes (National Audit Office, 1989: 17).

The terms of the review were to assess progress on management reform, to isolate barriers to further reform, and to make recommendations for action to the prime minister. The review was carried out by Kate Jenkins, Karen Caines and Andrew Jackson – all members of the PMEU – under the supervision of Ibbs and Sir Robert Armstrong (cabinet secretary and head of the home civil service), and took the form of a 90-day scrutiny. Richard Luce (minister for the civil service) may have known of its existence. The Treasury was not formally involved. In conducting the review the PMEU team carried out interviews with 150 ministers, officials, managers of large-scale enterprises in the public and private sectors and high-flyers who had recently left the civil service. They concluded their work on 20 March 1987 (Efficiency Unit, 1988: 33).

Because of the radical nature and sensitivity of some of its conclusions, the team made sure that its ideas were cleared with the prime minister before drafting its report (Flynn *et al.*, 1990: 161). The first version of the review was presented to Thatcher by Ibbs in May 1987, and was more radical than the Next Steps document which was finally published. In particular, the team favoured abandoning the constitutional convention that ministers are responsible for all actions undertaken by officials in their name (Hennessy, 1990: 620). The core idea of the Next Steps report – creation of 'executive agencies' to handle the service delivery function of departments – was contained in this draft.

In fact, the report was considered so sensitive that it was kept secret on Thatcher's personal instructions (Butler in Treasury and Civil Service Committee, 1988; Hennessy, 1990: 618). Moreover, an election – which in fact took place on 11 June 1987 – was pending, and the usual summer break was about to intervene. For these reasons, and possibly others, the issue was shelved until the late summer. In July, however, the MPO in the Cabinet Office, under Anne Mueller, identified 12 possible candidates for agency status (Cabinet Office, 1991; *Financial Times*, 7.8.87: 6).

Initially, discussions only took place at official level. The Treasury seems to have been drawn into policy making intermittently from about August onwards. Discussions were certainly fairly well developed by the time ministers were informed of the nature and progress of the review. The draft report was said to be 'endorsed' by ministers in late October 1987 (Cabinet Office, 1991: 3; Walker, 1987). However, it is not clear whether this endorsement took place in cabinet committee, or in a more informal meeting. Nigel Lawson (chancellor of the exchequer) claims that he and other colleagues were informed of the contents of the draft report 'out of the blue' by Number 10 when the report already had Thatcher's 'enthusiastic' backing (Lawson, 1993: 391). Once the matter was considered at ministerial level, positions began to harden.

Lawson, in line with Treasury concerns, claims to have persuaded Thatcher that the matter of maintaining effective control of agencies' expenditure had to be addressed. From this point, the issue was discussed more widely across government departments, with the Treasury acting as main protagonist. From October 1987 to January 1988 the matter mainly reverted to being handled at official level. A 'long battle' (Lawson, 1993: 392) or 'lively debate' (Butler in Treasury and Civil Service Committee, 1988: 57) ensued. Very top civil servants were drawn in. Press leaks suggest that the long battle/lively debate was at its height in late November/early December.

The Treasury's main concern was that creation of executive agencies within the civil service could weaken its control over budgets, manpower and pay. It also sought to ensure that if executive agencies were created it would be closely involved in overseeing their implementation. Formally, it was in favour of 'the maximum possible degree of delegation that is consistent with those central controls which remain essential' (Treasury and Civil Service Committee, 1988: 68).

The outcome of discussions at official level was a lengthy concordat negotiated in late December 1987/early January 1988 by Sir Robin Butler, who was to take over as cabinet secretary in January 1988, on behalf of Number 10 and the Cabinet Office, and Peter Middleton (permanent secretary to the Treasury) on behalf of the Treasury. It stated that each agency would be subject to financial targets agreed with the Treasury (Lawson, 1993: 392). It did not, however, undermine the principle of creating executive agencies. In January/ early February 1988, Butler discussed the proposals with the civil service trade unions (*Financial Times*, 19.2.92).

The consequence of these discussions was that the document finally agreed was somewhat different from the original draft submitted to Thatcher in May 1987 (Flynn *et al.*, 1990: 163). However, the main proposal to create separate agencies within the civil service was retained. The issue did go to a cabinet committee consisting of almost the entire cabinet (*Financial Times*, 5.2.88; 13.2.88), and was formally ratified by cabinet on 18 February. The Next Steps report was published that very afternoon.

Exit from the cabinet system

Publication of the Next Steps report was accompanied by a Commons statement by Thatcher which fully endorsed its main points (Privy Council Office, 1990: 4). The report stated that changes implicit in it could only take place 'if a strong lead is given from the centre' (Efficiency Unit, 1988: 11). It recommended that a full permanent secretary be designated 'project manager' to implement the changes (Efficiency Unit, 1988: 13). Peter Kemp was appointed to this position and, backed by his two superiors (prime minister and cabinet secretary), oversaw the formative implementation stages of the programme. Within five years, more than two-thirds of the civil service had been removed from the day to day control of traditional government departments. In addition, agencies employing more than half of all civil service staff had taken responsibility for their own pay and grading arrangements (Office of Public Service and Science, 1993: 6–8). The Next Steps initiative thus represents the greatest change in the structure of the civil service to have taken place this century.

Analysis

The outcome of this case was determined mainly by the very small group of people involved in it. They were predominantly officials. The issue was slightly delayed by external factors in summer 1987, but largely kept to a regular timetable. Some elements were selected out of it as a wider group of people became aware of the nature of the reforms being proposed, but the core proposal to create executive agencies survived.

The key shaping points in policy development were launch of the review on 3 November 1986, development of the scrutiny and drafting of the report from November 1986 to May 1987, acceptance of the report's main proposals by Thatcher in May 1987, inclusion of a wider group of ministers in October 1987, and agreement of the Butler–Middleton concordat at the turn of 1987–8. The effective final decision point was neither cabinet nor cabinet committee, but much the same group of people as controlled policy development throughout. Cabinet was merely brought in formally at the end to endorse a set of proposals which had already been largely decided.

The number of key actors was decidedly limited. The issue arose at the very centre of the cabinet system, and was only at a late stage taken into the wider government system. The main initiators were officials in the Prime Minister's Office: Ibbs and other members of the PMEU, backed by the prime minister. Their initiative took place in the context of a widespread recognition of the need to review existing programmes. Policy development was organised by the PMEU team – Jenkins, Caines and Jackson – and overseen by Ibbs and Armstrong. Some liaison with Thatcher took place. This group shaped the detailed framework of proposals within which subsequent policy development took place. It set the agenda to which others had to react. Thereafter, the range of participants was widened to include Mueller and members of the Cabinet Office's personnel and management division, Lawson, other ministers, and Treasury and other officials. Important roles were played by Butler and Middleton. However, throughout the momentum of the exercise was provided by the central actors involved in policy initiation.

A number of lessons about cabinet system operations can be drawn from the case. This issue took an unorthodox route through the cabinet system. Despite being a radical change in policy, it did not substantially involve ministers collectively either in cabinet or in cabinet committee. It also stayed mainly outside formal cabinet system machinery. Cabinet ministers were involved in policy development, but not until after an established set of proposals had already been endorsed by the prime minister. Much of this involvement appears to have been on an informal basis. Procedure was not, therefore, constraining in this case, though it did marginally slow policy development in summer 1987. Instead the issue was ably managed by central actors, who determined when to hold it back and when to introduce it into the system.

One of the major reasons why Thatcher, aided by members of the PMEU in particular, was able largely to develop policy from the centre was that matters relating to the civil service come substantially within the policy domain of core cabinet system institutions, and very often do not require legislation (as in this case). Hence, collective initiative and participation are likely to be limited. The position of the prime minister, in particular, is strong because as senior minister for the civil service, matters to do with its structure, operation and efficiency come largely within his or her domain. In effect, the prime minister is lead minister on these issues. Thatcher thus had a substantial resource base in this sphere. Indeed, as was noted in Chapter 3, this resource base has been strengthened in recent years, and was an important part of the context within which this issue was shaped. Concentration of responsibility also assisted the speed with which the issue was handled.

In relation to individual factors, the case reveals an important division in responsibility for operation of the civil service at the cabinet system level. The core actors and institutions are the prime minister and his or her advisers, the cabinet secretary and his advisers and the Treasury. Within this context, this case illustrates the power potential of a prime minister and those surrounding him or her. While the Treasury is often considered to be in a strong position, in this instance it did not have a veto, and could do little more than blunt the impact of the initiative (Thain and Wright, 1995). Equally, the famed resistance of the civil service to reforms which might negatively affect its own methods of working (Kellner and Crowther-Hunt, 1980) is not substantiated in this case.

The NHS review, 1988–9

Origins

The National Health Service (NHS) review was partly consequential on policy change elsewhere, and partly of external generation. It was consequential on two main types of previous policy change. One was government attempts since the mid-1970s to limit public expenditure growth, the other was its concern to inject business principles into all parts of the public sector. By the late 1980s, these policy initiatives had generated a perceived cash crisis in the NHS, and had also partly restructured it through introduction of general management principles. The result was widespread public concern at alleged 'under-funding' of the NHS, and an internal NHS structure which both provoked professional dissent, and made possible a further stage of reform.

Public concern developed substantially at the end of 1987. By December, the NHS was at the centre of media debate, and evidence of internal discontent was increasingly prevalent. The issue took top position on newscasts, and dominated such routine political matters as prime minister's questions in the House of Commons. In opinion polls, the NHS climbed from a concern rating of 32 per cent in November 1987 to 52 per cent in December. It climbed further to 64 per cent in January 1988, at which point it removed unemployment from the position of chief voter concern that it had held for the previous seven years (*Sunday Times*, 31.1.88).

By the start of 1988, the ramifications of previous policy change and media and public disquiet had thus contributed to a substantial NHS crisis. Although pressure on health secretary John Moore mounted, no major initiative was announced. The fact that Moore himself was ill with pneumonia may have contributed to his lack of action.

Entry into and treatment by the cabinet system

The issue thus entered the government machine at cabinet system level when prime minister Margaret Thatcher seized the initiative and launched a major NHS review programme. She did so following informal discussions with senior ministerial colleagues (*Sunday Times*, 31.1.88). Policy makers felt constrained to act by political crisis, and viewed the issue as high priority. They had no solution in mind at point of entry into the cabinet system.

The need to act was first emphasised by Moore himself, who in mid-January clearly became convinced that major reform had to be undertaken, and started to send briefings to Thatcher. On Friday 22 January, he met Thatcher to urge a review. She remained cautious (*Sunday Times*, 31.1.88). However, over the weekend pressure for action continued to mount through media coverage of the issue. On the night of Sunday 24 January, at a routine meeting to discuss the forthcoming budget, chancellor of the exchequer Nigel Lawson took the opportunity to suggest that an NHS review be launched. 'Margaret,' Lawson (1993: 614) writes, 'appeared to agree.' By the morning of Monday 25 January, Thatcher was on the verge of being persuaded. Following her regular meeting with leader of the House of Commons John Wakeham and party chairman Peter Brooke, she called Moore and chief secretary John Major to 10 Downing Street to discuss the matter. These meetings confirmed her decision to order a review to 'think the unthinkable' (*Sunday Times*, 31.1.88). The review itself was announced by Thatcher that evening during a live interview on the BBC *Panorama* programme. No formal cabinet system, or even wider governmental, machinery was used to take this decision.

In the interview, Thatcher announced that she would take personal charge of the review and dismissed the option of a royal commission on the grounds that it would take too long (*The Times*, 26.1.88). At the start, it was expected that proposals for NHS financing would be published within the next few months, possibly in the form of a green paper. In fact, the review took a year to publish any proposals, and when it did so they took the form of a white paper which said a great deal about NHS structure but little new about finance.

The review team set to work immediately, meeting for the first time on Wednesday 27 January (*The Times*, 28.1.88). It was extremely small, consisting at the start of Thatcher, Lawson, Major, Moore and Tony Newton (health minister). Also in regular attendance were Sir Roy Griffiths, J. Sainsbury executive, deputy chairman of the NHS Management Board and health service troubleshooter throughout the Thatcher years, and John O'Sullivan from the PMPU (Lawson, 1993: 614–15). The one major change to the team's composition was made on 25 July 1988, when a cabinet reshuffle split the DHSS in half and left Moore in charge of social security. Kenneth Clarke, who had previous experience in the DHSS, was elevated to health secretary, and brought into the review team in place of Moore. David Mellor was also appointed to the Department of Health (DoH), taking Newton's place in the team.

The review team never gained a formal footing. In its first days, it was stated that the team would steer events 'for a few weeks' until a proper cabinet committee had been set up (*The Sunday Times*, 31.1.88). However, this transition never took place. Instead, the team operated in much the same fashion throughout. Lawson (1993: 615) states that it met every week, and more frequently towards the end. Thatcher (1993: 616) reports that she chaired 24 ministerial meetings during the period of the review. Both accounts support the notion of a close-knit group meeting largely in secret on a regular basis.

The start of the team's deliberations was accompanied by a public relations offensive which saw Thatcher meet the 1922 executive, and Moore address a private meeting of the 92 Group of Conservative parliamentarians. Launch of the review was also the trigger for proposals on NHS reform to flood the political arena. Some were clearly likely to gain more attention from the review team than others. Notably out of favour were health workers' unions, as well as the doctors' 'union', the British Medical Association (BMA). In favour were Conservative MPs and right-wing think tanks, such as the Centre for Policy Studies (CPS), the Institute of Economic Affairs (IEA) and the Adam Smith Institute (ASI). Ideas such as health vouchers, compulsory medical insurance and reformed management structures were quickly floated by these individuals and bodies (*The Times*, 5.2.88). The CPS, and in particular David Willetts, was very close to the review team throughout (Griggs, 1991). Proposals from these outside bodies seem to have fed directly to Moore and the PMPU. However, the detailed work was undertaken by officials in the DHSS, Treasury and PMPU.

Thatcher was clearly the leading figure in the early stages of the review team's work, and remained key throughout. She considered NHS reform to be the government's top priority, and was determined to take personal charge of policy making in this sphere. By late February, three main options were being considered (*The Times*, 23.2.88). The first was a hypothecated health tax with the possibility of opt-out, raised by ex-cabinet minister Sir Leon Brittan in a Conservative Political Centre pamphlet published on 11 February. The second was introduction of an NHS internal market, proposed on an experimental basis in an IEA pamphlet published on 15 February. The third was health management organisations (HMOs) on the American model, strongly supported by a CPS pamphlet co-authored by Willetts and published on 25 February. The second of these three options had been considered for insertion in the Conservatives' 1987 general election manifesto, but ruled out as untimely (*The Times*, 23.2.88). Indeed, it had first been floated by an American health economist in 1985, and had formed part of the context in which Thatcher and then secretary of state Norman Fowler conducted a series of long-range discussions in the summer and autumn of 1986, culminating in a Fowler paper discussed by ministers in January 1987 (Thatcher, 1993: 607).

In February 1988, a white paper was expected by October at the latest, and possibly as early as July. However, in spring 1988 the work of the review team did not progress as quickly as had been hoped by some of its members. As early as 7 February, *The Sunday Times* reported that civil servants were jeopardising the review, claiming that it would take at least a year to produce necessary basic data about the NHS. As the review progressed it became clear that DHSS (later DoH) officials were indeed finding it difficult to produce the information required by the review team. The reason for this is just as likely to have been genuine problems in amassing detailed statistics as deliberate sabotage.

The result is that the work of the team became bogged down in the spring and early summer of 1988 (Griggs, 1991). At the time of the cabinet reshuffle, *The Times* (26.7.88) reported that progress was so slow that some analysts questioned whether the review was happening at all. Even Thatcher (1993: 614) had begun to feel that the team might be losing its way. Lawson (1993: 619) reinforces this view, claiming that DHSS and DoH papers were so weak that much analytical work had to be undertaken by a hand-picked team of Treasury officials headed by Hayden Phillips, on secondment from the Home Office.

Nevertheless, considerable work was undertaken in the DHSS/DoH. At the start, Moore commissioned 12 background papers on consultants' contracts, financial information, efficiency audit, waiting times and scope for increased charging (favoured by Lawson and the Treasury). In mid-March, he produced a paper on long-term options for the NHS. Of the 18 or so proposals listed in it, only two were thought to be realistic: reform of NHS finance and reform of NHS structure. Meanwhile, to focus ideas, in spring 1988 Thatcher held two seminars on the NHS at Chequers. In March, a hand-picked group of doctors was invited; in April a similar group of NHS administrators. The second of these two seminars, held on 24 April, considered the same three options as had resurfaced by the end of February, though by now they had been repackaged into five main alternatives (*The Times*, 26.4.88). All of this activity was brought together by Moore, who submitted a paper to the review team in mid-May (*The Times*, 16.5.88). It contained two main proposals: an internal market and tax breaks for private health insurance. The latter idea was supported by CPS and IEA pamphlets released on 16 May. Initially, Moore's paper was broadly approved by the review group (*The Times*, 16.5.88). However, it provoked a split when the Treasury, in a Lawson memorandum to the group, objected to the idea of tax breaks for private health insurance (*The Times*, 8.6.88). Thatcher (1993: 613) had a different concern, suspecting that a Treasury–DHSS alliance might be developing to undermine her own radicalism.

The review group's loss of momentum in the spring and early summer of 1988 seems to have contributed to Thatcher's decision in July to split the DHSS in two, and bring in Clarke as health secretary. With this change, the review group's concentration on structural reform was confirmed: Clarke ruled out radical reform of funding (*The Times*, 5.9.88; 12.10.88). More generally, health reform seems to have been more clearly driven from the DoH once Clarke had been made secretary of state. In September, once ministers had returned from their summer break, the work of the review group became more focused.

In developing structural reforms, the review group thus increasingly focused on the idea of an NHS internal market. Creation of GP fundholders, a notion said to be Clarke's 'brainchild' (*The Economist*, 4.2.89), came to be viewed as central to NHS reform. Indeed, this was the key innovation which made feasible pursuit of the internal market option. Reports in early September indicated that the review process was 'gathering pace' (*The Times*, 9.9.88). Thatcher chaired a meeting to consider progress, bringing in a wider group of ministers than had previously been involved in the details of the review (*The Times*, 9.9.88). The first authoritative, and accurate, summary of the NHS review team's conclusions came in Clarke's speech to the Conservative Party conference on 13 October. At this stage, it was clear that the Treasury still needed to be convinced of some of the proposed details of the NHS reforms.

Within the DoH, pilot internal market schemes still seemed the most likely initiative (*The Times*, 14.10.88). In addition many key aspects of reform, such as the element which eventually became NHS trusts, still had to be worked out in detail. Nevertheless, the main lines of policy change were now in place, and a bland commitment to NHS reform was included in the queen's speech of 22 November. At this final stage of policy development, the key actors appear to have been Thatcher, who continued to chair review group meetings, Lawson and Clarke. However, although Thatcher was an important contributor to debate, she was not an initiator of material brought to it. Instead, this function was undertaken chiefly by Clarke's team from the DoH, which worked on detailed papers for discussion by the review team. As a result, policy making was in many ways directed from the DoH, and defended in the review group by Clarke. Lawson could call on substantial Treasury resources in assessing proposals made by the DoH team. Thatcher, by contrast, relied chiefly on the limited resources available in the Prime Minister's Office. The most important of these appears to have been Griffiths, with PMPU support. Clarke, an able minister heading a well-resourced team, usually managed to maintain his department's line. In particular, he resisted Treasury attempts, backed by Thatcher, to secure increased control of the health budget.

The final struggle was between the DoH and the Treasury, over the likely cost of reform. In the event, tax concessions for the over-60s were included in the package unveiled as the white paper *Working for Patients* (Department of Health, 1989) on 31 January 1989, but no other financial reforms were announced. The white paper, which had been ready in draft in December 1988, contained little more than a sketch of NHS reform, promising that the details would be filled in later by means of a series of working papers.

Although the white paper went to cabinet committee and was almost certainly endorsed by cabinet, formal cabinet system procedures were largely bypassed by the entire review process. As *Working for Patients* was not considered to require legislation, the issue cannot even have troubled legislation committee.

Exit from the cabinet system

After just over a year, the issue of NHS reform left the cabinet system to be implemented by the DoH. In truth, much of it had been determined by the DoH, notably once Clarke had become secretary of state.

Analysis

This case looks, at first glance, like an example of prime ministerial government in action. Thatcher herself took charge of a major review of health policy, and prompted submissions from a wide array of Conservative thought, including the think tanks which became so prominent in the 1980s. Yet the outcome of the case was not primarily determined by Thatcher, or by new right think tanks. With the minor exception of tax breaks for the over-60s, the only one of many radical ideas to feature in *Working for Patients* was an internal market for health care, which had been discussed in ministerial circles for years. Although the cabinet system considered many schemes for NHS reform in 1988, that which it finally chose was thus in some ways quite organic and limited. The outcome of this case was therefore determined in part by the changed climate that Thatcherism promoted in the 1980s, and in part by the innate conservatism of the British civil service, notably in this case Treasury and DoH officials.

Key shaping points were Thatcher's decision to launch an NHS review, the failure in the early stages to make progress (which contributed to a sense that the review needed to be refocused), the replacement of Moore by Clarke in order to facilitate this, and the subsequent decisions he took to concentrate the work of the review team on structural change. The Treasury evidently applied a veto on major change to the NHS's financial regime but it is not clear when this happened, or even whether anyone fought particularly hard against it.

The key initiating actors were, in the first place, Thatcher and Moore and their officials, and later Clarke and his aides. The key organising actors were Thatcher and her staff. These actors drew in others, notably the members of the review committee. The key initiating and organising actors set the terms of debate and developed items for discussion. However, while the prime minister took the lead, she did not have the specialist information resources necessary to formulate and evaluate policy. It was partly for this reason that she tended to call on outside bodies. Few proposals emanating from these sources were practical or viable. In the end, it took a strong-willed minister drawing fully on the resources of his department to pull the review together.

The case reveals a number of points about operation of the cabinet system. Initially, this issue took very odd pathways through the system. Indeed, Thatcher's review team never was given formal status, and operated very much as an *ad hoc* working group receiving administrative support from a number of quarters. However, this mode of operation did not actually succeed in generating tenable proposals for health reform, and was partially abandoned in July 1988. Once Clarke had been appointed health secretary, the reform process to some extent conformed more closely to normal British government procedures. The DoH became lead department, Clarke lead minister, and the issue was debated by cabinet system actors in a fairly normal manner. However, it is important to note that even at this point, the review team was not given formal status within the cabinet system. Throughout, it remained an informal body within which substantial ministerial debate took place.

The role of procedure was complex. For the entire duration of the review informal procedures were used by Thatcher to bypass standard cabinet system operations. However, when her review team failed to make much progress, she was forced to make something of a return to more orthodox modes of operating. Even then, no formalisation of the review was made. Furthermore, other elements of normal procedure became redundant when it was deemed that the reform programme would not require legislation, and would not therefore have to compete for time in the government's legislative timetable. The role of external factors was limited. Clearly they played a key role in getting health reform on the cabinet system agenda, but thereafter they do not seem to have been decisive. The role of individuals was more significant. Thatcher was clearly important not so much in launching the review – which had become almost inevitable by the time it happened – but in determining its mode of operation. Yet even in this latter regard she was forced to adopt more orthodox methods of procedure and cede some control to the DoH, because of her review team's lack of progress. Perhaps more important, therefore, was Clarke, who as health secretary managed the only real progress that was made by the review. His role was essentially to divert attention from the many schemes launched by outside bodies, and to focus the review team's work on practical ways forward. Lawson, representing the Treasury team, was clearly influential throughout.

This, then, was a policy initiative which was taken into the prime ministerial domain because of its high profile and extreme sensitivity. Initially, it was unclear what was to be done about it. Gradually, however, an agenda was developed, and a policy line established. Only at the end of the process do formal mechanisms of British government appear to have been brought into play, and then in no more than a token fashion.

Council tax, 1990–1

Origins

The origins of council tax were inherited, consequential on previous policy change, and generated from party sources. These categories overlap, for council tax was the chosen solution to the problem of community charge (or poll tax), which dominated the final phase of Margaret Thatcher's premiership. It was one of two main issues at the centre of the leadership challenge which she faced in November 1990. Once Thatcher herself had withdrawn from the leadership election, each of the remaining contenders declared in favour of a review of the tax. John Major favoured limited change. Michael Heseltine called for a fundamental review. Douglas Hurd's position was somewhere between the two. When Major became prime minister, and on 27 November 1990 appointed Heseltine environment secretary, the issue entered the government at cabinet system level. Throughout, it was handled interchangeably by the lead department, other relevant departments, and cabinet system institutions.

Entry into and treatment within the cabinet system

On entry to the cabinet system this issue was viewed as a matter of high priority on which ministers had to act. However, no solution to the problem of community charge had yet been envisaged. It was handled in three main phases of clarification, detailed policy making and decision.

The first phase covered the period from November 1990 to mid-January 1991. Heseltine led the review of the community charge, and on his first day at the DoE set up a working group of civil servants under Robin Young (under secretary), having first consulted Terry Heiser (permanent secretary) (Butler, Adonis and Travers, 1994: 171). From the very start there were important differences within the government, and even within the DoE, about the necessary extent of the review. Heseltine still favoured substantial reform, and was supported by his new minister of state, Sir George Young. However, his local government minister Michael Portillo, inherited from Thatcher, was a strong advocate of community charge. Heseltine's position was bolstered by a perception that a policy of marginal change was unlikely to satisfy Conservative Party and local government interests, and by DoE advice that attempts to amend community charge would be expensive and hard to administer. In addition, something had to be done quickly. A general election seemed likely to take place in 1991, the next community charge bills were due to go out in March 1991, and local elections were to be held on 2 May 1991.

A substantial review was thus quickly signalled. After two days in office, and one cabinet meeting, Major conceded that the review would be 'fundamental' (Hansard, 1990). On 4 December he met Heseltine to discuss the review's precise terms (*Guardian*, 5.12.90) and subsequently created a cabinet committee, with himself in the chair, to oversee the review process. It is not clear whether this was a standing or an *ad hoc* committee, though either one is likely to have been mirrored by an official committee. In addition to Major and Heseltine, the committee's membership included Norman Lamont (chancellor of the exchequer), Kenneth Baker (home secretary), John Wakeham (energy secretary) and Ian Lang (Scottish secretary). It is probable that Kenneth Clarke (education secretary) and David Hunt (Welsh secretary) were also members. From time to time Richard Ryder (chief whip) was drawn into the work of the committee, as was Portillo. Papers for discussion were produced mainly by the DoE working group, though the PMPU under its head Sarah Hogg also contributed ideas, and a Treasury team under Sir Terence Burns (chief economic adviser) and Andrew Edwards (head of the local government finance division) later helped to examine tax options (*The Economist*, 1991b).

During December, cabinet discussed local government finance and emergent options for change. By early January 1991, these included new powers for councils to raise revenue to reduce community charge bills (including a scheme to introduce a property-based tax alongside community charge), removal of education from local government control, and annually elected city managers. Other options, such as a local income tax, had either been ruled out or not even considered. By mid-January, the idea that community charge might be supplemented by other taxes or even abolished was therefore emerging as a serious option. Treasury opposition to further subsidies, problems of amending community charge, and its continuing unpopularity were making it increasingly evident that radical reform would be necessary. In mid-January Heseltine asked his officials to begin detailed work on alternatives to community charge (*Guardian*, 21.2.91).

During the second phase of policy development, from mid-January to 22 March 1991, the key issue was which elements of community charge, if any, should feature in a new package. Two completely separate strands of policy development took place during this phase. The first comprised continuation and clarification of the review. The second investigated a switch of local government revenue from local taxation to central government subsidy.

Strand 1 initially involved prioritisation of options. By early February 1991, the proposal to transfer education to central government control had been ruled out (*Guardian*, 8.2.91), following opposition from the DES and the Treasury. The idea of elected city managers seems to have disappeared at about the same time. This left the government free to concentrate solely on reform of community charge. By mid-February, some ministers on the review committee were beginning to favour a banded property tax based on floor space, with a personal premium levied on the number of adults living in each property (*Guardian*, 20.2.91). This was intended to generate between 50 and

80 per cent of the revenue raised by community charge, which would itself provide the remainder.

This dual tax proposal was soon floated with Conservative MPs, probably at a meeting of the party's back-bench environment committee. Reaction was mixed. Some MPs were concerned that community charge might disappear altogether; others were critical of the proposal to base valuations on the square footage of properties. Major also outlined options at a meeting of the government's parliamentary private secretaries (*The Economist*, 1991a).

By late February, a majority on the cabinet review committee had moved from supporting reform of community charge to favouring marginalisation of it. Some appeared to desire outright abolition, though others resisted this (*The Economist*, 23.2.91). Portillo and Lang were said to be fighting for survival of the principle that everybody should pay something (*Guardian*, 21.2.91). At this time party divisions were also serious, for the issue raised a Thatcherite rearguard action prompted by the fear that with community charge the Major government might abandon other articles of faith. However, events in the real world of politics soon impinged on such rifts. On 7 March 1991 the Conservatives lost their thirteenth safest Commons seat at the Ribble Valley by-election, following a campaign dominated by community charge. Defeat sharpened debate about its survival (cf. Ridley, 1991b).

Throughout this phase Heseltine and Major held a number of private meetings at Number 10 to agree further aspects of reform. Major, constantly accused of dithering, was now under substantial pressure to act. At this stage he actually intervened substantially to ensure that policy development continued at an appropriate speed. Consequently, the matter soon came to a head. On 12 March, Major, Heseltine and Lang had a private meeting in Downing Street. Having received reports that Heseltine intended to present only a property-based tax to cabinet on 14 March, Lang sought to save community charge from abolition. He reportedly secured an assurance that Heseltine was still working on a dual-tax solution. There were also rumours on 12 March that two junior ministers from the No Turning Back group, Christopher Chope (Transport) and Michael Forsyth (Scottish Office), were threatening to resign if community charge was abolished. The rumours were denied, but both ministers discussed the situation with Ryder in the evening (*Guardian*, 12.3.91). As it turned out, the issue was not brought to cabinet on 14 March. Instead, papers were only circulated to members of the cabinet review committee (Macintyre and Huhne, 1991), which met to discuss them prior to cabinet on 14 March. Three alternatives were said to have been presented by Heseltine: a straight property tax, a hybrid tax involving a stepped property levy with discounts for the size of household, and the dual-tax option of a stepped property tax coupled with a reduced version of the community charge. Although the latter option was said to be favoured by some ministers (*Financial Times*, 14.3.91; *The Economist*, 1991b), the weight of opinion in the committee favoured the hybrid tax (Macintyre and Castle, 1991).

Further rumblings on the back-benches took place. A letter to Major from 50 Conservative MPs expressed misgivings about any attempt to abolish community charge. On 18 March, Major met a delegation of Conservative MPs who were worried about the effects of a property tax on home owners in the south east. However, at this point the second strand of policy making was fused with the first in the chancellor's budget statement to cabinet on the morning of Tuesday 19 March. Revenue raised from a VAT increase of 2.5 per cent was to be used to increase government grants to local authorities by £4.3 billion, thereby reducing the average community charge bill by £140 in 1991–2. The importance of this switch was that it diminished the political impact of community charge, at least in the short term.

Strand 2 of policy making had been kept completely separate from the community charge review process. Key players in it were Major, Lamont and other Treasury ministers and their advisers. The idea of providing a subsidy had been part of the budget judgement since at least January. It seems to have crystallized between Lamont and Major before Christmas (Macintyre and Huhne, 1991). The option of switching resources was explored in detail by Treasury ministers at the annual Chevening pre-budget meeting on 13 January, when a figure of around £4 billion was agreed. Attention then turned to means of raising the revenue. A review of alternatives left an increase in VAT as the only serious option. In keeping with normal budget procedures (see Chapter 6) this switch was not revealed to cabinet until the morning of the budget, though Heseltine was informed earlier as a matter of courtesy.

Once the two strands had come together, the momentum behind a largely property-based tax became unstoppable. A further meeting of the review committee took place before broad proposals were put to cabinet on 21 March. Announcing them in the House of Commons, Heseltine referred to a 'local tax under which there will be a single bill for each household comprising two essential elements, the number of adults living there and the value of the property' (Hansard, 1991). His statement reflected difficulty in cabinet over the balance to be struck between property values and headcount. In addition, no decisions had been reached either about the criterion to be used for evaluating property values, or about whether there should be a banding scheme. Heseltine announced that extensive consultation would take place before cabinet reached a final decision. Although the cabinet compromise seemed to contain at least an element of community charge, the budget announcement had taken the sting out of the Conservative back-bench revolt and some ministerial opposition. The stage was thus set for phase three, which ended in May 1991 with effective abandonment of community charge.

To be able to announce the broad details of the new tax before the 2 May local elections, members of the review committee now needed to reach some speedy conclusions. Some progress was made on the banding system for property values and the extent of exemptions in informal ministerial meetings held during the Easter recess. More details were settled between Major and

Heseltine by means of contacts involving Wakeham and Ryder (*The Economist*, 1991a). The key points of decision centred on a series of cabinet review committee meetings in the second week of April 1991. On 9 April the committee met to consider how much of the community charge should survive, but remained split on this issue. However, after Lang withdrew his objection, the committee was able to move in its next meetings on 11 and 16 April to agree details of the proposed package. These included a household tax based on five bands of property values, with a discounted personal element for households with only one resident. It was agreed that the new tax should come into operation in 1993 (*The Economist*, 1991b; Wastell, 1991). It seems that at the 11 April meeting the committee dropped the idea that community charge should survive in any separate form. At the 16 April meeting, attention was paid to groups which should be exempted from the tax. Later that day, a delegation of back-bench MPs visited Major to press their objection to any tax involving a high property element. By this point, however, Major had been advised by Ryder that he could afford to get tough with dissenting back-benchers.

The matter went to cabinet on 18 April, and after lengthy discussion the package was agreed. At this meeting, opposition to the new tax finally gave way. Agreement was facilitated by Heseltine's assurance that the community charge principle that most people should contribute to the cost of local services would be maintained. It was also agreed that Scotland and Wales would follow the same approach as England, and that property values would be divided into seven bands (instead of five), with those living alone qualifying for a 25 per cent reduction.

Exit from the cabinet system

Council tax was announced on 23 April, just in time for the local elections. Some details remained to be decided, notably the number of bands, and the basis on which properties would be valued. Legislation was introduced in autumn 1991, and council tax came into operation in April 1993.

Analysis

The factors which mainly determined the outcome of this case were political. The Major government faced substantial external, and some internal, pressure for reform of community charge. It also faced internal commitment to the principles of community charge. For this reason, development of the new tax took time, and an early wide-ranging package of reform was diluted. In the end, however, ideological considerations were overcome by pragmatism. The issue moved through the cabinet system at a regular pace, although on occasion it was both slowed by internal opposition, and speeded up by external factors.

Key shaping points were the circumstances of the Conservative leadership election in November 1990 (including Major's victory and his appointment of Heseltine to the DoE), ministers' acceptance by mid-January that the review must significantly dilute community charge, the review committee's choice on 14 March of a hybrid tax, Lamont's budget proposals of 19 March, and the decision of the cabinet review committee on 11 April to abandon community charge. Although the issue was considered by cabinet on 18 April, the main parts of the package had already been decided by then. The final decision point was thus cabinet committee, followed by cabinet endorsement.

Key actors were Heseltine, Major, Lamont and other members of the review team, plus officials in the DoE and Treasury in particular. Key initiating actors were Heseltine, Robin Young and the review team in the DoE, who supplied raw material for discussion, and to some extent set the pace for the review. It is remarkable that detailed alternatives to community charge only began to be considered in January. The centre of the cabinet system also took the initiative on occasion, and obliged the lead department to respond to directions from above. Consequently, other key actors who also had a measure of initiative were the prime minister and members of the cabinet review committee, including other implicated departments. The Treasury team, with the prime minister, dominated the second and important facilitating strand of policy making contained in Lamont's budget. Key organising participants were located chiefly in the DoE (strand 1) and Treasury (strand 2). As time pressures generated by the local elections became more intense the prime minister became a key organising participant, intervening to ensure that a fixed timetable was met.

A number of lessons about cabinet system operations can be drawn from the case. To some extent, the issue took orthodox pathways through the system. However, because it was politically hot it was drawn into the cabinet system from the very start, and before long developed an unorthodox strand which resulted in the Lamont budget announcement. Thus, although the case reveals extensive use of both formal and informal structures, and thereby seems to be a classic case of the use of cabinet machinery to ensure full consultation, on closer analysis this impression is misleading. Most ministers involved in the review knew nothing of the budget strand, which remained as exclusive as ever. On at least one occasion minutes of the cabinet review committee were circulated to members only, and not the rest of the cabinet. Major also frequently met Heseltine and others in small groups to determine strategy or details.

Procedure was constraining in this case, chiefly because technical aspects of the new tax were difficult to work out. A move away from the dual-tax option was perhaps inevitable given the severe difficulties of levying community charge. Moreover, the task of evaluating the impact of each proposed variation in the proposed tax, undertaken by the Treasury, was time-consuming, and at times slowed ministerial deliberations. The impact of party in this case was substantial. Conservative back-benchers and the mass party were an obvious constraint on ministerial manoeuvre. In addition, ministers who had previously taken a strong public stance on community charge were hard to move. Each of these factors imposed a significant limitation on the pace of policy development. Individual opportunities are most clearly revealed in Major's ability to influence policy. He and Lamont were the only people who had a real grasp of both major strands of policy development, and were thereby in important positions. Heseltine was also key.

In the end, however, this issue was driven by events, political pressures and approaching deadlines. Initially, there was no clear view of the review's precise remit and even Heseltine's attention appears to have wandered to secondary matters when the single central issue was community charge. Major's stance was always unclear, and in large part he and others seem to have been carried along by time pressures and events. As public attitudes towards community charge worsened, the argument for abolition gained ground. Similarly, the timing and pace of the decision were affected by bad publicity surrounding the government's indecision and Major's alleged 'dithering'. Ministers thus found themselves in a situation where abolition was the obvious choice. Their main task was simply to look decisive in making it.

Pit closures, 1991–2

Origins

The pit closures crisis of autumn 1992 was predominantly consequential on previous policy change. Its immediate origins can be traced to electricity privatisation in 1990. When the 14 privatised electricity companies chose to switch from coal- to gas-fired power stations, a major problem for the coal industry was in prospect. An excess of coal supply, much of it bought cheaply from abroad, compounded problems of declining demand (Parker and Surrey, 1993: 402–3). The future for deep-mined coal thus looked bleak. Until April 1993 the electricity companies were contracted to buy 65 million tonnes of coal per annum from British Coal (BC). However, by that date, at the latest, new contracts had to be negotiated to cover subsequent purchases. This was the key factor in development of the issue (Trade and Industry Committee, 1992a: para. 1). An important background factor was the government's commitment, announced in 1988, to privatisation of the coal industry. From mid-1989 a group of officials in the Department of Energy (DEn) developed privatisation plans for introduction in the next Parliament (Parkinson, 1992: 280–1). If the coal industry was to attract potential buyers it would need to be made profitable, either through substantial efficiency gains or through capacity cuts (*Financial Times*, 13.5.92; 14.10.92; 17.10.92). There was, then, also an element of party drive to the issue.

Entry into and treatment within the government machine

The issue was not activated until the late summer of 1991, when John Wakeham (energy secretary), his officials and BC opened contract negotiations with the electricity companies. The government accepted the market conditions under which energy supply was increasingly operating and the DEn was well aware, through internal studies, that there was certain to be a significant fall in demand for coal (Employment Committee, 1992b: 17). On the basis of these understandings, options such as subsidising coal or limiting permissions for gas-fired electricity stations were effectively ruled out (Employment Committee, 1992b: 266). Throughout, the central policy aims were to agree the best possible contracts, and to deal with consequent social and economic costs.

By January 1992, it was evident that new contracts would mean major job losses and a significant redundancy package. At both ministerial and official level, consultations thus took place between the DEn and the DEmp, with occasional BC involvement. At this stage, when matters were discussed in only the most general terms (Employment Committee, 1992b: 203; 1992a: para. 15), it seemed likely that contracts would soon be settled substantially at interdepartmental level. By late March 1992, a deal was said to be close (Bowen *et al.*, 1992).

At this point, however, the April 1992 general election intervened. On winning it, prime minister John Major abolished the DEn, and placed most of its functions in the DTI, which thereby became lead department on the issue. Timothy Eggar (energy minister, DTI) took responsibility for the negotiations at junior ministerial level. The significance of the general election was that it not only retarded policy development, but, according to press reports, also allowed the electricity companies to reopen the negotiation process and seek a more advantageous settlement (Bowen *et al.*, 1992). Eggar and Michael Heseltine (trade and industry secretary) were immediately briefed on the situation by officials (Trade and Industry Committee, 1992b: 2), but decided not to alter the general thrust of policy. Two distinct, if overlapping, objectives thus faced the DTI: negotiating new contracts and addressing the matter of redundancy.

In negotiating new contracts, Eggar and later Heseltine attempted to increase the target for coal use, but without success. By early June, the parameters of the settlement were thus clear. The generators would probably agree to buy 40 million tonnes of coal in year 1, and 30 million per annum thereafter. About 30 pits could close (Bowen *et al.*, 1992). However, these 'base' contracts were in general outline only, with the result that the DTI's initial aim of announcing the closure programme to Parliament before the summer recess was shelved (Trade and Industry Committee, 1992b: 2). Instead, during the summer efforts continued to conclude the negotiations and achieve a more generous settlement, and DTI ministers and officials pursued alternatives such as new overseas markets for BC (Employment Committee, 1992b: 272). Heseltine also sought legal advice on whether he could bring all the principal players together and force a settlement, but on 7 September was told that he could not (Employment Committee, 1992b: 262). Consequently, on 10 September, with contracts 'almost' finalised, Eggar accepted the settlement on offer as 'fair and reasonable' (*The Times*, 11.9.92).

In addressing the matter of redundancy, DTI ministers and officials were obliged to deal with other departments, notably the DEmp. From mid-June 1992, affected departments were made increasingly aware of the likely scale of job losses, and DTI and DEmp officials began to prepare a statement to the House of Commons. Much drafting was undertaken through correspondence and informal contacts (Employment Committee, 1992b: 235, 203), though one or two formal meetings also took place. At the end of July Eggar sent a letter to ministers in all affected departments seeking ideas for a redundancy package (Employment Committee, 1992b: 263). Thereafter, much work was conducted through ministerial correspondence between ministers, often at junior level, in the DTI, DEmp, DTp, DoE, Scottish and Welsh Offices and Treasury.

Entry into and treatment within the cabinet system

It is difficult to date precisely the issue's entry into the cabinet system, though possible to say that on entry policy makers had to act and had a solution, but viewed the issue as medium priority. On 17 June it was discussed at a meeting of cabinet's EDP committee (Employment Committee, 1992b: 275). Although it is not clear what happened at this meeting, it was certainly around this time that efforts to seek as generous a settlement as possible and to pull together a redundancy package began. In August, the Treasury was involved. A letter sent by Tim Sainsbury (industry minister, DTI) to Michael Portillo (chief secretary) on 1 September to request more funds was circulated to Major, Tony Newton (leader of the House of Commons) and other ministers (Beavis and Harper, 1992). At this stage, then, cabinet system engagement was intermittent and secondary. Policy development continued to centre on the DTI, with other departments being drawn in on its initiative.

In fact, cabinet system involvement does not appear to have been substantial until after 10 September, when the DTI accepted the contract settlement. Thereafter in September, Major chaired at least two Downing Street meetings on pit closures. At the first, he and others were not convinced of the case for closures, suggesting that detailed aspects of the issue had not yet been considered collectively. At the second, Heseltine made a new presentation and satisfied his colleagues that there was no alternative to pit closures. At this meeting, Major sided with other ministers in demanding better redundancy terms from the Treasury. It is not clear whether these meetings were cabinet committees. Around this time, the prime minister also met a number of ministers individually to discuss the matter.

On 16 September the wider context changed abruptly when the government was thrown into crisis by sterling's enforced exit from the ERM. Policy making nevertheless continued, and on 2 October the remaining barrier to completion of the package was overcome when the Treasury finally cleared an enhanced redundancy package (Trade and Industry Committee, 1992b: 10). On the same day Major, Heseltine and Eggar confirmed the decision to press ahead with the closures. Major, advised by Wakeham (now leader of the House of Lords) and Heseltine, was said to have considered the political implications of the programme, and concluded that the government could weather the probable stormy reaction (*Guardian*, 19.10.92). Once this decision had been reached, it remained to be decided when to make the announcement to the Commons, which pits would face closure, and when they would close.

However, the timing of the announcement was forced upon the government when the issue became a matter of public debate. Sainsbury's letter to Portillo had already been leaked in the press on 18 September (*Financial Times*, 18.9.92). Because of the ERM crisis, reaction to it then had been muted. A far greater reaction ensued when on 8 October the press claimed that, during the coming week, BC was expected to announce the closure of 20 pits with the loss of 20 000 jobs (Helm, 1993: 416; Trade and Industry Committee, 1992b: 4). Against a background of intense media interest the original plan, which seems to have been to present the pit closure programme to cabinet at its first regular meeting after the summer recess the following Thursday (*Financial Times*, 16.10.92) and then to Parliament on its return the following week (Hansard, 1992: col. 205), was therefore quickly altered. Final touches were put to the announcement at a meeting on 8 October at the Conservative Party conference. According to Bowen *et al*. (1992), this was an 'ad hoc' committee, the membership of which included Norman Lamont (chancellor of the exchequer), Kenneth Clarke (home secretary), Heseltine, Wakeham, John MacGregor (transport secretary), Ian Lang (Scottish secretary) and David Hunt (Welsh secretary). Gillian Shephard (employment secretary) was not present. The next morning, Major, Heseltine and Eggar met (Jones and Prescott, 1992). At one of these meetings, it was decided to prepare for the possibility of making the announcement on 13 October, one week before Parliament resumed after the summer recess. DTI and DEmp officials were informed of this tentative schedule on 9 October (Employment Committee, 1992b: 235). The final decision on this date was made by Heseltine alone on Sunday 11 October (Trade and Industry Committee, 1992b: 10–11), although he had little freedom of manoeuvre.

The DTI did not receive the definitive list of closures from BC until 12 October (Employment Committee, 1992b: 263), and only then informed the DEmp that an announcement would be made on the following afternoon. As Shephard and Michael Forsyth (minister of state, DEmp) were absent, they were informed by fax (Employment Committee, 1992b: 235). On the morning of 13 October Heseltine, in passing at the end of business, informally told some members of OPD, cabinet's defence and overseas policy committee, of his imminent announcement (Wastell, 1992). This was the first knowledge that some cabinet ministers had of it.

Only on the afternoon of 13 October did the DEmp receive BC's list of closures and Heseltine's statement. Shortly thereafter, Heseltine announced at a press conference that 31 of BC's 50 pits were to close and 30 000 miners would be made compulsorily redundant. BC produced a list of pits and proposed dates of closure, indicating that some would close 'immediately' (Employment Committee, 1992b: 236). As it meant by this the following Friday, in the first tranche of closures BC was not observing the DEmp's statutory redundancy notification period of at least 90 days. Interdepartmental coordination had clearly broken down.

The announcements provoked a public outcry, and gathering concern among Conservative back-benchers in their constituencies (as Parliament was still in recess). The situation was considered at length at a 'tense' Thursday cabinet on 15 October. Shephard was said to be aggrieved that she had not been part of the group which had agreed the closure programme announcement (*Financial*

Times, 16.10.92). Cabinet agreed to further money for retraining in affected areas. Otherwise, it appears to have endorsed the closure programme. Despite this, the Tory back-bench revolt gathered pace, making it increasingly clear that the government might face a Commons defeat on an opposition motion scheduled for debate on Wednesday 21 October. The government therefore altered its position significantly over the weekend of 17–18 October.

On 16 October Lord Walker was asked by both Heseltine and Michael Howard (environment secretary) if he would coordinate a regeneration programme for areas affected by pit closures (Employment Committee, 1992b: 46–7). On Sunday 18 October, at about 2.30 p.m., Heseltine met Major, having already split the list of closures in two in order to allow some pits a stay of execution while policy was more fully explained. Major called a special cabinet committee meeting for 6 p.m. that night, and an emergency cabinet for 9.30 a.m. the following day. Those who attended the special cabinet committee included Lamont, Douglas Hurd (foreign secretary), Clarke, Wakeham, Hunt, Shephard, Portillo and Richard Ryder (chief whip). Ryder emphasised the certainty of a Commons defeat on Wednesday (*Financial Times*, 20.10.92; *Guardian*, 20.10.92; Jones and Prescott, 1992). At Monday's emergency cabinet tentative conclusions agreed the night before were turned into firm proposals. Many ministers were later reported to believe that they had agreed a full-scale review (Macintyre and Castle, 1992). Following the cabinet meeting, Major and Ryder fulfilled a long-standing engagement by lunching with the 1922 executive. Naturally, pit closures were the main point of discussion and Major outlined the decisions reached by cabinet that morning (*Guardian*, 20.10.92; Jones and Prescott, 1992). A number of executive members were also of the opinion that a wide-ranging review had been promised (Macintyre and Castle, 1992).

Later that afternoon in the House of Commons, Heseltine announced a temporary reprieve or moratorium for 21 pits. The other 10 were scheduled to close after the statutory consultation period. He also announced an extra aid package and Walker's appointment as coordinator of the assistance programme. However, Heseltine gave no hint of a reprieve for all pits, or of a wide-ranging policy review (Hansard, 1992: cols 205–7). The back-bench rebellion thus appeared to be weakened, but not undermined. At least seven Conservative MPs still intended to vote against the government, and 10 to abstain. With a 21-seat majority the government would thus be defeated. Ministers therefore spent the next two days desperately trying to assemble a majority. Concessions and clarifications were drawn from them in a series of meetings. The Tory rebels and whips were in constant contact. Major, Wakeham and especially Heseltine were centrally involved. The Conservative whips were also in contact with MPs from the Ulster Unionist Party (UUP).

On the morning of 20 October, the first significant meeting took place between Heseltine and the 1922 executive. Conservative back-benchers were still not content with the government's position, and the 1922 executive refused to back Heseltine's policy until he had conceded a thorough review of pit closures and of energy policy generally (*Financial Times*, 21.10.92; *Guardian*, 21.10.92; Jones and Prescott, 1992). It only finally did so when this concession was made. Heseltine also liaised with Tory rebels on an individual basis. A new position was announced that afternoon by Major. A review would take place 'in the context of the Government's energy policy'. The 21 pits would be safe until the review had been debated in the House (Hansard, 1992: cols 313–18). Later, at 4.30 p.m., further clarification was given by Wakeham in the Lords, where the government was defeated on the issue by 100 votes to 125. In the evening Heseltine addressed the party's back-bench trade and industry committee (*Financial Times*, 21.10.92; *The Times*, 21.10.92). Some rebels announced that they would now support the government, but others refused to concede and pressed for an independent review (*Guardian*, 21.10.92).

On 21 October, the Commons debate on the opposition motion took place against the background of a major protest march in London. In the course of the debate Heseltine, opening for the government, and Hunt, summing up, announced further concessions as whips liaised with recalcitrant Tory back-benchers. The government promised to produce a white paper on the closure programme and energy policy, to employ outside consultants Boyds to review the viability of the 21 pits, and to provide an energy interconnector with Scotland for Northern Ireland (Hansard, 1992: cols 447–59). The latter measure had long been sought by UUP MPs, all eight of whom subsequently abstained on the opposition motion. That motion was defeated by 320 votes to 307. Six Conservatives voted against the government and five abstained.

Exit

During the subsequent few months the pit closure review took place. A white paper, endorsed by cabinet, was finally published on 25 March 1993. It proposed that 18 pits should be closed or mothballed, and one placed in development (Department of Trade and Industry, 1993). On 29 March the government's proposals were approved in the Commons by 320 votes to 295. On the same day, the electricity companies announced that they had finally agreed a new five-year deal with BC which was worth much the same as the agreement which had led to announcement of the closure programme in October 1992. On 1 January 1995 BC's remaining pits were privatised, at least 12 months later than originally intended.

Analysis

In the long term, the government achieved its policy aims in this sphere, though with some delay. Pits were closed and BC was privatised. The factor which mainly determined the outcome of the case was thus ministers' perception of the stark economic reality (which they never questioned) of a changed market for coal following electricity privatisation. However, difficulties were generated by ministers' misjudgement and mishandling of the political dimension of pit closures. In passing through the cabinet system, this issue was significantly disrupted by external pressures. For a while, the closures programme was diluted by these pressures, but in the end the impact was slight.

Key early shaping factors were the government's commitment to market forces and the 1992 general election, which both slowed and reopened aspects of policy development. Three important points of negative decision, when alternative options were ruled out, were at the beginning of the negotiations, in April 1992 when Heseltine and Eggar assumed policy responsibility, and in September 1992 when Major and other ministers were convinced of the case for pit closures. Policy development slowed in summer 1992, as the two key issues of contracts and the redundancy package were explored. Only on 10 September did the government agree the contracts, and only on 2 October, following interventions by the prime minister and other ministers, did the Treasury agree to fund the redundancy package. Thereafter, having cleared these hurdles, policy development was quickened in response to media pressure. In a matter of days, between 8 and 11 October, many overt decisions were taken but they only concerned details and presentational matters. In this short period, interdepartmental coordination was poor. Policy development then went into reverse in the face of public and Conservative back-bench pressure. Key shaping points in this phase were the special committee meeting on 18 October, the meeting between Heseltine and the 1922 executive on 20 October, the various contacts made with back-benchers throughout 20 and 21 October, and finally the Commons vote on 21 October. Final decisions were taken partly in cabinet, and partly almost on the hoof by Heseltine in particular.

Key actors involved in originating and developing the policy came from BC, the electricity companies, the DEn and, later, the DTI. The key individuals were initially Wakeham, and later Eggar and Heseltine, aided by their departmental officials. Colleagues in the DEmp and other departments were drawn in, or at least kept informed. Later, the Treasury was centrally involved. Throughout, however, the DTI was the main organiser of policy development. Key cabinet system actors such as Major and Ryder were only brought in once the issue had been substantially determined. Even then their involvement was only partial. The issue did not go to cabinet until it had become a hot political issue. Also drawn in at a very late stage were Conservative MPs, who might have possessed a veto but never successfully applied it.

The case reveals many aspects of cabinet system operations. This issue took an orthodox route, being largely set by the lead department before being brought into the cabinet system for consideration. Procedures helped to shape outcomes both at the time of the shift in departmental responsibilities in April 1992 and during the summer recess, when little consultation could take place with the parliamentary party over critical aspects of policy development. Procedures also failed badly in this case. Ministerial correspondence, a well-established feature of the cabinet system, generated coordination problems. Relevant ministers and departments were not brought together successfully when time pressures mounted. More widely, the cabinet system failed to spot and deal with a hot political issue. Party was clearly a crucial constraint on ministerial action in this case, revealing the problems of a small Commons majority. Overall, once alternative options had been ruled out, the weight of external factors left little room for individual manoeuvre.

9

□

Lessons from the cases

Our 14 case studies of cabinet system operations have already been analysed individually in Chapter 8. In this chapter we draw comparative lessons from them, employing an institutional approach consistent with that developed in Part 1. This approach enables us to isolate and assess the role of the individual. We also draw lessons from our cases about the effect on policy outcomes of other factors, such as procedure, party and tone of administration. However, before progressing to detailed comparative analysis, we draw some summary lessons from the cases.

Summary lessons from the cases

In drawing those lessons, we concentrate on four main aspects of the progress of issues through the cabinet system. Summarised in Table 9.1, these are origins (column 1), state of play at entry into the system (columns 2–4), treatment within the system (columns 5–6) and impact of the system on policy outcomes (column 7).

Column 1 indicates the extent to which cabinet system actors are constrained by the issues which capture their attention. The origins of an issue form a key part of the context within which cabinet system actors first address an issue, and help to condition the way in which it is subsequently handled. The origins of our cases are varied, and reveal no clear pattern. Only one – the Next Steps report – originated from within the state. Although the origins of this case were also partly consequential on previous policy change, the scope for initiative here was greater than in any other case. In all other cases key initiating actors were severely constrained either by outside (party/external) factors or by earlier policy commitments (inherited/consequential). This lesson is clear: very few issues arrive *de novo* in the cabinet system; all carry considerable baggage.

Columns 2–4 demonstrate further the constraints within which cabinet system actors operate. At point of entry of an issue into the cabinet system they

Table 9.1 Aspects of case study progress through the cabinet system.

	State of play at entry into the cabinet system					Cabinet system treatment	
	(1) Primary origins	(2) Required to act?	(3) Solution at entry?	(4) Priority	(5) Pathway	(6) Final decision point	(7) Cabinet system impact
Industry white paper	Party	No	Yes	Medium	Orthodox	Cabinet	Dilution of initial policy line
Reform of Official Secrets Act	Party, inherited	No	No	Low	Orthodox	No final decision point	Policy halted in cabinet system
Direct elections to European Assembly	External, inherited	Yes	No	Low	Unorthodox	Parliament	Dilution of initial policy line
Chrysler UK	External	Yes	No	High	Unorthodox	Cabinet committee/ informal	Policy substantially made in cabinet system
IMF crisis	Inherited, consequential, external	Yes	Yes	High	Orthodox	Cabinet	Policy continuous with initial line
Trident	Inherited	No	No	Medium	Unorthodox	Cabinet committee	Policy continuous with initial line
Employment bill	Party	No	Yes	Medium	Orthodox	Cabinet committee	Policy continuous with initial line
Falkland Islands	Inherited	No	Yes	Low	Unorthodox	No final decision point	Policy neglect in cabinet system
Community charge	Party, external	No	No	Low	Orthodox	Cabinet committee	Policy refined in keeping with initial line
Sterling's entry into ERM	External, inherited	No	Yes	Medium	Unorthodox	Informal	Policy stalled in cabinet system
Next Steps report	State, consequential	No	No	Low	Unorthodox	Informal	Policy almost wholly made in cabinet system
NHS review	Consequential, external	Yes	No	High	Unorthodox	Informal	Policy substantially made in cabinet system
Council tax	Inherited, consequential, party	Yes	No	High	Unorthodox	Cabinet committee	Policy substantially made in cabinet system
Pit closures	Consequential	Yes	Yes	Medium	Orthodox	Cabinet committee/ informal	Marginal dilution of initial policy line

reveal whether policy makers were required or simply chose to act, whether a solution to the problem had already been developed before the issue reached the cabinet system agenda, and whether cabinet system actors viewed the issue as high, medium or low priority. At this stage the situation of greatest constraint is likely to exist when cabinet system actors are required to act on an issue which is high priority. (Whether or not a solution has been developed is less relevant to the nature of initial constraints on cabinet system actors.) We have four cases of this kind: Chrysler UK, the IMF crisis, the NHS review and council tax. Each was driven to a considerable extent by external factors. In three of the four cases – the exception is the NHS review – the momentum of the issue's progress through the system was substantially out of the control of cabinet system actors. In no other case – with the exception of pit closures at the finish – was this true (though other constraints did of course exist in all cases).

Columns 5 and 6 provide machinery of government indicators, and shift the focus of interest from constraints to procedural matters. Although they are merely descriptive, these columns reveal the flexibility and variety of cabinet system treatment of issues. In terms of the model developed in Chapter 4, only six of our 14 cases can be said to have taken orthodox pathways through the cabinet system (and, as is noted below, even these were unorthodox in marginal ways). The rest were unorthodox to a substantial extent. Similarly, the range of final decision points is substantial and certainly undermines traditional accounts. The fact that only two of our cases were finally decided in cabinet was perhaps predictable: it has long been recognised that power has shifted from cabinet to its committees. Yet only five further cases were fully decided in cabinet committees. In as many cases, final decisions were taken at least partly in informal arenas.

Column 7 lists cabinet system effects in summary form, and shifts the focus of interest again, this time to impact. Here, we seek to make an overall judgement of cabinet system treatment of each issue. Was policy at exit from the cabinet system largely continuous with policy on entry? Was policy chiefly made within the cabinet system? Was the initial policy line substantially expanded or diluted within the cabinet system? In each case, our interest is not policy success or failure, for such matters can only be judged with the benefit of hindsight. Instead, it is a summary result of cabinet system activity. This column reveals that the cabinet system generally had a significant effect on our cases, but that that effect was sometimes positive and sometimes negative. On the negative side, the system operated to stop, stall and dilute issues. On the positive side, it worked to refine and expand them. In four of our cases, policy was largely made in the cabinet system. Three were cases which would normally be expected to have been determined largely in a lead department. Only one – the Next Steps report – fell firmly within the policy domain of cabinet system actors.

Analytical lessons from the cases

Our main concern in this chapter is not to summarise lessons from the cases, but to draw analytical points from them. Our approach is similar to that adopted in Part 1: we work from broad institutional considerations to reach a point at which the role of the individual can be assessed. In this chapter we also examine factors about which we were not able to generalise in Part 1. First, we consider whether the cases conform to our orthodox model of cabinet system operations (see Chapter 4). Then we highlight what they reveal about the system's semi-formal and informal aspects, also discussed in Chapter 4. In line with the analysis conducted in Chapters 4 and 6, we also investigate the effect of procedures on policy outcomes. Finally, building on Chapter 7, we examine the role of party, tone of administration and (at greater length) the individual in shaping policy outcomes. In evaluating individual impact, we apply an institutional analysis which is entirely consistent with that used throughout the book. It leads us to conclude that, while the role of the individual can be important, it is in many instances quite limited, and should not therefore be exaggerated.

Pathways

The case studies reveal that the exact workings of the cabinet system vary substantially across issues. Our cases show significant departures from the orthodox pathway outlined in Chapter 4 (see Figure 4.1 for a summary). As has already been shown in column 5 of Table 9.1, only six of our 14 cases largely followed the orthodox pathway. Even these six all departed from it to some extent. Indeed, two of the six have important irregular features. Although in the IMF case the issue followed a mainly orthodox route, policy making also featured a highly irregular pathway developed by the prime minister in pursuit of the sterling balances strand of policy. This strand was highly secret, and did not involve liaison with other departments (including, at the start, the Treasury). In the case of community charge, the way in which the issue was handled in the lead department (before it had entered the cabinet system) involved bringing in outside assessors and concentrating activity in small study groups. At this stage there was little liaison with other departments, and policy making was completely unorthodox. Although the issue was handled in a mainly orthodox manner in the cabinet system itself, its unorthodox departmental treatment had a significant impact on policy development within that system.

Our other eight cases were unorthodox in many ways. Only the most salient aspects are worth mentioning. In the case of direct elections to the European Assembly, the issue was taken completely out of the ambit of central government by external and party political factors. It then pursued a very irregular pathway through party, the mechanisms of the Lib–Lab pact and Parliament.

In the case of Chrysler UK, the negotiations which characterised the entire case required special – and unorthodox – machinery. In addition, the issue was removed from an orthodox arena at the very end of its cabinet system treatment in order for one minister, Lever, to seek a politically workable solution. In the case of Trident, special high-security pathways were pursued and formal cabinet system pathways were hardly engaged. In the case of the Falkland Islands the issue made an orthodox start, but failed fully to pursue an orthodox pathway. There were two elements to this failure. The lead department had difficulty in placing the issue on the cabinet system agenda. Cabinet system actors themselves failed to prioritise the issue. In the case of sterling's entry to the ERM, the issue never entered the formal cabinet system. In the case of the Next Steps report, the issue was wholly contained within the cabinet system. It hardly engaged formal cabinet machinery, and was initially pursued with little consultation with departments. In the case of the NHS review, policy was driven from within the cabinet system and not through either the lead department or a formal cabinet committee. Finally, in the case of council tax, the issue originated at cabinet system level and continued to be driven from there, with the result that the autonomy of the lead department was severely constrained.

It is clear that the orthodox model of pathways through the cabinet system has to be qualified. The system is in fact characterised by great irregularity. Irregularities arise for many reasons: the nature of the issue, circumstance, choices taken by key individuals. Indeed, the very great flexibility of the cabinet system is revealed. One notable lesson from the cases is that cabinet system actors often play a far more initiatory and directive role than the orthodox model allows.

The cases also reveal the importance of semi-formal and informal aspects of cabinet system operations. Extensive use of semi-formal groups is to be found in all of them. Some among many examples are the ministerial and Treasury negotiating teams established during the Chrysler and IMF crises, the ministerial group under Callaghan and the Duff and Mason working parties in the Trident case, the crucial Chequers meeting in the community charge case, the economic seminar in the ERM case, the 90-day scrutiny team which was instrumental in drafting the Next Steps report, and the semi-formal NHS review group. From these examples alone, the importance of semi-formal groups is evident. Very often such groups helped to predetermine issues by setting the policy agenda which later other actors were obliged to respond to. It is worth noting that not all these groups centred on the prime minister. Some centred on ministers, some on officials.

The cases also provide evidence of the importance of informal relations in the cabinet system. Such relations act as a key lubricant to activities taking place at formal and semi-formal levels. They often serve either to clear or block a pathway, or to mobilise support for one side or another. They can even be effective points of decision taking. Among many examples of informal relations to be found in the cases are the redrafting of the industry white paper by the PMPU and Cabinet Office; Lever's intervention in the Chrysler case; Callaghan's contacts with world leaders (which were later followed up by Lever and Hunt) and his conversation with Crosland on the way home from a European summit in the IMF case; similar contacts between government leaders in the Trident case; Prior's lobbying of E committee in the case of the employment bill; Ridley–Thatcher conversations in the Falklands case; Jenkin's initial conversation with Thatcher and Lawson's subsequent contacts with her in the case of community charge; almost the entire saga of the ERM case; Ibbs' approach to Thatcher in the case of the Next Steps report; connections with think tanks and the involvement of Willetts in the case of the NHS review; and the many informal ministerial conversations which took place in the cases of council tax and pit closures. This lesson is clear: there can be no proper understanding of the workings of the cabinet system unless attention is paid to its less formal aspects.

Procedure

Our cases demonstrate that procedures shape outcomes. Our definition of procedure is broad, and comprises the constitution (that is the membership and remit) of any governmental group involved in handling an issue, its members' interpretation of their remit, the timetable set for or by that group, the methods used by it to process business, and established general government routines (which almost by definition are not manipulable in the short term). Such procedures affect outcomes by limiting or creating opportunities for individual initiative. Procedures may, of course, themselves be manipulated in an attempt to influence outcomes. However, our argument is more general. Even if no explicit manipulation takes place, procedures can still have important consequences. Some of the more evident examples are as follows.

Industry white paper

The constitution of the departmental group, and its interpretation of its task as implementing a radical version of a manifesto commitment, meant that the outcome of its deliberations was inevitably distanced from the acceptable government line. Procedures in the cabinet system were then used to bring policy back into line. Membership of the relevant ministerial cabinet committee was changed when Callaghan was appointed to it, and its chair was switched from Short to Wilson. Redrafting of the white paper was then entrusted initially to official and ministerial cabinet committees under Foot, and subsequently to Cabinet Office and PMPU personnel under Hunt and Donoughue. These procedural manipulations helped greatly to shape the outcome of the case.

Reform of the Official Secrets Act

The procedure of placing policy development in two separate groups under two separate lead departments had clear consequences for progress of this issue. The two groups considered diametrically opposed aspects of the issue simultaneously. This inevitably led to a situation in which ministers were presented with contradictory information and advice. Had only one strand been pursued, the outcome of the case may well have been different. As it was, the issue lacked focus and clarity when presented to ministers, and thus got nowhere.

Direct elections to the European Assembly

In this case, it was not so much government procedures which were significant, but rather those inherent in the Lib–Lab pact and in the timetable imposed by the EEC. Each had an impact on the outcome of the case.

Chrysler UK

At different stages in development of this issue, the constitution of the negotiating team was changed to include Ross, Millan and Lever. These were the three key changes in membership which significantly affected the flow of the issue, illustrating very clearly the way in which procedural changes create opportunities for individual initiative.

IMF crisis

Standard cabinet system procedures, including extensive use of full cabinet and full discussion of the options, were exploited by Callaghan to construct a majority for the Treasury view. This use of regular cabinet system machinery generated collective agreement without ministerial resignations. It was crucial to the decision that was taken. Callaghan's primary aim throughout was to keep the government together. He adopted procedures likely to ensure this.

Trident

The constitution of both ministerial and official groups, and especially the membership and remit of the Duff and Mason groups, were significant factors in shaping the outcome of the case. The procedure of setting up two official working parties, which were then drawn together at official level behind a single recommendation in favour of Trident, meant that ministers were faced with limited choice. More generally, the fact that policy development as a whole was restricted to a very small group of ministers and officials served effectively to exclude many alternative viewpoints.

Employment bill

The use of orthodox procedures helped to shape the outcome of this case. Departmental lead on a policy secured collective agreement, with the result that in the end the departmental line was maintained (even against prime ministerial wishes).

Falkland Islands

In this case, procedural failings were a feature. Coordination of intelligence information was poor, and did not provide ministers with a clear picture of developments in the south Atlantic. FCO ministers did not manage to push the issue on to the cabinet system agenda. Their perception was that the members of ODP would not be supportive. In this instance, a failure to follow normal procedures was decisive in generating a policy vacuum.

Community charge

The constitution and remit of the departmental study groups in the DoE, combined with their working methods of considering each option in turn according to a particular interpretation of their task, served significantly to shape the recommendation that was finally presented to the prime minister and ministers at Chequers. The nature of that meeting, and the manner in which it was conducted, were also important. DoE ministers and officials sought to sell an option. They did not invite colleagues to consider the issue in the round. The study groups' work was also affected by a clear and limiting timetable. In this case, procedures strongly affected policy outcome.

Sterling's entry into ERM

In this case, procedures were used to stall an issue. Thatcher set up a ministerial group to investigate the possibility of sterling entering the ERM, but it produced what to her was the wrong conclusion. The fact that this issue never went into the formal cabinet system aided her in exercising her veto. Although the prime minister manipulated procedures substantially, she failed in the end to stop sterling from entering the ERM.

Next Steps report

Key procedural aspects of this case were the composition and remit of the scrutiny group. These set the framework for further policy development and created the opportunity for the prime minister to endorse the policy line which had been established. Subsequently, negotiations between the Treasury and the Cabinet Office were largely focused on details. A negative procedural point is that little collective discussion of the report took place.

NHS review

In this case, procedures were manipulated by the prime minister, who largely bypassed formal cabinet system procedures by setting up a semi-formal working group. It was only when the departmental contribution was increased in the second half of the review that real progress was made and a solution was found.

Council tax

Time targets forced central actors to keep the pressure on policy development. As time pressures became more acute, others were forced to give way and to agree to the emerging policy line.

Pit closures

Outcomes were affected by general government procedure over the summer. The failure to consult back-benchers is partly explained by the intervention of the long parliamentary recess. This made the task of gauging Conservative parliamentary opinion difficult. Extensive use of ministerial correspondence was an important factor in the breakdown of collective policy making which took place prior to announcement of the closures.

Our cases demonstrate that procedures do matter. We do not claim that they determine outcomes, merely that they help to shape them. In some cases, such as community charge, the impact of procedures on policy outcomes was substantial. Thus procedures, which are often neglected, need to be considered alongside other factors which shape the framework within which individuals act. Procedures shape outcomes by privileging distinct views and interests and by either creating or restricting opportunities. They are also open to management and manipulation. They are therefore a form of cabinet system power potential which is often most easily exploited by central actors, notably the prime minister and his or her advisers. However, our cases show that others, often in quite secondary positions, also have the ability to exploit this potential.

Party

Many of our cases illustrate and confirm the point made in Chapter 7, that cabinet system–party links are close and persistent. However, they are not always important. Party factors shaped the development of policy in all our cases except Trident and Next Steps. In the Trident case, Labour ministers found themselves pursuing a policy line which was directly contrary to the party's stated position. In the case of Next Steps, policy development was of little concern to the Conservative Party, and it was not therefore drawn in by policy makers. In all other cases, party played a part in policy development, though the extent to which it did so varied greatly. In some, party had a direct impact on the details of policy outcomes. In others, it shaped the context in which policy development took place. Only two main areas of party impact are investigated here: origins, and key considerations shaping policy outcomes.

Party was an important element in the origins of five of our cases (Table 9.1, column 1): industry white paper, OSA reform, employment bill, community charge, and council tax. In three of the five, party was also important in shaping policy outcomes. The employment bill, community charge and council tax were all affected significantly by Conservative Party concerns. In the other two cases, by contrast, party concerns succeeded in placing an issue on the agenda, but did not have much impact thereafter. The industry white paper was substantially diluted in the cabinet system. OSA reform was halted in it. In a further three cases – direct elections to the European Assembly, the Falkland Islands and pit closures – party was not a significant originating factor, but became important in shaping policy outcomes. In the case of direct elections to the European Assembly, party was the determining factor in shaping the final decision. In the case of the Falkland Islands, the lobby in the Conservative Party, and notably in Parliament, contributed to ministers' reluctance to confront the issue. In the case of pit closures, back-bench pressure induced the government to make important concessions in the timing and staging of its programme. Indeed, like council tax, pit closures involved persistent liaison with the parliamentary party, and showed how close contacts between ministers and government back-benchers can be. Council tax also reveals the extent to which ministers now seek to anticipate likely back-bench reaction.

It is worth noting that although four of our cases – the industry white paper, direct elections to the European Assembly, the IMF crisis and pit closures – illustrate the difficulties (noted in Chapter 7) of a small parliamentary majority, three others – reform of the Official Secrets Act, Chrysler UK and Trident – indicate that it is not always constraining.

Tone of administration

We argued in Chapter 7 that different administrations have different tones. We analysed tone of administration in terms of prime ministerial style and mode of cabinet system relations, and plotted all 11 post-war administrations on a matrix (Figure 7.1). In seeking to determine the impact of tone of

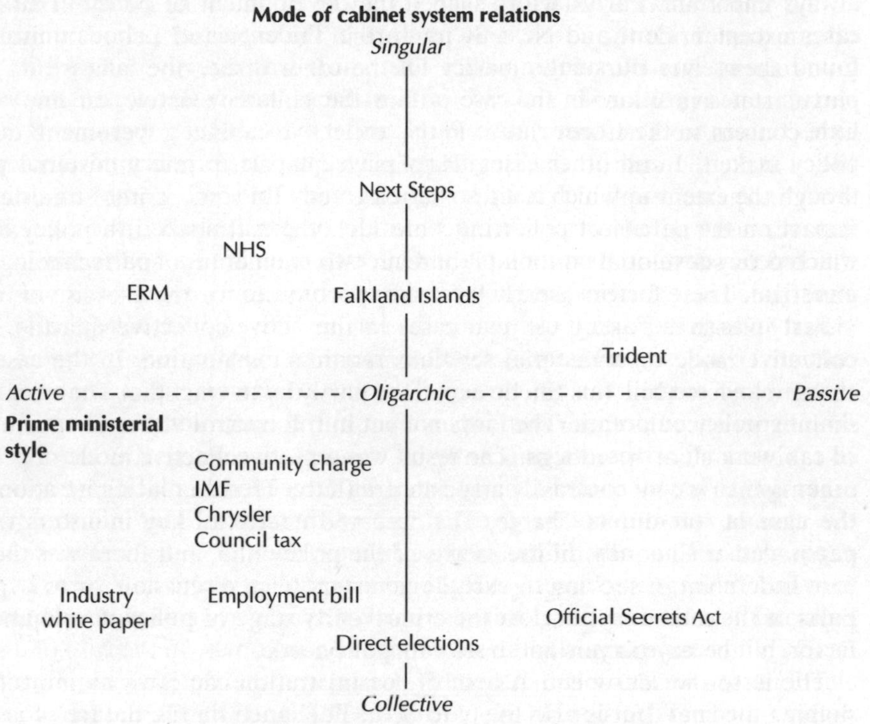

Mode of cabinet system relations
Singular

Next Steps

NHS

ERM　　　　　Falkland Islands

Trident

Active - - - - - - - - - - - - - - - - - - *Oligarchic* - *Passive*

**Prime ministerial
style**

Community charge
IMF
Chrysler
Council tax

Industry　　　Employment bill
white paper　　　　　　　　　　　　　　　　　　Official Secrets Act

Direct elections

Collective

Figure 9.1　Tone of administration characterising our 14 cases

administration on policy outcomes, we engage in a parallel exercise by plotting our 14 cases on the matrix developed in Chapter 7 (Figure 9.1). Although our placings are not pinpoint accurate, they do reflect relatively secure judgements.

These rather crude estimations demonstrate that tone of administration is by no means constant across cases, and that in terms of impact it is therefore itself affected by the nature of the issue at hand. Tone of administration is constraining, but not in an unvarying way. This point can be illustrated by investigation of the Thatcher administration, which many accounts place high on the singular and active dimensions. Indeed, many former ministers of the Thatcher years – Prior (1986), Gilmour (1992), Lawson (1993), Howe (1994) and even Thatcher (1993) herself – as well as many commentators on those years – Riddell (1983), Jenkins (1987) and Young (1991) – are united in characterising her administration in this way. We do not want to suggest that actors' perceptions are unimportant. Clearly, they can crucially shape strategies. Nevertheless, our seven cases from the Thatcher years demonstrate that issue can be an important influence on individual relations within the cabinet system.

Our cases provide us with seven instances of the tone of the Thatcher administration. Of the seven, only four are in the expected 'prime ministerial government' quartile of the matrix. Of the other three, one falls within the singular/passive quartile and two within the collective/active. In line with expectations, no Thatcher case is in the 'collective cabinet government' quartile. Taking the case in the singular/passive quartile, prime ministerial passivity requires explanation. In the case of Trident, prime ministerial intervention and objective-setting were highly constrained in a policy area marked by substantial continuity, bureaucratic momentum and technological expertise. These factors greatly limited opportunities for the exercise of individual initiative. Taking the two cases in the active/collective quartile, the collective mode of ministerial relations requires explanation. In the case of the employment bill, this can be explained partly by the fact that Thatcher was an inexperienced premier who was not yet in full control either of cabinet or of cabinet system operations. The result was a more collective mode of policy making than is conventionally associated with the Thatcher administration. In the case of community charge, Thatcher and nearly all key ministers were persuaded at Chequers of the merits of the policy line, and there was therefore little point in seeking to exclude ministers from discussion, or to bypass parts of the cabinet system. At the critical early stage of policy development, nearly all the key players had been brought on side.

The lesson we draw is that tone of administration can have an impact on policy outcomes, but is also likely to be itself shaped by the nature of issues passing through the cabinet system. Two more general points are that there is a prime ministerial effect, but it is neither unidimensional nor absolute and that, on the basis of even the crude plotting undertaken here, any simplistic notion of prime ministerial government is not sustainable.

The role of the individual

In line with the approach adopted in Part 1 we come, finally, to evaluate one of the most variable influences on policy outcomes in the cabinet system, that of the individual. Throughout, a central theme of our analysis has been that actors' attitudes, preferences and strategies are shaped by institutional considerations. We build on this theme in examining the roles of individuals in our cases.

Our approach focuses on outcomes, and analyses individual actions according to institutional criteria. We judge observed individual activity against the kind of activity that might normally be expected of an individual occupying a given position. Did the minister's or official's action conform to type? If it did, we hold the individual to be unexceptional, and to have had no significant impact on policy outcomes. If it did not, we hold the individual to be exceptional, and assert that he or she may have had a significant impact on policy outcomes. It is

266

important to note that even in these latter cases the issue of individual impact is framed in the conditional. An individual's action has only been identified as potentially significant. Actual impact has yet to be determined.

Central to our attempt to identify instances of actual individual impact is the concept of institutional prediction. We hold there to be two main dimensions to this concept. The first relates to an actor's ends, and focuses on the policy line which he or she seeks to promote. The second relates to an actor's means, and focuses on the strategy employed by him or her in pursuing those ends. According to the institutional theory which we employ, both means and ends are institutionally shaped. Not only the goals an actor seeks, but also his or her ways of seeking them, are influenced by the institution to which he or she belongs. Institutions have established policy positions (ends), and accepted ways of pursuing them (means). Once this point is established, the concept of institutional prediction and its two dimensions follow. We therefore attempt in this section to identify individual action which is exceptional on one or both of these dimensions. Having done so, we consider whether it had a significant impact on outcomes.

Ours is not the only means of evaluating individual impact, but it is consistent with the approach adopted throughout this book, and it does enable us to draw conclusions which are methodologically grounded. Our approach is also not exact. Indeed, whether an individual did or did not act in conformity with established institutional policy positions and modes of promoting them is essentially a matter of judgement. However, in analysing our 14 case studies of cabinet system operations we have found most individuals' actions to be readily classifiable. Where they are not, we say so.

In judging individuals' institutional affiliation within the cabinet system, each case clearly has to be taken on its merits. However, we can make one broad generalisation at the outset, between inner and outer core actors. All cabinet system actors are core in the sense that they operate at the very heart of British government. Some, however, operate in the inner core and are those actors whose attitudes, preferences and strategies are comprehensive across the range of government concerns. They comprise the prime minister and members of the prime minister's private office, cabinet secretary and deputy secretaries in charge of Cabinet Office secretariats, government business managers and their support staff, and those senior ministers who chair a significant number of cabinet committees. On the basis of institutional position, this group of individuals can be expected to be concerned chiefly with overall strategic issues which reflect the unity and success of the government. They seek to balance factional and departmental pressures, to effect coordination of distinct policy lines, to ensure efficient despatch of business within the cabinet system, and to manage presentation of the government's case in order to maximise its perceived success.

Outer core actors are those with access to the cabinet system whose attitudes, preferences and strategies are partial when judged in terms of cabinet system activity as a whole. These actors do not have the overarching perspective held by inner core actors. They include departmental ministers and their senior officials, who can be expected to promote a departmental line, plus other players who are from time to time drawn into the cabinet system, such as major party figures and interest group leaders. If acting institutionally, these individuals can be expected to conform to the known interests or established policy line of the constituency which they represent.

Of course, an individual may have more than one institutional affiliation, and this may generate conflicting lines of expected behaviour which the individual must resolve. An individual may, for example, be both a departmental minister and a central actor. Chancellors of the exchequer are sometimes in this position. Alternatively, an individual may hold a ministerial post and be an important member of a party faction. In the 1970s Tony Benn and Michael Foot clearly experienced this conflict. It could be argued that Margaret Thatcher experienced a similar conflict in the 1980s, though in her case the party faction to which she related was not strongly organised and did not, therefore, provide her with a clear institutional affiliation.

Our hypothesis, then, is that where an individual can be shown to operate outside what would be predicted in terms of institutional affiliation, then that individual is attempting to make an individual contribution to policy development. At this point, the actor is trying to create or exploit an opportunity on a purely individual basis. He or she may or may not be successful in the attempt. The individual can therefore be said to matter only if his or her action has a significant impact on the final outcome of policy, that is if policy is altered as a direct result of his or her initiative.

Once an individual behaves in a way which is not predictable on the basis of his or her institutional position, the deployment of personal skills and resources becomes critical to individual success. Naturally, other actors may themselves respond in an unpredictable manner, opening up the opportunity for them to exploit their own skills and resources. In essence, policy making at this point resembles an unpredictable game, in which personal attributes are to the fore. The kinds of personal skills and resources which are likely to be conducive to success were analysed in Chapter 7. As has already been stated, the impact of an episode of this kind on policy outcomes may be entirely insignificant.

This, then, is the means by which we assess individual impact. In conformity with this approach, we classify our 14 cases into three groups. The first comprises cases in which individuals acted in line with institutional prediction. The second comprises cases in which individuals acted unpredictably, but had no significant impact on policy outcomes. The third comprises cases in which individuals acted unpredictably, and did have a significant impact on policy outcomes. As can be seen from Table 9.2, eight of our 14 cases fit the latter classification. In all cases of individual unpredictability, we identify the individuals concerned.

Table 9.2 Classification of cases in terms of individual actions and impact.

Individuals acted in line with institutional prediction

Industry white paper
Reform of Official Secrets Act
Pit closures

Individuals acted unpredictably but had no significant impact on outcome

IMF crisis (*Callaghan, his advisers, Crosland and social democratic group*)
Trident (*Callaghan, Owen*)
Employment bill (*Thatcher, Howe, Hoskyns*)

Individuals acted unpredictably and had a significant impact on outcome

Direct elections to European Assembly (Callaghan)
Chrysler UK (Wilson)
Falkland Islands (Carrington, Thatcher)
Community charge (Jenkin, Baker, Waldegrave, Heiser, officials, Thatcher, Whitelaw, *Lawson*)
Sterling's entry to the ERM (Lawson, *Thatcher*)
Next Steps report (Ibbs, Jenkins, Caines, Jackson, Thatcher, Butler, Armstrong)
NHS review (Clarke, *Thatcher, Moore*)
Council tax (Major, Treasury officials)

Italicised names identify individuals who acted unpredictably but had no significant impact on policy outcome.

In engaging in detailed analysis of the role of the individual in the cabinet system, we begin by investigating those three cases in which individuals acted in line with institutional prediction.

Industry white paper

In this case, two individuals appear to have played significant roles. One is Benn, who as industry secretary acted in clear opposition to the established departmental policy line, and in evident contravention of established ways of doing things. However, Benn can in fact be identified as acting in a predictable sense on the basis of his institutional affiliation to a Labour Party faction. For him, this affiliation was more important than his ministerial position. It shaped his conduct substantially. The second individual is Wilson, whose strategy in organising the reception and processing of the draft of what was to become the 1974 industry white paper is in fact typical of a central actor concerned to maintain the unity of the government, and to produce an acceptable raft of policies on which to fight an imminent election successfully. What Wilson did could be very much predicted on the basis of his institutional position.

Reform of the Official Secrets Act

This case was also wholly predictable on institutional grounds. It failed to reach a positive outcome because no individual was able to act independently of institutional interest and break the institutional deadlock. The only possible exception is Callaghan, who was personally antipathetic to reform. However, his position can be interpreted as that of an experienced central actor immersed in the institutional culture of secrecy characteristic of British government.

Pit closures

Again, this case was predictable on institutional grounds. The important decision of Heseltine and Eggar not to explore alternatives to pit closures was in keeping with the established line of departmental policy. Both ministers maintained this line throughout, though they did try to expand the policy field by exploring complementary options. None of their explorations was successful; thus, institutional policy continuity was maintained. Central core actors also acted predictably. Major accepted the departmental line, and attempted to determine the best way of despatching policy. The 1922 committee also acted predictably in representing the concerns of back-bench Conservative MPs. Once external events took over inner core actors, such as Major, Wakeham and Ryder, entered a negotiating situation in an attempt to hold the government and party together. Heseltine's key involvement in this situation remains predictable, as his central concern was to maintain the thrust of his department's policy.

In three of our 14 cases, an individual or some individuals did act out of line with institutional prediction, but had no significant impact on policy outcome.

IMF crisis

Callaghan and his immediate advisers in the PMPU and Cabinet Office all acted outside their predicted institutional roles in pursuing the sterling balances line of policy development. Many other ministers also acted unpredictably. Chief among them were Crosland and the other members of the social democratic group, who had no institutional basis for the initial line of resistance which they took to the IMF's loan conditions. In the end, however, each of these ministerial initiatives was insignificant. The left-wing group in the cabinet acted predictably in conformity with the policy line of an established Labour Party faction. It too had no impact on policy outcomes. In the end, the Treasury line prevailed.

Trident

This case was also unpredictable on institutional grounds. Callaghan's decision to handle policy development in a secret working group which had no formal cabinet system status was out of line with the procedure established by his immediate predecessors (and, as it turned out, with that followed by his immediate successor). It had no significant impact on policy development. In addition, Owen's attempt with the help of his FCO policy unit to develop the Cruise alternative to Trident was also an unpredictable individual initiative. The attempt entirely failed.

Employment bill

This case was predictable until Thatcher, accompanied by Howe and backed by Hoskyns, moved outside her institutional remit as a central actor and sought to undermine the departmental policy line by exploiting links with organised groups in the parliamentary party. In this way, she was clearly acting outside established ways of doing things. Prior responded by also acting unpredictably. He sought to counter Thatcher's personal initiative by canvassing and mobilising support in unorthodox ways. Prior's individual response was effective in countering Thatcher's initiative, and ensured that the initial, departmental policy line was pursued to a successful conclusion.

In eight of our cases, an individual acted out of line with the institutional prediction with significant consequences for policy outcome.

Direct elections to the European Assembly

This case was predictable on many counts. Wilson's initial acceptance that progress needed to be made was in keeping with existing treaty obligations. He also operated in the European arena as a central actor in a bargaining game. The FCO line was predictable, as was the Home Office commitment to a first-past-the-post mode of election. However, the key decision to allow a free vote in the House of Commons, though predictable in terms of central actors' ends, was highly unpredictable in terms of means. Callaghan's primary aim – to maintain the unity and ensure the survival of his government – was very much the priority that a prime minister is expected to take. His concession of a free vote in the House of Commons was, however, unpredictable in its suspension of the cardinal cabinet system convention of collective ministerial responsibility. This concession was critical to the final outcome of the case. It is worth noting that Foot's actions, though not predictable on the basis of his central actor role, can be explained institutionally by his commitment to organised groupings of the Labour left. In a position of institutional conflict, Foot chose to honour his links with the wider PLP.

Chrysler UK

This case was also predictable on many counts. All departmental ministers acted in conformity with existing departmental policies or interests. Wilson displayed a central actor's concern to maintain the unity of his government, being interested primarily in wider political factors. However, his decision to commission Lever to take part in a bargaining game, though in conformity with central actors' predictable ends, was an unpredictable means of pursuing them. This decision was also critical to the outcome of the case. Healey's role in the case merits comment. He was subject to an institutional conflict between his roles as leading Treasury minister concerned to control public spending, and as central actor. His decision to act on the basis of the latter commitment cannot really be identified as unpredictable.

Falkland Islands

Development of this issue was unpredictable in two main ways. The first was Thatcher's unwillingness to address the issue speedily in the autumn of 1979. The second was Carrington's failure in the second half of 1981 to push the FCO policy line sufficiently hard to ensure that it secured the necessary collective hearing. Both actors failed to act in line with established ways of doing things. Although it is hard to make a definitive judgement in this case of policy neglect, it seems likely that these two institutionally unpredictable actions may have had some impact on the Argentine decision to invade the Falklands. They certainly affected the lack of preparedness on the part of the British, and can therefore be identified as significant.

Community charge

This case was unpredictable from the beginning. Jenkin's decision in September 1984 to reopen the policy area was entirely unpredictable. The established institutional position was that the issue had been thoroughly considered in two reviews, and was now off the agenda. This institutional position applied at both cabinet and departmental level. Party pressure for reform of the rates was not substantial. Subsequently, Baker, Waldegrave and Heiser operated outside normal departmental procedures in setting the remit, membership and working methods of the two study teams. This contributed significantly to the narrowing of options to one only, the per capita tax which was presented to ministers at Chequers. Given the impact on party and the electorate of Scottish revaluation and any possible English revaluation, Thatcher's decision at Chequers to sanction community charge was not unpredictable for a central actor. It could only be said that Thatcher was acting outside the remit of a central actor if she had been presented with a full review of all the options, and had herself chosen the policy to be pursued. From this point, Thatcher acted partly predictably for a central actor in that she sought to ensure efficient processing of a departmental policy which had secured priority on the cabinet system agenda. However, she and other central actors, such as Whitelaw, were unpredictable in the sense that they failed to fulfil one of the major tasks of a central actor, which is to take full account of the political implications of policy. In this context, Thatcher's enthusiastic embrace of the per capita tax option became significant. Lawson's pursuit of his own critique of community charge was unpredictable but insignificant.

Sterling's entry to the ERM

This case was also unpredictable from the start. Lawson's decision seriously to pursue ERM membership did not reflect either existing policy or the Treasury line. One of his few early supporters, the governor of the Bank of England, also acted outside the institutional prediction. These individual initiatives were significant in that they succeeded in converting the policy line of both the Treasury and the Bank in favour of ERM membership. In this context Thatcher's veto, applied at the ministerial meeting in November 1985, was a further unpredictable initiative in that it involved a central actor in deliberately undermining the collective ministerial view, and thereby threatening the cohesion of the government. Thatcher's intervention affected development of the issue, but not its eventual outcome. Her subsequent refusal to allow the issue to return to the cabinet system agenda was also unpredictable. Howe, Hurd and Major acted entirely predictably. The key significant individual in this case was therefore Lawson, not Thatcher, because it was his personal initiative which succeeded in transforming the Treasury line, and building the coalition necessary for ERM membership.

Next Steps report

In this case, it was predictable that Ibbs should commission a review of existing progress on management reform, given the evidence coming to him. What was not predictable was his decision to select a 90-day scrutiny as the form that the review would take. Such scrutinies had been conducted within the civil service ever since 1979. Their established mode of operation was to subject an area of departmental business to fundamental review. Once this procedural decision had been taken, a radical solution to the perceived problem was always a possibility. The exact content of that radical procedure was not predictable either, and for this Ibbs, Jenkins, Caines and Jackson were responsible. The prediction of Thatcher's institutionally conditioned behaviour relates to her role as ministerial head of the civil service. Viewed from this perspective her behaviour was not institutionally predictable. In agreeing to exploration, and later acceptance, of the Next Steps proposals, she allowed a move to take place which was radically at odds with the well established policy line of previous years. A break with the concept of a unified civil service was the result. Butler also acted unpredictably, and it seems likely that Armstrong did too. Significant individual impact was the cumulative result.

NHS review

In this case, it was not unpredictable that Thatcher should initiate a policy review. What was unpredictable was her decision to place the review team at the centre, rather than in the relevant department. Moore also acted unpredictably in going outside established fora of advice, but in the end his actions were insignificant. Thatcher's behaviour never became institutionally predictable, but when her original initiative failed more responsibility for policy development was taken by the relevant lead department. Clarke then acted unpredictably in pursuing a more radical solution than his departmental position would lead one to predict. In terms of outcome, Clarke was key.

Council tax

This case was in many ways predictable. In fact, the entire central strand of policy making conformed to institutional expectations. Major operated as a typical central actor both in commissioning a review, and in keeping it under close scrutiny. Council tax was one of the main government priorities, and had to be completed by a set time without splitting the government or the party. Hence, his interventions in the passage of the issue were highly predictable. Heseltine's personal animosity to community charge happened to coincide with the DoE's departmental line, which was that further reform of community charge was not viable. Given the history of local government taxation reform, it was almost inevitable that some kind of property tax would be selected. Lang's position reflected his role as a kind of central actor within the Scottish ministerial team. His defence of community charge was driven by factors within that team, and his eventual capitulation came only when he became convinced that he could sell a property tax to the Scottish party. In this case, unpredictability lay in the second strand of policy making contained in Lamont's budget. Major was unpredictable in developing this strand. Indeed, his was an important example of prime ministerial initiative. Lamont might be said to have been unpredictable, in that he was prepared to act more as a central actor than as a Treasury man. However, he is better viewed as an individual with conflicting institutional loyalties. By contrast, his officials clearly acted unpredictably.

Using institutional criteria, we have isolated significant individuals. These are individuals who not only seized an opportunity, but who also had an impact on policy outcomes. In fully six of our 14 cases, individuals did not have a significant impact on outcomes, which were instead shaped largely by broader institutional and contextual factors. In the remaining eight cases individuals were able to exploit opportunities successfully and to have a significant impact on outcomes. The range of formal positions held by these individuals varied. However, in six cases the prime minister was a significant actor, twice being singularly so. Although this indicates that the prime minister is in a strong position to have a significant impact on policy outcomes, our cases clearly reveal that others may also be similarly positioned. They also reveal the constraints on significant action on the part of any cabinet system actor.

The perspective taken by many traditional accounts of the cabinet system is that individuals are critical to policy outcomes. We do not deny that there is truth in these claims. Indeed, our analysis provides some support for them. However, we do hold that such claims must be analytically grounded, and have deployed the concept of institutional prediction as a means of doing this. On this basis we also make the further point that individual impact in the cabinet system should not be exaggerated. If individual actions are judged according to the criterion of predicted institutional response, our cases show that a significant individual impact on policy outcomes is by no means always registered even in high-profile cases. Individuals may of course be significant in other ways, by affecting the wider context and institutional framework within which they and others operate. However, such exercises of individual initiative are not susceptible to precise analysis. Individual impact on outcomes is. It is also one of the most important and commonly accepted indicators of individual significance.

Conclusion

In this chapter, we have presented some of the main lessons which may be drawn from our 14 cases. We have examined six key issues: pathways taken by business passing through the cabinet system, semi-formal and informal aspects of that system, and the impact of procedure, party, tone of administration and the individual on policy outcomes. Each element of our analysis reinforces the argument developed throughout this book, that the contemporary cabinet system is a complex set of organisations and positions which can only be understood as a whole. It operates at formal, semi-formal and informal levels and is structured not only by distinct values and practices, but also by a range of networks and processes. Its links with the rest of the government system, and with the outside world, are also complex. Some contacts, such as those with elements of the governing party, are persistent and often pressing.

One of the primary values of case-study analysis is the possibility it presents for evaluating the role of the individual. An element of cabinet system operations which we found difficult to analyse in the general terms of Part 1 has been subjected to sustained examination in Part 2. By means of our case studies, we have shown that individual initiative is always constrained and dependent on a wide range of conditioning factors. Even when opportunities for individual initiative do exist, few actors are either willing or able to overcome the confines of expected patterns of behaviour.

The central theme of our analysis of the role of the individual in the cabinet system is therefore constraint. All individuals operate within the margins of defined roles, and in keeping with established lines of policy. The scope for and incidence of genuinely individual contributions are far less substantial than is often suggested. In this regard, the impression given by memoirs, diaries, biographies and the media clearly requires qualification. The individual inevitably looms large in such accounts. Yet when a broader analysis is conducted, and consideration is given to wider institutional and circumstantial factors, the picture changes. The individual still has a place, but it is more often in the shade than in the sun.

□

Conclusion

By examining the British cabinet system as a complex set of institutions, we have been able to chart changes in the power potential of cabinet system actors during the course of our period 1974–95. Part of our concern has been to validate the argument that a more partial approach can only yield partial understanding. More importantly, we have sought to document shifts in power potential within the cabinet system over the past 20 years. In many ways those shifts have been substantial: the power potential of cabinet system actors has been significantly extended and substantially redistributed in our period. Despite this, central actors remain deeply constrained by both institutional and wider contextual factors. Alongside our central theme of enhancement of the power potential of cabinet system actors has therefore been a clear recognition of the constraints to which they have always been, and continue to be, subject.

In the context of constraint, in this concluding chapter we address four issues which arise in relation to the extension of power potential which cabinet system actors have experienced during our period. We look first at the extent to which the power potential of cabinet system actors as a group has been enhanced. Secondly, we analyse shifts in the distribution of power potential within the cabinet system. In these two ways, we provide a summary account of change in our period. We then, thirdly, consider ways in which the increase in power potential of central actors can be explained. Finally, we consider future challenges to the cabinet system.

Enhancement of the power potential of cabinet system actors

Enhancement of the power potential of cabinet system actors as a group, or extension of the capacity of the system as a whole, is reflected in many developments documented in this book. They include the creation of new organisations, the location of new functions and activities at the centre, the extension of existing functions, the selective development of cabinet system involvement in the wider governmental system, and the increase in staff numbers which have been witnessed in our period. Of these, the acquisition and development of functions, and the increased involvement in the wider government system, are most significant.

Organisational developments within the cabinet system have been extensive. They include creation of the PMPU in 1974, of the PMEU (in the Cabinet Office) in 1979, of the science and technology secretariat and of the MPO in 1983. Each of these last three new organisations was drawn into the most important new organisation of all, created as OPSS in 1992 and re-established as OPS in 1995. OPS has expanded the central executive territory by drawing in new functions and staff from other departments, notably the Treasury. Creation and development of these organisations has established a range of new positions at the very heart of British government. Each has had an impact on the operation not only of the cabinet system, but also of the wider system of central government.

Paralleling these organisational changes are far more significant changes in cabinet system functions. A substantial range of new functions has been located in the system. In addition, existing functions have been expanded. Examples of new cabinet system functions are responsibility for government efficiency, civil service management and public service standards. Examples of substantially enhanced cabinet system functions are found in the spheres of EU policy coordination, national security information and policy and government presentation. In general terms, this expansion in functions has extended cabinet system actors' involvement in the wider governmental system. Other changes have also extended cabinet system oversight capacity. The efficiency drive launched in 1979, the successor FMI and Next Steps programmes, and the Citizen's Charter initiative have all increased central oversight of departments (see Chapters 2 and 5), as have changes in the management of business flows above the level of department (see Chapters 3 and 4). More generally, rule changes have enhanced the ability of central actors to police divisions of functions both within and between departments.

Further indication of the extension of cabinet system capacity is to be found in its increased staff numbers, which have grown substantially in both the Prime Minister's and Cabinet Offices. In the Cabinet Office, growth in the course of 20 years has reached nearly 300 per cent. A large part of this increase directly reflects the increase in functions now undertaken at the centre. However, it is important to note that the vast majority of Cabinet Office staff now work in OPS, and are not therefore all engaged in high-profile cabinet system activity (see Chapter 2). Indeed, the number of staff involved in what have traditionally been central cabinet system tasks, such as those undertaken by the secretariats, has fallen during our period. We believe that no straightforward conclusions about cabinet system activity can be drawn from this decline. Indeed, we maintain that the power potential of the central state has increased *despite* a fall in staff numbers at the very centre, and *because of* a rise in staff numbers in other parts of the cabinet system.

Expansion in cabinet system capacity has been partnered by enhancement of its position in relation to other central government agencies. In part, this has been a product of growth. New functions and new oversight capacities have inevitably highlighted the presence of the centre. In part, it has been a product of regularisation and systematisation. Even in spheres of activity in which it has long been involved, the cabinet system has developed more directive potential. Facilitative links have become more focused on cabinet system actors and agencies (see Chapter 4). Networks in which the cabinet system is involved have become more concentrated at the centre (see Chapter 5). In general, the centre has been extended in such a way that more communication lines and information flows run into and out of it. The contrary trend, which has seen business of a less central nature increasingly devolve to departments (Chapter 2), has not undermined this expansion of central capacity. It has simply meant that the cabinet system has increasingly devoted its energies to genuinely core aspects of politics and policy, with the result that the division of responsibility between the cabinet system and departments has become more coherent.

In our terms, developments in the period since 1974 constitute an important alteration in the disposition of central government. At its core a formidable central machine has emerged. That machine has, of course, been built over a period of years. We do not claim that its creation has been a feature solely of our period, rather that the gradual pattern of growth documented in Chapter 1 has continued during our period. The cumulative outcome of that growth has now reached a point at which a substantial central executive, centred on the Prime Minister's and Cabinet Offices, exists. Indeed, part of our aim has been simply to reveal the significance of this development, though we have also had wider ambitions. Our first point is, then, that during our period the centre has been extended and the combined power potential of those who operate within it has been enhanced. This is of course not to say that the actual exercise of central executive power has been more directive in the contemporary period than in earlier ones. Real exercises of power are a function of individual dispositions to exploit power potential, and of the institutional context and wider circumstances in which they seek to do so. They cannot, therefore, be generalised. It is also not to say anything about the external constraints within which all cabinet system activity takes place. In all periods, these are key conditioning factors.

Change in the distribution of power potential within the cabinet system

Overall enhancement of the power potential of cabinet system actors has been partnered by change in its internal distribution. Some have gained more than others. Some have even seen their power potential diminish during our period. The major trend change is an extension of that which has affected the cabinet system as a whole. Just as the capacity of the centre has been enhanced, so the capacity of those at the centre of the centre has also been extended. In the past 20 years, core cabinet system positions have experienced an enhancement of power potential.

This point emerged very clearly from our analysis of networks and tasks (see Chapter 5). In virtually all of our eight networks, the centre of gravity has moved towards the centre of the state in recent years. We were thus able to show in Table 5.1 that core positions within the cabinet system are now strongly advantaged. Similarly, our analysis of business transacted by the classic arenas of the British central executive, cabinet and cabinet committee demonstrated that these collective arenas have declined in usage (see Chapter 2). The overall result has been an increase in the power potential of central actors. The core positions which have been particularly advantaged by change during our period are the prime minister and officials in the Prime Minister's Office, and the cabinet secretary and officials in the Cabinet Office. In this context the creation of OPS and the formalisation of the position of coordinating minister have been important. Relationships between this minister, the prime minister, and their lead officials, are now crucial to the operation of the contemporary cabinet system.

An important element of change in the power potential of central actors has been its regularisation. Expansion of central capacity both before and after 1974 has taken place in a largely *ad hoc* fashion. New functions and oversight capacities have been developed piecemeal at the centre. However, in time attempts have usually been made to impose some pattern on all elements of cabinet system activity. The period since 1974, like many earlier periods, has been marked by systematic attempts to impose some order on the gradual central accretion of functions which has taken place. The change in the position of central actors during our period has thus been regularised through institutional change.

This process of regularisation has been particularly characteristic of the Major administration. Its approach can partly be seen as a tidying-up operation following the extreme semi-formality and informality of the Thatcher years, though it amounts to far more than this. The Major period has in fact witnessed a substantial consolidation of changes which have taken place incrementally since 1974, and especially since 1979. The system of ministerial standing committees has been streamlined through consolidation of overarching domestic and overseas committees in EDP and OPD, reduction in the number of standing committees, and redistribution of responsibilities between them. Business has also been concentrated in formal ministerial standing committees of cabinet, with the result that the use of *ad hoc* and official committees has experienced a precipitate decline. Similar changes have been made to the organisation of Cabinet Office secretariats. On the domestic side, the economic and home and social affairs secretariats have effectively been fused, thus accentuating the distinction between domestic and overseas business. When these developments are analysed together, what emerges is a cabinet and committee machine which is both leaner and sharper and in which activities are drawn more clearly into formal structures. Consolidation is further reflected in the creation of OPS within the Cabinet Office. This has provided a new location for many functions which have been brought within the centre over a period of years. The placing of the OPS under a cabinet minister has served to regularise this accumulation of functions. Under Major and cabinet secretary Butler, the cabinet system has thus become more institutionalised and more firmly embedded in the established framework of government. Theirs has been a period of great significance, akin to the period of expansion and consolidation which took place under Attlee and cabinet secretaries Bridges and Brook.

Explaining contemporary cabinet system change

Change since 1974 in the overall extent and internal distribution of cabinet system power potential can be explained in a number of ways. Most explanations reflect long-term and global trends, though local factors have also been important.

The first long-term and global trend is an increase in government functions of a cross-departmental nature, which has almost inevitably required the placing of activities at a level above departments. This increase has taken place for a number of reasons. The growing interdependence of global politics means that personnel in national executives are not only increasingly involved in international issues, but also required to coordinate responses across a wide range of domestic policy. One indication of this is the finding of a recent OECD report that overseas aspects of policy are increasingly impinging on domestic policy questions and issues to such an extent that in all states central executives are having to enter previously autonomous spheres to ensure cohesiveness in policy making (Organisation for Economic Co-operation and Development, 1990: 4). A blurring of boundaries has in fact characterised most policy areas, and has provoked corrective action on the part of many central executives. It has been particularly marked in states, such as the British, which are involved in major supranational organisations, such as the EU. In addition, states in many parts of the world have taken an enthusiastic interest in the new public management, and have developed a series of initiatives aimed at improving the efficiency and effectiveness of public bureaucracies (Greer, 1994). The effects have been centralising in many of them, as attempts to make bureaucracy-wide changes have been made.

The second broad trend has been a recent increase in the importance of functions that have traditionally been undertaken by cabinet system actors. Across the world, the positions of heads of state or government have been particularly enhanced, though others have also benefited. The rise of international summitry is one aspect of this trend (Dowding, 1993; Lee, 1995). In Britain, it has provided the centre with new reasons for drawing policy into its domain. Similarly, the increased importance of global markets has made elements of economic and financial policy, such as those relating to exchange rates and currency movements, a central concern of governments throughout the world. In Britain it has prompted increased prime ministerial involvement in the form of Callaghan's economic seminar, which has been retained in one form or another by both of his successors. Increased media interest in a small number of key actors is also a feature of all contemporary states. In Britain, it has provided the centre with good reasons to draw the government presentation function to the heart of the cabinet system (Foley, 1993).

The third major trend has seen a transfer of central government activity from departments to the centre. In this respect, the precise details of change may differ from state to state. However, a basic administrative logic means that activities which are relevant to the general work of government gradually become located at the centre. In Britain, shifts in the location of responsibility for civil service organisation and management are examples of this kind of change.

In this context of important trends affecting government systems the world over, the influence of local factors is almost certain to be slight. Nevertheless, one which merits attention in the British case is the unbroken period of Conservative government which has existed since 1979. For a number of reasons, we do not believe this to have had a major impact on the structure of the central state. Many trends are international. Moreover, the changes which have taken place since 1979 are part of a cumulative trend which can be traced to 1916. However, 16 years of single-party government have certainly affected the way in which central actors operate. The sheer longevity in office of many ministers has generated an unusual degree of informality among both ministers and officials. It may also have facilitated consolidation of processes of change.

A further local factor which is sometimes held to drive change is the role of key individuals in promoting it. As we have said on a number of occasions, individuals such as Wilson, Callaghan, Hunt, Thatcher, Armstrong, Major and Butler have certainly helped to effect change, and have clearly been instrumental in facilitating it. However, whereas the pace and details of change bear the marks of individual initiative the direction of change does not. For this, deeper and more long-term factors are responsible. Not the least important of these are the continual attempts to manage problems of capacity, competence, coordination and direction which have driven change throughout the twentieth century (see Chapter 1).

Challenges facing the contemporary cabinet system

The contemporary cabinet system is an executive office in all but name. The power potential of actors within it has been enhanced and redistributed during our period, effecting an important shift in the disposition of central government. Yet change generates new challenges, and requires that they be addressed. The record of the twentieth century suggests that the cabinet system will change and adapt further in years to come.

In considering the challenges which face the contemporary cabinet system, it is necessary to reconsider the principles on which the system operates. The point we made in Chapter 1 was that these have been largely unchanged for many decades. They both predate creation of the modern cabinet system in 1916, and have continued to underpin its operations in the modern period. Indeed, all seven of the principles which we described in Chapter 1 remain substantially intact, though some have been compromised at the margins. Most notable in this regard is the challenge posed to exclusiveness by the open government initiatives of the Major administration. Some principles have in fact been reinforced during our period. Executive power has become more focused on a prominent individual and the key staff surrounding him or her. The state remains compartmentalised, though departmentalism, which has been strengthened in subsidiary spheres, has also been seriously challenged in wider areas. The emphasis on the unity of the group remains central to British governing practice, even though the frequency of collective engagement through cabinet and committees has declined. Thus, while the underlying principles of the British central executive remain intact, they are not necessarily secure. The most obvious challenges to them come from four main sources.

The first derives from the internal changes which we have documented. The strengthening of the centre which has taken place throughout the twentieth century has been substantial. It could of course be reversed, but the impulsion given to this change by long-term and international trends makes this seem unlikely. Moreover, there are identifiable ways in which the British central executive could be further strengthened. There is, for example, a case for bringing the government's legal service under the direct responsibility of cabinet system law officers, in order to ensure that a resource which is often used by all departments is effectively deployed. Similarly, as government increasingly operates by contract, an oversight function to ensure proper standards and procedures for setting and monitoring contracts might sensibly be placed at the centre. Indeed, to some extent this function is already undertaken on a purely advisory basis by the development division of OPS (Cabinet Office, 1994a: 34–5). In addition, the increased use of information technology for the creation and dissemination of documents within Whitehall is certain to raise security questions, and could require that a policing function be created in the cabinet system. In many ways, then, the centre has been, and is likely to continue to be, strengthened. The problem for the principles on which the

British central executive operates is that further strengthening could place the historic cabinet system tension between singular leadership and the principles of collective and individual responsibility under severe strain.

The second challenge derives from changes which have been sponsored by the centre, and which affect the structure of the entire British state. The Next Steps programme is the core part of a series of reforms of British machinery of government which could substantially affect the operation of the cabinet system. By 1995, nearly 65 per cent of civil servants were located in executive agencies (Cabinet Office, 1994a: 13). By the year 2000, more than 90 per cent of civil servants could be employed by such agencies (Conservative Party, 1992: 228), leaving between 25 000 and 50 000 civil servants in departments to set and monitor the frameworks within which agencies are expected to work, and to provide ministers with policy advice. The potential effects on the cabinet system of small, policy-centred departments have not yet been fully explored. This development opens up a series of possibilities for radical reform, including amalgamation of departments, and creation of a smaller cabinet able to focus increasingly on strategic issues. The administrative logic inherent in these possibilities may, however, be resisted for political reasons.

The third challenge is essentially of external derivation. Generalised calls for more open government, which are partly responsible for the Major administration's initiative in this sphere, and a more specific assertion of parliamentary rights through the select committee system, could oblige the central executive to introduce clearer mechanisms of accountability than currently exist. Only some elements of the cabinet system currently come within the range of parliamentary accountability. The prime minister and other cabinet system ministers are accountable to Parliament through ministerial questions. Structure of government and civil service management functions fall within the remit of the Treasury and civil service select committee. Reform in this sphere could take the form of a more substantial oversight capacity, possibly by means of an extension of the select committee system, to cover the whole of cabinet system business.

The fourth challenge to the contemporary cabinet system concerns coherence and has both internal and external sources. Within government, complexity of administration across departments is a continuing problem and requires renewed efforts at coordination. From outside, the increasingly intrusive attention of the media obliges ministers and those who speak for them to ensure that a clear and consistent message is presented. Meeting this challenge implies further central development of the coordination and presentation functions of government. Michael Heseltine's appointment as deputy prime minister is merely the latest attempt to address this problem. Enhancement of cabinet system capacity in this area seems certain to bring into question the principle of departmental autonomy.

All four challenges strike at the underlying principles of the British cabinet system. One of the major issues facing it in the years ahead is the extent to which these challenges will require overt recasting of those principles.

Bibliography

☐

Alderman, R. K. and Cross, J. (1985) 'The reluctant knife: Reflections on the prime minister's power of dismissal', *Parliamentary Affairs*, vol. 38, pp. 387–408.

Anderson, B. (1991) *John Major*, Headline, London.

Andeweg, R. (1993) 'A model of the cabinet system: The dimensions of cabinet decision-making processes'. In Jean Blondel and Ferdinand Müller-Rommel (eds), *Governing Together: The Extent and Limits of Joint Decision-Making in Western European Cabinets*, Macmillan, Basingstoke, pp. 23–42.

Armstrong, K. and Bulmer, S. (1995) 'The United Kingdom'. In Dietrich Rometsch and Wolfgang Wessels (eds), *The European Union and Member States: Towards Institutional Fusion?* Manchester University Press, Manchester (in press).

Bagehot, W. (1963) *The English Constitution*, C. A. Watt, London.

Baker, D., Gamble, A. and Ludlam, S. (1992) 'More "classless" and less "Thatcherite"? Conservative ministers and new Conservative MPs after the 1992 election', *Parliamentary Affairs*, vol. 45, pp. 656–68.

Baker, K. (1993) *The Turbulent Years: My Life in Politics*, Faber & Faber, London.

Barber, J. (1992) *The Presidential Character*, 4th edn, Prentice Hall, New Jersey.

Barnett, J. (1982) *Inside the Treasury*, Andre Deutsch, London.

BBC (1988) *The Very Model of a Modern Mandarin*, BBC2, London, 20 December.

Beavis, S. and Harper, K. (1992) 'Treasury blocks aid funds as thirty pits are marked for axe', *Guardian*, 18 September.

Beer, S. H. (1965) *Modern British Politics: A Study of Parties and Pressure Groups*, Faber & Faber, London.

Bender, B. G. (1991) 'Whitehall, central government and 1992', *Public Policy and Administration*, vol. 6, pp. 13–20.

Benn, T. (1989) *Against the Tide: Diaries 1973–76*, Arrow, London.

Benn, T. (1990) *Conflicts of Interest: Diaries 1977–80*, Hutchinson, London.

Benn, T. (1992) 'Debate'. In Martin Linton (ed), *The Guide to the House of Commons*, Fourth Estate, London, pp. 54–6.

Biffen, J. (1992) 'Debate'. In Martin Linton (ed.), *The Guide to the House of Commons*, Fourth Estate, London, pp. 52–3.

Blackstone, T. and Plowden, W. (1988) *Inside the Think Tank: Advising the Cabinet 1971–1983*, Heinemann, London.

Blake, R. (1985) *The Conservative Party from Peel to Thatcher*, Fontana, London.

Borthwick, R. (1988) 'The floor of the House', in Michael Ryle and Peter G. Richards (eds), *The Commons under Scrutiny*, 3rd edn, Routledge, London, pp. 53–75.

Bowen, D., Castle, S., Warner, J., Macintyre, D., Faith, N. and Cathcart, B. (1992) 'Who killed King Coal?', *Independent on Sunday*, 18 October.

Bradshaw, K. and Pring, D. (1973) *Parliament and Congress*, Quartet, London.

Brazier, R. (1988) *Constitutional Practice*, Clarendon Press, Oxford.

Brown, A. H. (1968a) 'Prime ministerial power (Part I)', *Public Law*, pp. 28–51.

Brown, A. H. (1968b) 'Prime ministerial power (Part I)', *Public Law*, pp. 96–118.

Browning, P. (1986) *The Treasury and Economic Policy: 1964–1985*, Longman, Harlow.

Bruce-Gardyne, J. (1986) *Ministers and Mandarins: Inside the Whitehall Village*, Sidgwick & Jackson, London.

Burch, M. (1980) 'Approaches to leadership in opposition: Edward Heath and Margaret Thatcher'. In Zig Layton-Henry (ed.), *Conservative Party Politics*, Macmillan, London, pp. 159–85.

Burch, M. (1983) 'Mrs Thatcher's approach to leadership in government: 1979–1983', *Parliamentary Affairs*, vol. 36, pp. 399–416.

Burch, M. (1990) 'Cabinet government', *Contemporary Record*, vol. 4, no. 1, pp. 5–9.

Burch, M. (1993) 'Organising the flow of business in Western European cabinets'. In Jean Blondel and Ferdinand Müller-Rommel (eds), *Governing Together: The Extent and Limits of Joint Decision-Making in Western European Cabinets*, Macmillan, Basingstoke, pp. 99–130.

Burch, M. (1995) 'The prime minister and Whitehall'. In Donald Shell and Richard Hodder-Williams (eds), *Churchill to Major: The British Prime Ministership since 1945*, Hurst, London, pp. 104–36.

Burch, M. and Moran, M. (1985) 'The changing British political elite', *Parliamentary Affairs*, vol. 38, pp. 1–15.

Burch, M. and Wood, B. (1990) *Public Policy in Britain*, Blackwell, Oxford.

Burk, K. and Cairncross, A. (1992) *'Goodbye Great Britain': The 1976 IMF Crisis*, Yale University Press, London.

Burnham, J. and Jones, G. (1993) 'Advising Margaret Thatcher: The Prime Minister's Office and the Cabinet Office compared', *Political Studies*, vol. 41, pp. 299–314.

Butler, D., Adonis, A. and Travers, T. (1994) *Failure in British Government: The Politics of the Poll Tax*, Oxford University Press, Oxford.

Butler, D. and Butler, G. (1994) *British Political Facts 1900–1994*, Macmillan, Basingstoke.

Butler, D. and Kavanagh, D. (1974) *The British General Election of February 1974*, Macmillan, London.

Butler, D. and Kavanagh, D. (1992) *The British General Election of 1992*, Macmillan, London.

Butler, Lord (1975) 'Reflections on cabinet government', interview with Norman Hunt. In Valentine Herman and James E. Alt (eds), *Cabinet Studies: A Reader*, Macmillan, London, pp. 193–209.

Cabinet Office (1991) *Setting Up Next Steps*, HMSO, London.

Cabinet Office (1992a) *Questions of Procedure for Ministers*, Cabinet Office, London, mimeo.

Cabinet Office (1992b) *Ministerial Committees of the Cabinet*, Cabinet Office, London, mimeo.

Cabinet Office (1993) *Central Intelligence Machinery*, HMSO, London.

Cabinet Office (1994a) *The Civil Service: Continuity and Change*, Cm 2627, HMSO, London.

Cabinet Office (1994b) *Ministerial Committees of the Cabinet*, Cabinet Office, London, mimeo

Cabinet Office (1995a) *The Civil Service Year Book*, HMSO, London.

Cabinet Office (1995b) *Ministerial Committees of the Cabinet*, (Cabinet Office: London), mimeo, April.

Cabinet Office (1995c) *Ministerial Committees of the Cabinet*, (Cabinet Office, London), mimeo, July.

Callaghan, J. (1987) *Time and Chance*, Collins, London.

Carrington, Lord (1989) *Reflect on Things Past*, Fontana, London.
Castle, B. (1980) *The Castle Diaries, 1974–76*, Weidenfeld & Nicolson, London.
Castle, B. (1984) *The Castle Diaries, 1964–70*, Weidenfeld & Nicolson, London.
Chancellor of the Duchy of Lancaster (1993) *Realising our Potential: A Strategy for Science, Engineering and Technology*, Cm 2250, HMSO, London.
Channel Four (1993) *Dispatches: A Tax Too Far*, Channel Four Television, London, 10 March.
Civil Service Department (1969) *Information and the Public Interest*, Cmnd 4089, (HMSO, London).
Clark, A. (1993) *Diaries*, Phoenix, London.
Clarke, P. (1992) *A Question of Leadership*, Penguin, London.
Cockerell, M. (1988) *Live from Number 10: The Inside Story of Prime Ministers and Television*, Faber & Faber, London.
Cockerell, M., Hennessy, P. and Walker, D. (1985) *Sources Close to the Prime Minister: Inside the Hidden World of the News Manipulators*, Macmillan, London.
Coleman, B. (1988) *Conservatism and the Conservative Party in Nineteenth Century Britain*, Edward Arnold, London.
Conservative Party (1979) *The Conservative Manifesto 1979*, Conservative Central Office, London.
Conservative Party (1992) *The Campaign Guide: 1992*, Conservative Central Office, London.
Contemporary Record (1989) 'Symposium: The 1976 IMF crisis', vol. 3, pp. 39–45.
Cosgrave, P. (1985) *Thatcher: The First Term*, Bodley Head, London.
Cox, G. W. (1987) *The Efficient Secret: The Cabinet and the Development of Political Parties in Victorian England*, Cambridge University Press, Cambridge.
Crenson, M. A. (1971) *The Un-politics of Air Pollution: A Study of Non-decisionmaking in the Cities*, Johns Hopkins University Press, Baltimore.
Crick, M. and Van Klaveren, A. (1991) 'Mrs Thatcher's greatest blunder', *Contemporary Record*, vol. 5, pp. 397–416.
Crosland, S. (1982) *Tony Crosland*, Jonathan Cape, London.
Crossman, R. (1963) 'Introduction'. In W. Bagehot, *The English Constitution*, C. A. Watts, London, pp. 1–57.
Crossman, R. (1975) *The Diaries of a Cabinet Minister*, vol. 1, Hamish Hamilton and Jonathan Cape, London.
Crossman, R. (1976) *The Diaries of a Cabinet Minister*, vol. 2, Hamish Hamilton and Jonathan Cape, London.
Crossman, R. (1977) *The Diaries of a Cabinet Minister*, vol. 3, Hamish Hamilton and Jonathan Cape, London.
Cunningham, C. M. and Nicholson, R. H. (1991) 'Central government organisation and policy making for UK science and technology since 1982'. In Sir Robin Nicholson, Catherine M. Cunningham and Philip Gummett (eds), *Science and Technology in the United Kingdom*, Longman, London, pp. 27–43.
Daalder, H. (1964) *Cabinet Reform in Britain 1914–1963*, Stanford University Press, Stanford.
Dean, M. (1978) 'The nine lives of a cabinet minister', *Guardian*, 11 February.
Defence Committee of the House of Commons (1981) *Fourth Report: Strategic Nuclear Weapons Policy*, HC paper 36, session 1980–1, HMSO, London.
Dell, E. (1991) *A Hard Pounding: Politics and Economic Crisis 1974–1976*, Oxford University Press, Oxford.
Dell, E. (1992) 'The Chrysler UK rescue', *Contemporary Record*, vol. 6, pp. 1–44.
Department of the Environment (1981) *Alternatives to Domestic Rates*, Cmnd 8449, HMSO, London.
Department of the Environment (1983) *Rates*, Cmnd 9008, HMSO, London.

Department of Health (1989) Working for Patients, Cm 555, (HMSO, London).

Department of Industry (1974) *The Regeneration of British Industry*, Cmnd 5710, HMSO, London.

Department of Trade and Industry (1993) *The Prospects for Coal: Conclusions of the Government's Coal Review*, Cm 2235, HMSO, London.

Devereau, M. (1992) 'Do we need government information services?', *RIPA Report*, 13.

Dillon, G. M. (1989) *The Falklands, Politics and War*, Macmillan, London.

Dilnot, A. and Robson, M. (1993) 'The UK moves from March to December budgets', *Fiscal Studies*, vol. 14, pp. 78–88.

Donoughue, B. (1987) *Prime Minister: The Conduct of Policy under Harold Wilson and James Callaghan*, Jonathan Cape, London.

Donoughue, B. (1988) 'The prime minister's day: The daily diary of Wilson and Callaghan, 1974–79', *Contemporary Record*, vol. 2, no. 2, pp. 16–19.

Donoughue, Lord (1994) 'The 1975 Chrysler rescue: A political view from Number Ten', *Contemporary Record*, vol. 8, pp. 77–83.

Dowding, K. (1993) 'Government at the centre', in Patrick Dunleavy, Andrew Gamble, Ian Holliday and Gillian Peele (eds), *Developments in British Politics 4*, Macmillan, Basingstoke, pp. 175–93.

Drewry, G. and Butcher, T. (1991) *The Civil Service Today*, 2nd edn, Blackwell, Oxford.

Dunleavy, P., Jones, G. W. and O'Leary, B. (1990) 'Prime ministers and the Commons: Patterns of behaviour, 1868–1987', *Public Administration*, vol. 68, pp. 123–40.

Dunleavy, P. and Rhodes, R. A. W. (1990) 'Core executive studies in Britain', *Public Administration* vol. 68, pp. 3–28.

The Economist (1991a) 'The cursed tax', 9 March.

The Economist (1991b) 'The new men at work', 27 April.

Edwards, G. (1992) 'Central government'. In Stephen George (ed.), *Britain and the European Community: The Politics of Semi-Detachment*, Clarendon Press, Oxford, pp. 64–90.

Edwards, J. L. J. (1984) *The Attorney General: Politics and the Public Interest*, Sweet & Maxwell, London.

Efficiency Unit (1988) *Improving Management in Government: The Next Steps: Report to the Prime Minister*, HMSO, London.

Ellis, E. L. (1992) *T.J.: A Life of Dr Thomas Jones, CH*, University of Wales Press, Cardiff.

Employment Committee of the House of Commons (1992a) *Employment Consequences of British Coal's Proposed Pit Closures: Report*, HC paper 263-I, session 1992–3, HMSO, London.

Employment Committee of the House of Commons (1992b) *Employment Consequences of British Coal's Proposed Pit Closures: Minutes of Evidence*, HC paper 263-II, session 1992–3, HMSO, London.

Expenditure Committee of the House of Commons (1976) *Eighth Report: Public Expenditure on Chrysler UK Ltd*, HC paper 596, session 1975–6, HMSO, London.

Fay, S. and Young, H. (1978) *The Day the Pound Nearly Died*, Sunday Times Publications, London.

Flynn, A., Gray, A. and Jenkins W. I. (1990) 'Taking the Next Steps: The changing management of government', *Parliamentary Affairs*, vol. 43, pp. 159–78.

Foley, M. (1993) *The Rise of the British Presidency*, Manchester University Press, Manchester.

Foster, C. D., Jackman, R. and Perlman, M. (1980) *Local Government Finance in a Unitary State*, Allen and Unwin, London.

Fowler, N. (1991) *Ministers Decide: A Personal Memoir of the Thatcher Years*, Chapman, London.

Franklin, B. (1994) *Packaging Politics: Political Communications in Britain's Media Democracy*, Edward Arnold, London.

Franks, Lord (1983) *Falkland Islands Review*, Cmnd 8787, HMSO, London.

Fry, G. (1988) 'Outlining the Next Steps', *Public Administration*, vol. 66, pp. 429–34.

George, S. (1990) *An Awkward Partner: Britain in the European Community*, Oxford University Press, Oxford.

Gill, P. (1994) 'The intelligence services'. In Patrick Dunleavy and Jeffrey Stanyer (eds), *Contemporary Political Studies 1994*, Political Studies Association, Belfast, pp. 170–80.

Gilmour, I. (1992) *Dancing with Dogma: Britain under Thatcherism*, Simon & Schuster, London.

Gordon Walker, P. (1972) *The Cabinet*, revised edn, Fontana/Collins, London.

Granada Television (1976) *World in Action: Chrysler and the Cabinet: How the Deal Was Done*, Granada Television, Manchester.

Greenaway, J., Smith, S. and Street, J. (1992) *Deciding Factors in British Politics: A Case-Studies Approach*, Routledge, London.

Greer, P. (1994) *Transforming Central Government*, Open University Press, Buckingham.

Griffith, J. A. G. and Ryle, M. (1989) *Parliament: Functions, Practice and Procedures*, Sweet & Maxwell, London.

Griggs, E. (1991) 'The politics of health care reform in Britain', *Political Quarterly*, vol. 62, pp. 419–30.

Gummett, P. (1991) 'History, development and organisation of UK science and technology up to 1982'. In Sir Robin Nicholson, Catherine M. Cunningham and Philip Gummett (eds), *Science and Technology in the United Kingdom*, Longman, London, pp. 14–26.

Haines, J. (1977) *The Politics of Power*, Coronet, London.

Hammond, T. and Thomas, P. A. (1989) 'The impossibility of a neutral hierarchy', *Journal of Law, Economics and Organisation*, vol. 5, pp. 155–84.

Hanham, H. J. (1966) 'Opposition techniques in British politics (1867–1914)', *Government and Opposition*, vol. 2, pp. 35–48.

Hansard (1990) *House of Commons Debates, 1990–91*, vol. 181.

Hansard (1991) *House of Commons Debates, 1990–91*, vol. 188.

Hansard (1992) *House of Commons Debates, 1992–93*, vol. 212.

Harris, R. (1990) *Good and Faithful Servant: The Unauthorized Biography of Bernard Ingham*, Faber & Faber, London.

Headey, B. (1974) *British Cabinet Ministers: The Roles of Politicians in Executive Office*, Allen & Unwin, London.

Healey, D. (1990) *The Time of My Life*, Penguin, London.

Heclo, H. and Wildavsky, A. (1981) *The Private Government of Public Money: Community and Policy inside British Politics*, 2nd edn, Macmillan, London.

Heffer, E. (1991) *Never a Yes Man*, Verso, London.

Helm, D. (1993) 'Energy policy and the market doctrine', *Political Quarterly*, 64: 410–419.

Henderson, N. (1987) *Inside the Private Office: Memoirs of the Secretary to British Foreign Ministers*, Academy, Chicago.

Hennessy, P. (1979) 'Planning for a future nuclear deterrent', *The Times*, 4 December.

Hennessy, P. (1986) *Cabinet*, Blackwell, Oxford.

Hennessy, P. (1990) *Whitehall*, revised edn, Fontana, London.

Hennessy, P. and Arends, A. (1983) 'Mr Attlee's engine room: Cabinet committee structure and the Labour government, 1945–51', *Strathclyde Papers on Government and Politics*, no. 26, Strathclyde University, Glasgow.

Hermann, M. G. (1986) 'Ingredients of leadership'. In Margaret G. Hermann (ed.), *Political Psychology: Contemporary Problems and Issues*, Jossey-Bass, San Francisco, pp. 167–92.

Heseltine, M. (1987) *Where There's A Will*, Hutchinson, London.

Hill, M. (1972) *The Sociology of Public Administration*, Weidenfeld & Nicolson, London.

Hill, C. (1991) *Cabinet Decisions in Foreign Policy: The British Experience October 1938 – June 1941*, Cambridge University Press, Cambridge.

Hogwood, B. (1987) *From Crisis to Complacency? Shaping Public Policy in Britain*, Oxford University Press, Oxford.

Hogwood, B. (1992) *Trends in Public Policy: Do Governments Make Any Difference?* Open University Press, Buckingham.

Hogwood, B. W. and Mackie, T. T. (1985) 'The United Kingdom: Decision sifting in a secret garden'. In Thomas T. Mackie and Brian W. Hogwood (eds), *Unlocking the Cabinet: Cabinet Structures in Comparative Perspective*, Sage, London, pp. 36–60.

Howe, G. (1994) *Conflict of Loyalty*, Macmillan, London.

Hunt, Lord (1989) 'Access to a previous government's papers'. In Geoffrey Marshall (ed.), *Ministerial Responsibility*, Oxford University Press, Oxford, pp. 72–6.

Ingham, B. (1991) *Kill the Messenger*, Harper Collins, London.

Ingle, S. (1987) *The British Party System*, Blackwell, Oxford.

James, R. R. (1987) *Anthony Eden*, Macmillan, London.

James, S. (1992) *British Cabinet Government*, Routledge, London.

James, S. (1994) 'The cabinet system since 1945: Fragmentation and integration', *Parliamentary Affairs*, vol. 47, pp. 613–29.

Jenkins, P. (1987) *Mrs Thatcher's Revolution*, Jonathan Cape, London.

Jenkins, S. (1985) 'The "Star Chamber", PESC and the cabinet', *Political Quarterly*, vol. 56, pp. 113–21.

Jennings, Sir I. (1936) *Cabinet Government*, Cambridge University Press, Cambridge.

Johnson, C. (1991) *The Economy Under Mrs Thatcher: 1979–1990*, Penguin, London.

Jones, G. W. (1985a) 'The prime minister's aides'. In Anthony King (ed.), *The British Prime Minister*, 2nd edn, Macmillan, London, pp. 72–95.

Jones, G. W. (1985b) 'The prime minister's power'. In Anthony King (ed.), *The British Prime Minister*, 2nd edn, Macmillan, London, pp. 195–220.

Jones, G. W. (1987) 'The United Kingdom'. In William Plowden (ed.), *Advising the Rulers*, Blackwell, Oxford, pp. 36–70.

Jones, M. and Prescott, M. (1992) 'Oh what a shambles: British Coal pit closures', *Sunday Times*, 25 October.

Kaufman, G. (1980) *How to be a Minister*, Sidgwick & Jackson, London.

Kavanagh, D. (1981) 'The politics of manifestos', *Parliamentary Affairs*, vol. 34, pp. 7–27.

Keith, A. B. (1938) *The British Cabinet System*, Stevens, London.

Kellner, P. and Crowther-Hunt, Lord (1980) *The Civil Servants: An Inquiry into Britain's Ruling Class*, Macdonald, London.

Kelly, R. (1989) *Conservative Party Conferences: The Hidden System*, Manchester University Press, Manchester.

King, A. (1981) 'The rise of the career politician in Britain: And its consequences', *British Journal of Political Science*, vol. 11, pp. 249–85.

King, A. (1991) 'The British prime ministership in the age of the career politician', *West European Politics*, vol. 14, no. 2, pp. 25–47.

King, A. and Sloman, A. (1973) *Westminster and Beyond*, Macmillan, London.

Klein, R. and Lewis, J. (1977) 'Advice and dissent in British government: The case of the special advisers', *Policy and Politics*, vol. 6, pp. 1–25.

Knoke, D. (1990) *Political Networks: The Structural Perspective*, Cambridge University Press, Cambridge.

Knoke, D. and Kuklinski, J. (1982) *Network Analysis*, Sage, Beverley Hills.

Labour Party (1974) *The Labour Party Manifesto 1974*, Labour Party, London.

Lawson, N. (1993) *The View from No.11: Memoirs of a Tory Radical*, Bantam, London.

Lee, J. M. (1974) ' "Central capacity" and established practice: The changing character of the "centre of the machine" in British cabinet government'. In B. Chapman and A. Potter (eds), *WJMM: Political Questions: Essays in Honour of W J M McKenzie*, Manchester University Press, Manchester, pp. 162–89.

Lee, M. (1986) 'Cabinet procedure', *Public Administration*, vol. 64, pp. 347–9.

Lee, M. (1990) 'The ethos of the Cabinet Office: A comment on the testimony of officials', *Public Administration*, vol. 68, pp. 235–42.

Lee, M. (1995) 'The prime minister and international relations'. In Donald Shell and Richard Hodder-Williams (eds), *Churchill to Major: The British Prime Ministership since 1945*, Hurst, London, pp. 200–24.

L'Etang, H. (1969) *The Pathology of Leadership*, Heinemann, London.

Lipsey, D. (1983) 'The making of the budget', *Sunday Times*, 13 March.

Macintyre, D. and Castle, S. (1991) 'Death of Thatcherism', *Independent on Sunday*, 17 March.

Macintyre, D. and Castle, S. (1992) 'Walking over the viper pit', *Independent on Sunday*, 25 October.

Macintyre, D. and Huhne, C. (1991) 'How Major staged his budget coup', *Independent on Sunday*, 24 March.

Mackintosh, J. P. (1962) *The British Cabinet*, Stevens & Sons, London.

Mackintosh, J. P. (1977) *The British Cabinet*, 3rd edn, Stevens & Sons, London.

Madgwick, P. (1991) *British Government: The Central Executive Territory*, Philip Allen, Hemel Hempstead.

Malone, P. (1984) *The British Nuclear Deterrent*, Croom Helm, London.

March, J. G. and Olsen, J. P. (1989) *Rediscovering Institutions: The Organizational Basis of Politics*, The Free Press, New York.

Marsh, D. (1992) 'Youth employment policy 1970–1990: Towards the exclusion of the trade unions'. In David Marsh and R. A. W. Rhodes (eds), *Policy Networks in British Government*, Clarendon Press, Oxford, pp. 167–99.

Marsh, D. and Rhodes, R. A. W. (eds) (1992) *Policy Networks in British Government*, Clarendon Press, Oxford.

Marsh, I. (1990) 'Liberal priorities: The Lib–Lab pact and the requirements for policy influence', *Parliamentary Affairs*, vol. 43, pp. 292–321.

Marshall, G. (1989) 'Introduction'. In Geoffrey Marshall (ed.), *Ministerial Responsibility*, Oxford University Press, Oxford, pp. 1–13.

McEldowney, J. F. (1994) *Public Law*, Sweet & Maxwell, London.

McIntosh, M. (1990) *Managing Britain's Defence*, Macmillan, Basingstoke.

McKenzie, R. (1963) *British Political Parties: The Distribution of Power within the Conservative and Labour Parties*, 2nd edn, Mercury, London.

Metcalfe, L. and Richards, S. (1990) *Improving Public Management*, 2nd edn, Sage, London.

Miers, D. and Page, A. (1990) *Legislation*, 2nd edn, Sweet and Maxwell, London.

Miller, C. (1990) *Lobbying*, Basil Blackwell, Oxford.

Minister for the Civil Service and Chief Secretary to the Treasury (1994) *The Government's Expenditure Plan 1994–95 to 1996–97: Cabinet Office, Chancellor of the Duchy of Lancaster's Departments, Privy Council Office and Parliament*, Cm 2518, HMSO, London.

Ministry of Defence (1963) *Central Organisation for Defence*, Cmnd 2097, HMSO, London.

Ministry of Reconstruction (1918) *Report of the Machinery of Government Committee*, Cd 9230, HMSO, London.

Mitchell, A. (1982) *Westminster Man: A Tribal Anthology of the Commons People*, Thames Methuen, London.

Moran, Lord (1968) *Winston Churchill: The Struggle for Survival, 1940–65*, Sphere, London.

Morrison, Lord (1964) *Government and Parliament: A Survey from the Inside*, 3rd edn, Oxford University Press, London.

Mosley, K. R. (1969) *The Story of the Cabinet Office*, Routledge & Kegan Paul, London.

Müller, W. C., Philipp, W. and Gerlich, P. (1993) 'Prime ministers and cabinet decision-making processes'. In Jean Blondel and Ferdinand Müller-Rommel (eds), *Governing Together: The Extent and Limits of Joint Decision-Making in Western European Cabinets*, Macmillan, Basingstoke, pp. 223–56.

Müller-Rommel, F. (1993) 'Ministers and the role of the prime ministerial staff'. In Jean Blondel and Ferdinand Müller-Rommel (eds), *Governing Together: The Extent and Limits of Joint Decision-Making in Western European Cabinets*, Macmillan, Basingstoke, pp. 131–52.

National Audit Office (1989) *The Next Steps Initiative*, HC paper 410, session 1988–9, HMSO, London.

Naylor, J. F. (1984) *A Man and an Institution: Sir Maurice Hankey, the Cabinet Secretariat and the Custody of Cabinet Secrecy*, Cambridge University Press, Cambridge.

Norton, P. (1975) *Dissension in the House of Commons: Intra-Party Dissent in the House of Commons Division Lobbies, 1945–74*, Macmillan, London.

Norton, P. (1980) *Dissension in the House of Commons, 1974–79*, Clarendon Press, Oxford.

Norton, P. (1985) 'Behavioural changes: Backbench independence in the 1980s'. In Philip Norton (ed.), *Parliament in the 1980s*, Basil Blackwell, Oxford.

Norton, P. and Aughey, A. (1981) *Conservatives and Conservatism*, Temple Smith, London.

Norton-Taylor, R. (1988) 'Picking the lock of Britain's security', *Guardian*, 6 April.

Office of Public Service and Science (1993) *Next Steps Review*, Cm 2430, HMSO, London.

Organisation for Economic Co-operation and Development (1990) *Aspects of Managing the Centre of Government*, OECD, Paris.

Owen, D. (1987) *Personally Speaking to Kenneth Harris*, Weidenfeld & Nicolson, London.

Owen, D. (1992) *Time to Declare*, Penguin, London.

Parker, M. and Surrey, J. (1993) 'The October 1992 coal crisis and UK energy policy', *Political Quarterly*, vol. 64, pp. 396–409.

Parkinson, C. (1992) *Right at the Centre*, Weidenfeld & Nicolson, London.

Parris, H. (1969) *Constitutional Bureaucracy: The Development of British Central Administration Since the Eighteenth Century*, George Allen & Unwin, London.

Part, A. (1990) *The Making of a Mandarin*, Andre Deutsch, London.

Peters, B. G. (1994) 'Development of theories about governance: Art imitating life?', paper presented to conference on 'Ten Years of Change', University of Manchester, September.

Pinto-Duschinsky, M. (1972) 'Central Office and "power" in the Conservative Party', *Political Studies*, vol. 20, pp. 1–16.

Pliatzky, L. (1984) *Getting and Spending: Public Expenditure, Employment and Inflation*, revised edn, Blackwell, Oxford.

Pliatzky, L. (1989) *The Treasury under Mrs Thatcher*, Blackwell, Oxford.

Plott, C. and Levine, M. (1978) 'A model of agenda influence on committee decisions', *American Economic Review*, vol. 68, pp. 146–60.

PMS (1995) *Parliamentary Companion*, no. 22, PMS Publications, London.

Pollitt, C. (1984) *Manipulating the Machine: Changing the Pattern of Ministerial Departments, 1960–83*, George Allen & Unwin, London.

Ponting, C. (1986a) *Whitehall: Tragedy and Farce*, Hamish Hamilton, London.
Ponting, C. (1986b) 'The document Benn couldn't disclose', *New Statesman*, 14, 21, 28 February.
Prior, J. (1986) *A Balance of Power*, Hamish Hamilton, London.
Privy Council Office (1990) *The Next Steps Agencies: Review*, Cm 1261, HMSO, London.
Public Accounts Committee of the House of Commons (1987) *Thirteenth Report: Financial Management Initiative*, HC paper 61, session 1986–7, HMSO, London.
Punnett, R. M. (1976) *British Government and Politics*, 3rd edn, Heinemann, London.
Quinlan, Sir M. (1994) 'Changing patterns in government business', *Public Policy and Administration*, vol. 9, pp. 27–34.
Radcliffe, Lord (1976) *Report of the Committee of Privy Councillors*, Cmnd 6386, HMSO, London.
Rallings, C. (1987) 'The influence of election programmes: Britain and Canada 1945–1979'. In Ian Budge, David Robertson and Derek Hearl (eds), *Ideology, Strategy and Party Change: Spatial Analysis of Post-War Election Programmes in 19 Democracies*, Cambridge University Press, Cambridge, pp. 1–14.
Ranelagh, J. (1992) *Thatcher's People: An Insider's Account of the Politics, the Power and the Personalities*, Fontana, London.
Rawlinson, P. (1989) *A Price Too High: An Autobiography*, Weidenfeld and Nicolson, London.
Redmayne, M. (1972) 'Whips and backbenchers', interview with Norman Hunt. In Dick Leonard and Valentine Herman (eds), *The Backbencher and Parliament: A Reader*, Macmillan, London, pp. 74–9.
Rhodes, R. A. W. (1988) *Beyond Westminster and Whitehall*, Allen & Unwin, London.
Rhodes, R. A. W. and Dunleavy, P. (eds) (1995) *Prime Minister, Cabinet and Core Executive*, Macmillan, London.
Riddell, P. (1983) *The Thatcher Government*, Martin Robertson, Oxford.
Ridley, N. (1991a) *'My Style of Government': The Thatcher Years*, Hutchinson, London.
Ridley, N. (1991b) 'Why rebates are the poll tax's saving grace', *Guardian*, 12 March.
Rippon, Lord (1992) *Making the Law: The Report of the Hansard Society Commission on the Legislative Process*, Hansard Society, London.
Robinson, A. and Sandford, C. (1983) *Tax Policy-Making in the United Kingdom: A Study of Rationality, Ideology and Politics*, Heinemann, London.
Rose, R. (1980) 'British government: The job at the top'. In Richard Rose and Ezra N. Suleiman (eds), *Presidents and Prime Ministers*, American Enterprise Institute for Public Policy Research, Washington.
Rose, R. (1983) 'Still the era of party government', *Parliamentary Affairs*, vol. 36, pp. 282–99.
Rose, R. (1984) *Do Parties Make a Difference?*, 2nd edn, Macmillan, London.
Rose, R. and Karran, T. (1987) *Taxation by Policy Inertia*, Allen & Unwin, London.
Roskill, S. (1970) *Hankey: Man of Secrets, Volume I 1877–1918*, Collins, London.
Roskill, S. (1972) *Hankey: Man of Secrets, Volume II 1919–1931*, Collins, London.
Rush, M. (1984) *The Cabinet and Policy Formation*, Longman, London.
Schattschneider, E. E. (1960) *The Semisovereign People: A Realist's View of Democracy in America*, Holt, Rinehart & Winston, New York.
Seidman, H. (1970) *Politics, Position and Power: The Dynamics of Federal Organization*, Oxford Univerity Press, New York.
Seldon, A. (1990) 'The Cabinet Office and coordination 1979–87', *Public Administration*, vol. 68, pp. 103–21.
Seldon, A. (1994) 'Policy making and cabinet'. In Dennis Kavanagh and Anthony Seldon (eds), *The Major Effect*, Macmillan, London, pp. 154–66.

Seymour-Ure, C. (1989) 'The prime minister's press secretary', *Contemporary Record*, vol. 3, pp. 33–5.

Seymour-Ure, C. (1991) *The British Press and Broadcasting since 1945*, Blackwell, Oxford.

Simon, H. A. (1947) *Administrative Behaviour: A Study of Decision Making Processes in Administrative Organization*, Macmillan, New York.

Sisson, C. H. (1959) *The Spirit of British Administration*, Faber & Faber, London.

Smith, D. (1992) *From Boom to Bust: Trial and Error in British Economic Policy*, Penguin, London.

Smith, M., Marsh, D. and Richards, D. (1993) 'Central government departments and the policy process', *Public Administration*, vol. 71, pp. 567–94.

Steel, D. (1980) *A House Divided: The Lib-Lab Pact and the Future of British Politics*, Weidenfeld & Nicolson, London.

Stephenson, H. (1980) *Mrs Thatcher's First Year*, Jill Norman, London.

Street, H. and Brazier, R. (1985) *De Smith: Constitutional and Administrative Law*, Penguin, Harmondsworth.

Thain, C. and Wright, M. (1990) 'Haggling in Mr Clarke's Turkish bazaar', *Public Money and Management* (Winter), 51–5.

Thain, C. and Wright, M. (1992) 'Planning and controlling public expenditure in the UK, Part I: The Treasury's public expenditure survey', *Public Administration*, vol. 70, pp. 3–24.

Thain, C. and Wright, M. (1994) 'Haggling in Mr Clarke's Turkish bazaar'. In Norman Flynn (ed.), *Change in the Civil Service: A Public Finance Foundation Reader*, CIPFA, London, pp. 49–56.

Thain, C. and Wright, M. (1995) *The Treasury and Whitehall*, Oxford University Press, Oxford.

Thatcher, M. (1993) *The Downing Street Years*, Harper Collins, London.

Theakston, K. (1987) *Junior Ministers in British Government*, Blackwell, Oxford.

Thelen, K. and Steinmo, S. (1992) 'Historical institutionalism in comparative politics'. In Sven Steinmo, Kathleen Thelen and Frank Longstreth (eds), *Structuring Politics: Historical Institutionalism in Comparative Analysis*, Cambridge University Press, Cambridge, pp. 1–32.

Thompson, H. (1995) 'Joining the ERM: Analysing a core executive policy disaster'. In R. A. W. Rhodes and Patrick Dunleavy (eds.), *Prime Minister, Cabinet and Core Executive*, (London: Macmillan) (pp. 248–74).

Thomson, A. (1989) *Margaret Thatcher: The Woman Within*, W. H. Allen, London.

Trade and Industry Committee of the House of Commons (1992a) *British Energy Policy and the Market for Coal: Report*, HC paper 237, session 1992–3, HMSO, London.

Trade and Industry Committee of the House of Commons (1992b) *British Energy Policy and the Market for Coal: Minutes of Evidence*, HC paper 237-I, session 1992–3, HMSO, London.

Treasury (1961) *Control of Public Expenditure*, report of the Plowden committee, Cmnd 1432, HMSO, London.

Treasury (1976) 'Control and presentation of public expenditure', *Economic Progress Report* 80 (November), pp. 1–3.

Treasury (1981) 'Public expenditure: Planning in cash', *Economic Progress Report*, vol. 139 (November), pp. 1–2.

Treasury (1992) *Budgetary Reform*, Cm 1867, HMSO, London.

Treasury and Civil Service Committee of the House of Commons (1988) *Civil Service Management Reform: The Next Steps: Minutes of Evidence*, HC paper 494-II, session 1987–8, HMSO, London.

Turner, J, (1982) 'Cabinets, committees and secretariats: The higher direction of war'. In Kathleen Burk (ed.), *War and the State: The Transformation of British Government, 1914–1919*, George Allen & Unwin, London, pp. 57–83.

Van Mechelen, D. and Rose, R. (1986) *Patterns of Parliamentary Legislation*, Gower, Aldershot.

Vickers, Sir G. (1967) *The Art of Judgment: A Study of Policy Making*, Chapman Hall, London.

Wade, H. R. and Forsyth, C. F. (1994) *Administrative Law*, Clarendon Press, Oxford.

Wakeham, Lord (1994) 'Cabinet government', *Contemporary Record*, vol. 8, pp. 473–83.

Walker, D. (1987) 'Secret plans to reform Whitehall left in limbo', *The Times*, 12 October.

Walker, P. (1991) *Staying Power*, Bloomsbury, London.

Wass, D. (1984) *Government and the Governed: BBC Reith Lectures 1983*, Routledge, London.

Wastell, D. (1991) 'Tory whips to crack down over local tax', *Sunday Telegraph*, 14 April.

Wastell, D. (1992) 'John Major steps into the minefield', *Sunday Telegraph*, 18 October.

Watkins, A. (1992) *A Conservative Coup*, Duckworth, London.

Wildavsky, A. (1975) *Budgeting: A Comparative Theory of Budgetary Processes*, Little, Brown, Boston.

Wilkinson, M. (1993) 'British tax policy, 1979–90: Equity and efficiency', *Policy and Politics*, vol. 21, pp. 207–17.

Wilks, S. (1984) *Industrial Policy and the Motor Industry*, Manchester University Press, Manchester.

Willetts, D. (1987) 'The role of the prime minister's policy unit', *Public Administration*, vol. 65, pp. 443–54.

Wilson, H. (1974) *The Labour Government 1964–70: A Personal Record*, Penguin, Harmondsworth.

Wilson, H. (1976) *The Governance of Britain*, Weidenfeld & Nicolson and Michael Joseph, London.

Wilson, H. (1979) *Final Term: The Labour Government 1974–1976*, Weidenfeld & Nicolson and Michael Joseph, London.

Wilson, S. S. (1975) *The Cabinet Office to 1945*, Public Record Office Handbook, no. 17, HMSO, London.

Wilson, T. (1991) 'The poll tax: Origins, errors and remedies', *Economic Journal*, vol. 101, pp. 576–82.

Wright, M. (1977) 'Ministers and civil servants: Relations and responsibilities', *Parliamentary Affairs*, vol. 30, pp. 293–310.

Wright, M. (1980) *Public Spending Decisions*, Allen & Unwin, London.

Wright, M. (1988) 'Policy community, policy network and comparative industrial policies', *Political Studies*, vol. 36, pp. 593–612.

Young, H. (1991) *One of Us: A Biography of Margaret Thatcher*, final edn, Macmillan, London.

Young, H. and Sloman, A. (1984) *But, Chancellor: An Inquiry into the Treasury*, BBC, London.

Index

□

see conventions
see ethos
see operating codes
Varley, Eric, 162, 179–85

Wakeham, John, 105, 213, 222, 233, 240, 243, 246, 248–51, 270
Waldegrave, William, 128, 214–18, 272
Walker, Peter, 203–4, 216, 250
Walters, Sir Alan, 29, 30, 222–4
Warren, Sir Alfred, 118
Wass, Douglas, 188
Wellbeloved, James, 97
Welsh Office, 103, 247
whips, 39, 76, 96–7, 111, 118, 250
whips' office, 38, 119
Whitelaw, William, 105, 127, 138, 196, 200, 203–4, 213, 215, 222, 272

Whittome, Alan, 188
Wigg, George, 97
Willetts, Davids, 234
Williams, Francis, 20
Williams, Shirley, 161, 167, 169, 183, 189, 190
Wilson, Harold, 2, 23, 28, 29, 77, 98, 146, 158–64, 165, 171, 172–3, 177, 179–85, 186, 193–4, 269, 271–2, 282
Wilson, Tom, 214–15
Witteveen, Johannes, 189–90
Wyndham, John, 21

Yeo, Ed, 188
Young, Sir George, 239
Young, Robin, 239, 244
Younger, Sir George, 204, 215–16